Complete Book of
HUNTING

An Outdoor Life Book

Also by Clyde Ormond

Bear!

Complete Book of Outdoor Lore

Hunting in the Northwest

Hunting Our Biggest Game

Hunting Our Medium Sized Game

Outdoorsman's Handbook

Small Game Hunting

The Sportsman's Companion (co-author)

Complete Book of
HUNTING

By CLYDE ORMOND

Drawings by Douglas Allen

OUTDOOR LIFE • HARPER & ROW
NEW YORK

Designed by Jeff Fitschen

To my Grandchildren

Contents

Part II—HUNTING GAME BIRDS

Introduction

HUNTING HAS ALWAYS been one of man's deepest instincts and has fulfilled one of his greatest needs. This was true in past ages when man hunted for food. It was true when man no longer was forced to hunt for his food but began hunting for sport. And it is equally true today when urban man seeks the renewal of body and spirit that hunting affords.

Man in his quest for civilization and progress has inexorably diminished the natural habitat of wild birds and game. He has done this by clearing lands for farming, building great dams and flooding wildlife lands for more power and irrigation, mining ever more remote areas and building access roads, and whittling down vast forests to meet the increasing demands for more lumber.

The number of huntable birds and game depends primarily on available range—specifically, on the availability of winter range. Without adequate food, sufficient range, and suitable habitat, no game species can endure. More, when the food, range, and habitat of one species is upset and greatly altered, it affects the entire pattern of wildlife balance.

The days of open hunting for all species are now gone, but there is still wonderful hunting in North America for everyone who wants to hunt. We will have to accept certain limitations, and we will have to make the effort to conserve the wildlife that is left.

We have demonstrated the capacity for doing this. While the environment of America's wildlife is rated as only "fair," the fact remains that we have, by sound management practices, actually saved many wildlife species from extinction. The population of many game species has increased, and many new species have been introduced. Numerous areas of wildlife habitat have been saved from needless exploitation, and, with revenue collected from hunters, vast areas of new bird and game habitat have been purchased.

From the experience of the past, it is now obvious what the future of hunting in North America holds, and what some of the basic limitations may well be.

First, game populations will be managed more vigorously than in the past—that is, populations will be based on available and determined ranges. Once the carrying capacities of the ranges are reached, surpluses will be harvested on a sustained-yield basis. For the hunter, this means that his chances to hunt a species will more often depend on his luck in drawing a permit in a lottery. Further, his "lucky" permit for a species will, to a greater extent, be for a specific area where a certain number of a species is to be harvested. There will be less and less general open hunting.

Again, when the needs of agriculture, mining, lumbering, power, and development have outweighed the benefits of a game species, and the habitat of that species has been depleted, there will be a greater trend towards the introduction of another, more suitable species into the disrupted areas. As a broad example, where great dams and other construction in a remote area have driven a species such as elk into wilder country, deer or black bear, which are more amenable to contact with man, may be transplanted into the area. Or where water impoundments are created by large dams, the hunting may be shifted from big game to waterfowl.

Transplanted game birds and animals will become more common. Experiments have proven that such species as antelope, elk, deer, wild sheep, goats, and many upland birds can be successfully transplanted. The outstanding example has been the introduction of the Chinese pheasant from Asia into the farmlands of America.

There is also a growing trend toward sheer trophy hunting—that is, hunting only the largest and noblest male animals. This trend is certain to increase, and is beneficial to the species. The oldest, largest game animals have served their greatest use to the herd, and harvesting them will not affect propagation as would the taking of the younger, more virile males. At the same time, the average hunter, as his annual opportunity to hunt every species diminishes, will come to regard the trophy he does get with more esteem.

In the future there will be more "handicap" hunting, as represented by the Wyoming One-Shot Antelope Hunt, the Muzzle-Loaders Only Deer Hunt, and others. Archery and camera hunting are bound to increase as a means of conserving game populations. Such handicap hunting clearly demonstrates that the allied values of the sport are as important as the final kill.

A final trend which appears certain is the involvement of more hunters, on a year-round basis, in the conservation movement. If hunting is to continue to be the great sport which it has always been, it will no longer be possible for the hunters of America to concern themselves with their wildlife only during hunting seasons, then forget it during the remainder of the year. Instead, hunters will become more active in sportsmen's organizations. They will become more and more involved in politics and those decisions which affect wildlife. Hunters will support with time, money, and effort the movements and organizations dedicated to the conservation of wildlife and the acquisition of more suitable habitat. They will come more and more to look upon wildlife and its habitat as their own.

I

HUNTING
GAME ANIMALS

1

Pollution and the Hunter

ONE OF THE GREAT "causes" which has united the American people is the drive to conserve our natural resources and halt the pollution of our environment. The danger has been slow in manifesting itself, and acceptance of the hard facts has been even more delayed. During the period of our country's development, while we were gradually depleting our resources and contaminating the environment, the public remained largely apathetic. Natural resources were long considered to be inexhaustible. Pollution was vaguely thought of as affecting someone else.

In 1970, it became painfully apparent that pollution and despoliation of the environment had reached the point of being a danger to our actual survival. Americans reacted.

Some politicians have tried to take the credit for this new and concerted fight against pollution, but hunters and fishermen started the fight at least seventy years ago. A relatively few dedicated sportsmen vainly tried to persuade Congressmen to legislate against pollution of our streams, and for the conservation of our natural resources. Theirs was a small voice, crying in a wilderness of apathy, in a nation dedicated to industrial expansion. The price we were paying for dumping industrial wastes into the streams, ravaging the wildlife, and cutting down the forests was considered small compared to the "progress" we were making industrially and financially. Politicians, concerned for their own political survival, could count more votes among those who made a profit from ravaging the natural resources than from the relatively few who wanted the forests, streams, and wildlife conserved for the ultimate good of the people. The public, by its silence, *condoned* the pollution of the environment.

3

Hunters were among the first to foresee the depletion of many wildlife species, and their efforts alone have been largely responsible for saving numerous species from extinction. As an organized body, hunters have willingly taxed themselves through license fees and excise taxes upon guns and ammunition to purchase additional breeding and nesting grounds, and suitable habitat, for wildlife. They often have renounced the immediate pleasures of hunting to conserve game and provide better sport for the future. Now that conservation and halting pollution have become a national cause, hunters must continue to play an even more active role.

There are vital things which hunters can do to help. In organizations, they can keep an eye on the status of the country's wildlife. They must protect it equally from those who would exploit it for a fast dollar and individual gain, and from those other extremists who would permanently lock up areas of wildlife against all hunting. Wildlife is a fluid crop that cannot be saved and stored as other products are. It can only exist if it is used and harvested on a sustained-yield basis.

As individuals, hunters can maintain vigilance against forest fires. There is no blow to conservation quite like a great conflagration in a huge forest. The burning of a great forest not only destroys the trees whose green leaves provide man with oxygen; it also ruins the habitat of game, hastens the erosion of soil, and in general upsets the balance of nature in the wasted area for up to a hundred years.

The pollution caused by a forest fire is awesome. I have witnessed some of the great forest fires in Alaska and Canada, where smoke reduced visibility to a hundred yards over an area of a hundred miles. Such a fire, if caused by the thoughtless act of a hunter, would nullify any life-long effort he could otherwise make in his fight against pollution.

The individual hunter can aid the cause by keeping hunting areas clean. A basic rule in the past for disposing of garbage, litter, and other waste in a hunting camp was to bury them. While still a valid method for many forms of waste and litter, burying will no longer serve to dispose of others. For example, buried glass bottles remain a permanent part of the landscape. Tin cans which contained food are often dug up by bears and varmints and become pollutants. The great Primitive Areas, such as the Bob Marshall Primitive Area in Montana, now require that the hunter or camper carry out all bottles and tin cans. If it is impossible to haul out tin cans, it is better, before burying them, to burn them in a hot fire. This destroys the paper covering and burns up all food scents which attract animals.

Garbage which will burn should be burned before leaving a campsite. Only small fires should be built, both for cooking and warming, as they are less apt to get out of control than are large fires. Such fires should be made of the driest woods, which will cause less air pollution. Never throw camp refuse in lakes or streams.

Human waste should be buried in pit latrines. Nothing is more sickening to the hunter who loves the hills and game than to find his pet hunting area or campsite defiled by waste, advertised by white flags of used toilet paper. Latrines should be kept away from springs, creeks or any source of water. They should be so placed that subsequent runoff, rain, or stream overflow will not reach them and the contents should be buried deeply enough so that uncovering is impossible.

The things an individual hunter can do to cleanup the landscape are endless. He can refrain from defacing living timber. If he must "chip out" a blaze to mark game he has killed so that he can return, he can use low bushes for the blazes—not timber where the scars will remain. He can bring the feet, antlers, and legs of a game-kill to camp where unwanted parts can be burned, not leave them to be scattered by coyotes and other varmints. The hunter can destroy or keep the film backing used in an instant-picture camera, since elk and deer will chew on them for the saline chemicals they contain, and die from poisoning. He can use mild soap at camp instead of strong detergents which pollute lakes and streams.

Already there are many groups dedicated to cleaning up the outdoors. Some of these are groups of youths who make expeditions into the outdoors to pick up tin cans, bottles, and other refuse left by their unthinking elders. This attitude must grow, and hunters of the future must adopt it, if the great hunting areas are to be cleaned up and kept free of pollution.

2

Planning the Hunting Trip

THE REAL PURPOSE of any big-game hunting trip is to have an enjoyable and rewarding experience in the outdoors. In addition, every hunter hopes to climax such an experience by taking a prized game animal. That is the unsurpassed thrill of any hunt.

To harvest both these pleasures from your trip, it is wise to do some thoughtful and early planning. Careful preparation not only assures your own enjoyment, but it is the best guarantee for the success of the hunt and the safety of yourself and your hunting companions.

When planning any hunting trip, always consider the following factors: the trophy wanted; the right hunting area; a congenial hunting partner; and provisions for shelter, food, and warmth.

THE HUNTING PARTNER. Perhaps the most important is the wise choice of a hunting partner. Solo hunts in settled areas—taking off into the hills alone and getting back to nature—are fine experiences. But in big hunting country, where the remaining concentrations of our big-game supply are found, hunting alone is not sensible. It is far safer, especially when after the larger species of game, to hunt with a partner and it is less laborious to be able to share the necessary heavy chores. But most important, a hunting trip, like any satisfying experience, must be shared with someone to be completely enjoyed.

Unless the partner has been on previous hunts, good questions to ask about him are: How stable a person is he? How does he react to unavoidable inconvenience? How dependable would he be if the chips were down and someone's life depended upon his decisions and courage?

The partner who qualifies in such vital respects, and loves the outdoors, is apt to have the numerous other qualities which will make him a prized companion.

For short hunts near settled areas, a party of two hunting companions is ideal. It is indicative of the importance of good hunting partners that in many instances the same two fellows hunt annually, over a period of many years. Often they are far apart in financial, social, and occupational status, but as hunting companions their likes and interests are the same and they make a fine partnership.

For the big hunts, or any type of big-game hunting where an extra member won't crowd the party, three members are better, psychologically, than two. A third hunting partner acts as a buffer when the hardships of a hunting camp cause tempers to get raw, or physical discomforts or lack of success in bagging game cause people to become discouraged. For wilderness hunts into big country, four hunters make an ideal group. Each has a hunting partner, and partners can alternate.

CHOOSING A HUNTING AREA. The game one wishes to hunt is, of course, a fundamental consideration. No hunter should ever plan a hunt with the simple hope that he will bag anything that jumps up, or that he is "out after everything." Well in advance of his hunt, he should determine what species he wants most, then route the hunt into a region where he is most apt to find that species. Additional species should be regarded as a bonus.

Broadly speaking, the best areas for any game species are those regions where game has been hunted the least. There the biggest trophy heads will be found. Competition with other hunters will be less keen. There will be less danger. And the game itself, in proportion to the degree it has previously been in contact with man, will be less wary. In this respect, a costly trip into a wilderness area may be far less expensive in the long run than one or more unsuccessful trips into areas where the chances are slimmer.

I learned this the hard, "cheap" way on elk. When I was a boy, elk country was a two hour's drive from home. I felt then, as so many hunters do, that I couldn't afford a pack trip into real wilderness elk country, but that I could afford one or even several short trips close to home. For six years, partners and I went into this nearby area and hunted our hearts out trying to bag that first prized wapiti. At the end of the sixth year, the nearest I'd ever come to elk was stale tracks and the sight of an elk carcass at somebody else's camp.

The next year I decided to put the same amount I had spent the past six years into one good hunt in country where I could bust an elk, even if I had to lay off hunting for the next five. That year, in Idaho's vast

Selway Forest, I killed my first bull. Oddly enough, I returned there for the next twelve years and never missed getting one.

SOURCES OF HUNTING INFORMATION. In choosing a region in which to hunt any game species, one of the hunter's best tools is a good map. Some of the best maps for the purpose are the hunting maps published by the state game departments especially for hunters. These usually are available free by early fall in states having shootable numbers of any game species. The interested hunter may obtain one simply by writing the Fish & Game Department at the capital of the state or province in which he wishes to hunt.

Having obtained such a map, it is wise to keep it for the next season. Often the new maps are not available while the hunt is in the planning stage; but usually only minor changes will be made from the map of the previous season.

Another good source of information about possible game areas is the official census of game published by the Fish & Wildlife Service, Department of Interior, Washington, D.C. This brief game-count by states gives the estimated game population of all states, the annual estimated kill, and the trend as to increase or decrease. A study of such a census often gives the nonresident hunter a fair notion of a region where his chances at a species will be optimum.

The periodic kill-report of a state, or the country, published by the big outdoor journals, is another source of reliable and broad information.

A fine, dependable source of local information is the game warden or conservation officer. Such men are in constant touch with the game situation in their individual hunting areas, and will usually advise hunters whom they know to be good sportsmen of choice hunting areas.

Again, much valuable information may be had from local ranchers, sportsmen, and other inhabitants of an area who are obviously honest and sincere. In depending upon this source of information, the stranger should beware of the ubiquitous Hot Stove League. Tips "privately" given, usually in return for a favor or a drink, are often biased, exaggerated, and in many cases manufactured out of thin air purely to send a hunter on a wild-goose chase.

Once the beginning hunter has made a hunt, then experience begins to help him. But for both veteran and tyro, all the above sources of information—except the last—will help him to find a suitable game region where his chances will be good.

EARLY PLANNING. It is hard to stress too much the necessity of planning the big-game hunt *early*. Winter and spring months are not too soon to plan for the fall hunt.

First, one's vacation time should be arranged, if possible, to coincide with a known game season. Often by planning early enough, the annual vacation can be made to fit the hunting season. This frequently entails added work or favors to the company or the boss, but it is worth it.

Next is the important matter of hunting licenses. The minor difficulties of getting the proper hunting licenses apply most to the nonresident hunter. Increasingly, in the management of big game, the states and provinces are determining the annual hunter harvest of game on the survival-potential of a species' population on its winter range. This system often will not permit open hunting. Licensing is done on a permit basis.

Whenever the number of hunters is top-heavy in proportion to the intended game-kill, the applications for permits are heavy, often running several dozen to one; then permits are decided by a public drawing.

In many states, application for special permits is open to resident and nonresident alike. In others, preference is given to the resident over the nonresident hunter. Each state has its own system of licensing, and the regulations regarding licenses should be known early.

As one specific example of special licensing, Wyoming has had for a great many years a law prohibiting the sale of more than a given number of nonresident hunting licenses. This number has varied from 2,500 up to 4,500. These nonresident licenses are for antlered bull elk only, plus deer and black bear; and they also permit the nonresident hunter to hunt game birds and to fish. These licenses are in great demand and are normally sold out soon after they become available on January 1st. Every year, hunters expecting to hunt that state, some of whom fly in from long distances, are disappointed. They complain to their outfitter, "We thought that *some* way you'd be able to get us licenses." One outfitter used a stenciled "WARNING" on his stationery, reminding his clients to get their licenses early.

In planning the big-game hunt, nonresidents especially should investigate the matters of licenses and hunting laws early. Often the pertinent information will be contained right on the state hunting maps. Otherwise, when writing it is wise to ask for full information on licenses and hunting regulations in the state or province.

OUTFITTERS AND GUIDES.   Some states and provinces require the services of a licensed guide for the nonresident hunter. Such a service is considered by the game commissions to be necessary not only as a measure to prevent game-law violations but, equally important, to keep hunters unfamiliar with the country from becoming lost. In primitive country, the lost-hunter situation each fall is a serious business. The Forest Service, Fish and Game Departments, mounted posses, and state flying organizations have to donate time, money, and effort to retrieving lost hunters from rugged, remote mountain terrain. Requiring the nonresident hunter to employ a licensed guide or outfitter largely eliminates this problem.

Often the incoming big-game hunter, even when not required by law, prefers to hire a professional outdoorsman who can insure the success of the hunt. He knows the country—how to get into, around, and out of it in the easiest manner. He knows where the game is, and the best ways to approach it. He can lead the hunter to the best trophies. And as part of his services, the guide does much of the prosaic camp work such as tending horses and pack mules, logging up wood, setting up camp, and lugging things around. This leaves the hunter all his time to hunt and enjoy himself.

When an outfitter or guide is to be used, arrangements should begin well ahead of the season. Midwinter and early spring are not too soon. An outfitter takes care of hiring guides, wranglers, a cook, and other help, if necessary.

As with other personnel and services, the best comes high and is most in demand. Often with the best outfitters, the unknown nonresident hunter coming to a region for the first time can only make reservations if another party cancels. Good outfitters are often booked full for the next fall immediately after the current fall hunts. Their satisfied hunters simply say, "Well, write me down for next fall. And I'll likely bring a friend along with me, if you can handle that many." To get on the repeat list of such reputable outfitters one must arrange months in advance.

Lastly, all hunting equipment, personal gear, and necessary camp duffel should be obtained well in advance of any big-game hunt. This is important, not only in order to have the basic necessities ready when the hunt begins, but so that all gear may be checked beforehand for fit, condition, and suitability.

3

Clothing and Equipment

IF EVERY ITEM a big-game hunter needs on a ten-day hunt were tabulated on a strip of paper, the list would look as long as a polygamist's clothesline. However, when properly packed, the total duffel need be neither heavy nor bulky—if sensible items are chosen.

On a recent polar trip of a month's duration, neither my partner's nor my own gear—exclusive of the sleeping bag which the outfitter provided each of us—exceeded 66 pounds. This gear included a heavy rifle each, and we had everything needed for a good hunt. Again, on another British Columbia big-game hunt of three weeks we agreed on a duffel limit of 150 pounds per man for the chartered plane. My own gear, including a heavy press camera, weighed 108 pounds.

The beginning hunter tends to drag along everything except the kitchen sink. The veteran hunter tends to go light but right. Every item of his personal outfit is well chosen for its intended purpose, and his motto is, "If you don't use an item every day, leave it home." However, this precept must be modified somewhat in big-game hunting due to changes of weather, species of game, and changes of hunting terrain encountered during the hunt.

The fundamental gear for big-game hunting includes clothes, personal items, camp equipment and food (if the hunter isn't outfitted), and packaging for the same.

It is axiomatic that if a big-game hunter can be kept warm, dry, and well-fed, the chances of his hunt being a success are increased. Due to the storms of hunting country, the long hours on the trail or the chase, *keeping* warm, dry, and well-fed is temporarily impossible. But in choosing the equipment, some provision should always be made so that the hunter can *become* warm, dry, and fed without too much delay.

11

FUNCTION OF CLOTHING. Before getting into the various types of clothing suitable for big-game hunting, it would be well to understand the true function of proper body covering. No clothing, regardless of material, is either cold or warm, *per se.* Warm clothing is warm only in that it provides a layer of insulation next to the body, allowing the body heat to be retained, and inducing a feeling of warmth. Conversely, cold clothing does not insulate but allows body heat to escape, inducing a feeling of cold. This condition is aggravated both by body perspiration, which cools as it evaporates, and by wind.

For the big-game hunter, who fluctuates between strenuous effort and rest, between warmth and cold, clothing must perform three functions: It must provide a layer of insulation; a measure of thickness to absorb body perspiration; and some sort of shell, layer, or covering to keep wind from spoiling the effectiveness of the insulation.

Entirely waterproof clothing performs only one of these functions; hence it is either cold or hot depending on the weather and season. Wet or damp clothing likewise becomes cold.

In choosing clothing to fit the kind of weather and temperatures expected during a hunt, the advice of the outfitter, a hunting friend who has made such a hunt, or even the suggestions of the inhabitants of that particular area can be most helpful.

Make sure that all hunting garments are large and loose-fitting enough, so as not to hamper your movements while you are physically active. Plan to purchase any new hunting garment well in advance of the hunt, so that any alterations can be made, and the garment can be tried out before taking it afield—even if you just wear it around the house for a few hours to break it in.

UNDERWEAR, PANTS, SHIRTS. For warm-weather hunting, cotton underwear of the union-suit type is fine. The standard cotton shorts worn at home had best be left there. The big-game hunter needs the extra length for comfort in cool weather and high altitude and for leg protection against brush, sudden wettings, and the friction and galling of horseback riding.

Next in underwear warmth are the thermal knitted cotton garments, either in two-piece or union-suit style. This type of quilted knit provides an added measure of thickness which absorbs perspiration and provides added insulation. It is good for cool fall days and is easily laundered even at camp.

For cold weather, snow, and freezing nights, underwear of the laminated kind, which has an outer layer of wool and an inner layer of cotton (to prevent itching), is one of the most useful ever developed. These should be purchased in two-pieces so that one may be worn at a time, depending on the weather and the hunter's activity.

12

In the Far North, the standard fall and winter underwear has long been the double-barreled, trap-door, heavy woolen "Long Johns." I've been told by Canadian bushmen that, with the first heavy frosts, natives often sewed them on for the winter and emerged, as if from hibernation, in the spring. They're fine cold-weather garments, though not as adaptable as the duotype.

For the coldest weather, such as that encountered hunting elk in deep snow and high altitudes and polar bear in the Arctic, the warmest underwear is the quilted type insulated with down or Dacron. The down-filled kind is warmer, though more expensive and harder to launder. Such garments are usually worn over a light suit of cotton underwear and will keep the hunter warm in subzero temperatures. The cotton garment is easily laundered and prolongs the "sweetness" of the insulated one. I know several hunters who wear the shirt part of down-insulated underwear as an outer garment while hunting rams at elevations of 10,000 to 12,000 feet, where it is cold even in early fall, and every additional ounce of weight the sheep hunter carries is a burden.

Hunting pants include pants of cotton twill and duck, denim jeans, light woolen pants, heavy mackinaw-cloth woolen pants, and down-insulated pants made for subzero temperatures.

Except for the extremes of hunting temperatures, perhaps denim riding pants, often called Levi's, and heavy woolen pants are the most usable. Levi's are inexpensive, tough, blend fairly well in color with rocky, mountainous terrain, and are cut to protect the groin when horseback riding. Heavy woolen pants are best in cold weather when walking in snow. Woolen pants are "warm and dry even when they're cold and wet," and they don't swish noisily like Levi's.

The two best materials for the hunting shirt are cotton and wool. Cotton hunting shirts are fine for mild weather, such as the antelope and deer season in September. For colder weather, woolen hunting shirts are best.

FOOTWEAR. The feet are critical areas for the hunter. Unconditioned feet will swell. They will sweat and are very apt to blister. Toenails will be blackened by poking toes violently forward into new hunting boots while hiking down steep hills. Crippled feet will put a hunter out of sorts and commission as fast as anything you can name, so great care should be taken to obtain the right kind of footwear.

Nylon and cotton socks are fine for mild-weather hunting. Light woolen socks are even better, and may be doubled as temperatures get colder. Heavy woolen socks are best in uninsulated hunting pacs and boots, or when walking in deep snow. Their bulky tops help keep the snow off the pants and legs.

Weight of the hunting boots is a vital consideration, and whenever possible it is wise to choose the lighter weight. Extra ounces multiplied by the number of steps a big-game hunter takes in ten miles of walking in mountainous country add up to a prodigious tonnage.

For mild-weather hunting in muskeg, where the feet are constantly wet, moccasins made of heavy moosehide are fine after you become accustomed to wearing them. They are easily dried without stiffening each night, and are usable again next morning. The light rubber Bar-Flex type of moccasin many Canadian hunters wear over heavy woolen socks are likewise fine for mild weather. They are better for climbing rocks in sheep and goat country than the moosehide variety as their cleated soles stick tightly to slick and uneven surfaces.

For average big-game hunting, two basic types of boots are most often used. One is an all-leather boot, usually from 8 to 10 inches high, which is best when equipped with "cord," neoprene, or rubber-cork soles. The other is a leather-top, rubber-bottom hunting pac, of similar height, for rain, light snow, and muskeg.

Any boot of this kind should be purchased one-half size larger than the hunter's dress shoe. This added dimension takes care of the inevitable foot swelling during hard walking, and allows for the use of heavy socks and often felt innersoles, which in themselves protect and insulate the feet.

Shoe pacs with leather tops and rubber bottoms are ideal for mild-weather hunting in rain, light snow, or muskeg.

For dry, cool weather, the all-leather hunting boots with composition soles and tops that are not over 10 inches high can't be beat. Such boots should have heels which are square-cut on the face, not continuous with the sole or cut at an oblique angle. A squarecut heel is vital for climbing in rocky country, especially when going downhill. The square face of the heel will prevent small rocks from "rolling" beneath the boot and causing dangerous falls.

For wet, mild weather, leather-top, rubber-bottom pacs are the best footgear yet developed. However, for cold weather, pacs are an abomination. They become sweaty, clammy, and colder than the left nostril of a hound.

Where real cold enters the hunting picture, the best bet is to go to hunting boots insulated with foam rubber or other material.

For the most extreme cold, two other types of footgear represent the best developments yet. A pair of 12-inch felt gaiters worn over a pair of heavy woolen socks and inside a pair of 4-buckle rubber overshoes, or arctics, will keep most men's feet warm down to zero. For subzero use, Eskimo *mukluks* are the very best, the only type of footwear that will keep the feet from freezing during long hours of outside exposure. *Mukluks* are hair boots of nearly knee height, worn over an inner boot having the hair turned inside.

GLOVES. The hands and fingers are also critical areas in cold weather. Good hunting gloves should provide both protection and warmth.

In mild weather, authentic buckskin gloves (the short ones, not the fancy gauntlet type which habitually collects twigs and leaves in the cuffs) are the best possible hand covering for work around camp, handling horses, ropes, and saddles, and for hunting on horseback.

Next in warmth, most inexpensive, and one of the most usable gloves ever developed are knitted brown jersey gloves. Their one fault is that they are not waterproof. A pair of these jersey gloves worn inside a pair of leather mittens will keep the hands warm in very cold weather. Even better is a pair of rabbit-lined leather driving gloves.

For extreme cold the warmest mittens ever invented are down-filled mitts of gauntlet design. The uppers come well over the wrists, shutting out any draft, and the hands have an inside pocket, enabling the fist to be doubled, and a mouton backing for wiping snow and moisture off the nose and face. Such down mitts often are used in combination with a pocket hand-warmer which is heated by lighter fluid and carried in the coat pocket.

HUNTING COATS. The choice of a hunting coat largely depends on the type of foliage encountered, the degree of cold and storm expected, and the wearer's physical conditioning.

15

The most useful mild-weather hunting coat is a denim jacket which matches the denim Levi riding pants. Such a coat is tough as boiled owl, resists snagging on limbs far better than most materials, is trim, lightweight, inexpensive—and you seldom see a big-game hunter wearing one. The reason? The virtues of the denim jacket haven't been discovered by the average hunter.

However, consider that many guides, horse wranglers, and stockmen in the West habitually use a denim jacket while riding horseback. There's no better garment made for riding through snaggy brush. Woolen, nylon, cotton, and down coats in such terrain will soon be torn to ribbons. But an old "ducking jumper" takes it and wants more. For colder weather, such horsemen simply buy the kind with flannel lining.

Other suitable hunting coats include heavy woolen shirts with the tails cut square so they may be worn outside the belt, down vests and coats, and for the most extreme cold, down-filled, hooded, and fur-ruffed parkas.

One of the most useful coats for average big-game hunting conditions is the woolen cruiser-stag made of heavy mackinaw-type cloth, with double thicknesses at the shoulders and cuffs for added warmth and wind protection. The coat has ample pockets for the numerous small articles the big-game hunter habitually lugs along. It is usually red to conform to the hunting regulations of many states.

One other coat which should *always* go along on any big-game hunt is an entirely waterproof raincoat. Unless the raincoat is hooded, a rubber rain hat and rubber pants should complement it. A most useful type of waterproof rain pants used in the West are rubber "lambing chaps," which can be made up by any good canvas-and-awning house and cost around $10.

HEADGEAR. In cold weather one fact should be kept in mind. The human brain is used more than the extremities; therefore more blood circulates through it. More body heat may be lost by having a cold head than by having cold hands. It is odd, but by keeping the head warm, the hands and feet are kept correspondingly warmer. In choosing headgear this fact is worth remembering, especially for older, balding men whose heads have a tendency to grow up through their hair.

Hunting caps are made of nylon, cotton twill, corduroy, wool, and leather. Some are down-filled. Most are red or flame orange to conform to hunting laws, and most have earflaps in case of wind or sudden drops in temperature.

One of the best mild-weather hunting caps is a nylon ski cap such as professionals wear. For colder weather a woolen or down-filled cap should be chosen. Such a cap should always be equipped with earflaps and a stiff

16

peak long enough to keep the direct rays of the sun, twigs, rain, etc., out of the eyes. Even in the Arctic, where a hunter wears a fur-ruffed parka, such a cap is useful in wind, especially if he uses eyeglasses, to keep the fur out of his eyes.

CHANGE OF CLOTHES. It is wise to make everlastingly certain that on any prolonged big-game hunt you take along one complete change of clothes (except rain gear and a heavy outer coat). Mild mishaps such as falling into the creek, getting caught out in sudden storms, or tearing the seat out of the britches while straddling logs all have a way of happening around a hunting camp. Also, after a few days of hard hunting and sweating, and without the convenience of the home tub, most hunters begin to acquire an aroma comparable to that of an old soured churn. A quick dip in a creek or lake, plus fresh clothes, makes one more acceptable in woods society again.

BEDDING. Closely allied to the matter of clothes is the hunter's bed. The only suitable bed is a good sleeping bag. Dacron and similar synthetic fibers make good filling for bags meant for use in mild weather. But the only really good sleeping bag for the big-game hunter is a down-filled bag. Regardless of the warmth of the autumn days, the nights of big-game hunting seasons range from cool to downright cold, often below zero. A down-filled bag will keep the hunter warm where others won't, and is least expensive in the long run.

The sleeping bag should be of a size to fit the hunter, and should have either a cotton sheet or inner liner, which is easily laundered and will keep the down bag clean. In extreme cold, even the down bag may be warmed by the addition of a woolen blanket folded and placed inside.

Some pillows meant for sleeping-bag use are of the rubber, blow-up type. Others are integral with the air mattress. Experienced outdoorsmen find few of these adequate. The best is a small feather-filled or foam rubber pillow, rolled up inside the bag and ready for use when the hunter is tired.

The rubber air mattress has long been the standard item for use with the sleeping bag and is still the difference between an outdoor night of comfort and a night of misery. It should only be blown up enough so that when lying on your side you can just bump your hip on the ground if you bounce gently up and down. Too much air is like sleeping on a plank. Plastic air mattress are not worth packing to the hills; they won't take the hard use in a hunting camp.

Recently an invention has come along which threatens eventually to replace the air mattress in those hunting camps where portability to and

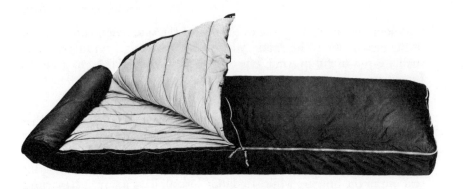

Down-filled sleeping bags are best for cold nights in big-game country. Oblong-shaped Eddie Bauer bag (*above*) is warm at 30 degrees below zero; compact Alaska mummy bag (*below*), for milder weather, is comfortable at 25 degrees above zero.

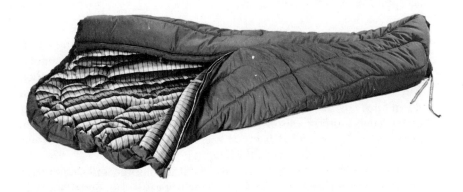

from camp is no great problem. That's the insulated, folding camp cot. This item has four aluminum leg bars which set into light side rails built right into the cot with spring tension. This lifts the cot approximately 8 inches off the ground, protecting the sleeper from moisture and insects. Its down or Dacron insulation is not only comfortable but eliminates that coldness of a rubber mattress long thought to be unavoidable. The entire cot folds neatly inside a small package about 30 inches long and 8 inches wide. It is easily carried on horse, car, boat, or plane.

RIFLE AND SCABBARD. In ninety cases out of a hundred, one rifle, proper'y sighted in beforehand and carefully taken care of during the trip, is all any big-game hunter needs. Some hunters say that a spare rifle should be carried along, just in case, and they cite instances where a rifle has been put out of commission.

During my own forty-two years of hunting big game from Mexico to Alaska I've seen two instances of this. One rifle's scope crosshairs suddenly snapped for no apparent reason. Another fine rifle had its stock broken off at the grip because a knot-headed horse suddenly barreled the wrong way around a pine tree and hooked the rifle butt along the bole. In both instances, the hunters were with partners who had rifles; in addition, the guide accompanying them had his rifle to be used as a spare.

The biggest drawback to lugging along two or three rifles is the matter of transportation. Once you arrive at road's end the rifle often has to go on a horse. Seldom are there more than enough available riding horses to have a spare, and two scabbards on one horse is like hauling a bicycle in the back of a station wagon for emergency. Among the numerous outfitters who have packed me into the hills, I know only one who, if he had to pack a hunter's *two* rifles, would not lay back his ears and bellow his head off.

The rifle scabbard is another important item. Regardless of the outfitter's policy, it is always smart for the hunter to provide his own. It should be made of heavy cowhide, fit the rifle, and cover the gun at least as far as the grip. Those short, surplus military scabbards advertised at army stores are useless for anything except lever-action carbines.

EQUIPMENT AND FOOD. The question of camp equipment and food is answered in advance if the hunter makes reservations with an outfitter who furnishes everything except personal items—as most of them do. This, of course, should be ascertained in advance. However, usually a "furnished" hunt includes all personnel such as guides, wrangler, cook, etc., and all camp equipment and food.

When the hunting party goes on its own, all such items must be furnished by the party. Transportation of the gear to and from the hunting camp must also be considered.

Beginning hunters often make major mistakes in selecting food and equipment. One of the best ways of avoiding error is to include in the party, if possible, an experienced hunter or camper, then heed his suggestions. The twin mistakes of the tyro are that he usually takes too much food and equipment, and much of it of the wrong kind.

The basic camp equipment for any hunt includes tent, stove, lantern, axes, saw, shovel, waterproof tarp, and camp cooking and eating utensils. The type of gear depends upon the number in the party, the kind of country, the season of year, and the length of the intended hunt.

TENTS. For mild weather, a baker-type tent will do for two people. The cooking fire is placed before the open front; the hunters sleep at the sloping rear, and the reflected heat of the fire provides the needed warmth. For three or four hunters, in mild weather, the baker tent may be augmented by a 7-by-7-foot tepee tent, which will sleep two of the party. Allow 25 square feet per person for sleeping space.

However, for big-game hunting in any area and for any size party, no tent yet devised surpasses a good wall tent with a stove. Such a tent provides ample head room and is easily heated. A white tent is far more cheerful inside than a colored tent.

An 8-by-10-foot wall tent will accommodate two hunters, if they don't mind being a bit cramped. Sleeping bags are piled up during the day to provide room and laid back down at night. A tent of 12-by-14-foot size is ideal for four hunters.

A tent should be entirely waterproof, and this should be determined in advance. The best way to make sure is to set the tent up on the lawn and turn the hose on it. One leak in a tent, especially if it occurs during violent rain and over *your* bed, can spoil a hunting trip.

Most veteran outdoorsmen immediately upon buying any wall tent will have a canvas shop sew an additional foot or two of canvas around

A favorite of big-game hunters, the wall tent is easily heated and has sufficient headroom for cooking indoors.

the bottom edge, extending the tent height. This allows standing room inside so that no one has to go around humped over.

For milder-weather hunting, and a party of two men, several other forms of tents may be used. These include the explorer tent, the forester tent, and their variations.

The explorer tent has a high front and a sloping ridge which tapers at the rear. It is set up by staking down the bottom edge, then erecting the front upon two shear poles and stretching the ridge tightly to the rear.

A forester tent is somewhat similar in shape but is set up with the two shear poles in front, and the ridge stretched over another pole reaching from the front shear to the earth behind the tent. In stretching the forester tent tight, two angles of roof are created in the fabric, quite like the two pitches of a large dairy barn. Both tents are light, snug, and easily set up.

In an emergency, pup tents or ponchos offer some protection. These are simple A wedges of canvas or rubberized material stretched tightly over some form of ridgepole.

For those camper-hunters who want to use their house trailer for hunting, there are several types of tents available. These are usually awnings that fasten to the trailer contour. Some have a tent that can be erected adjacent to the trailer and the awning can be stretched between. For mild weather, when the hunter wishes to camp at his car, the trailer type of tent or an umbrella tent with an awning is commonly used.

STOVES. Camp stoves come in a variety of types. Some stoves are made of welded iron and must be hauled intact. Folding sheet-iron stoves have ingenious arrangements whereby they may be taken down, folded flat, and hauled as a neat bundle. Some have telescoping stovepipes, others have standard lengths of 4-inch pipe used with a fireproof pipe collar.

Outdoor magazines continuously advertise these camp stoves and they are entirely suitable. Also, the military developed several compact folding sheet-iron stoves during World War II, and some are still available in army surplus stores. Many veteran outdoorsmen have their own stoves made to their specifications. When one does this, and doesn't mind a bit of extra weight, it is an advantage to have the top made of heavier metal than the sides to prevent buckling when heated.

A two-burner gasoline stove makes a fine addition to the wall tent and metal stove. During mild days, or when one is in a hurry, say, to get a quick lunch, the gasoline stove can be quickly lit, used, and turned off. An adequate tent warmer can be made by cutting two holes in an inverted No. 2 washtub, one for the pipe and one for feeding wood. Cut the hole for the wood on three sides only, leaving a hinged door that can be closed.

21

Two-burner gasoline stove is clean and fast for cooking outdoors in mild weather.

LIGHTS. The standard camp light has long been the gasoline lantern. It is better to use the single burner—fewer mantles to carry along, less to get out of order, and the light is nearly as adequate.

Electric camp lights—the big ones run on a single large battery—are being increasingly used. Small gas-operated lamps using a disposable cartridge are making an appearance in hunting camps. They are perhaps safer than gasoline lanterns but are far more expensive to operate.

AXES AND SAWS. Camp axes for logging up stove wood and tent poles, and for clearing down timber around camp, vary in size and utility. For most camps, two such cutting tools will suffice. One is a double-bitted ax with 2½-pound head and 28-inch handle. The other is a Swedish bow saw with a 39-inch blade. Regardless of the amount of camp wood to cut and the size of the party, those two tools will handle the job best. An ax doesn't have to have a 5-pound head to be highly efficient. Two cutting edges on an ax make it virtually as effective as two single-bits. And nothing goes through stove wood faster than the ribbonlike blade of a bow saw.

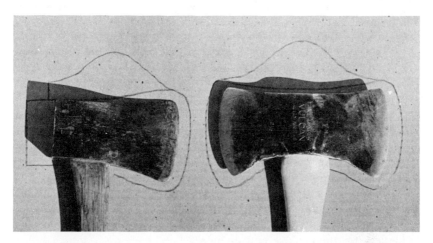

A sheath can be made for a single- or double-bit ax with the patterns shown above. Then leather is cut accordingly, riveted and equipped with a strap and buckle (*below*).

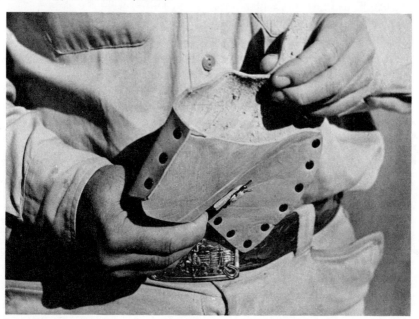

COOKING UTENSILS. Camp cooking utensils should include a large pail for carrying and heating water, a coffeepot of suitable size, pots for cooking vegetables, the equivalent of a 12-inch frying pan or skillet for each two people in the party, and if at all possible, a medium-sized Dutch oven. No better camp cooking utensil has ever been developed than the Dutch oven. It will bake, fry, broil, roast, and stew, and it retains an even heat.

Nesting aluminum kits are compact and easily packed. Most veteran campers find extensive use for the kettle, coffeepot, and inside pots, but immediately throw away the aluminum plates and cups. An aluminum coffee cup holds a scalding heat long after the coffee is too cold to drink, and an aluminum plate gets cold and greasy almost before the steak hits it. Such items are often replaced with enameled ware. The important thing is to make sure that each camper has an individual plate, cup, spoon, knife, fork, and a small bowl or dish for cereal, fruit, etc.

Cutlery for the cook should include a butcher knife, a long-handled fork and large spoon (slaving over a hot stove is *hot* on the hands), pancake or egg turner, and some kind of hotpad. Nothing is hotter than the handle of a cast-iron skillet or the lid of a Dutch oven.

With the cutlery should be included the necessary dishtowels and soap for laundering the dirty dishes. Incidentally, regardless of preferences, the man who does the cooking in camp *never* does the dishes. It is also an unwritten law in any hunting camp that the first one who complains about the cooking immediately has to take over the job himself.

Two men on a bow saw make short work of hefty stove logs.

Nested aluminum pots are easily packed, but many campers prefer enameled cups and plates which do not heat up and cool off so rapidly.

FOOD.   Grub lists for camping will be as varied as the people who make them. Camp food should include those basic items necessary to a well-balanced diet and be sufficiently ample to satisfy individual tastes, increased appetites, and possible emergency. It is a long way from a hunting camp back to the corner grocery.

Here is the simplest formula for taking the right foods to camp: Multiply the amounts of the same foods the hunter, or hunters, eat at home daily by the expected number of days of the trip; include two or three basic foods for use in emergency; and add a margin of twenty-five per cent. Do this for breakfast and supper, but alter the items of the noon meal, since hunters often skip lunch or just eat a sandwich.

Suppose four hunters are going and all agree that in the morning such things as juice, coffee, bacon, eggs, and toast would represent a good breakfast. Assume also that each man would eat about 6 ounces of juice, ½ ounce of coffee, a tablespoon of sugar for the two cups, 2 squirts of canned milk, 1/7 pound of bacon, 2 eggs, and 2 slices of bread with 2 pats of butter.

If these amounts are multiplied by four (hunters) times ten (ten-day hunt) the total amount will represent the amount of food needed for all breakfasts while on the trip. Naturally, someone will prefer ham to bacon, hotcakes to toast, and so forth. Such changes can be made and the items for which they are substituted decreased.

The items necessary for supper can be handled the same way, and the lunches arrived at similarly. It is wise, in making up the food list, to have each member of the party present, state his preferences, and help arrive at the total. When the list is tentatively completed, multiply each amount by an added one-fourth for a safety margin. At camp hunters eat ravenously and there is always the chance of running out of some items and having to substitute others. If the approximate balance of meat, vegetables, and fruit eaten at home is maintained, the diet won't be lopsided in any direction.

Meat is hard to transport on a hunting trip. Most wise campers plan on taking along fresh meat for the first day or so, then changing over to cured meat such as ham, bacon, and canned meats. Before these get monotonous, all hunters hope to have fresh liver, heart, and later meat from downed game.

Two of the best staples for an emergency are an extra bag of flour and potatoes. With these two items, and with any game in camp, a party could become snowed in or endure similar emergency for a month if necessary.

PACKING. Some form of adequate packaging is needed to protect the gear en route and for storing it at camp.

For sleeping bags, the Navy covers made for officers during the last war are among the best. These consist of a canvas bottom, sides that fold over, and straps that buckle the bedroll. A waterproof tarp of suitable size, folded around the sleeping bag and tied with nylon rope, is also fine protection for the bedroll. I've looked thirty years for an absolutely waterproof sleeping-bag cover to be used in transit in wet weather. The only one I ever found was made by a friend from the cloth top of a convertible.

For personal items and extra clothing, the Army and Navy duffel bags measuring approximately 30 inches long and 16 inches in diameter are among the handiest and safest containers. Leather-bound duffel bags of similar shape are now available.

Gasoline lanterns are best packed in plywood boxes which have room inside for extra mantles, funnel, and generator. Axes and bowsaws should be sheathed. Even a piece of burlap tightly wound around the ax blade will prevent accidental cutting of gear or people. And a fine sheath for the bowsaw is a length of old garden hose, split along one side, and tied with cord to the blade.

Dishes are best hauled in a box in which they fit snugly. Camp dish kits are often nested, then set inside a heavy-canvas bag sewed to fit and having a drawstring closure.

A fair makeshift box for hauling groceries is a wooden orange crate obtainable at many food stores. Two crates, filled with groceries and balanced as to weight, are often packed (after being wrapped in mantas) on a pack animal and successfully hauled to camp. Later, the orange crates can be nailed together for a cupboard for storing food in the tent.

The best possible container for packaging the food en route is a pair of wooden boxes, or "kitchens," made especially for the purpose. These boxes are usually made of light plywood and range in size from 20 to 24 inches long, 10 to 12 inches wide, and 15 to 18 inches high. Such a pair of grub boxes are the handiest things imaginable for hauling food in a truck, station wagon, or car. Where horse transportation is necessary at road's-end, the filled and balanced boxes are simply wrapped and become a pair of cargoes for a pack animal.

A similar pair of boxes called "alforjas boxes" are most useful, especially when horse transportation is used to reach camp. These are light rectangular boxes made to fit inside the canvas saddlebags used on a pack saddle. Some have hinged lids, others a canvas flap. Many alforjas boxes have open tops, permitting them to be used with loads that bulge or stick out on top. These boxes will carry food, clothing, quarters of venison on the trip back, or oats for the horses.

My own alforjas boxes measure 23 inches long, 11 inches wide, and 17 inches tall. They fit snugly into most saddlebags. On the ends of each one, 4 inches down from the top, I have attached hardwood cleats, diagonally. These are used when lashing the boxes onto a mule's spine without any available covering for the boxes. As an added protection to gear, I have a pair of rubber bags which slip inside the boxes. Any type of duffel, even delicate binoculars, cameras, and other breakables can be packaged inside the rubber bags and slipped into the alforjas boxes. Regardless of what the mule does, the gear will get to where it's going without damage or loss.

4

Rifles and Cartridges

IN THE RECENT past, the hunter with a preference for a certain cartridge had to accept any available rifle which would chamber it. Similarly, the hunter who preferred a certain type of action often was limited in his choice of cartridges which that action would safely handle.

Today, modern rifle and cartridge development has reached a stage where the big-game hunter can exercise his individuality in both rifles and cartridges, yet have them in combination.

The four basic types of actions in the big-game rifle are:

1. Lever
2. Bolt
3. Slide, or Pump
4. Autoloading

LEVER-ACTION RIFLES.   Various lever-action big-game rifles attained a degree of popularity before the turn of the century. Among these were the Winchester Models 1866, 1876, 1873, and 1886. None of them, however, reached the sustained acclaim of the Model 1894. This was partly due to the simple, sure functioning of that particular action. It was due to a far greater extent to the fact that the Model 94 was designed to handle a cartridge loaded with the new smokeless powder—all former lever actions had been made for black-powder cartridges.

Winchester's Model 94 was made to handle the .30/30, the .38/55, and the .32/40 smokeless cartridges. But of the three, the .30/30 soon became most popular and has remained so ever since. Even today, for some types of hunting, the old Model 94 full of .30/30 shells is hard to beat.

Lever-action rifles (*from top*): Winchester Model 94, Savage Model 99, Winchester Model 88, Marlin Model 336.

Other early lever-action rifles included the Winchester Model 1892, meant for short cartridges, and the Model 95, box magazine, which handle the .30/40 Krag, .35 Winchester, .405 Winchester, and .30 Government cartridges. The .405, incidentally, was President Teddy Roosevelt's favorite rifle.

In 1899 the Savage lever-action Model 99 repeating rifle was released, and like the Model 94 Winchester, the Savage 99 has retained its popularity to the present time.

The Savage was designed for a cartridge similar to the .30/30, which was the unique .303 Savage. The action differed from the Model 94 in that it was hammerless, had a rotary magazine, and side ejection of empty cartridges. It was a strong, safe action, sleek in appearance, and had excellent handling qualities. Of all the lever actions, the Model 94 and the Model 99 have been most popular. The Marlin Model 336 has also been a popular lever action.

Among the intrinsic drawbacks of the old lever action were the facts that its construction necessitated a two-piece stock; and the rear locking bolt would not permit the extended use of the higher-powered cartridges without "stretching" and creating excessive headspace. In the Model 94, an additional fault was that only blunt-end bullets could be safely used in its tubular magazine—otherwise there was danger, during recoil or bumping, of a sharp bullet point igniting the primer of the cartridge immediately ahead.

Today's versions of the popular lever-action rifles include the modernized Savage Model 99 and Winchester's new Model 88. In the Model 88, the three basic faults of the Model 94 have been corrected. The 88 has a one-piece stock, which is conducive to better accuracy; front-locking bolt-lugs which permit the use of higher-intensity cartridges; and a clip magazine which takes spitzer (sharp)-pointed bullets. The Savage Model 99 has now been modernized to accept a magazine loading clip, as well as the older rotary-type magazine.

In these two modern lever-action rifles, such adequate cartridges as the .300 Savage, .308 Winchester, and the .358 Winchester are available and safely handled.

The virtues of the lever-action rifle are that it is light, handy, permits fast successive shots, is useful for both left- and right-handed shooters, and is the handiest type of rifle yet devised for a saddle scabbard.

BOLT-ACTION RIFLES. This strong, simple action became popular among hunters who had been introduced to the Springfield, Krag, and Enfield rifles during their military service. The action is particularly suited to high-intensity cartridges, and it can be used with a rugged, one-piece stock.

Bolt-action rifles (*from top*): Winchester Model 70, Remington Model 700, Savage Model 110-MCL for the left-handed shooter, Weatherby Mark V.

This custom-built sporter combines a Model 98 Mauser bolt action, Vickery barrel, and Bishop stock.

The first commercial versions of the bolt-action rifle were Remington's Model 30 (a commercial form of the 1917 Enfield), marketed in 1921, and Winchester's Model 54 introduced four years later.

These two bolt-action rifles, and their military forebears, are the foundation of today's modern, highly efficient sporting rifles. Today there are a half-dozen American manufacturers making high-quality bolt-action big-game rifles. These include Browning, Colt, Harrington & Richardson, Savage, Remington, Winchester, and Weatherby. Four of the best are the Winchester Model 70, the Remington Model 700, the Weatherby Mark V, and the recent Ruger Model 77. The Weatherby Mark V is a custom-grade bolt-action rifle of great beauty and class. And the Ruger Model 77 incorporates several outstanding features not found in other modern bolt-action rifles. Two of the features are the integral scope bases, and a stock-screw which sets at an angle, binding the barrel-action to the stock in precisely the same position and tension after disassembly. The Savage Company has fulfilled a long-standing need by their introduction of a modern bolt-action big-game rifle in optional left-handed model—the Model 110-MCL. Weatherby also offers left-handed models, at higher cost.

Owing to the increased interest in bolt-action rifles, plus the availability of cheap military actions and machine-inletted stocks which take ninety per cent of the drudgery out of stock building, there has been an augmented interest in home remodeling of rifles. Also, with the ever-improving design in military rifles, many nations have taken to dumping their surplus of obsolete rifles on the open market; and needless to say, the United States has been the favorite dumping ground.

These cheap rifles often prove expensive in the long run. It is sufficient to say here that the cost of converting any military rifle to sporting use is often as much as the purchase price of a better, and new, factory sporting rifle. More, with the exception of a few such actions as the Enfield, Springfield, and Model 98 Mauser, old military actions are both unsafe and unsuitable for conversions. The majority of such "bargain" military rifles are junk.

Single actions, either converted or custom made, are generally unsuited to big-game hunting except for the experimenter or specialist.

SLIDE-ACTION RIFLES. The popularity of the pump-action shotgun, introduced just before the turn of the century led to the development of the slide-action rifle, namely the Remington Model 14, later developed into the Model 141. This rifle handled the .25, .30, .32, and .35-caliber Remington cartridges.

Over the years, the slide action achieved a considerable popularity, especially with shooters who liked the pump-action shotgun. The rifle was "fast" on deer-sized game, especially in brushy country demanding quick follow-up shots.

Today's modern slide action is best represented by Remington's Model 760 Gamemaster rifles. These are trim, clip-loaded, fast-handling rifles with bolts that rotate and head-lock into the barrels. This permits the use of the most modern cartridges including the .270, .30/06, .280, .300 Savage, .308 Winchester, and . 35 Savage. Another very recent and fine slide-action repeater handling the old standby .30/30 cartridge is the Savage Model 170, selling for just under $100.

Two popular slide-action rifles: Remington 760 (*top*) and Savage 170.

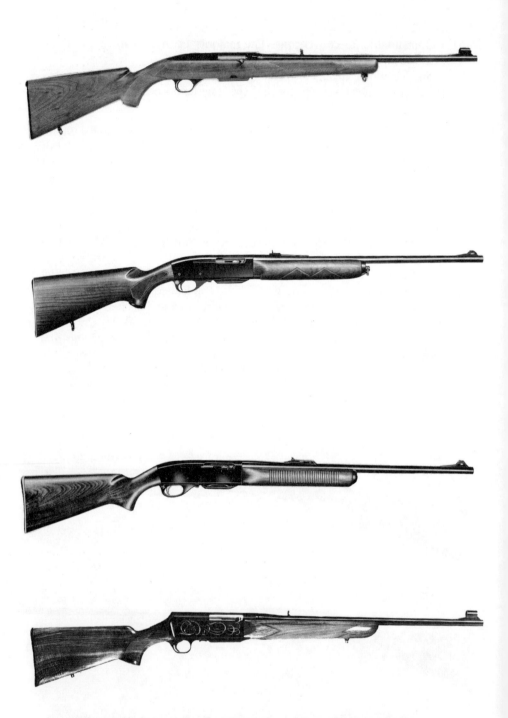

Autoloading rifles (*from top*): Winchester Model 100, Remington Model 740ADL, Remington Model 742A, Browning BAR.

THE AUTOLOADERS. In 1913, the Remington Model 8 Autoloading Rifle was introduced. This was a John M. Browning design which continued in popularity almost to the present day. It was redesigned in 1936 into the Model 81 Autoloader, and many of these old "corn-shellers" are still in use.

This autoloader used the same series of rimless cartridges as the slide action—the .25, .30, and .32 Remingtons, all comparable ballistically to the rimmed Winchester .25/35, .30/30, and .32 Special. In addition, the Models 8 and 81 used the famed .35 Remington cartridge, long known for its knock-down properties at close range on deer.

The Remington Autoloading Rifle of today bears little resemblance to the old Model 8 or 81. Instead, the Model 740 Remington Woodsmaster closely resembles the modern slide-action rifle and is available in much the same series of high-intensity cartridges.

In addition, three new gas-operated autoloading rifles have become available to the hunter. One is the Winchester Model 100, which in carbine length may be had with 19-inch barrel. A second, the Remington Model 742, may be had in either rifle or carbine with 18½-inch barrel. The most recent autoloader comes from the Browning Arms Company, and is called the BAR (Browning Automatic Rifle). Like the other two, the Browning is clip-fed, and has the additional virtue of being able to withstand the pressures of the most modern high-intensity magnum cartridges, including the 7-mm Remington Magnum, the .300 Winchester Magnum, and the .338 Winchester Magnum.

CARTRIDGES. Cartridges for big-game use are always being improved, developed, and replaced. A popular cartridge today becomes obsolete within a year or two. The trend in cartridge development is basically in the direction of improved bullets of reasonable weight driven at higher and higher velocities.

Following is a list of many of the standard, recent, or older big-game cartridges which have remained popular. The list begins with those usually considered minimum for deer, and shows also the bullet weights available for use on suitable big game:

CARTRIDGE	BULLET WEIGHT (grains)
.243 Winchester	100
6-mm Remington	100
.240 Weatherby Magnum	100
.250 Savage	100
.257 Roberts	100, 117
.257 Weatherby Magnum	100, 117
.25-06 Remington	120

6.5-mm Remington Magnum	120
.264 Winchester Magnum	140
.270 Winchester	130, 150
7-mm Mauser	175
.280 Remington	150, 160, 165
.284 Winchester	125, 150
7-mm Remington Magnum	125, 150, 175
7-mm Weatherby Magnum	154, 175
7 x 61 Sharpe & Hart	160
.30/30 Winchester	150, 170
.300 Savage	150, 180
.308 Winchester	150, 180
.30/06 Springfield	150, 180
.300 Winchester Magnum	150, 180
.300 Weatherby Magnum	180
.338 Winchester Magnum	200, 250, 300
.35 Remington	200
.350 Remington Magnum	200, 250
.358 Winchester	200, 250
.375 H&H Magnum	270, 300

To this list may be added the various wildcat cartridges which duplicate or exceed the ballistics of the above cartridges, as well as other obsolete or near-obsolete cartridges. Also, additional bullet weights for the above cartridges are available from several bullet makers for handloading.

HUNTING SIGHTS. Sights for big-game rifles are of three types—open sights, peep sights, and telescopic sights.

Standard sighting equipment on factory rifles usually consists of open sights. The front sight is some form of bead, round or square, and may be red, white, or plain black. The rear sight consists of an element set solidly into a slot in the rifle barrel, with an extension strap of thin steel upturned at the end. This vertical upturn has a U or V notch in which the front sight is aligned. Elevation adjustment is made by spring-lifting the rear of the sight upon a series of elevated notches. Each notch, depending upon the length of the rifle barrel, represents several inches change. Windage adjustment is obtained by moving the entire rear sight sidewise with a brass punch and a hammer.

In the more recent factory open sights, adjustments for windage and/or elevation may be made by movable elements within the sight, which are tightened by setscrews. These sights are easier to adjust.

Good cartridges for most medium game (*left to right*): .25/06, .264, .270, .284, 7-mm Remington Magnum, .30/30, .308, and .30/06.

Some suitable big-game cartridges (*left to right*): 7-mm Remington Magnum, .30/06, .300 Winchester Magnum, .300 Weatherby, .338 Magnum, .350 Remington Magnum, and .375 H&H Magnum.

Standard open sights: the flat-top (*top*) and the semi-buckhorn both come with a V or U notch and elevation adjustments.

Open sights are useful at reasonably short ranges, and for young shooters. The eye attempts to focus upon three separate objects at once—the rear sight, front sight, and target. Older men, whose eyesight is less keen, often have difficulty making this quick visual adjustment.

A better sight is the peep sight. This has a relatively large opening, or aperture, and is normally set as far to the rear in the sighting plane as possible (usually on the rifle's receiver) so that the eye looks not *at* the sight but *through* it. A normal eye will "center" such an aperture naturally without actually seeing it. The peep sight is used in conjunction with a front sight similar to that used with open sights. The eye must only focus on two objects, the front sight and the target.

Generally peep sights are accurate at longer ranges than are open sights, and are more useful to the older shooter whose eyesight is beginning to lose flexibility. Peep sights are adjustable for both windage and elevation. In the better models, this is accomplished by micrometer-like knobs, with each click representing a fraction of a minute-of-angle, itself practically one inch per hundred yards.

In adjusting both open and peep sights for elevation or windage, the rear sight is moved in the direction of the change desired. That is, if a rifle in trial shoots left, the rear sight must be moved right in order to correct the error. If the rifle shoots high, the rear sight must be lowered.

The peep sight is more accurate at long ranges than the open sight, and has adjustments for windage and elevation. *Redfield Gunsight Co.*

Telescope sights are the finest type and are useful for most forms of big-game shooting. The scope has four basic virtues. It enables the shooter to see better because of its light-gathering qualities, enabling him to sight accurately in dim light. The magnification of a scope sight helps greatly in correct bullet placement and game identification. Perhaps its greatest asset is that the shooter focuses upon only one object—the target. The scope's reticle appears to be superimposed upon the target. Lastly, the scope makes a fine substitute binocular. In hunting big game, the scope will be used ten times for looking, spotting, and identifying game, to the one time it is used in shooting.

The real turning point in scope use by the average American big-game hunter occurred in 1933. Before that time, scopes were high-priced, usually imports, and generally mounted high on the rifle. The best grades, suitable for big-game hunting, were beyond the purse of the average hunter and therefore beyond his interest. In 1933, however, Bill Weaver of the W. R. Weaver Company, El Paso, Texas, perfected and placed on the market his "3/30" scope. This glass sight was equal to the expensive scopes in optical qualities. It would withstand the recoil of heavy rifles. It could be mounted low on the rifle barrel. And most of all, it cost only a fraction of the price of other good scopes—$27.50.

The famed "3/30" caught the fancy of American hunters, and we have become increasingly a country of scope users. Today, American-made scopes are among the world's best, and the younger generation of big-game hunters is coming to regard the scope sight as an integral part of the rifle. For hunters over fifty-five years of age, with normal eyesight, a scope sight is almost a must for accurate shooting, since at that age man's eyesight has lost its power of "accommodation."

For most big-game hunting, scopes of 2½ to 6 power are best. For average use the best is 4 power. A majority of hunters like the crosshair reticle, as it permits easy holdover and visibility at distant game. For shooting in dark woods, at reasonably close ranges, or for running game, many prefer a post reticle, or dotted crosshair.

Competition is so keen among scope makers that fine hunting scopes, in single power, may be had from several reputable makers at around $50 for a 4-power glass. Among these are high-grade 4-power scopes by Weaver, Bushnell, Leupold, Bausch & Lomb, and Lyman. There is no need to go higher in price, and it is difficult to obtain any higher quality than the products of these makers.

In the past few years there has been an increased interest in variable scopes. These are scopes which may be changed in power, usually from a low of 2 or 3 power, to a high of possibly 9 or 10 power.

The earlier variable scopes had several drawbacks. They were large and bulky due to their large objective lenses, considered necessary at that time. Also, as the power increased the width-of-field decreased, and the apparent size of the reticle changed. Owing to their bulk, the early variable scopes didn't ride well in a saddle scabbard. They were more susceptible to bumps, mainly because there was more to bump. Finally, they were more expensive than fixed-power scopes. The manufacturers of modern variable scopes reduced or eliminated many of these faults. In many of the newer variables a power range of from 2 to 7 power is possible in a scope no larger or heavier than the earlier 4-power scopes. Examples of smaller variable scopes include the Weaver V7 and Leupold's Vari-X 2 x 7.

The advantages of variable scopes certainly outweigh the faults. One scope of several selective powers of magnification will cost far less than separate single scopes. A variable scope permits the use of the same rifle for more types of game without a change of sights. As one example, a .243 with scope turned to 9 power is nearly ideal for shooting chucks; with a twist of the wrist the same .243, using heavier bullets and with scope set at 4 power, becomes an adequate deer outfit. As another example, a .284 Winchester with scope set at 3 power represents an almost ideal combination for running deer in somewhat open country; when set at 6 power it is similarly ideal for a ram perched upon a bluff 350 yards away, or an antelope buck at 400 yards which is watching and cannot be approached any closer.

Often the cost in ammunition spent in resighting a rifle whose scopes must be changed to fit the game hunted will pay the difference in price of a variable scope. Finally a variable scope on the big-game rifle often eliminates the need for lugging a pair of binoculars around as it can be used in spotting game.

At this writing, Bushnell, Leupold, Weaver, Bausch & Lomb, and Redfield all make fine variable scopes. Each has its individual advantages and selling points—such as the Command-Post of the Bushnell, the nitrogen-filled fogproofing of the Leupold, and the fine eye-relief of the Weaver. Prices for variable hunting scopes currently begin around $80.

All quality scope sights now have coated lenses and are adjustable for windage and elevation. Gradations, both for windage and elevation, are normally in fractions of a minute-of-angle. Dials under the adjustment-knob covers plainly indicate which direction to turn the knobs for a desired correction.

Scope Mounts. No scope will perform better than the rigidity of the mounts allows. Two qualities to look for in any mount are lightness and rigidity. There are three basic types of scope mounts. One is a mount composed of two separate bases having detachable or integral rings for encircling and holding the scope. These bases are fitted to the rifle contour, usually at the rear of the receiver and at the receiver ring, and

This Weaver Model K6 scope has a split-ring mount which consists of two bases attached to the rifle which dovetail with rings that hold the scope.

are screwed tightly at these points. Many modern rifles are tapped-and-drilled at the factory to accommodate such bases. The scope is fitted into the rings and they, in turn, are screwed solidly to the bases, with the scope forming a connecting bridge.

Another, and one of the most solid types, is an actual bridge mount. This differs from the two-base mount in that a metal connecting bridge is shaped integral with the bases. In other words, the ends of this metal strip become the terminal bases, and have similar rings for holding the scope. Some bridge-type mounts are screwed solidly to the rifle. Others have dovetail arrangements whereby the bridge-and-scope may be removed by turning one portion of the mount laterally.

The bridge mount is strong and solid because it has a connecting piece between the two rings which is screwed firmly to the rifle.

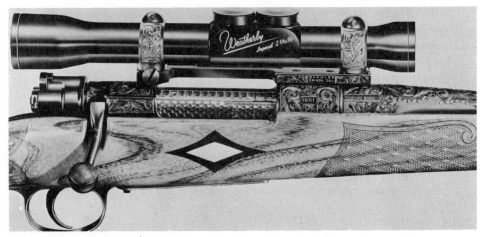

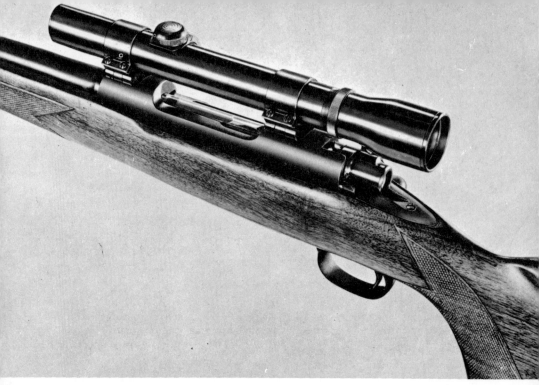

This Weaver pivot mount allows the K3 scope to be swung to one side so iron sights can be used.

The third type is a pivotal mount which swings the scope out of line so that iron sights may be used—usually if the scope is put out of commission by snow, fog, or damage. This is accomplished by a hinged arrangement in the base. The base in one model is a flat longitudinal element which fits the contour of the receiver's side. The hinge works on the order of the hinge in a piano cover.

All these mounts serve their purposes. The bridge type is considered the most rigid of all. Regardless of the type of mount, all hunting scopes should be mounted low on the rifle.

RIFLES FOR WOODS, PLAINS, AND MOUNTAINS. Often the beginning big-game hunter, and sometimes the veteran as well, will have only one rifle which must serve regardless of the game hunted or the terrain. Often this is an advantage in that an increased familiarity with the single weapon will result in better shooting. Many big-game hunters, however, own several rifles for various conditions.

Broadly speaking, the big-game rifle will be used for mountain, plains, or timber hunting.

Rifles for woods hunting should have adequate knockdown power (precise bullet placement is often difficult), fast sighting equipment, a fast-working action, and shoot bullets of relatively large diameter and weight. Thus the woods rifle is often a slide, lever or autoloader with either open or peep sights, or a low-power scope. It should fit the shooter well for fast handling.

Accuracy, flat trajectory, and retained punch at long ranges are the features to look for in a plains rifle. For these reasons, it is often a bolt action, sling equipped, with a scope of medium to high power. This is a rifle for precision shooting.

The basic difference between the plains rifle and the mountain rifle is weight. Both should shoot straight and flat. But in the mountains, a lightweight rifle makes climbing a lot easier. Rifles for mountain hunting should have short barrels, light stocks and scopes. Barrel length should not exceed 22 to 24 inches. The recoil of an adequate cartridge should be absorbed by a light recoil pad.

Recently both Remington and Winchester have added light mountain rifles in carbine lengths to their list of fine bolt-action rifles. Remington's Model 660 carbine, Model 788 carbine, and Winchester's Model 670 carbine and Model 88 carbine all make fine mountain rifles. Some models will accept cartridges of sufficient power for the heaviest game.

Light mountain rifles in carbine length (*from top*): Remington Model 660, Remington Model 788, Winchester Model 670.

5

Sighting in
a Rifle

A RIFLE IS of no value in hunting until it is sighted in. Also called zeroing in, this means aligning the sights so they coincide with the line of the bullet's flight at some reasonable range.

It is important in sighting in to understand the pull of gravity on a bullet in flight. The basic principle is that a bullet fired from a horizontally held rifle, above a flat earth surface, will strike the ground at the same time as a bullet held at the rifle's muzzle and dropped at the same instant. The first bullet will drop to the earth several hundred yards away, while the second bullet will drop straight downward. Both bullets will fall at an identical rate of speed. According to the formula "distance fallen equals ½ the acceleration of gravity, multiplied by the time squared," both bullets will fall 16 feet during the first second of free fall.

The path of a fired bullet is never flat, but follows a downward curve as velocity falls off. This path, called the trajectory, traces the pattern of an inverted catenary curve.

Sights are mounted on the top of a rifle, a scope sight about 1½ inches higher than the bore. If the sights are thus mounted, they are parallel to the bore. With the bullet dropping down from the bore for every yard it travels laterally, its flight will never coincide with the line of the sight at any distance, unless compensation is made. In short, the rifle will not shoot where one looks.

Since the flight of the bullet curves, beginning below the line of the sights, and since the target is usually a distant spot, the bullet must start under the line of sight in order to intersect it. It then rises upward, becomes level with the line of sight, continues above it, and finally descends, usually at a distance of several hundred yards, until it again

44

coincides with the line of sight. Normally, the second intersection of bullet with line of sight will be at the range at which the rifle is sighted in.

When sighting in, adjustments are made on the sights so that the line of sight dips down into the line of the bullet's flight. In other words, if the sights are held horizontally, as they are in most forms of shooting, the bore points mildly upward so that its line of flight will intersect the line of sight and hit the target.

If a rifle is not sighted in, the line of sight and the line of bore are parallel to each other. The bullet, acted on by gravity, will drop below the line of sight and miss the target.

With the rifle sighted in (for 200 yards in this diagram), the bullet will cross the line of sight at 25 yards, travel above the line of sight in a slight arc, and cross the line of sight at 200 and be on target.

BOLT-ACTION RIFLES. There are several ways to sight in a rifle. The necessary equipment includes a benchrest, a table on which a rolled tent or heavy coat can be placed, or another means of holding the rifle motionless. A rolled tent over which the shooter can sight and from which he can shoot prone will suffice. A safe backstop for the target and bullets is also necessary.

One of the best methods of sighting in is to zero the rifle at 200 yards but do the initial sighting and test-firing at 25 yards. As indicated above, the bullet from many modern rifles which comes up into the line of sight at 25 yards will fall back down into the line of sight at just over 200 yards, a good range to sight in for most hunting purposes.

To begin, remove the bolt from the action in order to bore sight. Look through the bore until the target, at a measured 25 yards, appears in the

45

exact center of the barrel. A 2½″ square of black paper thumbtacked to a sheet of yellow typing paper makes a fine sighting in target. It will appear as a small dot, with the aperture of the barrel appearing much larger around it.

When the target appears in the precise center of the bore, set the rifle perfectly still in that position. It will remain still if held by sandbags on the benchrest or if nestled into the folded tent. With the bore exactly on target, adjust the sights until they too point perfectly at the target at 25 yards.

Most modern rifles are now used with scopes. Adjustment for windage and elevation is made by turning two dials. With iron sights, move the rear sight in the direction appropriate for moving the bullet upon the target. If the bullet hits low, move the rear sight up to move the bullet upward. This applies to both open and micrometer sights.

When the bore and the sights coincide on the target, it is time to

---

HOW TO SIGHT IN A BOLT-ACTION RIFLE FOR 200 YARDS

1. With the target at 25 yards, rest the rifle on a rolled tent or other solid support and remove the bolt. Bring the bull's-eye into the center of bore. Then adjust the windage and elevation crosshairs so they also line up with the bull's-eye.

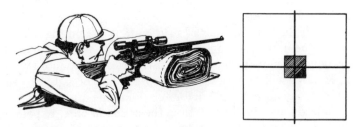

2. Replace the bolt, and fire three test shots.

test-fire. Fire three trial shots to compensate for errors of aim and allow for inaccuracies in the rifle. Next, draw lines between all shots to make a triangle. Mark the exact center of this triangle with a pencil. This spot is where the rifle will currently target, and it may be somewhat off from the point of aim. Finally, make adjustments in the sights until the rifle prints its bullets exactly on the target at 25 yards. The rifle is now sighted in at 25 yards. With cartridges of around 3,000 foot-seconds velocity, the rifle will also be sighted in at just over 200 yards, the desired range.

For example, a .243 Winchester shooting 100-grain factory ammunition and sighted in perfectly at 25 yards will be ¾ inches high at 50 yards, 2 inches high at 100 yards, 2¼ inches high at 150 yards, 1¾ inches high at 200 yards (very close to the desired setting), ½ inches low at 250 yards, 4 inches low at 300 yards, and 9¾ inches low at 350 yards. Other factory loads of comparable velocity and bullet shapes will have similar trajectories.

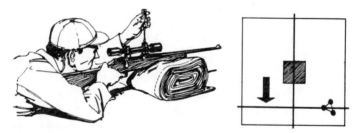

3. Draw lines between the three bullet holes and mark the center of the group. Then adjust the elevation knob so the horizontal crosshair bisects the center of the group.

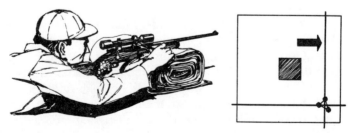

4. Adjust the windage knob on the scope so the vertical crosshair bisects the center of the group. The rifle is now sighted in for 200 yards.

47

To conclude the process, test-fire several more shots at 200 yards. The bullets should print about 1¾ inches high. If they do, leave the setting just as it is and remember when shooting at game that the rifle shoots a trifle high at 200 yards. Since many trajectory tables are calibrated for ranges of only 100, 200, and 300 yards, I find it advantageous to finish sighting in by lowering the sights to print at 200 yards. Then, by reading the trajectory tables, one can tell where the rifle will shoot at 100 and 300 yards without further firing.

OTHER ACTIONS. The above formula for sighting in applies to bolt-action rifles whose bores may be opened so the shooter can look through the barrel. The process is similar for lever-actions and other types whose bolts cannot be removed. However, in these cases it is relatively difficult to get the first shots on the paper. If you look over the barrel and not through the bore of one of these actions, keeping both eyes open and above the barrel, you can fit the rifle onto the target fairly close, from the standpoint of windage, by virtue of stereoptic vision. To get similar results on the 25-yard target for elevation, keep the eyes just to the left of the barrel and sight along it until the barrel appears to point at the bull's-eye. Now, adjust the sights until they point at the target at the same time the barrel points at it. Test shots fired from this point generally land quite close to the point of aim. When this occurs, complete the sighting in process with the same final steps used for bolt-action rifles.

SIGHTING IN FOR MAXIMUM RANGE. Many hunters like to sight in by zeroing the rifle and its current load for the longest distance they ever expect to shoot. With the rifle sighted perfectly for that distance, they memorize the trajectory height for intervening distances and shoot accordingly.

For example, a hunter may elect never to shoot from over 300 yards away at the deer-sized game for which his .284 Winchester is well adapted. He may further decide to use only 125-grain factory ammunition with its initial velocity of 3,200 foot-seconds. He sights in perfectly, shooting at 25-yard targets or using another method, so that his bullets strike the point of aim at exactly 300 yards. From a trajectory table available in many gun magazines or gun company catalogues, he finds the trajectory height over that range. In this case it is 5.3 inches midway. When actually shooting at game, if the hunter estimates the distance between himself and the animal at 300 yards, he holds dead on. If the animal is half this distance or nearly so, the hunter holds a few inches lower than he knows his bullet will hit. If the game is 100 yards away, or out at 200 yards, he holds accordingly: about 2 to 3 inches low. This, for all practical purposes, insures a clean hit on deer-sized game and is a good way to sight in for open country where long shots are taken.

Following are some mid-range trajectories of popular big-game calibers, with the rifle sighted in to strike the point of aim at 300 yards:

CARTRIDGE	BULLET WEIGHT	TRAJECTORY HEIGHT
.243 Win.	100 grains	5.5 inches
6 mm Rem.	100	5.5
.264 Win. Mag.	140	4.9
.270 Win.	130	5.3
.270 Win.	150	6.3
.284 Win.	125	5.3
.284 Win.	150	6.3
.30/30 Win.	150	11
.30/06	150	6.5
.30/06	180	7
.300 Win. Mag.	150	4.8
.300 Win. Mag.	180	5.3
.308 Win.	150	7
.308 Win.	180	7.4

When using scope sights, the line of sight is approximately 1½ inches above the line of the bore with many mounts. Remember when sighting in this way to subtract half of this 1½ inches from the mid-trajectory height, shooting at midway, if the rifle is zeroed at 300 yards. The reason for this is that the line of sight and the line of the bore are separated by 1½ inches at the shooter's end, but coincide at the 300-yard mark.

SIGHTING IN FOR 200 YARDS. Another method of zeroing, useful to those who have only 100 yards of sighting in range, is to find the mid-trajectory height of the particular cartridge at 200 yards and sight in so the bullets strike that high at 100 yards. Then the rifle will be sighted in at 200 yards. The bullet drop for longer ranges can be determined later from a ballistics chart.

For example, the popular .30/06 rifle shooting a 180-grain factory load of 2,700 foot-seconds velocity will shoot 2.9 inches high at 100 yards, when sighted in for 200 yards. If one has only 100 yards of available range, he can sight in so the bullets hit 2.9 inches high at 100 yards, and he will know that they hit correctly at 200 yards. Using a ballistics table, he finds that he will hit about 9 inches low at 300 yards and approximately 26 inches low at 400 yards. These figures vary somewhat according to bullet type and some other factors, but generally they will be more accurate than the average shooter's ability to hold.

SIGHTING IN HIGH.   A final procedure for sighting in is perhaps the easiest. First, get on the paper, using one of the previous methods, at 100 yards. When this is done, adjust the sights until they print the bullets just 3 inches high. Most modern cartridges, sighted for 3 inches high at 100 yards, will then deliver their bullets to the point of aim just beyond 225 yards. The bullets will drop about 5 to 7 inches low at 300 yards, depending upon the shape, sectional density, and allied factors affecting sustained flight. Several of the most popular modern cartridges for game hunting now approximate the 2,800-3,000 foot-second mark in muzzle velocity. Although some cartridges will be less and some more, for sighting in the differences are not important.

From these figures, the shooter will find that he can hold almost dead on for ranges up to 250 yards or more and still get a good hit, on game the size of deer or larger. He will, of course, have to learn to judge the bullet-drop for the longer ranges and hold over accordingly. When the shooter determines the setting for a certain rifle or load he has just sighted in, he should copy the setting for that particular combination in a notebook.

OPTICAL AIDS.   Recently, optical devices have been designed to help sight in a rifle without too many initial test shots. These gadgets work on the principle of collimation, or making the line of the bore and the line of the sight parallel before any firing is done.

One of these devices is a tube somewhat like a very short scope sight, with internal optics and a tiny grid usually calibrated for inches per 100 yards. It is held by bore-studs so that it stays in a vertical position above the muzzle of the rifle. The shooter sights through his scope, so that the reticle appears to be superimposed upon the grid. He then adjusts the windage and elevation so that his sights zero upon the grid. For practical purposes, the line of sight and the line of the bore are now parallel, and the rifle, except for differences caused by gravity, will shoot fairly close to point of aim at 25 yards. Necessary adjustments are made after test-firing, as explained.

One of the best of these shot-saving devices is the Bushnell Bore-Sighter, which is available with studs for all calibers.

RETAINING THE SIGHT-PICTURE.   Part of the difficulty of sighting in, especially for the beginner, is obtaining and retaining the same sight-picture each time he fires. If he does not see the identical picture of the sights in relation to the target each time, his shots will vary with a confusing result. The Winchester Arms people have a little tip for determining just how well a shooter sees a sight-picture, particularly valuable for the beginning shooter. It requires a partner, a benchrest or table for holding the rifle perfectly still, a target on a backstop, and a 3-inch cardboard disc.

Now proceed as follows: Punch a tiny hole into the disc at the exact center and nail on a handle, to make it like a fly-swatter. Use an unloaded rifle. Have your partner stand at the target and hold the disc by the handle. Move the rifle around on the rest until the sights point exactly at the center of the paper target. Next, have your partner move the disc in front of the target, shifting it about until the disc is also centered precisely in the sights. With this accomplished, have your partner make a pencil mark through the hole in the disc onto the paper target and move the disc away. Repeat this process three times.

At this point, there will be three marks on the paper target. Draw lines from each mark to form a triangle. If the triangle is too large to be covered by a quarter, you are not seeing the same sight-picture each time and need more practice.

To practice retaining the sight-picture, have a partner stand by the target with a 3-inch cardboard disc attached to a stick. The disc should have a hole in the center. Use an unloaded rifle. Move the rifle on its rest until the sights point exactly at the bull's-eye. Then instruct your partner to shift the disc until it is centered in the sights (1). Have him mark the spot with a pencil (2). Repeat this procedure two more times. Then join the three pencil marks (3). If you are taking a proper sight-picture each time, you should be able to cover the triangle with a quarter. If not, you need more practice.

6

Pack Outfits

BOTH HORSES and mules are used as pack stock in the United States and Canada; in Mexico and the Southwest, burros are often packed. Each of the three has certain advantages and drawbacks.

Horses weighing 1,200 to 1,400 pounds, which are broad-chested and "mountain broke," make fine pack animals. A heavy horse is necessary for packing large loads. A broad-chested beast can keep its wind because of its large lung capacity. And a horse that has been raised and broken in mountain country learns the knack of traversing a rough mountain trail much quicker and is more dependable than one born and raised in level country. The casualty rate during hard mountain use is far less among horses of this type.

Mules have definite advantages for trail use. They are smaller than horses on an average but far tougher. Mules with short backs and of good size, say 900 pounds, can carry up to 200 pounds all day without tiring excessively. They have very small hoofs, which enable them to dig into the uncertain footing of rocks and rocky slides. And mules follow other animals in a pack string better than horses.

One of the greatest advantages of mules in mountain-trail work is that in a mishap or emergency a mule will not get as excited as will a horse. When a horse goes down on its back or becomes tangled in gear, it will probably die unless gotten out quickly. A mule simply lies there philosophically and waits for help.

The big drawback of mules in a pack string is that, as a breed, they're hard-headed and smart, and you never know just what one will do. Whatever it does will be with the speed of lightning—suddenly rearing back, bucking, or kicking anything within range. And when a mule kicks, it never misses. For these reasons, mules are not as safe as horses.

The burro does a lot of packing in Mexico, but for packing big-game hunters into mountain country it isn't used much. Mainly, the burro is too small, too slow, and too stubborn. As with a mule, one often has to knock a burro down three or four times to get its attention.

HANDLING PACK STOCK.   Pack stock has to be well fed to do heavy work. At a mountain hunting camp animals are turned loose to graze each night. This forage is supplemented by oats and baled hay, hauled in at great expense. One riding horse is tied up or corraled at night for the horse wrangler to use in finding the others next morning.

To keep them from wandering too far, horses are hobbled across the forelegs with a strap-and-chain arrangement. Animals that learn to lope off with only a simple hobble are cross-hobbled, with one end of the strap-and-chain buckled to the forefoot and the other to the opposite hind foot.

One animal in the bunch is belled. This is always a horse or mare that has a tendency to stay close to camp. Mules especially will follow a mare, and will be close to the belled animal the next morning. Horse wranglers sleep soundly while the horse bell is clanging within earshot of camp. But the minute the bell stops, a good horse wrangler will wake up. Often it means that his nags have struck off for the next county.

Pack animals are approached, saddled, and loaded from the *left* side. They are never bridled but are handled by ropes tied to rope hackamores or leather halters. On the trail, pack animals are joined together by a 6-foot rope. The rope is not tied solidly, so that in case one animal falls it won't pull the entire string with it. A good method is to attach the halter

A pack string loaded with food and equipment ready for the trail out of camp in western big-game country.

rope to three strands of baling twine. A strong pull from the horse will break it. Such an arrangement is necessary on dangerous mountain trails.

Often in rolling country with a gentle pack string the packer will turn each animal loose. He rides ahead and the animals follow, with the hunter bringing up the rear to encourage laggards. Nose baskets may be used to prevent the animals from grazing.

All animals of a pack string are steel-shod for mountain work. A good pair of shoes will last about thirty days of hard use. Where the country is largely rocks, shoes often have to be replaced in two weeks.

Catching, feeding, and packing the horses in the morning is hard and time-consuming work. If a loaded pack string is ready to hit the trail by nine o'clock, it is considered an early start. And once on the trail, the string is not stopped except for emergency or to retie packs until it reaches the destination. When loaded animals are delayed they will lie down and roll with their packs and mess up the outfit. They want to get there and be immediately unloaded—their real incentive while on the trail.

A good pack string will cover fifteen miles a day on moderate mountain trails. Ten to twelve is a good average, but on easier trails it may make twenty miles if absolutely necessary. I've been on longer rides in a day with a string but don't recommend trying it.

Other basic facts for the neophyte to remember around saddle or pack stock: Never mistreat any animal. Don't let an overheated animal drink—it's apt to founder. Use no more than 2 quarts, or four double-handfuls, of oats at a feeding. Too much oats will founder an animal. Perhaps the best suggestion of all is to stay away from the kicking end of *any* beast. With unfamiliar animals, stay away from the grazing end, too.

PACK SADDLES. The best way to get a quick understanding of the difficulties of packing stock is to take a good look at the back of a horse or mule—a soft, hide-covered section which is in motion when the animal walks. On this flexible, undulating surface, which is tender and easily injured, packs of varying weights, sizes, and shapes must be loaded. They must be fitted not only to ride securely but so they won't injure the animal.

The device that makes this possible is the pack saddle. There are four basic types: the *aparejo*, the sawbuck, the Decker, and the Springerville. The sawbuck and the Decker are based upon the *aparejo*, the Springerville pack saddle is derived from the sawbuck.

The Aparejo Saddle. The *aparejo*, the first known form of pack saddle, originated in Arabia. The Moors brought it to Spain in the 8th century, and the Spaniards, during their early settlement of America, brought it with them into South America and Mexico.

In Mexico the natives gradually began making two styles of *aparejo* pack saddles. One was made of matting from the fibers of the *agave* plant. Saddles of this type were used mainly for light loads on burros. The other type, made of rawhide, was used for hauling heavy loads such as ore from mines.

The basic design of the latter type of *aparejo* saddle was simplicity itself. Two pieces of rawhide 24 inches wide and from 58 to 62 inches long were sewed together and placed over the saddle pad. On each side, a few inches from the center line, round holes approximately 8 to 10 inches in diameter were cut out of the top layer of rawhide. Grass was stuffed through these opposing holes to provide protection between the load and the animal's back. A cinch held this stuffed rawhide saddle in place. A crupper went around the horse's tail to prevent the load from slipping over its head. The loads were lashed to this simple saddle.

By the time of the Spanish-American War in 1898, two changes had been made in the *aparejo* saddle by the American cavalry. A breast strap had been added to keep the load from slipping back when going up steep hills, and the crupper had been changed to a breeching, as it was discovered that a burro could support more with its rump than with its tail.

In the light of today's pack saddles, the chief shortcoming of the *aparejo* is apparent: it had no "horns"—either wooden crosspieces, or iron rings—upon which to hang things. This lack gave rise to the sawbuck saddle.

The Sawbuck Saddle. This pack saddle consists of a pair of elongated wooden pads, shaped to conform to the sides of an animal's back on each side of the spine, to which two pairs of wooden crosspieces are bolted. The packs are attached to the tops of these crosspieces.

This combination of pads and crosspieces is the saddle's tree. Onto this tree the straps holding the rigging—the cinches, breast strap, and breeching—are riveted and looped. Most sawbucks are double-rigged, that is, they have two cinches. This helps to keep the saddle from turning and more evenly distributes the load on the animal.

A variety of loads may be packed on a sawbuck saddle. The most common arrangement is to use the saddle with a pair of heavy-canvas saddlebags, called panniers. These vary in size, but are usually about 24 inches long, 16 inches high, and from 10 to 12 inches deep. Each pannier is equipped with a heavy leather loop at each end which hooks over the crosspieces. These are of such a length that the pannier rides just above the outer bulge of a pack animal's side. Also, one of a pair of panniers has a long strap attached on its outside, the opposing pannier a buckle. After the two panniers are loaded, they are strapped together over the top of the saddle.

Canvas panniers are lashed to the crosspieces of the sawbuck saddle, and trophy antlers are tied on top. Care should be taken that points do not gouge the animal.

Homemade wooden alforjas boxes serve for packing gear on the trail and for storing it in camp. Wooden cleats on the sides are for supporting the boxes in sling ropes.

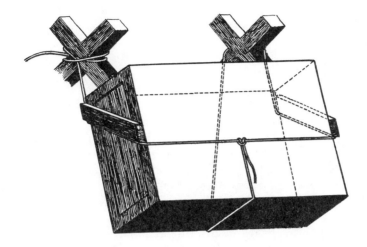

Alforjas box lashed to a sawbuck saddle with the basket hitch. Another box of equal weight must be slung on the opposite side to balance the load.

It is important that the weights of the loaded panniers match exactly. If they don't the animal's back will be ruined. If possible, weigh the packs in advance. Where this can't be done, stand behind the loaded beast (far enough not to be kicked) and have someone rock the loads sidewise. A pair of evenly balanced packs will rock as far to one side of the animal as to the other. Uneven packs will rock farther to the heavier side. By this method experienced packers can judge within a pound or so of any weight difference. Sometimes it's necessary to put rocks in one pannier to balance the load.

In most heavy packing, top packs are necessary. These are small bundles of light gear or odd-shaped duffel which won't fit into panniers. Such bundles are usually wrapped in canvas and loaded on top of the saddle between the pairs of loaded panniers. Many times a pair of uneven loads can be balanced by placing the top pack farther to one side than the other.

With the top pack in place, a canvas tarp is thrown over the entire pack, tucked in at the front, rear, and sides, and tied down with a suitable hitch (usually a diamond hitch). The animal is then ready for the trail.

Sawbuck saddles used in this fashion have made western history. In many areas today, only sawbuck pack saddles are used and their owners swear by them.

The Decker Saddle. Because the sawbuck must be loaded with packs of equal weight, which is often difficult, another type of pack saddle—the Decker—was developed in the Northwest. It is especially good for packing game meat. Instead of wooden crosspieces, the Decker saddle has a pair of iron rings at the top. Panniers cannot be used with a Decker saddle. Instead, loads are lashed to the saddle with sling ropes looped through the iron rings and fastened with a single ingenious hitch. Top packs, covering, and final diamond hitch are used as with a sawbuck saddle.

The virtues of the Decker saddle are that loads of uneven shapes may be packed, since they do not have to fit inside panniers. Also, loads of differing weights may be packed on either side in perfect balance. This is possible by lowering the lighter load and raising the heavier. Due to the roundish shape of the pack animal, the lighter load naturally rests farther *out* on its circular belly, and the heavier load rides higher and closer to the spine.

The sling hitch holds the two cargoes in place upon the saddle. Both for speed in handling and safety in a possible emergency, the sling hitch should be tied so it can be immediately untied with only a single hard jerk on the rope's running end. A packed animal that has fallen on its back usually dies unless the load can be quickly released.

Loaded alforjas boxes also can be packed on a Decker saddle. Each is wrapped in a manta (a square of canvas measuring 6 by 6 feet) and lashed on. If provided with hardwood cleats on each side, they can be lashed to the saddle without covering. In this case the lash rope goes across the box, holds tightly under each cleat, and the sling arrangement holds the weight.

The Springerville Saddle. The third type of modern pack saddle is a simple improvement upon the standard sawbuck. This is the Springerville saddle, which is different from the sawbuck in that the crosspieces extend approximately 10 inches below the wooden pads of the tree rather than being cut off at the point where they are fastened to the pads. The extension of these crosspieces provides extra protection for the animal, keeping the packs from rubbing against its sides. Springerville saddles are used most often in heavily forested country, such as the heavy oak brush of the Southwest, where trees may crush packs and animals.

SHORT-CUT PACKING. There's no better way of packing in a buck deer on a saddle horse than to "buttonhole" the buck onto the horn of a stock saddle and bring it in. This is done by cutting a small aperture, or buttonhole, in the meat of the deer's abdominal wall exactly at the point of the sternum, or rear of the rib cage. Slip this hole over the horn of the stock saddle and tie the hind legs down to the cinch ring on one side. Tie

The Springerville pack saddle, a modification of the sawbuck, with sling ropes ready to receive gear.

Irregular-shaped bundles can be lashed to a sawbuck or a Decker saddle with the barrel hitch. Again, load on the opposite side must be of equal weight.

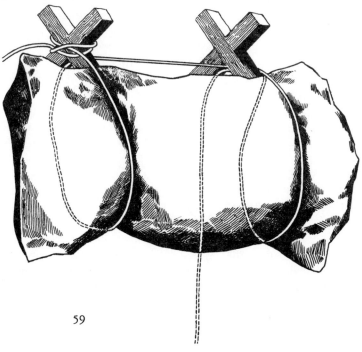

the forelegs down similarly to the opposite cinch ring and tie the antlers up and toward the rear so that they cannot under any circumstance gouge the animal.

A professional packer won't do it that way. Moreover, he'll laugh at you if he catches you at it. But, as I say, it is a good compromise and will let you get the job done if you know only a little about horses, saddles, and the real art of hauling odd-shaped packages on animals.

HANDLING SADDLE HORSES.   Since much of today's big-game hunting is done on saddle horses, the hunter should learn as much of basic horsemanship as possible. In this way he not only can help with the necessary chores, but can save his mount from injury and often himself from accidents.

Horses for dude hunters will be "broken" in advance. This means they will be conditioned to halters, bridles, saddles, and to being ridden. As with pack stock, saddle horses are approached, bridled, saddled, mounted, and handled from the left side. Cinches should be tightened just before mounting each morning and checked periodically throughout the day—working horses get thinner during the day due to sweating and exertion. The right stirrup length for any rider is approximately the length of his extended arm. When the rider stands up in the stirrups, he should have about 3 inches of daylight showing between his britches and the saddle.

Rifle scabbards are fastened fore and aft to the saddlestrings, usually in the "Northwest" position with rifle butt forward on the left side and gun barrel going under the left stirrup; on the right side, butt to the rear and muzzle pointing forward under the right stirrup.

Hunting horses should always be ridden with loose (unknotted) reins. When the hunter dismounts, loose reins will fall to the ground and somewhat deter the horse from running off. It tends to step on the reins as it walks or runs, jerking on the bit which in turn hurts its mouth. Inexperienced riders should leave the halter or hackamore on under the bridle. This allows the halter rope to be used for tying up the mount if the hunter wishes to hunt on foot or scout for game any distance from the horse.

In steep or boggy country, a rider should dismount and cross on foot, allowing the horse to cross by itself. A riderless horse has better balance in treacherous footing and more confidence if the rider crosses a dangerous area ahead of it. It is safer, too, for the rider.

Finally, a hunter should *never* shoot at game from the back of a horse. He can't hit anytning that way because of the horse's movement. Moreover, it is sheer cruelty to shoot over a horse's head; the blast will deafen it. Many a rider has been thrown from shooting on horseback.

7

Outfitters and Guides

THE SUCCESS OF a big-game hunt into those areas requiring a guide or outfitter depends largely on his skill and dependability. This is especially true of hunting trips into the most remote and inaccessible of our remaining wilderness areas.

It is also true that the hunter has a corresponding responsibility. He must bring to the hunt his own enthusiasm, the proper equipment, and a fair degree of hunting and shooting skill. He must be willing to adapt to unfamiliar living conditions, and he must expect a certain amount of hard physical effort.

But despite the hunter's part in the hunter-outfitter association, the guide or outfitter either makes or breaks the hunt. The choice of a guide or outfitter, therefore, is one of the most vital the hunter has to make. And one of the best ways of making a sensible choice is through a basic understanding of the viewpoint of each of the parties.

The outfitting business is relatively new and its origin is easy to trace. It wasn't too many years ago that hunters in remote areas bordering on farmlands simply rented available stock from ranchers to bring in their downed game. Hunters at that time hunted fairly close to home, and, due to slow transportation, meager sports dollars, and relatively few hunters, the sport of big-game hunting was not the big business it is today.

With the gradual but increasingly heavy boom in hunting came a thinning of the larger, most prized species of big game in marginal areas. Agriculture ate up other fringe lands. Game herds moved farther back into more remote regions and were harder to reach.

While this was taking place, means of transportation speeded up, leisure increased, and sporting dollars became more numerous. The appeal of red-blooded recreation to urban people became stronger. The result was a great upsurge in nonresident big-game hunting. Today, it is fundamentally as easy to hunt out of one's own state, or even in another country, as it once was to hunt ten miles from home. This transformation has occurred within the present generation.

In any activity, sport or otherwise, when strangers come into a region there is need for local services from those familiar with the area. This is especially true of big-game hunting. It was only a single step from renting a horse from some local rancher to carry out a deer, to the natural question, "Why not hire somebody to do *all* the arranging on this end of the hunt?"

So outfitting was born. The use of a professional guide came about in a similar manner.

THE OUTFITTER.   Like a fence, the guide-hunter relationship has two definite sides. An understanding of this vital association might well begin with some of the professional outfitter's problems.

Today's big outfitter, catering to hunters in such remote areas as the hunting country of the West, Canada, and Alaska, has an investment of anywhere from $50,000 to well over $100,000. This generally includes horses and mules averaging from $125 to $250 per head; riding gear (saddle, bridle, blanket, etc.) which costs at least $150 per rider; and pack saddles, completely rigged, at another $75 to $100 each.

The transportation end of outfitting often includes light aircraft, motorboats, jeeps, snowmobiles, bush tractors, and trailers. Often in some areas, the outfitter himself must lease other equipment from companies or other outfitters.

Other necessities include cook and dining tents of enormous size for base camps; smaller tents for camp personnel and hunters; dishes and cooking equipment; stoves; rope; horseshoe and horeshoeing equipment; canvas for mantas and coverings; axes, saws, camp tools, and all sorts of small items.

This overall tonnage has to be transported, including the pack and riding stock, to and from the hunting country each season. Heavy trucks, pickup trucks, and automobiles are also part of the investment.

Personnel is another expensive item in the large outfitter's operation. Help includes guide, cook, horse wrangler, packer, and all-round flunky. These are largely professional services. Cooks who can feed and keep happy gangs of hunters eating from before daylight to after dark every day for a month cannot be employed for the same amount as a cook back in town. Neither can guides who usually work from before daylight to any time during the night they happen to get in.

Food for hunters and personnel adds up to a prodigious amount, since appetites are pronounced. Feed for hard-working animals includes high-priced baled hay and oats, truck-hauled great distances over mountain roads.

But perhaps the biggest expense of the large outfitter is unseen by the majority of hunters. This is the very real expense of feeding, storing, and caring for the pack stock and equipment for the *other* eleven months of the year after hunting season is over. Usually, caring for the animals and gear of an outfitting operation involves ownership of a ranch, costing an additional $50,000 to $100,000. Repairing and replacement of broken equipment during the off months also runs into money. Just as a small example, one outfitter told me that annually he had to replace one in seven of his riding and pack animals—that's the mortality rate for good animals. Another said the previous winter he had repaired and replaced nineteen riding bridles which dude hunters, unfamiliar with how to care for such gear, had broken.

Depreciation and wear on all such outfitting equipment is severe, to say nothing of equipment that is somehow lost. Worse is the increase in the cost of equipment. Rope, as one example, costs just double what it did a few years ago. Trucks, horseshoes, camp tools, cooking equipment, and anything made of metal are correspondingly higher.

But the saddest fact in the hard life of today's outfitter is that this increase in his cost of operation must be balanced against a constantly decreasing number of days in the annual hunting season. Where once it was several months, the hunting season now, in many areas, is an average of six weeks or even thirty days.

From this short period of time, the professional outfitter must recover enough cash from his clientele to support his operations for the entire year and make a profit if he is to remain in business.

Specifically, the thirty-day hunt must be broken down into, say, four seven-day hunts. If the outfitter has been fortunate enough to "book full" and averages a minimum of four hunters for each hunt, then it boils down to the blunt fact that each dude hunter must pay roughly six per cent of the outfitter's annual investment, depreciation of capital, and profit. With fewer hunters, he pays more.

That is the fundamental reason why an outfitter's charges for an all-furnished hunt into remote areas after the more desired species of big game seem so exorbitant. It is sufficient to say here that were it not for the fact that such outfitters cater to summer fishing parties, do summer dude ranching, or have some other source of income from their stock, they could not operate.

THE HUNTER'S VIEWPOINT. On the opposite side of the relationship is the hunter. Here are his basic problems:

The average hunter is not rich. In the United States, exclusive of Alaska and Hawaii, there are over sixteen million licensed hunters. A majority of these are big-game hunters. This means that one of every ten people is a hunter, and there are not that many rich people.

The *average* hunter must save his money, often for several years, in order to make one trip after really big game. This is especially true of easterners who come to the West, Canada, or Alaska after several species on a combined hunt.

The average hunter, because of this, is usually middle-aged or more before he can afford to take big-game hunts involving outfitting operations into remote areas. He is often soft physically, unaccustomed to living in the country and under conditions involving hardship and discomfort, and has no real notion of just what a big-game hunt into wild country entails.

However, he has the enthusiasm and the money to take on the hunt. Above all, he wants to bag a trophy. He feels, after the years of effort and saving, that he is paying the outfitter to make certain he accomplishes this.

In short, the hunter-outfitter association brings closely together two entirely different types of individuals: one who is physically soft, knows little of the outdoors and less about hunting; the other, a rugged individual who can lick the wilderness with nothing more than his Levi britches and a Dutch oven. Thus unfortunate misconceptions arise. And too often, through the failure of each to understand the problems and real contribution of the other, both the relationship and the hunt go sour. Yet, despite the dissimilarity of viewpoints, each has a real need for the other, and couldn't get along without him.

The best outfitters and guides are tolerant of their guests. They realize that while a beginning hunter may not know too much about horses, hunting, and outdoor living, he is successful and knowledgeable in a field about which an outfitter knows little.

In fairness I must say that in forty-two years of big-game hunting and knowing many guides and outfitters, I have had dealings with only two who weren't reliable and who did not live up to their agreements. That is largely because I've dealt only with reputable, top-flight outfits. All except the two were fine men, skilled in their complex jobs, dependable, and went all out to provide a grand hunt. During this time I must admit, however, that I've witnessed some gross mistreatment of dude hunters by fly-by-night, chiseling outfitters. These are the relatively few vulturelike outfits of which the big-game hunter must beware.

Fortunately, the situation is being overcome. In many states and areas, vast improvements has been made through newly formed packers' associations and by the steady struggle of the reliable outfitters to clean out their own ranks.

CHOOSING A GUIDE OR OUTFITTER. As suggested in an earlier chapter, the best assurance of getting a good guide or outfitter is to begin arrangements early. One advantage of this is that the outfitter, once contacted, immediately puts the hunter's name in his little black book as a prospect.

Some of the best outfitters, who plan to build a repeat business and stay with outfitting exclusively, make annual spring trips about the country, contacting hunters who have hunted with them as well as new prospects. They also show movies of their operations to local sportsmen's groups. These pictures, usually accompanied by a running lecture by the outfitter himself, show the hunting country, the general mode of his operation, and the game potential there. An outfitter will often travel considerable distance out of his way just to make a prospect's acquaintance and offer his services. Even when a hunt isn't arranged at the time, chances are good that the two parties may come together for a future hunt.

Another way of learning about a guide or outfitter is by contacting a friend who has hunted with him, or arranging one's own hunt with such a friend as a partner. Contacts often are made by letter through business acquaintances and casual friendships acquired through travel. Once the subject of big-game hunting comes up in a group, information has a way of cropping up, and the alert hunter should take advantage of it.

The serious hunter, however, should not wait for any chance information. Once the region he wishes to hunt is decided upon, he should immediately write to the fish and game department of that state or province and ask for a list of the licensed guides and outfitters operating there. Most states with sufficient big game to warrant the use of outfitters will not only have a list of such personnel but also require that the guides and outfitters be bonded in order to operate. The fact that an outfitter is bonded is some assurance that he will be reliable, since he is financially responsible to the state for what he does. The beginner who has no previous experience with outfitters should never settle for an outfit whose name does not appear on the accredited list of the state.

Many of the best guides and outfitters regularly advertise, at least until they have built up a clientele. Some do even after there is no apparent need for advertising, simply to keep their names before the public and replace clients who can't make hunts every year. The very fact that such outfitters do pay heavy money for advertising is some assurance that they are not of the fly-by-night variety—especially those who advertise in the better outdoor journals.

A final way of making a contact in any hunting area is to locate on a map a town adjacent to that area and write to the Chamber of Commerce or similar civic group for information about reliable outfits operating in that region.

Once the guide or outfitter is contacted, the procedure for ascertaining his reliability, skill, and general standing is the same as in any other business transaction. You write to him. You ask for references. You ask for a list of satisfied customers. Then you write directly to enough of them to give you a fair cross section. And from this information you sort the kernel from the chaff.

There are definite indications in each of the above to establish an overall picture. The man's character will be revealed in his return letter. If the reply is neat, orderly, and gives forthright information, that's one indication.

His reply will usually include information about his hunts and operation, perhaps with pictures of equipment, game previously taken, hunting country, and base of operations. Also included will be a list of his prices. All these help to bring into clear focus the overall picture of the outfit, especially the fees. Any hunter should beware of prices which are in any way "cut-throat" competition with those more or less standard to other operators giving similar services.

In the hunter's first letter to any prospective outfitter, one of the most pertinent questions should be about the outfit's past record. That is, what percentage of all hunters booked scored on the various species of game—say for the past three or four years. It should be borne in mind when asking this, that no outfitter can ever have a perfect record. Big-game hunting just isn't that sure-fire. But on an average, his record should show at least around fifty per cent hunter-success on the big species of game before I would be interested further. Perhaps this high a success-ratio is rough on the beginning outfitter and the outfitting profession. But it is equally rugged on the hunter who must pay the top outfitters' high fees; and the records of the top-flight outfitters are usually much higher than fifty per cent.

In all such correspondence, facts should be looked for and promises disregarded, or the rash ones looked upon with suspicion. The big, established outfits, fine as their record of hunter-success is, can only promise to provide the hunter with good hunting country, good guides and other help, good equipment, a fine hunt, and a memorable experience. The best ones, with few exceptions, never promise the hunter his game. Any promises that the hunter will "surely" get his trophy are regarded by veteran hunters with skepticism and usually mean that the guide or outfitter intends (for a price, of course) to kill the hunter's game illegally himself.

From the personal letters of past customers, the hunter gets a real indication of the outfit's true work. Replies from satisfied clientele generally will be specific as to game and general conditions, and direct in their recommendation.

All this close screening of guides and outfits naturally entails a similar obligation on the hunter's part. He should never expect an outfitter to be more reliable or honest than himself. He should be willing to furnish the same type of reference for himself which he expects of another, and in any arrangement make his word as good as his bond.

Fees. It is difficult to list a set of standard fees for guide services or overall outfitting charges. Hunts vary according to species of game, distances, transportation, and equipment. However, a few current examples will give the beginner a fair notion.

At this writing, simple guide service (in which no equipment is furnished) for one relatively numerous species of game such as deer, antelope, or moose, will run $30 a day and up per man.

For furnished hunts after a single, fairly numerous and easily reached species such as deer, fees begin at around $35 a day per man. This is if the hunting country is close to the outfitter's base of operations and is easily reached.

Hunts after a really big species such as elk, or a combination of species such as elk, deer, and black bear involving pack stock, will average between $50 and $70 a day per hunter. Such hunts usually are for a minimum of seven to ten days and a minimum of four hunters.

Special hunts after a prized species such as sheep, where the hunter of necessity must go alone with a guide, not hunt as part of a party, often cost $75 a day.

Alaskan and Canadian hunts for a mixed bag of several species, for such game as grizzlies, caribou, rams, black bear, and goats, currently cost from $100 to $150 a day per hunter. These hunts normally run three weeks and cost approximately $2,500 as a package. Short hunts for one species, such as rams, are normally for ten days and cost about $1,250 to $1,500. Coastal trips after brown bear will cost approximately $2,000.

The standard charge for polar-bear hunts is $2,500. This usually involves airplanes, and is one case where some guides will guarantee the hunter a legal bear, not a cub.

Once the decision is made, all arrangements with the guide should be made in writing. All such important factors as dates, fees, equipment each is to furnish, and where the hunt both originates and terminates, should be written into the agreement and agreed upon by both parties before signing.

The normal arrangement is to deposit one third of the hunt's total cost with the outfitter upon signing the agreement. This the hunter forfeits if for any reason he cannot go on the hunt. The outfitter or guide refunds this deposit only if he cannot provide the hunt. Cancellation of a hunt by the hunter is no grounds for expecting his deposit back.

Hunting with a good outfitter in primitive country after the prized species of big game, when each of the partners has an understanding of the problems and joys of the other, is one of the finest experiences on earth.

8

How to Set up a Hunting Camp

THE FIRST THING to do before setting up a hunting camp is to ascertain whether camping is permitted. Most camps for hunting big game will be located on public lands such as the National Forests where camping is generally open to the public.

In certain areas, however, and especially during a dry season, portions of such public lands are closed to camping or have restrictions imposed. It is well to learn of these in advance from the nearest agency office. If a camp is to be set up on private lands permission must be obtained in advance from the landowner.

A hunting camp should be pitched near but not within a game area so that the noise of camp activity does not frighten away the animals. This is especially important when hunting elk and other species which spook easily. An elk camp should not be placed closer than a mile from where game is known or thought to be, and there should always be a high ridge or a hill between.

WATER AND WOOD. The two basic necessities for any big-game camp are a suitable supply of water and ample firewood. In the habitat of the larger species of big game, the water problem tends to solve itself. Moose, elk, caribou, and grizzly country is normally watershed country where rivers and lakes are born. In such country there is usually ample fresh water. Moreover, the water found in high mountainous country has not been contaminated with sewage and pollution and is safe and pure. Higher country is largely wooded country, and the problem of firewood is easily solved. Most of the wood there will be pine, fir, spruce, and aspen.

Wood for the fire doesn't mean simply nearby timber. It means dry and standing timber. Down timber is no good as it takes up moisture from the earth. Attempts to use it result in ninety per cent smoke and ten per cent heat. A short walk into nearby timber will show whether there is dry wood, and whether it is handy enough to be dragged to camp or snaked with a horse.

Camps set up for hunting mountain sheep and goats, which range above water and timber, likewise are set up below the game habitat, to keep from alerting the game and for the convenience of wood and water.

For hunting whitetails in brushy country, mule deer in sagebrush country, and game such as antelope in semibarren desert areas, the problems of water and wood become more acute. Often the hunter has to camp close to the game, take what wood is available (such as sagebrush, willows, etc.) and haul his water supply along with him.

Incidentally, for desert hunting there is no better way of hauling water than to bring it from the last available source in the 10-gallon milk cans dairy farmers use. These cans are rugged, galvanized against rusting, and watertight. On desert hunts it is often best not to depend upon any available wood, except for occasional warming fires, but to use artificial fuel such as gasoline. A sagebrush fire is a two-hunter fire—one to find fuel and one to stoke—in case you haven't tried building one.

SELECTING A CAMPSITE. Choose a campsite close to the water supply and as close as possible to dry wood. Sandy beaches or shorelines of mountain lakes, so long as they are well above waterline, often make good campsites. So do the points of small promontories overlooking a creek or lake. The edge areas where timber meets meadow, small elevated river bars, or small humps of semi-open land near timber are suitable campsites if water is handy.

In each instance, camp should be set up on some kind of elevated ground. This insures that the earth will be comparatively dry, and that sudden storms won't drown out a camp by draining water under it. For this reason, it is never wise to camp in gully bottoms, however attractive they seem to be. Flash floods in mountain and desert country can suddenly send awesome amounts of water through such gullies.

If at all possible, the camp should be set up in a small clearing to let in sunshine and lessen fire hazard. In a clearing there are no trees to drip on gear after a rain or snowstorm. And a camp in the open is easy for hunters to find as the tents may be seen from a distance. Also, breezes can blow through a clearing, diminishing the insect problem.

With these basic conditions satisfied, if it is also possible to have level ground for the tents, so much the better. However, small dips and unevenness in the ground often can be fixed with a bit of elbow grease and a shovel. Check for level ground by filling a pan nearly full of water and setting it down on a stove or table. If it runs over one side, you will know it isn't level.

PITCHING CAMP. Once having chosen the campsite, the first thing to do is to unload the pack animals, if you are packing into a hunting camp. It is a cardinal sin to allow any pack animal to remain loaded for even a few minutes once it has reached its destination.

The next thing to do is to get a tent set up. In the mountains, storms come up out of nowhere and can saturate people and gear in minutes unless dry storage space is provided.

Miner's tents are pegged down at all four corners and their tops tied to the crosses of two shear poles (dry standing jackpines or large willows make good shear poles), and the poles stood erect.

A baker tent is pegged down at the rear; the flap for its open front is placed over a ridgepole set upon two sets of shear poles, stretched taut and tied. Often one end of the ridgepole can be attached to a standing tree. This eliminates any need of guy ropes to keep the shear poles from wobbling sidewise.

There are several ways of setting up a wall tent. In every case, the roof must be held solidly on a ridgepole and the guy ropes must be solidly

The wall tent can be pitched with a ridgepole supported by two sets of shear poles and guyed with ropes front and back. The guy ropes often double as clotheslines.

The pyramid tent, suitable for mild weather, can be supported by a single pair of shear poles.

anchored. The bottom edge of the test also must be pegged down securely to prevent wind from entering and heat from escaping.

The ridgepole should be straight, if possible, and as light in weight as is consistent with strength. Snowstorms in big-game country often deposit several inches of wet snow in a matter of hours, and this weight must be supported by the ridgepole.

One way of supporting the ridgepole is to cut it exactly the length of the tent, cut two upright poles 8 inches longer than the tent is high, and nail the ends of the ridgepole into the tops of each upright. Set the bottom ends of the uprights 8 inches into the ground at the exact middle of each end of the tent, stretch the entire tent over this pole arrangement, and peg it down solidly.

This method should only be used where a ridgepole of greater length than the tent can't be found. It has the disadvantage of having an upright pole right in the middle of the front opening where someone is always bumping into it.

A better way is to use a ridgepole about 3 feet longer than the tent. Cut a small hole in the ends of the tent at each apex just under the roof's center line. Run the ridgepole through these holes, allowing it to extend 18 inches at either end. Put the heavy end of the ridgepole at the tent's front where there will be the greatest strain. Next, tie together two sets of shear poles and slip them under the ridgepole at the front and back of the tent, raising the tent to its maximum height. Spread the shear poles so they form an inverted V and stand firmly on the ground. With the ridgepole and shear poles in place, tie down the side ropes tightly and the tent will support itself due to opposing strain on the ropes.

Ropes from the tent's roof may be tied either to long stakes driven into the ground at a suitable distance from the tent or to horizontal poles tied at suitable height either between two trees or solidly set stakes.

Lastly, peg the tent's bottom through the sewed-in loops. Pegs are made on the spot from small lengths of limbs, pine splits, or sharpened poles. So are any necessary stakes. For light tents such as the tepee, good tent pegs are 12-inch timber spikes, available at any hardware store. Such pegs will go easily into frozen or rocky ground where wooden pegs could not be driven, and come out as easily.

Before setting up any tent, check wind direction by watching treetops for movement, or wafting cigarette smoke. Tents should be pitched with their backs to the wind to keep wind and storm from blowing in the front opening. Campfires should be built so that smoke blows away from all tents. Sleeping tents should be set up behind or at the sides of the main wall tent—traffic is always heavy in front. Ample room for traffic should be left around all tents as toes have an affinity for tent ropes.

A most useful addition to the main tent is a "fly." This is a large tarp about 14 by 16 feet in size which is thrown over the ridgepole and guyed down, leaving a space between fly and tent roof for insulation in hot weather and protection against rain. Set high off the ground, a fly may be used as a temporary cooking tent, but it is perhaps most useful as a place to store anything from boxed food to baled hay.

In tying guy ropes, the tyro usually employs overhand and slip knots. These are fine except that when wet they are difficult to untie. Better knots for tying rope to any kind of pole or stake are a clove hitch or a double half hitch. The end should be left under the hitch in a loop. To untie, give the end a yank and the knot comes loose.

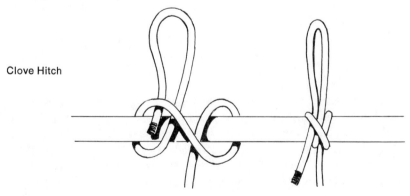

Clove Hitch

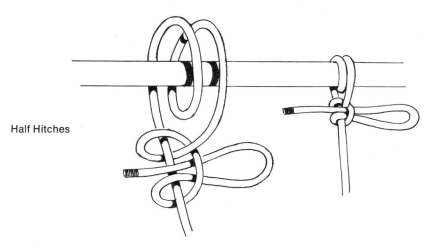

Half Hitches

The final chore in pitching a tent is to dig a trench around it. The trench is shoveled to a depth of 5 or 6 inches, and the end ditched away toward lower ground. Rain or melted snow will drain away from and not under the tent.

GARBAGE PIT AND LATRINE. A garbage pit and some form of latrine are necessary for sanitation. Both should be downwind and downstream of the camp, the latrine the farthest away, in a clump of trees if possible.

The garbage pit is simply a large hole dug in the ground. Vegetable peelings, food scraps, and anything which will decay are all thrown into this pit. (Garbage which will not decay, such as tin cans, glass bottles, and plastic containers, should be stored in a gunnysack brought in for the purpose, then packed out for disposal.) A thin layer of dirt spread on top each day over the accumulated refuse is the best guarantee against flies around camp. When camp is broken, the entire pit is filled and covered.

Camp latrines are of different kinds, depending upon the permanence of the camp and the availability of transportation. The simplest is a long smooth pole, anchored at toilet-seat height between two trees, with its middle over a hole in the ground. A better one consists of a folding box which stands rigidly upright when set up, with a holed top for a seat. Privacy is afforded by wrapping a large canvas tarp around four trees, or high stakes driven into the ground. Commercial latrines are available with folding seats, disposable plastic bags, and erectable "houses" of tubing and canvas to surround the sitter.

CAMP FURNITURE. Camp furniture is always a problem in big-game country. Most all of it must be designed and built on the spot of available materials. Exceptions are folding camp cots and alforjas boxes. The latter can be joined together and do service as a table. Also, wooden orange crates which serve as grub boxes going in, nailed together three or four high can become camp cupboards.

Sleeping bunks may be made at camp. Two 3-foot logs are sawed for each bunk. Onto these, laid lengthwise, slender poles such as 3-inch jackpines of 6-foot length are laid edge-to-edge, then nailed to the crosslogs. The outside poles should be about 5 inches thick and serve as "rails" to keep the air mattress, sleeping bag, and sleeper from rolling off. Where tent height will permit, double bunks can be made by using longer crosslogs and attaching their ends to four upright poles set solidly into the ground.

When sleeping bags must be laid directly on the ground, place dry grass or a thin layer of hay under them. If such material is unavailable, a tarp or sleeping bag cover should be used beneath the bag to insulate against cold and absorb ground moisture.

There are available today light folding tables which are hinged in the middle and may be horse-packed to camp. They are small and wobbly, however, and clumsy to carry as a top pack. Better ones can be made at camp if three 1 by 12 boards 5 feet long are hauled along. A frame of legs and side rails is built of available timber, then the three boards nailed on top. For solidity, the legs may even be set into holes dug in the ground.

A better table, requiring the same legs and frame, has a top made of slats and canvas. This top, made at home of course, is constructed of two layers of light canvas which are laid together and seams sewed across their width every 2 inches. Wooden laths slide into each of the pockets formed by these seams. The result is a flexible table top which can be rolled up for carrying. At camp it is simply unrolled upon the table frame.

A simpler top can be made entirely of small-diameter saplings laid edge-to-edge lengthwise on the table frame. The main trouble with this kind is that nothing ever stays upright on it except dishes and cans with large bottoms.

A handy washstand can be built just outside the tent by nailing two short sticks on opposite sides of a large tree. The sticks, which may be flattened with an ax to fit the tree better, extend parallel to the ground like arms and a board or pole surface is nailed or lashed across them.

An even simpler stand for a washbasin is made by driving three sharpened stakes solidly into the ground, with their tops far enough apart so that when spread a bit they will fit under the rim of the basin.

Chairs are always a problem in a big-game camp. Canvas folding chairs may be hauled along but are seldom strong enough for the hard use hunters give them. Permanent hunting camps solve the problem by having a large plank table built with benches on both sides, like the tables at public picnic grounds.

At most big-game camps, a length of log is sawed off squarely at both ends and used as a chair. Log chairs can be improved by nailing a short length of board across the tops of two logs, making a short bench for two

In grizzly country food should be stored on a high platform. This one was built on the sawed-off stumps of trees.

people. Usable stools can be made by spiking a piece of board to the top of a log of small diameter—like the old milking stool farmers once used.

In trimming off the branches of trees in the camp clearing, leave limb butts of 3 or 4 inches on trees near tents for use as hooks for hanging dishtowels, bow saw, packboards, and clothing.

Two of the most useful items to take along are a small sack of nails and a small roll of baling wire. The nails should be assorted and vary in size from 6-penny to 16-penny. Tables, beds, chairs, and cupboards can be nailed together and hangers for all kinds of gear can be made by driving single nails part way into trees. Wire can be used for clothesline, lantern hooks for the ridgepole, "doodle hooks" for the Dutch oven, and for toggling up the joints of log tables, chairs, and bunks.

Here are some additional suggestions:

Make sure that no dry trees are left standing which may fall on tents or people during a storm.

Clear away all grasses and shrubbery from around the tents—they are a fire hazard.

If there is a tall tree in camp, have the youngest member of the hunting party shinny to the top and tie on a large piece of white cloth, such as a dishrag. Such a beacon is often visible for miles in hunting country, with the aid of binoculars, and saves hunters from getting lost.

Make doubly sure that all fire is out in the tent before leaving camp. In addition, always tie down all tent flaps when leaving camp. The combination of untied flaps, fire in the stove, and the sudden appearance of wind has caused many a fire in camp—often hours after the hunters have left.

Cover all food supplies to protect them from animal pests. This applies also to hung quarters of game meat.

The things a camper can do to make his hunting camp more convenient and enjoyable are numberless. Often it is a simple little thing such as digging out the spring so that the water bucket will dip without muddying it; or making a small spout by chopping a V-channel into a wooden slab and setting it in the creek so that a pail may be set under it and easily filled.

Each time the camper goes afield he learns something new. And all the beginner needs to know are the fundamentals—his enthusiasm will take him from there.

9

How to Locate and Track Game

FINDING WHERE THE game is located in hunting country depends more on understanding its habits than being able to follow each consecutive hoofmark in a trail. An experienced hunter in strange country can often take one look around and estimate just where any game is apt to be. And by climbing the first big ridge in that area he can also tell what species is there and its approximate abundance. Such skill is not based on magic or exceptional vision but on past experience and close observation.

PATTERNS OF MOVEMENT. Here are generalizations which will help the beginner:

Generally game is found higher in summer than in late fall and winter. Game goes high in hot weather to escape heat and insect pests. Also, summer feed is more abundant higher up than in the parched regions below.

An early fall brings game down sooner than a late fall. A sudden violent storm also tends to move most game downward, just as clearing weather tends to move it upward.

The largest males of most species are found at the upper peripheries of their range. When traveling in a band, the biggest males ordinarily come last, with the females and small animals ahead. This applies to elk, deer, antelope, caribou, and moose.

Most game feeds in the early morning hours and again at dusk, either bedding down, shading up, or moving to slightly higher elevations during midday. Feeding game will normally be more in the open than will resting game. All game common to wooded country likes "edge" country—that is, areas where foliage meets meadows and similar clearings.

77

Browsing and grazing feed grows better where there is more sunlight, and the edge country offers immediate cover for concealment if enemies appear.

Many game species, when moving between patches of timber, stay just inside the fringe of such timber and will not cross openings unless absolutely necessary. Bears, especially, route their travels just inside the fringe of timber and through connecting timbered necks.

Game in wooded country will usually yard up and huddle during severe storm and move with increased vigor in clearing, colder weather.

Most game, if unmolested, tends towards a regular pattern of movement, often in a circuitous manner covering the main part of its food supply. Molested game tends to scatter.

With a knowledge of the basic traits of game, the hunter immediately narrows down the area where it might be within a large region. If, for example, he knows that most game moves more at the daylight-sunup and dusk-to-dark periods, he'd best be hunting for it then—not during midday when it is shaded up. And if the hunter also knows that at those times game will be feeding in edge country, then he will disregard other areas and look for it there—just as he will look for game at midday in shaded canyon apexes, north timbered slopes, and thick copses of foliage.

An experienced hunter will tell you that game moves higher in the daytime and descends at night. One reason for this is that game descends to drink at creeks at night, and ascends during the day to escape insect pests. The major reason, however, is that the enemies of most game approach it from below, and game attempts to elude them by following the course of air currents.

Warmed by the sun after a cool night, air rises during the day into the mountains. After sundown the cooling air currents descend into the valleys. Game has learned to utilize such air movement for its own protection.

When game descends at dusk, it carries with it its own scent in one small area of descending air movement; when it moves upward at daybreak with the ascending air currents, it carries its scent along with it, leaving no trace below for the benefit of predators.

DETECTING SPOOR. In order to survive, game animals must continue to do fundamental things. They must eat, excrete, rest, reproduce, dodge enemies, and remain within a habitat suitable for their species.

In doing this, game moves constantly about. Food, in game areas, is often widely spread. Also, the summer ranges do not always coincide with winter ranges. Resting places which offer concealment from enemies and pests are usually not the best grazing or browsing areas. The sexes of many game species separate during the summer months, and only find each other when the fall craze of reproduction is on. Places of concealment and cover constantly change as enemies threaten. This means game is always in a state of fluid movement, often overlapping as to species and habitat.

Any time game moves it leaves certain evidences which inform its enemies of its whereabouts. It must do so for its own survival and reproduction. As an example, the minute traces of scent which deer leave upon brush from the metatarsal musk glands during the fall rut tell passing bucks where the does are. The "flashing" of an antelope, caused by raising its white rump hairs, can be seen with the naked eye for two miles or more in bright sunlight. It tells the hunter and predatory coyote where the antelope band is located, but it also alerts other antelope of the danger.

The most obvious spoor which game leaves is tracks and excreta. This is a by-product of the intricate patterns of movement necessary to its life cycle. But such spoor is often misleading. A hunter can locate game better by being able to unravel a pattern of movement than by following a single trail.

The utilization of spoor, however, is not unimportant. Often a country gives all the appearances of having a game population yet is devoid of game. It would be useless to look for game there according to its basic behavior patterns.

Experienced hunters, therefore, generally look for sign, then having identified it as to species, probable quantity, and age, begin to look for the game itself. The general pattern of such spoor, combined with known game characteristics, helps lead the hunter to his quarry.

TRACKS. In tracking the first necessity is to identify the spoor. The novice looking at the hoofs of such medium game as antelope, sheep, goats, and deer is apt to say that they all look the same. There are, however, detectable differences; and these differences are not so much in the shape of the hoofs, as in the way the different animals strike the earth when walking or running. The resulting imprint, with its often minute

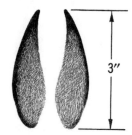

Tracks of a whitetail deer walking are pointed at the toe, and the hoof halves are slightly separated. Often, as here, the dewclaws fail to register.

3″

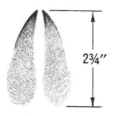

Antelope tracks are more widely spread than deer tracks and the imprint of the hoof halves are more parallel to each other.

2¾"

differences in shape and contour, gives the observing hunter his cue to the animal's identity. Often the type of country helps to corroborate this. Tracks that only *looked* like deer tracks, in flat desert country might well be antelope tracks. And those big blunt "buck" tracks, far up in the crags and intervening alps, might prove to be a ram's tracks. The terrain does help to identify the spoor.

In a general way, deer tracks will be very pointed at the toe, with the hoof halves only slightly separated. Often the rear portion of the hoof pad fails to make an imprint. This is because deer step daintily when walking, punching the tips of the hoof sharply downward.

Antelope tend to leave tracks in which the hoof halves are more parallel and more widely separated. Also, the outer edges of antelope tracks are a bit straighter and don't look as heart-shaped as a deer's. In mud, snow, or soft ground, a slowly walking deer will often show the imprint of its dewclaws (two small appendages above the hoof at the rear); but an antelope never will—an antelope doesn't have dewclaws.

The hoof of a Rocky Mountain ram is similar to that of a big mule-deer buck. But the imprint isn't. A big ram's track, due to the way he puts his heavy weight down, is almost square in contour. We measured several tracks of a big ram I killed this past fall; they averaged 2¼ inches wide by 2⅞ inches long. His hoofs were actually heart-shaped, but the toe points spread with its weight, wiping the earth at the hoof points into a nearly square imprint.

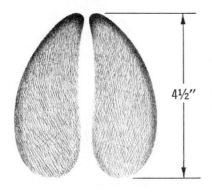

4½"

Tracks of a bull elk are roundish in contour. Only when walking in soft mud does the animal leave the imprint of its dewclaws.

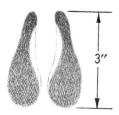

Tracks of the Rocky Mountain ram are rounded at the toes due to the weight placed on these points.

3"

Bull elk tracks are approximately the size of a coffee cup and quite roundish in contour. They resemble the tracks of a two-year-old steer. Cow elk tracks and those of calves are correspondingly smaller but also roundish. Only when walking in mud do elk show their dewclaw marks.

Moose tracks are larger, the big bulls' running to 6 inches, and have a tendency to splay, much like two spread fingers. Also, the dewclaw marks, of the big bulls especially, often show. The general impression an observing hunter gets is that moose tend to plant their hoofs farther *back*—not on their toes like elk.

Caribou tracks are virtually round in outside contour and unduly large compared to other species. The two big crescent-shaped halves of the hoof are something like two miniature kidney-shaped pillows.

Mountain-goat tracks resemble domestic-sheep tracks (in the few places where spoor may be found). They are rarely mistaken, simply because the cliffs and spires of goat country are not the habitat of other species.

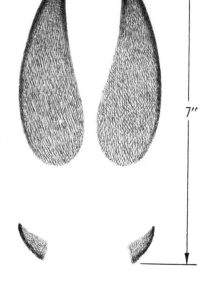

7"

Moose tracks are large, and the hoof halves tend to splay outward. The big bulls, because of their weight, often leave the imprint of their dewclaws.

Bear tracks are not hard to identify and, due to a bear's liking for trails, are often clearly imprinted in dirt and soft earth.

The forefoot track of a black bear will average around 5 inches wide and 3 inches long. The claw marks are set closely in front, each visible as a sharp, tiny V indentation. The rear tracks resemble those made by a man's wet bare foot. A 6-inch hind track is from a medium bear. Cub tracks are quite similar, and about the size of a large porcupine's tracks.

Grizzly tracks are similar in shape, except that the claws make their marks much farther out in front of the forepads than do a black bear's. A front grizzly track measuring 6 inches across the pad is a big grizzly. A hind track measuring 11 inches from heel to claw marks is also made by a big grizzly.

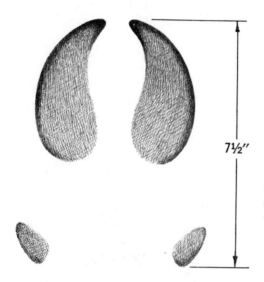

7½″

Caribou tracks are nearly round in outside contour, and the imprint of the dewclaws usually appears.

Brown bear tracks are like grizzly tracks only larger. Also, because of the weight of these large bruins, the imprints sink down deeply into moss and muskeg; and due to the animal's great width, a "ridge" is left between the right- and left-foot tracks in deeply worn trails.

Beginners often confuse domestic cattle and sheep tracks with those of wild game. Cattle tracks differ from those of moose in being round rather than elongated and splayed, and they are larger than elk tracks. Domestic sheep leave tracks that are far more blunt and more widely separated between the hoof halves than those of either deer or antelope. But domestic sheep seldom get into wild goat or wild sheep country.

Tracks of the black bear are characterized by a hind-foot track resembling a man's bare foot and a small forefoot track.

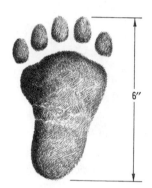

6″

The grizzly's tracks are larger than the black's and the imprints of the claws are farther from the forepads.

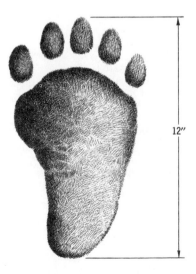

12″

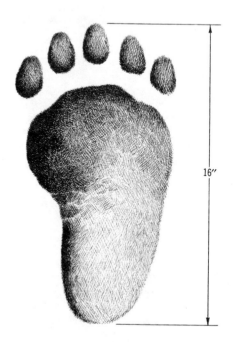

A full-grown Alaska brown bear leaves an enormous hind-foot track 14 to 16 inches long.

16″

EXCRETA. The dung of game animals is another way of identifying a species.

The kernels of deer dung are dark brown, almost black, are usually individually separated, and are about the size of a little fingertip. They are blunt on one end, sharp on the other, like a filbert.

Antelope dung is similar but smaller.

Elk dung is also dark brown with individual kernels which are almond shaped and elliptical, about the length of the first section of an index finger and about ⅝ inch in diameter.

Moose dung is larger, with kernels that are nearly an inch in diameter, lighter in color (almost olive), and pear shaped.

Sheep dung differs in that all kernels of a pile tend to stick together, resulting in a matted pile of flattened kernels.

Caribou dung tends to pile in a single mound, like that of domestic cattle.

Bear dung is found in piles. During autumn, that of black bears usually shows an abundance of berry seeds, that of grizzlies shows the purple coloration of a blueberry diet and similar seeds. An adult grizzly will leave up to 3 quarts of dung at a time.

The freshness of spoor, both tracks and dung, is misleading to most beginners. Hoof tracks in dry, dusty earth during clear weather often look as fresh after a whole week as if they were just made. The same track made during a rainstorm would look old and weathered down within ten minutes. Game dung several days old may look soft and fresh immediately after rain; conversely, dung left in below-zero weather may be frozen hard and look old in a few hours. But there's one infallible rule: if game dung is still steaming, the hunter is not too far from the animal that left it.

OTHER KINDS OF SPOOR. There are other signs left by certain species. Small spruce or pine trees of 2 or 3 inches diameter which are stripped of most of their bark to a height of 6 or 7 feet indicate that bull elk have recently rubbed off the velvet from their antlers there. Hairs and claw marks on sticky spruce trees show where a grizzly has rubbed the itch from its hide and marked the boundary of its domain.

If tracks meander aimlessly, the animal probably was feeding. If they head in a straight line, it probably was going to or from feed grounds, migrating, or changing areas. Great numbers of tracks of a similar species, all headed in the same general direction, mean the game was migrating. Fresh, bounding leaps mean the game was spooked, probably by the hunter's approach.

SPOTTING GAME. Two sensible approaches to the art of locating game are to move slowly and climb the first available ridge and scout for game from above. Most game has extremely keen eyesight and will pick up the hunter far quicker if he moves fast than if he pussyfoots along slowly. The enemies of most game stalk it from below. Therefore, game watches for enemies from below more than from above. Also, most game's vision is such that it is far easier for them to see straight ahead and below than upward. This is because the bony eye-orbit of most game animals hangs over the eyeball and obscures their vision.

Binoculars are one of the big-game hunter's most useful tools. In medium power, they give him vision equivalent to the game he seeks. Further, they allow him to hunt without moving and disclosing his presence. And if the hunter uses binoculars when hunting his game from above, during those hours when game moves and feeds most, he has the added advantage of spotting his quarry as it moves upward and downward.

Another specialized tool for locating game is the spotting scope. Once such an instrument was a cumbersome outfit, usually left at camp because of its bulk and weight. Today there are lightweight spotting scopes little more than a foot long. These can be toted in a rucksack or on a packboard and are worth the bother when hunting such keen-visioned animals as antelope and mountain sheep.

The best way to use high-powered binoculars or a spotting scope is to approach a ridge, crest, or any rise which permits seeing into the next basin, flat, or canyon—without showing one's self. This is best done by crawling the last few yards up to the crest, after having removed hat and eyeglasses. Hats, especially colored ones, are quickly spotted by game if they show over a ridgetop. Eyeglasses often reflect the sun's rays like a heliograph and fully advertise the hunter's presence. The spotting scope should be pushed up in front of the hunter as he peers over the crest.

With such an approach, and in such a position, any game within the basin immediately ahead is not normally alerted, and the hunter can make a minute, deliberate study. This should include *everything*. One of game's greatest protections is the coloration nature has given it to match the foliage and terrain of its surroundings. White "snow patches" with more scrutiny often become mountain goats. Black stumps are often black bears, immobile for the moment. And the gray shelving rocks of crag country often become mountain sheep or big mule-deer bucks after moments of hard study through the glasses.

Studying every inch of country thoroughly perhaps pays off best in ram hunting. A familiar tale of even the experienced sheep hunter is, "I glassed every inch of that country, and I'm telling you there was nothing there. *Nothing!* Then, right in front, almost under my nose, was this big ram. One minute nothing, the next there he was plain as the nose on your face."

Often with the more common species, and especially where excess weight would become cumbersome for the hunter, the rifle scope becomes a good substitute binocular for locating game, assessing its size and identifying objects not quite plain to the naked eye. The scope is one of the finest aids in locating game.

STALKING. One reads and hears so much about "good tracking snow" or snow "so dry you couldn't follow a track," that certain misconceptions have arisen about stalking game. Actually, tracking game belongs more to the realm of legend and history for it is a technique used successfully only in special situations and is unproductive most of the time.

Most game animals have senses far superior to man's. They see, hear, and smell better. They are faster on foot, and because of their coloration, are much better camouflaged. Moreover, their very lives depend upon outwitting their enemies, whereas man only practices stealth when he wants to sneak up on game. Game animals that have reached trophy proportions have not reached that size and age by being stupid. A six-year-old mule-deer buck has lived that long by outwitting enemies every day for six years.

All game knows that most enemies stalk it from its backtrack. Because of this, game tries to leave a backtrack that will be of least advantage to its pursuer. It plans this backtrack so that it can always look back from some vantage point and spot the enemy.

A big buck will cross small openings purposely but quickly enough not to be seen and hurry into cover for concealment. Once there, he will circle, strike off at a tangent or even sharply back, to some position from where it can watch that backtrack. If a pursuer crosses that small opening, its attention is focused straight ahead; but the buck sees it from a different direction and, unseen, continues with its zig-zag escape strategy.

This is why a crafty old buck continuously moves back and forth across small canyons. A scarlet-clad hunter who can't see, smell, or hear as well as the buck and tries to unravel his tracks will eventually show himself—simply because the buck has left its spoor in a visible spot.

In tracking game, even in ideal conditions such as fresh snow, it is far more productive to parallel the trail 50 or 100 yards to one side. An added advantage is that, if and when the game is approached, it will be in a quartering position or broadside, affording a better target than if approached from the rear.

10

Trophy and Range Estimation

THERE ARE FEW things more disappointing than for a hunter to wait all year for an expensive hunt, spot his game, estimate it as a prize, shoot it, and then come up to find that he has downed a scrawny trophy.

In addition to the inherent difficulties of appraising game at a distance, there is a definite mental obstacle as well. The hunter thinks, "I've waited all year to hunt. Here is a prize, and I may not get another shot." In the excitement induced by the year-long wait, the sudden appearance of game, and the fear that this chance may be the only one, his imagination runs wild. He does not see the game animal which actually stands before him, but a prize created by his dreams and desires.

I am convinced that the majority of the ranking heads in the record books were not taken by hunters who estimated their game carefully, killed it, then found it would "make the book." Usually the biggest heads are taken partly by luck, partly because the hunter merely guessed at the animal's size. The discovery that it would make the records came later.

The record elk head for one western state was taken by a hunter who was sick for the day and stayed in the tent. Hearing a sudden commotion just outside, he lifted the tent flap to see a huge bull elk splashing through the creek. The sick man simply laid down his reading material, hoisted his rifle, and shot the bull. It was his taxidermist who discovered that the bull was a record-buster.

I have a Stone ram head which rates fairly high in the records. This ram was taken out of a band of eleven rams, all within shooting distance, in British Columbia.

As my partner and I lay down to fire, I asked the Indian guide, "Which?"

Without lowering the binoculars, he said, "One there in front. One over there."

"Take your choice," I whispered to my partner, who had never killed big game any larger than deer.

My partner missed his, and after some terrible shooting at the other ram at long range across the basin I got it down.

Coming up to it, we laid the tape around its horns and I was immediately disappointed. Our outfitter had sworn there were rams in the area which would surely go 45 inches around the curl. Mine didn't quite make 40 inches. The first indication that it was a real trophy came later when the outfitter measured it and grinned widely. The conviction that the ram was a prize came when the taxidermist saw it, ran for his tape and record book, and we measured it again.

GAME SIZE AND HUNTING AREA.   A game animal is largely a product of what it eats. With many species, the runting of the young produces later adult animals of small size. This is especially true of deer. Antler development is determined by the incidence of certain minerals found in the game area. Deer need forage from a region high in limestone deposits if the antlers are to reach prodigious size.

Certain broad regions often produce a relatively smaller norm of the same species than do other regions. This often has nothing to do with the abundance of feed but with the type of feed available. In sections of Arizona the deer's antlers are skimpy. Mule deer in the Black Hills of North Dakota are smaller than the mule deer of other western regions. Oppositely, that strip of mountainous country on the border between Wyoming and Idaho produces some of the biggest mule-deer bucks on earth.

My son killed a young buck in that region which was only a two-pointer. However, the antlers measured exactly 19 inches around the outside curve, and the same distance across at their widest spread. That is big for any two-point muley. In previous years in the same country, my wife and I had taken two-pointers up to 16 inches around the curve several times.

As against this, my three-point mule deer in Arizona one fall was only 13 inches in width and a foot around the curve. I was advised that this was about average for three-pointers in that region. Such a wide divergence of size among the same species makes the estimation of an animal before the shot difficult indeed.

The relative length of the seasons also determines to some extent the size of trophy heads, and even the size of the animals themselves. In years of late spring following a hard winter, the heads are normally small that fall—especially if fall happens to come early. Antler development and growth depend on food, and there simply aren't enough days for the antlers to sprout from tender nubbins, grow, and become polished fighting gear for the fall rutting season. For this reason, in the same area and with the same species, there are years of good heads and years of poor heads. This is confusing to the hunter trying to size-up game.

METHODS OF JUDGING GAME.   Despite the difficulties, there are ways of appraising a game animal before it is shot. With observation and practice, these ways will pay off, and any hunter can become reasonably adept in using them.

Two of the best tools for estimating game are binoculars and a spotting scope. With them solidly set up, the hunter or guide can often make a fair judgment of the size and desirability of game at great distances. This not only saves time spent in wasted stalking, but prevents disappointment after the kill.

Such pre-assessment should, if possible, be done in advance of the stalk. Game will be farther away, it is true, but will often be standing or moving slowly. It is hard to estimate game breaking cover at close range. Under such a situation, the hunter has to make up his mind awfully fast.

Antelope.   Antelope are among the smallest of North American big game, and one of the most difficult to size-up in advance of the shot. First, because of their marvelous eyesight and flat-country habitat, pronghorns are normally seen and shot at long ranges. This adds to the difficulty. Again, the way buck antelope carry their heads habitually gives the impression that the horns are longer than they really are. That is a basic rule in antelope estimation—horns always measure less than they appear. This illusion is augmented by the mirages in antelope country. Mirages tend to extend any standing animal's height.

The basic method for appraising any big game's headgear is to compare the antlers or horns with the beast's body size. The antelope hunter who does this, and knows in advance the dimensions of an adult antelope, will come fairly close in his estimation of horn length—as long as he doesn't let the factor of *desire* affect his judgment.

Adult male antelope average 34 inches long and stand 36 inches high. Hog-dressed bucks will lose an average of 27 per cent in weight. As an example, two of the biggest bucks checked at a nearby station for an Idaho special antelope hunt weighed 90 and 95 pounds respectively. That meant a live weight of 123 and 130 pounds.

Pronghorn antelope are taken largely for trophies, and if the hunter will keep the above dimensions in mind, he can estimate horn size within reason. If a large buck measures 34 inches from brisket to rump, then it would take a 17-inch horn to give the appearance of being half the

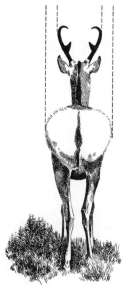

A full-grown pronghorn is trophy size if the horns are at least one-third of its body length (*above*), or if its horn spread exceeds half of its body width.

animal's length. Such horns are, of course, record size; and under close scrutiny very rarely will any buck antelope's horns ever appear to be half a body length.

In today's hunting, a 15-inch antelope is considered mighty good. Most good trophies will be in the 13-inch class. A 13-inch buck should have horns which appear to be at least one-third the animal's body length.

Mule Deer. Because of their variation in size between areas, deer are hard to estimate. First, the hunter should determine if the general run of animals in the region he wishes to hunt is large or small for the species. Then, as with other game, a comparison of the headgear may be made with the body size.

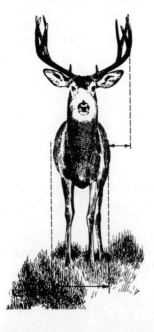

A mule deer is trophy size if the antlers are at least one-half the animal's height from withers to ground (*above*), of if either antler overhangs the body by at least half the body width (*left*).

As an example, if the mule deer in a certain region run large, and a big buck would stand approximately 4 feet high at the withers, then it would take an antler height of half that to be a 24-inch head.

One thing I've come to look for when sizing-up trophy mule-deer bucks is the amount of width between the antler and the body, as seen when the animal faces either away or towards me. Big mule deer in many western areas will have a rump width of around 18 inches, hair and all. If, as the animal faces away, there appears to be half that much width between antler-and-body on the outside, he is in the 30-inch class. This trick is most useful when hunting in snow, as such a space shows up well.

Whitetail Deer. These animals are somewhat more difficult to esti-mate in advance of the shot than are mule deer, for two reasons. First, whitetails are brush-loving deer. The hunter is more apt to come upon them partially obscured by foliage. Again, the hunter is far more apt to come upon his whitetail at close range, causing the animal to bolt suddenly from its place of concealment and making it difficult to estimate its size.

Secondly, the antlers of a whitetail do not stand upright in the same fashion as do those of the mule deer, but the beams point forward and assume more of a basket shape. The beam lengths, because of this, lie in a flat plane to the viewer and are hard to estimate.

The best procedure is to estimate the antlers in some way against a known body feature. While whitetails vary greatly in size, an average big buck may reach 15 inches in body width. The record antler width (inside spread) for this species ranges in the ranking heads from 16 to 23 inches. This means that if a whitetail can be sighted from the rear for even a fraction of a second, and his antlers appear to exceed his body width, he is probably a whopper.

Another way of getting a quick appraisal of a running whitetail buck is to estimate the height of his headgear against two body features—the uplifted tail or the vertical height between brisket and chin. If the antler height appears to be comparable to the tail length, or would fill the area between chin and brisket as the buck runs, it is apt to be outstanding.

Caribou. These may be sized-up in the same way as mule deer. Big bulls of several subspecies weigh up to 600 pounds or more and reach 5 feet at the shoulders. Caribou have antlers that are large in proportion to their body size, and it takes a bull with antlers approximately 5 feet around the outside curve to make the records. However, it doesn't take that much antler size to make a fine trophy.

A prized feature in any caribou head, and one that should always be determined in advance of the shot, is the presence of double shovels. The

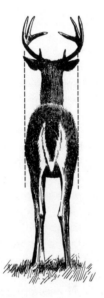

A whitetail deer is trophy size if the antlers approach the height of the body from withers to brisket (*above*), or if the antler spread exceeds the body width (*left*).

A caribou is trophy size if the antlers approach the animal's height.

normal caribou antlers have but a single brow point (often separating into many points after a palmation) coming down over the animal's nose. The incidence of two such shovels is one in several hundred, and is a prized feature.

Elk. These are also estimated by a comparison of the antlers to the body. Bull elk are larger than bull caribou, but have proportionately shorter legs and a deeper body. They, too, stand about 5 feet high at the shoulders and hips. From brisket to hams, elk measure 4 feet or a bit more. The largest cows of a band weigh up to 600 pounds. The largest bull of a band is the herd bull, and such a beast often weighs up to 1,000 pounds.

Incidentally, facilities for weighing elk and other large game in the wilds are usually nonexistent. However, by later weighing the dressed quarters at cold storage, a fairly accurate live weight of the animal can be established. It is generally agreed by outfitters and packers that a bull elk will dress off practically 50 per cent with the cape-and-antlers, legs, and most of the neck meat removed from the quarters.

I have an outfitter friend who annually weighs the trimmed quarters of elk at cold storage for his guests. Until 1960 the biggest bull's dressed

An elk is trophy size if the antlers approach body length.

quarters weighed 556 pounds. In 1960 one of his clients killed a prodigious bull whose dressed quarters weighed 573 pounds—which would mean that bull weighed well over 1,000 pounds on the hoof.

With such facts known before the hunt, the average hunter has a base for a reasonable appraisal of both the elk's size and the dimensions of its headgear. A trophy bull should be nearly as big as a small saddle horse. If his antlers are to reach 50 inches, they should appear to be about as long along their outside curve as the distance from his brisket to his ham at the belly line. Care should be given, in such an estimation, that his hind leg is not stretched out.

In today's hunting pressure, exceptionally large bull elk are kept thinned down in most areas. The seven- and eight-pointers are very scarce, and a six-point bull is considered remarkable. One feature to look for in any six-point bull is the length of the final point, or terminal tine. The biggest six-pointers usually have the longest terminal tines, and one a foot long is good. Ivory-tipped points are another prized feature in elk trophies.

Moose. There are three species of moose: the Shiras, Canadian, and Alaska moose. They range in size in that order, with the Alaska species largest. Both the Canadian and Alaska species measure over 7 feet high at the withers. As with other game animals, antler size is best estimated by a comparison with that height. Features with moose to appraise with special care are the number and symmetry of points, and the size of the palms. Points are counted, of course, and palms are judged in comparison to body height.

As field examples of how such comparisons turn out, my own 1955 Shiras moose, which placed first in Boone & Crockett competition, stood 6 feet high at the withers and had an antler spread of 52 inches. A Canadian bull moose which a partner killed measured 7 feet from his withers to his front foot as he lay on his side, had 24 points, and measured 52 inches spread also. He was considered fair. And an Alaska bull I killed in 1958 also had 24 points, a 58-inch spread, and was laughed at by the Indian guides as being but a "leetle one." He, too, stood over 7 feet high at the withers.

Sheep and Goats. Rams are estimated by the fullness-of-curl of their horns, and the horns' overall size compared with the body. Rams average from 200 to 300 pounds, depending upon species. Mountain goats are

A mountain sheep is trophy size if the diameter of its horn curl is about one-third the animal's height.

A mountain goat is trophy size if its horns are about one-fourth the animal's height. Note: Measurement does not include shoulder hump which is mostly fleece.

estimated by the size of their shoulder hump and the ratio of horn length to body height. Also by the fact that the big billies are usually alone.

Bears. All species of bears are generally estimated by their degree of lankiness according to the season, and most accurately by their tracks. A bear traveling alone is apt to be a boar. Yearlings usually travel with their mothers, until new cubs are born during subsequent hibernation. The remoteness of the area often indicates a bruin's sex and size. Smaller bears are likely to be seen closest to roads, outlying ranches, and forest refuge dumps. Pest bears are most apt to be sows and young bruins. Bears, especially grizzlies, that are come upon in the most rugged, remote regions, are apt to be boars and are usually very large.

Lanky-looking bruins are apt to be yearlings, sows with cubs, or young bears. Broad-shouldered black bears are boars and large for their species. This generality must be qualified in spring season as bears fresh from hibernation will be considerably smaller than after a summer fattening.

Grizzlies having the largest shoulder humps are the largest bears of their species. If they travel alone, they are probably boars. The males will have a proportionately larger breadth of skull than the females.

The best way to estimate any bear's size is from a clearly defined track. The rule-of-thumb is: Add one to the greatest width of its front pad in inches; convert the resulting figure to feet; and the result will be the size of its squared hide.

For example, a black bear whose front paw measures 5 inches across will "square out" as a 6-foot hide. This means that if the hide were laid flat, and the total of its width and its length were divided by two, the result would be 6 feet.

The formula is quite accurate and applies to all species of bear. For purposes of comparison, a 6- or 7-foot black bear is a large one; a 7- or 8-foot grizzly is also large; a 10-foot brown bear is a whopper; and a 9- or 10-foot polar bear is outstanding.

HOW TO ESTIMATE RANGE. If the interest around your hunting camp palls and you want to liven things up, just ask each person to estimate the distance to some object, say, 300 to 400 yards away. Heated arguments and money bets will quickly ensue, for the estimates will no doubt differ widely.

Estimating lateral distance is intrinsically difficult simply because man's stereoscopic vision is limited by the fact that his eyes are not set very wide apart. Even so, judging distances reasonably well is amazing when you consider that a person with one eye blinded has trouble estimating *any* lateral distance.

The normal difficulties of judging distances are compounded by weather, atmospheric conditions, the relationship of the sun's rays to the object, and the intervening terrain. In clear, sunny weather, distant objects usually appear closer than they are. Objects in fog or other conditions of extreme humidity appear to be farther away than they really are. When the sun's rays strike a distant object directly from behind the observer such as in early morning or late afternoon, the object will appear to be closer than if viewed at the same distance while looking into the sun. And distant objects over flat surfaces such as water are difficult to estimate, both as to size and range. Oppositely, if no terrain is between the viewer and an object at long range—such as game viewed across a great open basin—estimating distance is the most difficult.

Coupled to this is the fact that the first segment of an extended distance is proportionately easier to estimate correctly than successive segments of that distance. That is, the first 100 yards of a range is easier to estimate than the next 100 yards, and so on. This is because the farther one looks towards infinity, or the vanishing point of vision, the more difficult it is to judge the surface of the ground.

It is possible for anyone vastly to improve his ability to judge distances. No one will ever be able to estimate ranges with complete accuracy, but it is encouraging to know that the most accurate estimates are made by

Comparative sizes of three average species of North American bears (*from left*): black bear, grizzly, brown.

Comparison between an average 500-pound grizzly (*right*) and an exceptionally large specimen of about 1,000 pounds. A noticeable feature of a large bear is its greater skull width.

To estimate the size of a bear's hide, measure the width of its front paw or track in inches, add one, and change inches to feet. The result will be approximately the size of its "squared" hide. This brown bear's paw measures 9 inches, indicating a 10-foot hide.

the most experienced hunters who constantly practice some basic form of range estimation.

Memorizing Distances. One good way to learn how to estimate ranges is to memorize some segment of distance, then estimate any distance by multiples of that known distance. For example, how far can you throw a rock? Let us say it is 50 yards. This is determined by throwing a number of rocks, then either measuring or pacing the average distance. Incidentally, many men who have had numerous occasions to pace distances, such as ranchers who set fence posts a rod apart (5½ yard-long paces), can step within 5 per cent of a measured yard, time after time. And that is close enough for practical purposes.

Having established that you can heave a rock 50 yards (or any other known distance), keep looking at such a distance and throwing an occasional rock and pacing it off until you have a mental conception of 50 yards. With practice it can be done.

Then, if that buck you're hunting in the fall appears to be two long rock-throws away, he is right at 100 yards. If it would take you five consecutive throws with a rock to reach him, then he is approximately 250 yards away.

A similar way, which may be practiced and developed right in town, is to measure or learn the exact yardage of a city block, or memorize the length of a football field. Again, use your mental conception of such a known range in the hunting field and utilize it, in multiples, to determine any longer range.

The first 100 yards of a range is easier to estimate correctly than successive segments of that range. As the hunter's vision approaches the vanishing point, it becomes more difficult to judge the surface of the ground.

We live on an acreage which is just 80 rods, or 440 yards, long. (Over forty years of big-game hunting have convinced me that, under the less-than-ideal conditions of hunting, no big game should be shot at over 400 yards.) The neighbors' cattle and sheep often walk and feed along the boundary fence of this acreage. Each time I'm out at the shop, or shooting from the benchrest (approximately 40 yards inside the opposite boundary fence), and there happen to be animals along the other fence line, I simply aim the rifle scope, try to hold on an animal, and think:

"That is the outside limit. If that was a bull elk or moose, could you hold on his vital area?" Of course, my rifle is always empty. Such repeated practice helps greatly to establish a mental conception of 400 yards. It does this both in terms of individual rifle holding and size of image in the rifle scope.

A similar way of learning to estimate distances is to sight in all hunting rifles at a known range, say 200 yards. When doing this, also keep trying to get a mental conception of that range. Try visualizing the size of a deer, elk, bear, or caribou on the backstop of that range; then take these images of a known distance to the hunting field.

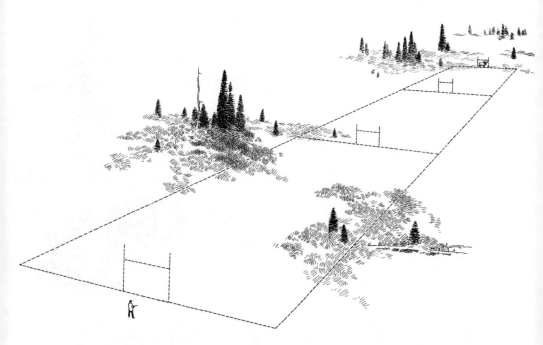

By remembering the length of a football field, or other convenient distance, a hunter can visualize it in multiples to estimate the range of a game animal.

Another practical way of learning range is to practice each time afield estimating the distance to a certain object; then carefully pace it off. To learn the distance of each pace, try to pace with the same stride every time; then measure an average stride after you get well under way. If your stride is 34 inches long, you take 108 of them to the object, and have guessed it to be 100 yards away, then you are a far better "guesstimater" than most.

Estimating with Scope Reticles. Much progress has been made with scope and binocular reticles to help in estimating ranges. One of the simplest improvements is the addition of a round black dot superimposed on the intersection of the cross hairs. Usually such a dot will cover so many inches per hundred yards. Assume that the dot will cover 3 inches per hundred yards. If, when aiming with the rifle solidly held, the dot covers the width of one of the 12-inch planks facing the backstop of the target range, that plank is 400 yards away. Utilizing such a fact in the hunting field involves a knowledge of the approximate size of game. Most hunters, especially experienced ones, have some basic knowledge of this and can apply it in practical fashion.

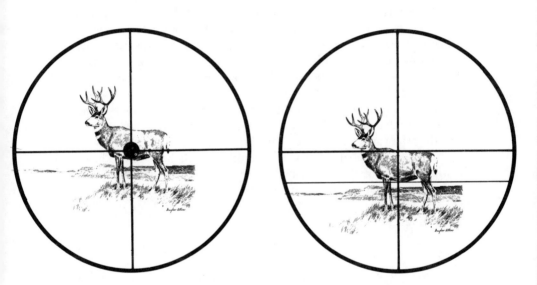

Range-finding with scope reticules: If a dot reticule which covers 3 inches per hundred yards covers half the body of an average mule deer (body is about 18 inches deep), the deer would be 300 yards away (*left*). If a pair of lateral crosshairs which spread 6 inches per hundred yards bracket the body of the same deer, it would be 300 yards away (*right*).

As an example, suppose the black dot of the scope just covers half the body of a standing mule-deer buck from withers to belly line. Such bucks have bodies around 18 inches deep. A reasonable estimate of the range would be 300 yards.

The standard post of a rifle scope makes a fair range estimator. To use the post for such a purpose involves some knowledge of game size. First, one has to learn just how many inches per hundred yards the width of such a post reticle will cover. The manufacturer will supply this information if asked; otherwise it is simple to determine. Lay the rifle solidly on a table or benchrest and aim it at a target backstop 100 yards away. Mark the edges—where the post edge cuts the target on both sides—and measure between. Many posts will cover from 4 to 6 inches.

In use, either estimate the animal's length in terms of multiples of the amount the post seems to cover or the width (depth) of its body and reduce it to number of 100 yards of range. If the 6-inch post covers a third of the length of a 3-foot-long antelope he is about 200 yards away. To estimate his relative width with the post, turn the rifle on its side, allowing the post to run longitudinally; then estimate how many widths he is high.

Still another type of rifle scope has a pair of lateral crosshairs set exactly far enough apart so that at a given range a known amount of inches will show between them. I have one whose crosshairs spread exactly 6 inches at 100 yards. If the top wire were laid along the back line of a buck with an 18-inch body, and the lower wire rested along the belly, he would be about 300 yards away.

A new type of scope is being developed which has two movable crosshairs and a pair of knurled ring collars, one denoting the game size, the other the yardage. The crosshairs are spread with the adjusting ring until one lies on the animal's back, the other on its belly line. Then the width in inches of the beast's body is set on one ring, and the range in yards is shown automatically on the other ring. Such scopes are somewhat bulky but are most useful at extreme ranges and for standing or slowly moving game.

11

Bow Hunting

THE BOW WAS the first mechanical weapon made by man and has been used in wars of conquest throughout ancient history. With the advent of black powder and arms suited to its use, the bow's popularity as a military and a hunting weapon began to wane. During the settlement of America, even the bows of the Indians gave way to powder arms when they were obtainable from the whites.

The situation held true during the decades when game was hunted primarily for food and, in fact, nearly to the present generation. Then a gradual shift in hunting objectives became necessary due to dwindling game supplies and a mushrooming population. Hunting purely for meat tapered off and was replaced by the more romantic pastime of hunting for sport and trophies. With this gradual change came a spirited revival of the bow.

Several additional factors have caused a recent upsurge in archery as a method of hunting. One has been the development of better equipment. Today one can do with the bow-and-arrow what no one in the early days of bow hunting believed possible. Camouflage clothing developed during World War II has been adopted by bow hunters, enabling them to stalk closer to game. The perfection of authentic-sounding artificial game calls such as bugles for elk, horns for moose, and natural-sounding calls for varmints has further helped the bow hunter to reduce the distance between himself and his quarry.

As a result, all species of North American big game have now been taken with bow-and-arrow. That this has been accomplished by expert archers, but not by average archers, poses a challenge for those with only moderate skills.

Two other developments have given impetus to the sport of bow hunting. The Pope & Young Club, emulating the Boone & Crockett Club, now ranks the best trophies taken with bow-and-arrow. And

107

archery clubs have sprung up all over the country, while courses in archery are now standard at most large universities. The archer who learns the skills of the bow at these places of instruction will find that his target shooting is readily adaptable to the hunting field.

A basic point to remember in bow hunting is that the bow is a relatively short-ranged weapon. The broadhead arrow does not kill with the same speed as a high-velocity bullet from the modern hunting rifle. For this reason, a high degree of hunting skill must be learned and practiced so that the archer will get close enough to his quarry to release a certain, humane shot.

THE AMERICAN BOW. History has given us four main bow types. It took American ingenuity, imagination, and practicality to choose the best points of each of three and combine them into a new creation which has proven superior to any of its progenitors.

From the Turkish recurve bow, the American bow designers took a partial recurve, for sweetness in pull. From the Indian flat bow, the Americans derived the principle that the flatter the bow the less was the expansion and contraction of the wood. They modified this feature while imparting to the whole some of the virtue of the English long bow's length. The result is a superior weapon known as the American semi-long bow.

Many woods have been used for making bows in the past. Among the most popular have been lemonwood, yew, osage, and bamboo. Among the first attempts at lamination was the use of sinew and rawhide, either from wild or domestic animals, for bow backing.

These materials were considered good bow stock until approximately two decades ago. I have a bow of beau d'arc (osage) backed with rawhide which was made and given to me by a hunting partner in 1946. This weapon is still as good as the day it was made and a fair bow even by today's standards.

The perfection of fiberglass marked another step forward in the making of better bows, and the best hunting bows today are of the wood-glass laminated type. Some archers claim that the very best bow obtainable currently is a lamination of hard-rock maple with fiberglass on the back and belly.

One of the best fiberglass products is known as Bo-Tuff. It is bonded into solidity and used in a lamination with a maple core for the limbs of a hunting bow. Such a bow generally has a grip of cherry, tiger, or another fancy wood to add to its attractiveness. A weapon of this design, with a pull of 40 pounds, has a far better cast than a 50-pound wooden bow of two to three decades ago. For this reason many male archers are

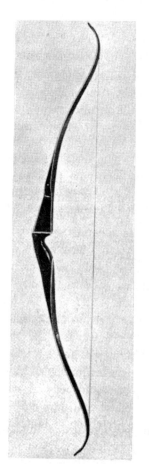

The modern laminated hunting bow is characterized by flatness, length and a partial recurve for extra power. *All photos courtesy of Bear Archery Co.*

using hunting bows with pulls of 45 to 48 pounds, although 50 pounds was the minimum for the older wooden bows. The mass production of such excellent weapons has largely eliminated the need for an archer to make his own bow.

The average hunter is best off buying a quality bow from a reputable maker. The real enthusiast can still begin with a stave and make his own, and a few custom makers supply special weapons at relatively high prices. Also, like boats and gunstocks, semifinished bows complete with accessory kit are available. All the buyer need do is finish and polish the bow.

Bow Size. The size of the hunting bow is important. Bow size is determined by arrow length, which in turn is determined by the bowman's reach. This is roughly the distance from his right eye to the knuckle of his left index finger minus 1½ inches.

The old standard for a medium to large man was a 28-inch arrow in a 6-foot bow. The formula was that for each inch reduction necessary in arrow length, a 2-inch reduction should be made in the bow's length. This ratio is not adhered to in today's modern bows. Today, a 69-inch bow is considered a "long" bow. Averages run from 62 to 66 inches, with 66 inches the most popular. These bows are used with 27- to 29-inch arrows. Two advantages of the shorter bow are that it is faster in delivery and less cumbersome while hunting in foliage. A disadvantage of too short a bow is its tendency to "stack up," or greatly augment its pull in the final stage before releasing the arrow. The pull, or weight, of hunting bows is determined by the strength and experience of the shooter and the hunting regulations of the various states.

Hunting bows for men will run from around 40 pounds on up, with a 50-pound bow a good average, especially for the larger species of big game. For the largest species, such as the dangerous grizzly or brown bear, more weight is required. Women archers, who hunt mostly for deer-sized species, often use bows in the 35-pound class where legal.

Most modern hunting bows have contoured grips and are designed to shoot the arrow through the bow's center line. This eliminates the problem of releasing the arrow from the side of the grip and off-center.

Some bows have sight windows and even can be equipped with special telescopic sights. Once accustomed to these sights, many big-game hunters will not hunt without them.

ARROWS. Broadhead arrows are the only type legally permitted in most states for hunting big game. Blunts and flu-flu arrows are used for game birds, rodents, and small game. Standard shafting for hunting arrows was for decades made of Port Orford cedar. A decade or more ago, aluminum shafts were introduced which were the equals of cedar and were less sensitive to changes in temperature and humidity. Today's best hunting arrows, however, are made of fiberglass.

Good broadheads are of two types, two-bladed and three-bladed, and may be barbed or barbless. For game hunting broadheads range from ⅞ inch to a full inch in width. For best penetration the heads should have a length-width ratio of nearly three to one. Extra-large broadheads, having any flat surface exceeding ½ inch, are not ideal since they have a tendency to wind plane. A very recent design in broadheads for game hunting is the snap-on head. With either type, all cutting edges are honed or filed razor sharp, both for added penetration and the sure cutting of blood vessels.

Standard wooden shafting in hunting arrows designed for bows of approximately 50-pound weight used to measure 11/32-inch diameter. Now many archers prefer fiberglass shafts of larger diameter for big-game hunting. The straightness, weight, spine (relative stiffness), fletching, and uniformity of shafts are all critical factors in accuracy. Any deviation will be greatly magnified in the way the arrow will perform after being released.

The best archers once weighed their wooden arrows and checked for uniformity on a spining scale before taking to the field, just as benchrest shooters meticulously weigh all bullets before loading. With today's precision-made fiberglass arrows, this is no longer necessary. The fletching on hunting arrows should be uniform and average about 3½ inches long.

BOWSTRINGS. The finest bowstrings today are made of Dacron-polyester fiber. For a few dollars the archer can buy strings of suitable length for his individual bow. It is no longer necessary to make one's own strings.

Bows should be left unstrung when not in use. The orthodox way to string a bow is to place the lower end inside the instep, grasp the grip and pull upward while pushing the opposite end loop into the groove with the thumb and forefinger. To unstring the bow the opposite procedure is used, leaving the end loop around the end.

For an archer with weak muscles an unorthodox way of stringing a bow of heavy weight is to step between bow and string with the right foot; place the lower end over the left arch; reach behind and grasp the upper end with the right hand; push with the right hand towards the left, and slip the loop over the end with left-hand fingers.

For hunting the long-accepted distance between string and grip was approximately a "fist-and-thumb," or 6½ inches. Recently, and due in part to the shaped grip of the modern bow, this distance is now from 7½ to 9 inches. Bows higher- or lower-strung than this have no added advantage.

Even though many modern bows have sighting arrangements meant to help aim the arrow, many of the best bow hunters rely more on instinct. That is, from practice they attain a mental image of distances and the correct hold to drive the arrow to that point. For them, shooting an arrow is much like shooting a rock from a kid's old-fashioned "flipper" or slingshot. In fact, early training and proficiency in hitting things with a flipper is a great help in archery.

ARM GUARDS AND GLOVES. Arm guards are of two types. One is the standard strip guard, reinforced with an internal steel stay running longitudinally and strapped around the forearm. A more recent type is a shaped and reinforced leather sleeve which opens under spring tension along an open side, then slips snugly into place around the forearm, covering most of it. Either type is suitable for hunting.

Protection for the fingers of the string hand takes the form of finger tabs, tips, and shooting gloves. All three are used and liked by hunters. Of the three, the leather fingertip is perhaps best.

The most necessary feature of both arm guards and tips is that they fit

111

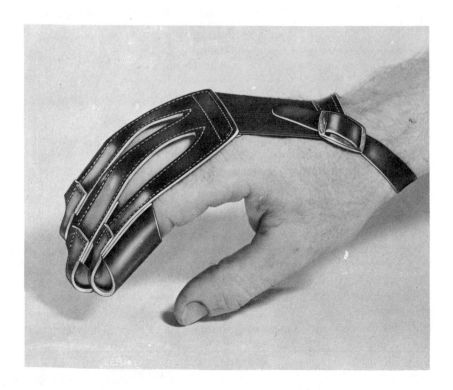

Leather fingertips protect archer's fingers from the bowstring.

well and prevent discomfort or injury from the bowstring. A slapping string causes flinching and spoils a "sweet" release.

QUIVERS. Quivers are of various kinds. Some hang from the hunter's belt, others are worn, and a recent plastic holder attaches to the bow and holds several arrows, presumably for fast successive shots. The most popular quiver is a leather pouch type which is worn diagonally upon the hunter's back. Some of these have a small pocket for carrying a hone or small file and a knife.

Some early settlers and Indians used to make their own noncollapsible quivers by lacing wet rawhide, such as green moose skin, over a split log of suitable diameter. When the rawhide dried, the log, by being split, could be removed from the solid quiver, which was then extremely hard. The fault of this quiver was that it allowed the arrows to rattle and was noisy.

That, briefly, is the basic archery equipment necessary for hunting. All items can be as elaborate or expensive as one wishes, but the beginning

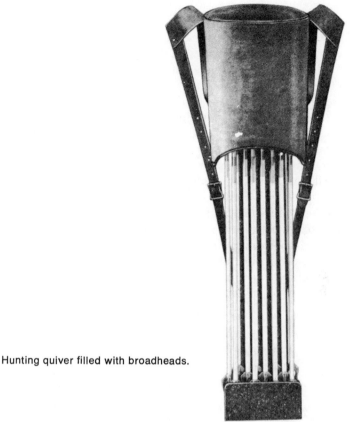

Hunting quiver filled with broadheads.

archer can start with a functional outfit which currently may be purchased retail for around $100.

As with handgun shooting, success with the bow-and-arrow requires extensive and continuous practice. The same outfit, with the substitution of target blunts for broadheads, can be used by the archer to obtain this necessary practice.

HUNTING RANGE. The entire technique of bow hunting revolves around the singular fact that archery hunting is a short-range proposition and, in the majority of successful instances, will be terminated with a shot at standing game.

In rifle hunting, ranges will reach a maximum of 400 yards. The maximum range for the average bow hunter seldom exceeds 50 yards if a high standard of sporting ethics is maintained.

It is true that in target archery targets are set up within many shooting courses at 80 yards and even further. Many an experienced archer hits those targets with regularity. Again, a few exceptionally skillful archers who have spent most of an active life shooting arrows can make spectacular hits at extreme ranges and can *shoot* an arrow as far as game can be hit with a rifle. This does not make the bow-and-arrow certain or ethical for use on game at such ranges, nor should any hunter attempt it.

Setting the outside range for hunting with the bow at around 50 yards gives the archer a ratio of approximately one in fifty chances at bagging game, as compared to that of the rifle hunter. In other words, under average hunting conditions, fifty times as much game might be located beyond 50 yards, in standing position and offering a shooting opportunity, as will be found at ranges under 50 yards. This is especially true in the more open game country of the West. This means that the archer must get *close* to his game, undetected.

Getting close to game, without being seen, smelled, or heard is accomplished generally by one of two techniques. Either the hunter stalks within close range of his quarry without alerting it, or he waits until game comes close to him.

Noted archer Fred Bear pulls a hunting bow to full draw.

STALKING. Stalking game with the bow-and-arrow involves a knowledge of game habits, an ability to detect winds and faint breezes in relation to a pattern, and an ability to interpret the sounds, contours, and objects of the forest. But more, the stalker must possess two fundamental qualities to a degree seldom needed by the rifle hunter—an infinite patience, and an ability to move *slowly*.

A neighbor who is a fine hunter and keen bow enthusiast, in telling of his recent elk hunt in the West, said, "I heard this big bull bugling and making a fuss in some chaparral and alders maybe 400 yards up the sidehill. He wasn't spooked and didn't know I was anywhere around. In a couple of hours I was up to the brush where he was polishing his antlers, and in range. . ." In such a situation with a rifle, the same hunter, within fifteen to thirty minutes, would have had the beast's heels in the air.

Because the special senses of most game are superior to those of man, the hunter must utilize the concealment of foliage and terrain. The biggest blessing to the bow hunter is foliage. By staying behind trees and brush, and moving slowly and quietly, the archer often can approach his quarry closely enough to release an arrow. *But*—and it's a big one—the blessing of thick foliage immediately becomes a curse, for it offers no opening through which a broadhead will fly. Unlike a heavy bullet, a broadhead cannot penetrate, or even touch, limbs and twigs and stay on course. The instant a broadhead touches such foliage it flies off at an acutely oblique angle.

The standard excuse and lament of game archers is, "I hit a damn limb!" Years ago while taking photographs with an exceptional archer hunting in a game concentration, I saw him miss four separate mule-deer bucks for the same reason. All were at 40 to 50 yards and standing. All his arrows were deflected off course.

It is difficult to reduce to words the minute details that make up a fine stalking skill. A few basic do's and don'ts will help: Hunt into the wind. Wind direction can be tested with a wet finger, or dry dust allowed to trickle down from the fingers. Don't cross openings in trees or foliage—rather, stay inside timber fringes and shadows. Move slower than you think necessary, and far slower than the quarry habitually moves. Stay low to the earth if game is suspected to be nearby. Freeze into immobility at the first sight of game, regardless of distance, and move only after ascertaining that it hasn't seen you. In instances where game detects the hunter, he should *never* make quick, excited motions which indicate to the game an intention to pursue. The best procedure is to give no indication that game has been seen, and slowly and unobtrusively move away.

Most game will detect movement far quicker than contour; based somewhat on this fact, the modern camouflage clothing available today

Camouflage clothing is basic equipment for the bow hunter, who must conceal himself yet remain within range of his quarry.

has proved to be one of the archer's most invaluable assets. The rubberized camouflage garments are fine as outer clothing during wind, rain, or stormy weather. In balmy weather camouflage clothing had best be of porous cotton so that it "breathes."

Many hunting bows are drab-colored. The glare from light-colored luminous bows will carry great distances and scare game. Bow socks are now available in camouflage cloth which simulates the coloration of autumn foliage, and similar ones can be made of white cloth for hunting in snow. Both effectively eliminate bow glare.

Arrows are often kept in their quivers during the stalk, but whenever game is suspected to be close by, broadheads should be nocked and carried at ready.

SHOOTING FROM BLINDS. The second successful method of bow hunting is to wait in some form of blind for game to pass. Natural spots for blinds are at canyon apexes, narrows in drainages, and points adjacent to game trails and areas which spoor indicates game to be using. "Blinds" here do not necessarily mean elaborate structures but any places of concealment the hunter can find. The very best are often log jams, down timber, clumps of brush, and similar natural-appearing foliage or obstructions.

One of the best aids to this form of hunting is camouflage cloth, sold especially for hunters. It can be purchased in strips about a yard wide by 10 yards long. The strip is simply wound around suitable brush or woven into tree clumps. If placed in a seemingly haphazard fashion, it looks like part of the landscape.

When trail watching for deer with bow-and-arrow, the archer can use two forked sticks to hold his bow at ready position.

Record Stone ram shot by Fred Bear is testimony to the archery skill and stalking ability of an expert bow hunter.

ACCURACY. How accurate is the bow-and-arrow as a hunting weapon? In a broad way, the average accuracy is comparable to the average accuracy possible with a suitable handgun. That is to say, the hunting ranges for game are comparable, and the aggregate scores of a reasonable number of fair pistol shots would be comparable to the aggregate scores of the same number of similarly skilled archers at the same ranges.

To settle such a controversial question, a pistol club in a neighboring state challenged an archery club to a shoot-off. The results were slightly in favor of the handgun enthusiasts. Neither group should shoot at deer-sized game beyond ranges at which they can keep all broadheads or bullets within an 8- to 12-inch circle.

Many states now set aside special archery hunts for many species of game. This has come about because of increasing interest and enthusiasm on the part of bowmen, better equipment, the proportionately smaller number of game animals taken as compared to rifle hunting, and the exceptional safety record established. These special archery hunts are generally set up in advance of rifle hunts in the same area, for obvious reasons; and to give bowmen a reasonable chance, the hunts are usually authorized in the areas of considerable game concentration. As one example of the trend, one western state had its first legal archery season in 1946. In 1961 there were at least eleven special archery hunts in the same state. By 1970 this number had nearly doubled.

Archers are an enthusiastic group, and firmly sold on their weapon for hunting purposes. Realizing the basic shortcomings of the bow for game hunting, as against the potential of the modern rifle, most archers hold to a code of high personal ethics in the matters of getting close to an animal before loosing an arrow and refusing chancy shots which may only wound it.

Many an enthusiastic bowman will hunt several successive seasons for a species before bagging his trophy or even releasing an arrow. "But," as one grinning archer told me recently, "when you *do* get him, it's all worth it!"

12

Deer

WHITETAIL DEER. The most popular and widely distributed big-game animal in the United States, the whitetail populates almost every area of the country except a long fingerlike strip of land stretching from California to Ohio. Whitetails also range over one third of Mexico and are found well up into the Canadian provinces. Only five states have no whitetail deer, or so few as to be negligible: California, Colorado, Kansas, Nevada, and Utah. Michigan, Wisconsin, Pennsylvania, Texas, and Minnesota have the most.

Whitetails are the smallest of the three major deer species (the mule deer and blacktail are the other two) and are divided into many subspecies, largely according to location. There is an extreme variation in size among adult whitetail deer. Exceptional bucks in some northeastern states often reach 300 pounds; the Coues deer of Mexico and Arizona seldom exceed 40 pounds.

The whitetail deer will face new demands in the future as hunters and hunting pressures increase. Its habitat is bound to be diminished by the spread of the human population and the attendant land needs of agriculture, mining, lumbering, and industry. The future for the whitetail deer, however, is bright, due to several factors.

Principal among these is a biological trait. The whitetail has the greatest potential for rapid reproduction of any big-game species in North America. Does of this species will begin breeding at the age of one and one-half years. The first fawn of a doe's reproductive years is apt to be a single, but from then on the average is twins, with triplets and even quadruplets not uncommon. Given any kind of a chance, such potential will rapidly save a species from near-extinction caused by disease, starvation, depredation, or overkill. Between 1937 to 1967 the whitetail population increased from 3 million to over 7 million.

The whitetail deer carries a graceful set of antlers—a single main beam on each side with several projecting tines. Information on how to measure a whitetail trophy can be found on pages 382–385.

A second factor is the whitetail's capacity to adapt to man. More than most big-game species, the whitetail deer can live and flourish virtually in man's backyard. So long as there is suitable habitat, and sufficient winter range, this species will thrive. This habitat is often the "edge" country where farmlands meet forest and brushlands. The brush-loving whitetail subsists where any kind of foliage grows, often thriving in croplands almost as well as in the natural cover they replaced.

These factors, plus the continuation of sensible game management, will keep the whitetail deer as America's number one big-game species.

The whitetail is distinguished from the two other deer species by several characteristics. Its hoofs are thinner and daintier. Antlers are arranged upon a single main beam. The musk glands occurring along the metatarsal bones are smaller. The most distinguishing feature, its big flaglike tail, gives the deer its name.

The innate characteristics of the whitetail resemble those of the Chinese pheasant, imported into this country to replace native upland birds which couldn't survive the increasing agrarian expansion of man. Both are wily, smart, and full of tricks. Both feed at the open edge-country of farmlands, love to lie low in concealment in the presence of danger, skulk through cover, and pit their wits against man's. Both "explode" from cover at close range.

The whitetail is largely a brush-country deer and spends most of its life span in or near heavily timbered, brushy or swampy country. Unlike its cousin the mule deer, the whitetail does not migrate from summer to winter ranges but will usually stay within a radius of a few miles.

Like other game species, the whitetail is largely nocturnal, and this fact gives the cue to the best hunting hours—early morning and late evening when it is feeding.

Before getting into the three best methods for hunting this deer, it would be best to understand those abilities in which the animal surpasses the hunter, and any possible departments in which it is weak.

First, the whitetail's hearing is far keener than man's. Its sense of smell, too, is far more acute. Its running speed is faster than any man's. In short, the whitetail can outsmell, outhear, and outrun the hunter, and any hunting procedure based on matching deer against hunter in any of these abilities would result in failure.

On the other hand, the deer's vision is relatively poor. The whitetail is not a long-distance runner like the antelope; it runs in short bursts of speed and does not run out of an area but prefers to circle about within it. Moreover, the whitetail, like the antelope, is mildly curious. And like all game animals, the males during mating season tend to lose a great amount of their caution.

Methods of Hunting—Driving. The three standard methods of white tail hunting are driving, stillhunting, and stalking. Driving is most often employed in areas of known deer populations and numerous hunters. The party is managed by one person; hunters are divided into "standers" and "drivers" who alternate positions, usually after one or more kills his deer.

Standers are posted along runways, deer trails, old forest roads, on high vantage points overlooking canyon bottoms, and similar places where deer are known to move. Their basic attribute should be the patience of Job since once they are posted it is a cardinal sin to move until the drive is over. Any motion is apt to frighten the oncoming animal from crossing in front of the stander.

The drivers circle to an opposite side of the general area to be driven. There they spread out in a mild V formation with the hunters placed closely enough together so that driven deer will not cut back between them.

Once in position, the drivers move toward the standers. Normally the game ahead will move forward so that the standers get their chance. Often deer will slip between the drivers, or around the outside of the driving line where the end drivers will get a shot.

Deer drives are the least thrilling form of deer hunting. They are also the most hazardous. But drives are often necessary; they are one of the results of increased population.

Stillhunting. Taken literally, the term "stillhunting" means that the hunter remains motionless and waits for the game to come into sight. He may then shoot, if he's within rifle range, or stalk his quarry until he is close enough for a killing shot. Stillhunting has also come to mean stalking quietly in search of the game.

When choosing to wait for his deer, the hunter should find a spot that will allow the game to approach him downwind. He should post himself against a tree bole, in a brush heap, or other concealed place. As in any other form of big-game hunting, the hunter sees best while he is immobile; the game sees worst while it is on the move. The deer's acuteness of hear-

Dressed in camouflage clothing, the author conceals himself in a natural blind for hunting whitetails.

ing and smell also have a bearing on the outcome. The stillhunter therefore must not make noise or smoke lest he give away his presence. If other hunters "play dog" for him, they will cause game to move more than normally, and this ups the posted hunter's chances.

Successful stillhunting depends on a thorough knowledge of the country, an understanding of the quarry's habits and weaknesses, and the sheer physical ability to stay in one spot without moving for hours at a time.

Stalking. Perhaps the most thrilling form of hunting is for the man to invade the deer's own bailiwick and try to outwit it by stealth and superior strategy.

The way to approach stalking is to *think* as a deer might and even ask yourself: "If I were being hunted in this area, with my life at stake and no other place to go, just how would I go about outsmarting somebody who was after me?"

It is surprising how a hunted man reacts in the same way as a hunted deer. Military men during wartime have discovered that the strategy soldiers use to evade an enemy has a striking resemblance to the tricks big game uses to accomplish the same purpose. Both utilize camouflage, lie low, and remain motionless to avoid detection. Both evade followers by suddenly angling off their main course, circling, and often coming upon the opponent from an unsuspected direction. When the chips are down, both will resort to fighting (according to their capabilities), or flight.

An understanding of all this vastly helps the stalker. He moves more slowly than a beginner might think necessary, knowing that fast movement is easy to detect. And, as a deer would, he moves inside fringing timber and behind the blind side of trees rather than in the open. The quarry's keen sense of smell is nullified by the expedient of hunting *into* any breeze, even if it means wide circling to hunt any particular spot where deer is thought to be. The stalker learns not only to refrain from making noise himself but to interpret any noise not in keeping with the surroundings as sounds made by game. He doesn't let his pants legs swish together as he walks; likewise he interprets the sudden snapping of a twig or tinkle of shale in windless woods as the sound of walking deer.

The stalker's strategy in this way becomes a thrilling game of hide-and-seek. The satisfaction he receives after coming into range of his deer on his own is usually far greater than that derived from shooting driven game.

Veteran whitetail stalkers employ a trick which takes advantage of the deer's natural curiosity. One old-timer said, "I've actually killed more whitetails that I've caught circling behind me than any other way. The smart little devils always seem to hear me comin', then sneak in behind me to see what it's all about. I always hunt awful slow, and keep watchin' where I've been."

Hunting in Pairs. Hunting with a partner is another productive method of hunting whitetails. The basic technique is to so hunt any area that while the game moves to protect itself from the sight or sound of one hunter, it inadvertently places itself where the partner might see it.

In hunting out a brush patch, for example, one hunter circles so as to be in a position to see the far end of the patch; then the partner pushes through the patch of foliage, flushing the game from the opposite end. When game is thought to be in a gully or canyon, one hunter works the ridge where he can look downward, the other hunts the canyon bottom hoping either to spot the deer at close range himself, or have it move into a position where the hunter at a higher elevation will see it.

Partner hunting is a cheery way of hunting. It lacks the hectic bustle and danger of the drive, yet offers fine companionship and a measure of protection against getting lost.

Rifles and Cartridges. Since most whitetail habitat is brushy and heavily foliaged, this deer is shot at relatively close range. The majority of whitetails are killed under 100 yards. The first shot at a whitetail is invariably the best shot though there is often the opportunity for quick succeeding shots. Like the ruffed grouse, a whitetail once startled and under way will quickly put any available tree or bush between himself and the hunter. This prevents deliberate follow-up shots.

These conditions dictate both the type of rifle best suited for hunting this deer and the overall requirements of the bullet. In order to get off a quick shot in brush, the rifle must be relatively short and lightweight. The bullet which does the work must be a fairly good brush-bucker and be able to plow through foliage and reach the target. It must have sufficient weight to penetrate well. Often the shot at whitetails will be a running shot; and while it is always necessary to aim for a vital area, the truth is that whitetail deer are often hit anywhere. The good whitetail bullet should do the job well on any solid body hit. The bullet should open up fast. With these conditions in mind, the hunter might well first select a suitable bullet or cartridge, then choose a rifle which will properly handle it.

Two rifle-cartridge combinations which have proven themselves as nearly ideal whitetail weapons are the old Winchester Model 94 lever-action rifle shooting the .30/30 cartridge, and the old Remington automatic "cornsheller" handling the .35 Remington bullet and cartridge.

125

The Model 94, in .30/30 cartridge, has killed more whitetail deer than any other rifle. The Remington, which was developed later, is equally popular for whitetails. It is significant here that the bullets which made this reputation, in both cartridges, were relatively blunt-nosed, and had well-exposed, softpoint tips. Even today, after decades of bullet and rifle development, these two combinations are still fine outfits for whitetail deer. Both handle and shoot "fast," with quick repeat shots. The bullets of both plow through brush well. Both are adequate to kill whitetails with any well-placed hit.

Other more modern rifles which are fine for whitetails are the Savage Model 99, Marlin Model 336, Winchester Models 88 and 100, and the Remington Models 760 and 740. Many whitetail hunters use modern bolt-action rifles such as the Winchester Model 70, Remington Model 700, Ruger Model 77, and Weatherby Mark V, especially if they have only one rifle and must use it on other species.

Some of the best cartridges for use on whitetails are:

.30/30 Winchester
.300 Savage
.308 Winchester
.30/06 Springfield
.35 Remington
.358 Winchester

In areas where heavy brush isn't too much of a problem, or where the rifle and cartridge must be used also on game shot at extended ranges, the following cartridges are entirely suitable:

.243 Winchester
6-mm Remington
6.5 Remington Magnum
.264 Winchester Magnum
.270 Winchester
.284 Winchester
7-mm Mauser
.25-06 Remington

Shotguns. As a safety measure, some states won't allow the use of rifles on deer, and a shotgun must be used with either buckshot or rifled slugs. Generally speaking, buckshot should not be used at over 40 yards, and even then buckshot fringes on being a game-crippler. The modern rifled slug is far better, more accurate, and may be used up to 100 yards. The best shotgun for deer is a 12 gauge, of magazine type, with a single sighting plane.

The vital areas to aim for on a deer are shown here. The heart-lungs area is best, neck or spine shots next best if the game is at close range.

Shot Placement. Generally speaking, the best spot to aim for on whitetails is the lung area, just behind the point of the shoulder. Standing shots often dictate where the animal must be shot, since brush may conceal part of the target. The spine, anywhere from hips to head, is a vital area. So are the heart and brain. Gut shots should be avoided if at all possible.

Often a shot animal is only wounded and must be followed and finished off. In such instances the real art of tracking comes into use, and the sign left by the animal must be unraveled step-by-step if the beast is to be found.

Generally speaking, the hunter should allow ten to thirty minutes before following an animal known to be wounded. An unpursued animal will travel slower, stop more often, and lie down quicker than one that is pursued.

Before taking up the trail, the hunter should always mark the spot where the game was last seen with a white handkerchief tied to a tree or bush. Often wounded game cannot be located by following spoor, but may be located by starting at the spot and moving in concentric circles. Often the starting point must be used several times, hence the necessity of marking it plainly.

Wounded game bleeds. Bright red blood on a trail means a lung shot and the game won't travel far. Heavy dark blood comes from muscle. Green fluid or bits of undigested forage mean a gut shot. A dragging track indicates a hit in that particular leg. Spots along the trail where the animal has laid down or stopped usually mean a hard-hit beast. If the animal heads steeply downhill, this means a hard hit. If a whitetail's flag dropped as it ran off, it was hard hit.

In following a wounded whitetail, the hunter should go slowly, looking ahead as carefully as he watches the spoor. His rifle should be at ready for a finishing shot if the game jumps up again and tries to escape.

Handguns. Hunting the whitetail with a handgun is feasible because it can be approached at close range in heavy cover. Once handgun hunting for any game was considered a stunt, practiced only for publicity by showoffs. This was true because the handguns of the past were inadequate for killing any species. But the recent development of handguns with the power of many medium rifles has changed the picture. The advocates of the handgun have sold the idea of using it on game to the game commissions and in many states handgun hunting is now legal.

With minor restrictions on species, caliber, and areas, twenty-two of the fifty states now permit handgun hunting of big game. Forty states permit handgun hunting of small game, and forty-six states permit handgun hunting of predators and unprotected species. Since regulations change from year to year, the hunter should check in those areas whenever he wishes to hunt, especially in those states whose regulations about handgun hunting are somewhat vague.

In general, the handgun hunter should use only the highest-powered weapons. He should set a self-imposed maximum range of 60 to 70 yards. Before attempting to hunt whitetails, he should graduate from a .22 pistol up through at least three successively more powerful cartridges.

When hunting whitetails with a handgun, the weapon should be held in both hands with elbows braced against knees.

White coveralls camouflage the hunter in snow. Heavy handgun should be carried in a shoulder holster.

And for any shot at game he should use a position permitting the use of both hands on the gun—such as sitting with elbows inside knees or offhand.

Bow Hunting. The whitetail is usually a short-range proposition, and it is a general rule-of-thumb that a bowman has to get within 40 to 50 yards of game if he is to be successful. Even a close approach does not always mean a chance to release an arrow. The bane of any bowman's existence is the seemingly inevitable presence of limbs or foliage between him and his game. And a twig the size of a finger will deflect an arrow. The archer's dream is for an open shot within 40 yards.

A partially open route to his target isn't enough. An arrow kills by hemorrhage, not by shock and tissue destruction as does a bullet. For this reason, the arrow must reach a vital spot or the deer is apt to escape only wounded. And since the arrow at best is only a slow killer, all chancy shots should be avoided. The high ethics of the bowman are one of his most necessary tools. Many an archer will turn down shot after shot at his deer simply because the outcome isn't certain.

MULE DEER. Subjected to the same pressures as the whitetail, the mule deer has not adapted as well and has left its ranges east of the Rocky Mountains and moved into the rough, broken country of the West.

Mule deer hunting will be good in the future, but will be more controlled. Populations will be determined by available winter ranges. Surpluses will be harvested on the basis of a given number of animals to be taken from specific areas.

Mule deer multiply by approximately 25 per cent annually, after normal losses to winter-kill, predation, disease, and aging. This is a rapid rate for hunting surpluses, and for reestablishment after any devastating loss. The species browses but does not seriously compete with domestic stock grazing within its range. Under wise game management, seasons are set early in the fall before deep snows. This adds to the rigors of hunting but reduces the "take."

Mule deer country is high watershed country with deep winter snows. Because of this, an unusually severe winter or loss of winter range will cut into the populations more than will hunting. Deep, crusting snows in late winter, and range fires in summer which wipe out vast bitterbrush and sagebrush areas, can devastate deer herds.

The game departments are doing a fine job of managing the current herds. As an indication of the current status of mule deer hunting, the forecast for the 1970 hunting season, in twelve top mule deer states, listed three states as "fair," seven states as "good," and two states as "excellent."

The question of artificial winter feeding of deer to provide more animals often comes up. Experiments with artificial feeding have been unsuccessful. The deer's digestive system needs natural foods. Deer will die after periods of artificial feeding.

Similarly, attempts to increase the deer herds beyond the capacity of winter ranges have failed. One of the worst disasters occurred in Arizona's Kaibab Forest, in the 1920s, when thousands of overprotected deer starved on winter ranges.

Although more and more hunters annually take to the tall timber after mule deer, the number of animals has increased slightly over the past decade. The current mule-deer population is estimated at over 1.5 million.

The main beams of the mule deer's antlers fork into two branches, and each branch displays two tines. Measure a mule-deer trophy according to the information on pages 386–389.

This species gets its name from its mulelike ears, which are proportionately larger than those of either the whitetail or the blacktail deer.

The points of the buck's antlers do not originate from a single main beam. Instead, the beam separates, forking out in several directions depending upon the number of tines. The number of points is no criterion of age in mature bucks. Four points plus a brow point on each side are standard for an adult. Antler development and number of points are directly related to sexual vigor and depend on the presence of limestone in the diet.

The metatarsal, or musk, glands on the mule deer are from three to four times as large as on the whitetail and have no white fringe hairs.

On the face of the mule deer is an identifying black patch, in the form of a solid U, which comes down the head from between the ears to a point midway on the face.

Mule deer taken in 1949 by author in Idaho's Caribou Forest measures 196 Boone & Crockett points.

The hoofs are generally larger and more blunt than those of its whitetail cousin to aid the deer in its broken-country travel. Because of these larger hoofs, the mule deer can handle deep snow better than the whitetail, which prevents the excessive "yarding up" in midwinter common to some whitetail regions.

Perhaps the most distinguishing characteristic of the mule deer is its tail, an insignificant little rope covered with slick short hairs ending in a tassel of black.

The mule deer's generally larger size, coupled with its stockier build, gives it a blockier, less dainty appearance than the whitetail, though it is by no means ungraceful. The high mountainous regions of the West produce some of the biggest deer, and mature bucks will weigh up to 300 pounds and over.

The mule deer is not a brush deer like the whitetail. Its habitat is broken country and mountainous regions. And while the whitetail tends to live out its life cycle within an area of a few miles, the mule deer will migrate. This migration is not comparable with the mass migrations of the caribou but is generally a gradual drifting between summer and winter ranges. In winter, concentrations of mule deer will be seen far down on desert sagebrush and bitterbrush areas and in areas such as the famed Salmon River Gorge which is only 3,000 feet in elevation. In summer, however, the mule deer move upward into mountain and timber country to escape heat, flies, and enemies. As an indication of how great this change in elevation may be, mule deer have often been seen in summer in Wyoming's Bridger Wilderness Area above timberline at 10,000 feet elevation.

Hunting the Mule Deer. The methods of hunting this deer differ from those used in hunting whitetails. Mule deer aren't driven. In much of the western country all deer-hunting seasons are set ahead of the deer's winter concentrations. Neither the deer nor the hunter population in any area is sufficient to make driving successful. For the same reason trail watching isn't popular. In most western mule-deer country, about all a trail watcher would see is pretty scenery.

The two most popular and successful methods of hunting mule deer are stalking and hunting on horseback. Much of the same caution, knowledge of game, and skill necessary to whitetail hunting can be applied to hunting mule deer. This includes hunting into the breeze, moving slowly and noiselessly, and correctly interpreting wilderness signs and sounds. Both types of hunting require a knowledge of the quarry.

There are major differences, however. Mule deer are generally shot at greater distances than are whitetails. They are hunted in more open country. They are come upon in a far more diverse habitat of elevations and intervening cover, which alters their general strategy of escape.

It is a cardinal hunting rule that the farther the hunted game is from the hunter, the more slowly it will react to danger and retreat. A stalked whitetail may burst from heavy cover at 60 yards on a dead run; a mule deer which spots the hunter at 200 yards is more apt to take a good look, then leave in a slow trot. This alters the necessary speed of getting into action and the type of weapon.

Stalking. One of the best rules for mule-deer hunting is to "go climb a mountain." Mule deer, like other species, see danger better from above. They retreat from danger by going higher. Thus the best technique is to hunt down upon them. Hunting from above has many advantages. The hunter can see better. He can approach closer, since the game looks for danger from below. In watching for danger from below, the quarry normally stops on the *upper* side of foliage, trees, and brush, revealing itself to the hunter. Also, the largest animals of this species will be found at the upper peripheries of their range. The does, fawns, and small bucks will be lower down. Hunting down gives the advantage of being at the general elevation of the big bucks, which are unmolested by the hunter moving lesser animals upward. Finally, hunting down makes it easier to get it back to camp—the way will be all downhill.

Like other deer species, mule deer are out in the open, feeding or moving about, in the daylight-to-sunup and the dusk-to-dark periods. In order to hunt mule deer from above, the hunter must do his climbing early in the morning. Daybreak is an ideal time.

Ridges are fine places to hunt for mule deer. So are points of timbered country overlooking canyons, and jutting promontories. At daybreak the game is most apt to be on the sunny sides and slopes leading off such ridges; with mid-morning the animals go up and over the ridges into the northern slopes for shade. Ridges give the game an opportunity to watch for danger from several directions at once, and provide an escape route in at least three directions.

Canyon apexes are also good places to hunt mule deer. So are the undulating little humps of land and complementing slash canyons leading off a main ridge. Edge country, where foliage joins open land, is good mule-deer country.

If the hunting season is during a mild, late autumn, most deer in an area will be relatively higher within their range. Heavy rain and snow will move the entire population lower. The does and fawns will come first, with the old mossback bucks bringing up the rear, often several days later.

A good general rule for normal fall hunting is that mule deer are apt to be found at the lower edge of the snow line. This is especially true if such foliage as mountain mahogany, bitterbrush, and aspens coincide with such an elevation.

Often in hunting mule deer in their mountainous habitat, the hunting camp will of necessity be considerably removed from the best deer country. This makes it difficult to utilize the best hunting periods, and it becomes necessary to hunt during midday. During the day, mule deer will gravitate to canyon bottoms, the northern slopes of mountains, and patches of heavy foliage for rest and shade. They particularly like aspen patches. A good way to hunt aspen patches during midday is with a partner. One hunter moves up through a patch in a gully; the other works the ridge overlooking the bottom. Any game in the aspen patch will be moved forward ahead of the first hunter. His partner on the ridge will then be in a position to spot it as it emerges from the patch.

When hunting heavily timbered canyon bottoms from a high ridge, the lone hunter often can spook game into view by rolling a heavy rock downward into the brush or trees. Another good way of making game move and disclose its presence is to throw a rock into such brush patches and groves of trees. It's best, if the hunter has a stout arm, to throw a rock across the gully and to the opposite side. The noise will often scare the game towards him.

Another place old trophy bucks like during midday is the rimrock overlooking big canyons. They will bed down just under such shelving rocks, after having scouted for danger in four directions from the ridge. In such a position they can see danger approaching from the canyon or the ridgetop. The smart hunter will continuously glass such areas.

Hunting mule deer from horseback is no different from any other method. The hunter determines the presence of game from its spoor, then rides to the choice areas. Mule deer often will not spook at the sight of a horse and rider as quickly as they would a hunter on foot.

In the lower country of the Southwest, jeeps are used instead of horses for getting around in deer country. When deer are located with binoculars, a stalk is made utilizing any cover to get close enough for a shot.

Rifles and Cartridges. The choice of a mule-deer rifle depends on a number of factors: the age and sex of the hunter, his accuracy with a rifle, the foliage in the region. It also depends on whether he hunts for trophies or for the skillet, on horseback or on foot, and for larger species of game besides the mule deer.

Young beginning hunters, women, and older men, should not choose as heavy a weapon as men in their prime, nor one with as severe a recoil. The rule-of-thumb is, the gun's weight should not exceed 1/20 of the hunter's weight.

The hunter's age, eyesight, and shooting skill have a bearing on the matter. If the hunter's physical capacities limit his ability with the rifle to 200 yards, then there is little need for a rifle-cartridge combination with 400-yard potential. He is better off with a lighter weapon having less recoil.

Probable foliage is another consideration. If the deer cover is expected to be intense, then a cartridge with a large bullet diameter and knock-down power is desirable. In open country, a cartridge with a smaller and flatter-shooting bullet is better.

The *kind* of deer hunted also has a bearing on the choice of a rifle. Hunters who prefer meat animals will not need the long-range rifles necessary for trophy hunting, since does and young deer usually are shot at closer ranges than are the wise old bucks.

Generally speaking, hunters on foot should choose lighter rifles than those who hunt on horseback, especially when after other species beside mule deer. The right rifle for mule deer in such instances is the rifle that is adequate for the biggest species hunted.

135

Lastly, the choice of a deer rifle is governed somewhat by a preference in the type of rifle action. Often the hunter is willing to compromise somewhat on a cartridge to get the rifle action he likes. Conversely, some hunters pick the best all-round cartridge, then get a rifle that will handle it.

Broadly speaking, the right rifle-cartridge combination for average mule-deer hunting will be a high-intensity cartridge with high velocity and keen accuracy handling a bullet of good sectional density (for retained velocity at long ranges) and weighing from 100 to 180 grains. The minimum caliber should be .24, or 6 mm, and the maximum need not exceed .30 caliber unless used for a combination of species.

Some fine mule-deer cartridges, beginning with the minimum, follow:

.243 Winchester, using 100-grain bullets
6-mm Remington, using 100-grain bullets
.25/06 Remington, using 120-grain bullets
.257 Roberts, using 100- or 117-grain bullets
6.5 mm Remington Magnum, using 120-grain bullets
.264 Winchester Magnum, using 140-grain bullets
.270 Winchester, using 130-grain bullets
7-mm Mauser, using 130- or 139-grain bullets (handloads)
.284 Winchester, using 125- or 150-grain bullets
7-mm Remington Magnum, using 150-grain bullets
.300 Savage, using 150-grain bullets
.308 Winchester, using 150-grain bullets
.30/06 Springfield, using 150- and 180-grain bullets

Five of the *best* all-around cartridges for mule deer in reasonably open country, under all hunting conditions, are the .270, 7 mm, .284, 7 mm Magnum, and .30/06.

There is usually better opportunity for a deliberate shot when hunting mule deer than when hunting whitetails. Ordinarily, the muley is located farther off, and either is standing or moving slowly. For this reason, scope sights are best. Scopes for the mule-deer rifle should be of good quality, mounted low and rigidly, and of medium power. A 4-power scope perhaps has the best all-round magnification, and the crosshair reticle is probably the best.

Several new variable scopes are fine, especially if the deer rifle must double on chucks or varmints where more than 4-power is needed. Also, there are some newly developed reticles which show much promise for mule-deer hunting. Some are double for range finding. Others have either a combination of post and crosshairs (one is elective), or converging post and crosshairs. The heavier, more easily seen reticle is valuable at dusk and early morning.

Any rifle for mule-deer hunting should be sling-equipped and fit well. It should also have a relatively light, crisp trigger-pull. Many a buck has lived to shed his trophy antlers still another year simply because a sloppy trigger-pull caused the hunter to veer from his aim.

The mule-deer rifle should be perfectly sighted in, in advance of the hunt. A good sighting-in range is 200 yards.

Bow Hunting. Bow hunting for mule deer is growing steadily in the West. The choice area for the bowman is semi-open country with numerous rolling hills, intervening gullies, and canyons where he can conceal himself while making a close stalk. Bow hunts are usually held in advance of the open season for rifles.

In bow hunting for mule deer, the ratio of kills to the number of hunters is very small but is increasing as archery equipment and know-how improve. Archers seldom spook the game sufficiently to be a hindrance to rifle hunters, and the bowmen have a fine safety record.

Shotguns. In the past, the shotgun has not been considered seriously for mule deer except on isolated occasions. The mule deer is long-range game, and there has been no need of hunting it with this short-range weapon. In some of the West's good deer country there are grouse, pheasants, and other upland birds. While hunting these, many hunters carry a few rifled slugs in case they see a deer.

The rifled slug is far superior to a load of buckshot. Due to its large caliber, such a slug has ample energy to down a mule deer up to 100 yards, especially in 12-gauge size.

Current indications are that the shotgun may be used more on mule deer in the West, as a safety measure, due to the increasing numbers of people and ranches in and near deer country. As one example, Idaho as early as 1960 set aside one management area for deer hunting with shotguns only.

Handguns. Hunting mule deer with a handgun is becoming increasingly popular. The best chances for success are in areas of heavy deer concentration. A skilled stalker doesn't want other hunters around who might spook game. In fact, some handgun enthusiasts wait until late in the deer season when the deer are migrating downward in groups and the ranks of hunters have thinned.

The handgun is perhaps used most for mule deer when hunters are stalking elk on horseback. In addition to an elk rifle, many a hunter carries a heavy pistol and uses it when he encounters a deer.

Three factory handgun cartridges are powerful enough for mule deer: the .357 Magnum, the more powerful .41 Magnum, and the most powerful .44 Magnum. With factory loadings, the .357 Magnum shoots a 150-grain bullet at 1,450 foot-seconds velocity, with a muzzle energy of nearly 700 foot-pounds. The new .41 Magnum shoots a 210-grain bullet at 1,500 foot-seconds, with a muzzle energy of 1,050 foot-pounds. And the powerful .44 Magnum handgun shoots a 240-grain bullet at 1,470 feet per second, with a muzzle energy of 1,150 foot-pounds. This places them in the class of low-powered rifles. However, since handgun ranges should always be short, and since all three are large-caliber cartridges, they are adequate for deer if used properly.

Development in handgun cartridges is steadily going on, and already several wildcat handgun cartridges will exceed the power of the .357, the .41, and the .44 Magnums. A recent improvement in pistol bullets is bound to cause handgun velocities to jump appreciably—the semijacketed bullets formed by swaging a metal cup over the base of lead bullets. This allows velocity to be increased without stripping lead inside the bore. Such bullets are available in .357, .41, and .44 calibers especially for the handgun enthusiast.

Handguns for hunting purposes should have long barrels, adjustable sights, hand-fitting grips, and sufficient weight to absorb powerful loads with safety. A handgun having a 6- to 7-inch barrel, square-topped patridge-type sights, and a crisp, light trigger-pull is most popular. Many hunters prefer it in single action.

A gun of this type weighs approximately 3 pounds. The only satisfactory way of carrying it while hunting is in a shoulder holster. This distributes the weight at the shoulders, where any burden belongs. It also protects the weapon from rain and snow, as it hangs under the armpit. This position is fast enough for hunting purposes and leaves both hands free.

Shot Placement. The best area to aim for on mule deer is the lungs-heart area, just behind the foreshoulder and just below midway of the animal. A bullet missing the exact spot by a few inches in any direction will kill the animal quickly.

A wounded deer should be approached slowly, with weapon ready for a finishing shot, and in a direction which will bring the hunter above and behind the animal. Mule deer are strong for their size, and a wounded buck can be dangerous. The hind hoofs of a deer can cut like knives; and a wounded deer can reach up and rake a hunter sitting on the animal's head. Bucks can gore a hunter to death with their antlers. It is best to finish off a wounded beast with a bullet, not cut its throat.

BLACKTAIL DEER. Here and there throughout the West, one still hears the statement, "I saw a blacktail." The person really means he saw a mule deer. The reason for the confusion is simple. Mule deer were once called blacktails. When the separate species of blacktail deer was determined, the name "mule" was given to the former. Today, the Columbia blacktail deer (*Odocoileus hemionus columbianus*) is a recognized species.

In some respects, the blacktail is like the mule deer; in others it resembles the whitetail. The blacktail is midway in size between the average whitetail and the average mule deer. The bucks weigh from 150 to 200 pounds. The *average* whitetail buck, if the Coues whitetail subspecies is included, does not reach this size. Similarly, the biggest mule-deer bucks found in British Columbia weigh close to 400 pounds.

The antlers of the blacktail are similar to those of the mule deer—that is, they fork instead of all points coming from a single main beam. The blacktail's ears are larger than the whitetail's but smaller than those of the mule deer; its metatarsal glands are midway in size between those of the other two species. Both the mule and the blacktail have a black patch on the upper part of the face. The tail is black on top and white on the underside.

The range of the blacktail consists of a thin, crescent-shaped strip of country generally coincident with the coastal slope along the Pacific Ocean, reaching from the middle of California northward to the islands off lower Alaska. The depth of this strip is greatest at the U.S.-Canadian border and reaches inland as far as the Washington-Idaho boundary.

Three of the blacktail's greatest enemies are the wolf, the cougar, and man. Wolves in its habitat have greatly decreased in number. Adult cougars kill an average of one deer a week, and deer hunters are on the increase.

None of these enemies, however, has succeeded in moving the blacktail deer from its coastal habitat. This region has a humid climate and heavy, lush foliage—the kind of country this woods-loving deer likes.

The problems confronting this species are much the same as those facing the whitetail and mule-deer herds, with one difference. The forest-loving blacktail actually prefers to live in areas of first- and second-growth timber now common to a continuous planting-and-harvesting lumber operation. The new, shorter growths admit sunshine into the cutover areas and induce the rapid growth of the best deer foods.

Hunting the Blacktail. A good experiment for the novice deer-stalker is to go with a hunting partner into typical deer country, have the partner post himself in one place while you circle out of sight to a position a half-mile away. Then see how close you can come to your partner's position without being detected. Use any strategy you wish.

Of course, a deer's faculties—with the possible exception of vision—are much keener than those of your hunting partner. But such an exercise will give you some conception of hunting techniques and the

139

strategy of your quarry. It will teach you that stalking deer in dense woods and heavy undercover demands the utmost caution.

Blacktails are like canny old mule-deer bucks in their escape strategy. Either they detect the hunter's presence at considerable distance and take off immediately, depending upon sheer distance to elude him; or they lie low in thick foliage until the danger has passed. Generally speaking, unless the rut is on, blacktail bucks will be found a bit removed from the does, in the more inaccessible places.

In the warmer areas of their range, blacktails will move from the brushy canyons during midday to the higher ridges where the breezes are cooler, or to areas near water, which similarly modifies the temperature.

When crusted snow is on the ground, stillhunting is more productive than stalking, simply because of the unavoidable noise made by walking.

Good areas to watch are known game trails, ridges where there is abundant spoor, canyon heads, and especially the low saddles and passes in hills where game normally crosses from one canyon or basin into the next unless pushed out of its normal behavior pattern by hunters.

A form of trail watching which is gaining in popularity is hunting from a "blind" near a spot where game is known to pass. Such a blind is usually not a permanent, elaborate affair, just a simple place of conceal-ment. Clumps of brush, piles of downed timber, log jams, and natural foliage are the best temporary blinds. Often such brush heaps and timber need some arranging for convenience and utility.

When rearranging natural blinds near a deer runway, do it at least two or three weeks in advance of the season. This gets rid of any man smell, and allows the game to get used to the new arrangement.

In conjunction with these natural blinds, more and more hunters are wearing camouflage clothing. Its value was learned during World War II when spotted-green camouflage suits saved the lives of many soldiers. Camouflage clothing can still be bought at army surplus stores. Manufac-turers of sport clothes also supply it. In the autumn, use the spotted brown and green pattern. When snow covers foliage and terrain, white coveralls such as painters wear, plus a homemade white cap, provide good concealment.

Hunting blacktails with a partner is frequently productive. One man takes the bottom of a canyon, arroyo, or small basin, while the other hunts along the rim or ridge above. Sometimes both skirt the side of a large canyon.

In brushy country especially this doubles the advantage, as two men separated can view more country than one. But most important, any game suspecting the presence of one hunter in trying to avoid detection will expose itself to the view or hearing of his partner.

Rifles and Cartridges. The most important qualification for the rifle used on blacktails is that it is handy, and that the hunter is entirely familiar with it. The same cartridges mentioned for whitetails will be satisfactory on blacktails, as indeed will most of the cartridges for mule deer. It doesn't take excessive power in a cartridge to kill a blacktail deer. It is the bullet-and-energy that reaches it that counts, especially in brushy country.

Handgun and Bow. Blacktails usually are found in country of thick foliage where ranges are apt to be short and hunting them with a handgun is feasible. Besides, restrictions against pistol ownership are not as stringent in the West as in the East, and handgun hunting generally is more prevalent. Likewise, the blacktail is a suitable quarry for the bow hunter, if he is a good stalker, as this woods deer can be approached close enough for a killing shot.

141

13

Elk

THE AMERICAN ELK, or wapiti, has been affected by encroaching civilization as much as any big-game species. Once considered a plains animal, its range included most of the United States. When population and land settlement created too much pressure, the elk didn't move in a mass migration into the Far North as did the moose. Instead it stayed and was slaughtered into near-extinction in the East, the plains of the Midwest, and the Southwest. The remaining bands gradually learned to condition themselves to man's pressure by retreating into the highest and most inaccessible regions where most of our elk population remains today.

The biggest area of elk habitat lies coincident with the Rocky Mountains in a long strip of country ranging from north-central Alberta, Canada, to near the Mexican border in New Mexico. Four other smaller areas virtually complete the elk range. These are West Coast spot areas overlapping the California-Oregon border, the Oregon-Washington border, Olympia Island, and an extensive region in Canada covering the central portions of Saskatchewan and Manitoba. States having the greatest elk populations are Wyoming, Colorado, Montana, Idaho, Washington, and Oregon. Due to the increasing popularity of elk hunting, the elk population is gradually diminishing.

In some areas, migration routes which the elk once used in descending to their winter ranges have been fenced off, as have the ranges themselves. But in Yellowstone Park and the Jackson Hole, Wyoming, area this attempt to help the elk is currently backfiring. As with other species, the winter range is the determining factor in the size of the elk population. At Jackson, Wyoming, the largest winter feeding grounds for elk in the world, thousands of animals annually congregate for refuge feeding. This has tended to create an artificial balance in that this man-fed herd can now survive during the winter but are eating their summer ranges—part of which are in Yellowstone Park—into depletion.

142

The regal elk, monarch of the high country, bears a set of stately antlers armed with long, deadly tines which are directed forward to inflict damage in the brawling battles of the rutting season. A mature bull's antlers may have a spread of as much as 50 inches. To measure your own trophy, see the scoring chart on page 390.

The future of elk hunting depends on sufficient range—principally winter range—and the remoteness of that range. Wild elk simply cannot tolerate contact with man. Although elk may stand and gape at visitors in national sanctuaries such as Yellowstone Park, they behave differently in their natural wilderness habitat. Spooked elk simply move on.

Industries such as mining and lumbering which require access roads through wilderness areas cannot coexist with elk. The roar of chain saws, trucks, and crashing timber, will drive the animals further into the wilderness. The building of great dams in the upstream watershed areas of the West, often flooding prime elk pasture land, will also force the animals to move.

Thus, elk hunting generally isn't going to improve. We do not see as many trophy elk in the wild bands as we did a decade ago. A six-pointer is considered very good today, and many hunters have to be satisfied with five-point trophies and smaller. There will be fewer open seasons on elk and more managed hunts on a permit basis, where a given number of animals (considered as increase) will be harvested by hunters drawing "lucky" permits.

But there are several bright spots in the elk picture. One is the outstanding increase in elk numbers in the states of Oregon and Arizona. Between 1937 and 1967, elk increased in Oregon from 18,000 to over 56,000 head. Arizona's elk during the same period more than doubled, from over 4,000 to over 9,000 head. Good game management there and elsewhere has made remarkable strides.

Another encouraging sign is that elk ranges in key areas are producing more food by a system of controlled, prescribed burning. Where foliage has been unduly high-lined, keeping the lower plants in the shade, the judicious burning of brush will produce a new growth of such edible plants as willow, serviceberry, and other high shrubs. Such burning is done in the early spring, under optimum conditions, while the snows still lie on the higher elevations—to prevent fires from getting out of control.

Elk are being successfully transplanted into many relatively small, remote areas where they once thrived, and into new areas where it once appeared they could not. One example of the latter is Afognak Island, off the coast of Alaska. The animals transplanted to that area are increasing in that hardiest of surroundings. I was at Seal Bay, Afognak Island, two years ago, and was shown two elk heads taken by a seal hunter. They were not large trophy animals, but both bulls had been in good shape when taken. The elk there have adapted to such an extent that they now eat the tender tips of the treacherous and miserable Devil's Club plant. Any animal which can survive on such food can lick many an adverse range problem.

The elk is an imposing and regal game animal that varies in size according to sex, age, and area. Large cow elk weigh from 500 to 600 pounds or more; mature bulls reach 1,000 pounds and exceptional animals in certain regions will weigh more. Both sexes are long-legged and rangy-looking. Bulls often stand 5 feet at the withers, appearing even taller because of their massive antlers. The elk is tan over most of its body, with a brown head and neck, and a yellowish rump, aptly named its "sunflower."

When elk are not moved by molestation, their life cycle conforms to a fixed pattern. In summer the bands range high, just under the remaining snow lines, feeding in alpine pastures where it is cool, free of flies, and the animals don't have to compete with domestic cattle for feed. The tender antlers of the bulls grow through the velvet stage and toughen.

With the first frosts and early snow the bulls remove the velvet from their massive antlers by rubbing them on small pine trees and begin bugling with the advent of the rut, or mating season. From early September till mid-October, they fight for the cows and will hold up to thirty or more females in a harem. The herd bull's mating call is his piercing bugle. The whipped bulls and young bulls just learning to bugle will challenge the mature herd bulls with the same piercing call—one of the most thrilling sounds in all the wilderness.

In regions where the elk are not bothered too much in winter by man, they will start moving downward with the first deep snows of October and November. Elk can predict a heavy storm as much as twenty-four hours in advance, and move with it or ahead of it.

Part of the famed Jackson Hole, Wyoming, elk herd on its winter feeding grounds at the foot of the Grand Tetons.

Where elk have become conditioned to winter feeding grounds, the animals often delay their downward migrations until their canny wisdom tells them the fall hunts are over. Then, with deep snow and the next roaring blizzard, they come down through the migration routes in a body. Often several thousand elk migrate single file over the same trail in a couple of days.

Elk differ from deer in one important respect. Ordinarily, deer remain in the same general area. If disturbed, they circle and filter back into the home region in a day or so. Disturbed elk, however, tend to head out in a straight line. They may not stop for five or ten miles and may stay in another area for a week or more.

HUNTING THE ELK. The three ways of hunting elk are bugling, stalking, and drift-hunting. Bugling for the bulls is the most thrilling

Bugling for elk on an artificial call requires skill and a thorough knowledge of elk habits.

of sports and very productive for the experienced hunter. An artificial bugle, or call, is used on which one can simulate the bugling of the wild bulls. Bugles are made of bamboo, elderberry stalks, metal conduit, or plastic water hose. Only bugles made of bamboo have perfect sound qualities. Such bamboo must be node-free and of sufficient length and proper diameter to make a call on which the four distinct tones of the bull elk's natural bugling can be duplicated.

The hunter bugles only from those locations in which a bull would normally bugle. His hope is that either the herd bull will consider it the challenge of a defeated bull trying to horn in, or that a defeated bull will hear and respond. In either case, if the call is authentic, a bull within a half mile or so will probably answer.

Good places to bugle are canyon heads, high ridges, rim country, and the apexes of slash-canyons. The best time is at sunrise. The hunter should be concealed from view when he bugles. Bugling should not be repeated oftener than at ten-minute intervals. If there is no answer to the second toot, the hunter should move quietly on, and try again within the next half mile or so.

The best weather for artificial bugling is a frosty, clear morning. It is useless to bugle in high wind, fog, or heavy rain as the animals are normally huddled. Not only will they refuse to answer but regard any such unnatural tooting with suspicion.

If a bull answers an artificial bugle once, and won't respond to a second calling, the hunter should not give up for thirty minutes but sit tight and as concealed as possible. Many times a bull, suspicious after a first call will circle and come silently into view from an opposite direction. He wants to size up an opponent unseen.

Stalking on Horseback. Elk are stalked on horseback in many areas except in late season. Occasionally, in deep snow, stalking is done on snowshoes. Horses are often needed to cover the necessary ground in hunting this long-legged species; and horses or mules are needed to pack in its meat quarters.

When stalking elk on horseback, first climb the big ridges leading upward out of camp. Then cross the long, undulating crests, the ridges and canyon rims, into the high timberline country. Utilize old game trails for getting to the upper elevations.

Study all canyon sides, brushy bottoms, promontories, open alps, and "patchy" country. Elk usually are spotted at great distances. They appear in dark, timbered areas as tan spots or simply shapes that don't belong to the landscape. Binoculars are a must for such hunting.

When the top country is reached, it is best to leave the horses just under the crest, tied so they won't leave, and cautiously climb to the crest on foot. Then study the next basin, slope, canyon, or creek bottom.

147

Often when riding through patches of timber, the hunter will unwittingly come upon elk. Many horses used to hunting elk will either stop short and turn their heads or turn their heads while moving. Invariably, if the hunter will sight between the pointed ears of a good hunting horse, he'll see the game which it has already spotted.

Elk move mostly between daylight and sunup, and between dusk and darkness. They feed most at these times, bugle most, move about most, and are in the open more. From around nine o'clock in the morning until four or five o'clock in the afternoon, elk head back into heavy timber and shade up for the day. They have learned that the thick foliage in heavy timber which enemies must traverse offers built-in protection—it makes for a noisy approach.

Therefore the two best hunting periods are daybreak and dusk. For the hunter on foot, especially if he is bugling for elk, these periods are best. The daybreak period is the better of the two. The bulls bugle more at that period of the day, and if a kill is made there is all day for the heavy work of dressing and hanging a large animal. Many a hunter has come upon his elk at dusk, several miles from a camp, and has either had to camp out at his kill overnight to take care of it properly or has hastily gutted it, neglected to hang the quarters or get the carcass off the ground, and has had a soured elk the next morning.

Using horses often makes daylight hunting for elk impossible. Camps with horses must be set far enough away from a game area to prevent spooking the game. Horses must be wrangled each morning, and intervening distances must be covered. Such country can't be ridden by average hunters in the dark. In short, the horseback hunter can't be in a game area by daybreak. Because of this, many horseback hunters consider the last hour of daylight worth all the others. One advantage is that the kill will cool out better during the night, if properly cared for in advance.

Often when a kill is made at dusk it will be pitch dark or even later before the hunter can care for it and head for camp. However, horses that wouldn't know their way at pre-daylight to elk, will have no trouble returning back to the camp oats from where they happen to be. Experienced horses often will bring in a hunter who couldn't find his own way.

However, not all horses will head for camp after dark if given their heads. For the unbelieving, it is quite an experience to ride some knotheaded old crowbait at night in mountain country and have it walk right off a trail, a high bluff, or even into a river—as this author has done.

Drift-Hunting. Drift-hunting means to take advantage of the normal movement of elk during the fall hunting season. That is, the general routes of the game, moving gradually downward after storm and late season in the high country, are ascertained; then the hunter plans his hunting so as to coincide with the areas in which the game may be expected to be during this normal movement. It does not mean hunting elk along a single migration route once they have been endangered by deep snows and are leaving a region *en masse* before being trapped by winter.

Stalking on Foot. In average elk country the game is located at long ranges except when spooked in timber. And stalking to within rifle range of elk is one of the most difficult of hunting arts.

Elk are normally spooky and will often choose to leave an area for no apparent reason. Impending weather changes will often make elk so nervous that they run from one elevation to another. And elk can detect danger by sight or sound for unbelievable distances. Elk will often spook

This superb six-point bull elk was in prime condition and its antlers were fully developed when it was brought down.

at the sight of a hunter or horseback rider at distances beyond a half mile. Often, after making up their minds, they will continue their flight for several miles, or into an adjoining basin.

Since the normal elk season is set to coincide with the rut, the sexes are mingled. One elk located, in the majority of cases, means a number of elk near by. The lone elk, located by sight or spoor, is usually a traveling bull, possibly whipped by the herd bull from a band and in search of other cows.

A traveling bull, except in instances where it may pause or approach in response to a call on an artificial bugle, is generally out of sight and range by the time the hunter has stalked to where it last was seen.

A band of elk usually has an old cow standing guard. When the elk are feeding, bedded down, or moving about, the cow will habitually be at some vantage point several rods removed from the band, in order to spot danger and warn the rest. The cow will stare hard at approaching danger, its ears will become erect, the yellow hairs of its sunflower-like rump will suddenly raise, or it will whirl away in an alerted manner. To warn its calves the cow elk will bark a warning which scarcely can be distinguished from the yapping of a small dog.

In stalking any elk, the hunter must first determine if he has been detected. If so, the elk have fled the area and his strategy must be to find them. If he is undetected, he must stalk to within range before they have moved.

Elk stalking is a slow process. Elk habitat is country of thick foliage and trees, and is therefore noisy. The hunter must move silently, utilizing all foliage and unevenness of terrain so as to approach unseen.

The relative elevations of hunter and game often indicate where startled elk will go. Elk startled in a canyon will move up one side of the canyon, the better to watch their backtrack. Elk startled on a sidehill, with the hunter on the crest above, will usually duck back into timber, cross the basin bottoms, and leave via the opposite crest. And elk spooked at the same level as the hunter will retreat in a generally upward route.

Elk seasons in most high country usually entail some snow. This in itself can be a great aid to the hunter. The lower edge of snow line is an ideal elevation at which to hunt unmolested elk. And startled elk will leave a readable trail in snow.

Two hunters can work patches of timber known or thought to contain elk. One hunter will circle and post himself at the timber's probable outlet. The partner follows the spoor, and spooks the game ahead of him. The likelihood of game being in a certain patch of timber is often authenticated by the presence of fresh tracks going into the area, but none coming out on the opposing sides.

Rifles and Cartridges. An elk is tough. A trophy bull especially is hard to put down and make stay down. Bulls with one leg shot completely out of commission will often travel five miles and then be lost. Bulls have been shot through the heart, and have wandered off for over a hundred yards. Elk have been gut shot and pursued for miles on end without the hunter ever catching up. In short, a bull elk is one of the three hardest animals in North America to *kill*.

The ideal elk cartridge should be at least .30 caliber. It should shoot a bullet of at least 180 grains in weight. And that bullet should be of proper type for deep penetration and expansion on elk; and travel at a minimum of 2,900 feet per second for that weight, proportionately slower for heavier weights in the same caliber.

With this as a basis, the following are good elk cartridges:

.300 H&H Magnum, using 180- and 220-grain bullets
.300 Weatherby Magnum, using 180- and 220-grain bullets
.300 Winchester Magnum, using 180-grain bullets
.338 Winchester Magnum, using 200- or 250-grain bullets
.350 Remington Magnum, using 200- or 250-grain bullets
.375 H&H Magnum, using 270- or 300-grain bullets

The popular .270 Winchester, the newer .280 Remington, and the old standby .30/06 represent the minimum in cartridges to be used on elk; and these should only be used by the experienced hunter with the patience and sheer guts to turn down *all* shots on elk until he is certain his bullet is going into the heart-lungs area.

The newer, fast-stepping 7 mm Magnum cartridges such as the 7 mm Remington Magnum, the Weatherby 7 mm Magnum, and the 7 x 61 Sharpe & Hart, when used with 160- to 175-grain bullets, are marginal elk cartridges. They perform well on the long-range open shots, but lack the bullet weight for heavy timber shooting.

The slower-velocity cartridges in .35 caliber, such as the old .35 Whelen and the .358 Winchester, are good elk cartridges for close range—for timber shooting up to 200 yards—but lack the punch for longer ranges.

The elk is a big animal, and looks big at long ranges in clear mountain air. The temptation for most hunters is to shoot at animals at extreme range. This is ethically wrong, and impractical, resulting in wounded and lost game. Elk should not be shot at ranges beyond 400 yards. The extra punch of the high-powered magnum cartridges recommended above is not to extend this range, but to do a better job within those liberal limits.

A low-powered scope, from 2½ to 4 power, is the best sight for the elk rifle. Due to the animal's considerable size, more magnification is not needed, and a low-powered scope is better for running shots than one of great magnification and small field of view. A rifle sling is a must.

Shot Placement. The best spot to aim for on elk is the lungs area, just behind the shoulder blade. This is a generous-sized target, and a lung-shot elk will not go far before it bleeds and dies from hemorrhage—if the shot doesn't tip it over in its tracks. Also, a lung-shot animal generally leaves a good blood spoor.

Shots directly through the shoulder should be avoided. The heavy shoulder blade often turns bullets from such cartridges as the .30/06 and .270. This is especially true of light, fast-expanding bullets meant for use on thin-skinned game such as deer.

When stalking in timber, the hunter occasionally encounters an animal partly concealed by timber or foliage. When necessary, a spine or neck shot will break the beast down, permitting a quick finisher after the hunter comes up. Most beginners, incidentally, don't know that the neck bone of an elk is approximately halfway down on the neck. They see the high brown ruff on top, and conclude that the bone lies nearly that high. They bang away, see the beast drop, and yell, "I gottim!" Then they find that the animal was only "creased," and immediately took off.

When a wounded elk must be followed any distance after a botched job of shooting, the same general procedure is followed as with wounded deer. Wounded elk will head for the most impenetrable cover, usually faster than the hunter can travel. They will double back or wade along the shoreline of a lake to throw the hunter off the trail.

Signs to look for are leaves and pine needles freshly turned over, and drops of blood on the ground and on bushes at animal height. Places to watch for blood especially are blowdowns where the animal may have crossed. Blood or intestinal juices from wounds will drain down and often smear big logs in contact with the beast's belly as it crosses. An elk can walk over high logs that a horse would have to jump.

Any wounded elk approached when down is dangerous, especially a male, whose antlers are like pitchforks. Any approach should be from above and behind. No attempt should ever be made to finish off a wounded elk with a knife. A shot into the neck or base of the head is better.

Bow and Handgun. The elk is too large, too tough, and must be shot at too great a range to be considered fair game for the average archer or handgun hunter. It is true that archers and handgun enthusiasts have killed elk. But there is where the matter should rest—with the specialists who have the enthusiasm, time to perfect their skill adequately to do the job, and the moral courage to turn down all shots at elk until the opportunity for a certain kill comes along. The sport is not sporting for the casual archer or pistol shooter. For the average hunter, the job of taking an elk with a rifle in wilderness country is big enough. So is the thrill.

14

Moose

THOUGH HOMELY as a mud fence, the moose's assortment of awkward features serve a number of useful purposes. Its lanky legs enable it to wade and feed in deep water, and cross deep snow, boggy areas, and windfall timber with speed. Its large splayed hoofs and well-developed dewclaws buoy it up in oozy footing. Its long, overhanging "Roman" nose is useful for stripping bark and for hooking over aspen limbs and branches which it pulls down to nibble. Its big ears endow it with a keen sense of hearing. And the ropelike "bell" of hair-and-hide drooping from its neck helps to drain off water when it raises its head from feeding on aquatic vegetation.

There are three species of North American moose: the Canadian moose (*Alces americana americana*), the Alaska moose (*Alces gigas*), and the Shiras, or Wyoming, moose (*Alces americana shirasi*).

The Shiras moose is smallest of the three. Adult bulls reach around 1,200 pounds in weight, stand 6 feet high at the withers, and have an antler spread of over 50 inches. The cows are approximately one-third smaller.

The largest is the Alaska moose. Trophy bulls of the Alaska species weigh nearly 1,800 pounds, stand 7 feet or more at the withers, and have antler spreads of well over 6 feet. The bulls on the Kenai Peninsula are regarded as the very largest. The Canadian moose ranges in size midway between the Shiras and the Alaska moose.

The migration pattern of the American moose has been most interesting. While elk migrated upward into the western mountains to escape extermination and molestation by man, moose migrated northward. Moose require a combination of cold weather and wooded country, and as the forests of northern United States were being cut, the species migrated northward ahead of the ax into timber country.

Today, the moose is found northward into Alaska where it was unknown a century ago. Its overall range includes all the wooded country

153

The moose's huge head is crowned with a pair of unmistakable antlers whose main beams separate into two branches. The smaller branch reaches forward and outward; the larger extends backwards and spreads into a large palm edged with numerous points. See page 392 for scoring data.

of Canada and Alaska and extends in an east-west direction from the Atlantic Ocean to the Bering Sea in the Arctic. This range extends southward as far as just inside the borders of the northern tier of states in the Great Lakes region, with a fingerlike strip of range dipping into the states of Montana, Wyoming, and Idaho along the Continental Divide. States with the greatest moose populations include Wyoming, Maine, Minnesota, Montana, and Idaho, in that order.

This species must remain in the vast wooded country of the North. For in addition to cold weather and wooded country, moose need a habitat with lots of rivers, lakes, and streams. Canada, Alaska, and the northern portions of some of our states are the only large areas left on the continent which provide this combination.

The moose benefits from the great forest fires which ravish the North. An advantage of forest burning is the elimination of great quantities of down timber and underbrush. This allows sunlight to penetrate and ultimately produces a new growth of plant life, some of which the moose finds edible. Thus moose have a special liking for old "burns." In the camouflage afforded by charred stumps they are protected from two of their enemies, wolves and man. Since wolves have now been reduced in numbers, they no longer pose a serious threat. Poaching is man's worst offense against the species, but with continued wise management the future of moose hunting looks favorable.

Despite the mass migration of the species during the early settlement of the country, the moose is not known as a migratory animal. Unlike the elk and mule deer which migrate downward to winter feeding grounds, the moose remains within the same general area the year round. Where 18 inches of snow will normally move elk, moose can survive in nearly twice that depth.

The Alaska bull moose, the largest big-game animal in North America, grows to a maximum of 7 feet high at the withers and may weigh 1,800 pounds.

The foods of moose are varied. A choice food in summer is the aquatic vegetation growing in lakes and streams; and during this season of the year most animals are seen at the edges of such water or feeding in it. Adult moose will stand virtually submerged in deep water, with nothing except their withers showing, and graze for long periods of time on the underwater growth.

With winter, and the water plants no longer available, the main diet of the moose is twigs, bark, leaves, and branch tips. Two of the favored winter foods are willows and quaking aspen. Another is the second growth following old burns in timbered country. Often to reach the tender tips of such foliage, especially in areas where aspens competing for sunlight are thick and high, moose will push over the younger trees with their heavy bodies. After nibbling the green branch tips, they allow the tree to flip back upward. It is a common sight in winter to see an old cow moose straddling such a young tree so her pair of 400-pound calves can nibble off the tender tops. Willows in meadows are especially good moose food and in the West are known as "moose pastures." So are lily-pad lakes.

During the summer and fall seasons, moose like to feed and wade in the water, where it is cool and there is freedom from summer flies. This does not mean that moose are low-country animals. They also like the high timbered plateaus, the jutting points and promontories adjacent to such water. Like other species, moose come down at night and go higher with early morning. In good moose country one may observe the big animals coming down from the timber at dusk to the edges of lakes and streams. There they feed until it is fully dark and remain until daybreak at the same elevation. With the coming of full sunlight, they move upward onto adjacent plateaus and wooded rolling hills where they shade up and rest.

Moose are relatively pugnacious. A cow moose with calves is dangerous. So is any bull during the rutting season. A bull, even in early spring when his antlers are tender and covered with velvet, may be pugnacious and willing to fight because of aggravating ticks boring into his hide.

Many a fisherman has run into a moose on a trout stream. Sometimes the moose can be bluffed out of the way. It is safer, however, to get out of the way yourself. Every summer anglers roost in trees for hours, waiting for some pugnacious old moose to leave.

HUNTING MOOSE. The two best areas for moose hunting are Canada and Alaska. Getting into moose country generally requires time, effort, a hunting camp, hunting partners, and for the nonresident, outfitters and guides.

The moose has legal protection now in all states except Wyoming,

Shiras bull and cow graze peacefully in favored moose country, which is usually grassy meadowlands near water.

Montana, and Idaho. In these states, hunting is allowed for a limited number of animals each fall, after the lucky hunters are determined by a public drawing from a list of applicants. The ratio of those who draw lucky permits to the number of applicants is exceptionally meager. And in Idaho, once a hunter has drawn a permit and taken a moose, he may not apply for the species thereafter.

The methods of hunting moose are determined by the area into which the hunter goes and the techniques of his guide or outfitter.

Moose are generally hunted by stalking the animals on horseback or on foot; by hunting lake edges, inlets, outlets, and adjacent creeks with a canoe; by spotting the animals with light aircraft, then stalking them; or by some form of calling.

Horseback. Combined with stalking, hunting on horseback is a productive method where large areas of wooded country must be covered. As with elk, the hunters ride the higher ridges (but generally at lower elevations), and glass for game from above. A high knoll overlooking river beds, small lakes, and creek bottoms are good places to anchor the horses and meticulously study the area in all directions with binoculars or spotting scope.

157

Such a study should not be hurried. It is surprising how well so large an animal can conceal itself. Its dark-brown coloration blends with dark timber, the dense shadows of thick conifers, and the charred stumps of old burns. One reason a bull moose can remain unseen is that he sometimes stands perfectly still for long periods of time; he does not step about or move his head as do other species. This habit is directly connected with the rut.

Alaska Moose with 63⅓-inch spread, taken by author in 1964 west of Beaver Creek region.

During the warm summer months, when the bull's antlers are changing from bloody, tender clumps into the polished fighting weapons necessary to the battles during mating season, he moves about relatively little. His chief interest is food. He must become strong and fat, and must rest in order to have the physical vigor necessary to reproduction. Often he will stand for hours in one position without moving. It is possible for a horseman to ride within two rods of such a beast, in heavy willows or timber, without detecting him unless his horse snorts, or points its ears in the animal's direction. And a hunter on foot can pass on one side of a clump of 12-foot willows without detecting a bull moose on the opposite side.

During the first part of September, the rutting season begins and the bull moose shakes off his lethargy. Instead of being a lazy, disinterested creature, he is suddenly crazed by the urges of reproduction. Where once he preferred to stand, he now travels far and wide in search of cows. Where once he would hide, in the grip of the sexual urge he now barges through the timber grunting challenges to all competitors.

This transformation is a big help to the hunter. So is the falling of the

This Shiras Moose, taken by author in Wyoming's Atlantic Creek area, took first place in 1955 Boone and Crockett competition with 173-6/8 score.

willow leaves shortly after the first heavy frosts. One week the willow pastures are an opaque field of green. Within a matter of days they are transformed into a field of bare willow stalks in which a 1,500-pound moose will be as prominent as a wart on the end of one's nose. Under such optimum conditions, the hunter with good glasses and a vantage point on some high knoll may spot his trophy miles away.

Stalking. Once the quarry has been located, stalking moose is comparable to stalking elk. The hunter studies the lay of the land; he finds a suitable approach route which will take advantage of the best cover, unevenness of terrain, and possible breezes; then he stalks noiselessly to within rifle range.

The moose's senses of hearing and smell are far more acute than his vision. A moose often will walk within 50 yards of a hunter standing motionless against a tree bole, but he'll stop at the snapping of a dry twig.

In a region with lots of lakes hunting moose from a canoe is productive. At daybreak or dusk the craft is paddled noiselessly along the shoreline and each succeeding bend in the lake's contour is watched as it comes into view. Moose are often found feeding in shallow water just off shore. When startled by the approach of the craft, they tend to whirl back towards shore and offer a moving target as they head into the timber.

Hunting the shoreline of lakes on foot is another fine way of locating game. Usually, if there are many moose in the region, their trails will be deep and easily read. The hunter works such trails at daybreak and dusk, always into the wind and watching not only the trail, but all adjacent water and timbered points as well.

When hunting sheep or caribou on the alpine plateaus, the timbered country below is hunted for moose both going up and coming down to camp in the evening. Hunting moose in the evening is made easier by this technique since the hunter hunts *downward* from a position of greatest advantage.

Artificial Calling. When the rutting season is on, trophy moose are hunted by artificial calling. One technique is comparable to the bugling for elk. A horn of birch bark is generally used to imitate the brassy love-call of the cow. Any bull in the immediate neighborhood is likely to come crashing into view. Even without an artificial call a bull may be successfully called simply by cupping the hands to the mouth and, in much the same manner in which a trumpeter uses a mute, calling, *Uh-waugh! Uh-waugh!*

Since trophy moose are hunted largely by outfitted parties, it is usually best to let an experienced guide do the calling. He knows the time, the probable places, and the circumstances under which calling will work. Good areas for such calling are just inside the concealment of foliage or timber around lake shores, and from low, timbered necks leading toward meadows.

Another form of "calling" is to dump a hatful of water in a slow dribble into a lake at dusk. This noise approximates the sound of a cow urinating—a noise which a rut-crazed bull cannot resist, and which at that time of a calm day will carry far. In this form of calling, the "art" of the dude hunter is probably as polished as that of his guide.

One of the best glasses for locating moose and for appraising size and trophy potential is a small spotting scope. There is at least one on the market which is just over a foot long and weighs approximately 1 pound. This instrument comes in 20 power, and together with a light tripod makes an adequate tool. Many a step and a lot of disappointment can be saved by the hunter who uses such a scope.

Rifles and Cartridges. In the Far North the standard rifle used on moose by natives and Indians has long been the .30/30. They need a rifle that is light and sure-functioning. Ammunition for it must be available at any outpost. Such men hunt for meat and dog food, and the smaller animals—young cows, yearlings, and "mulligan-bulls"—are invariably chosen. Once an animal has been killed the meat supply lasts for weeks or months, during which time they hunt for other meat.

Most neophyte moose hunters are after a mixed bag of game. This often includes moose, grizzly, sheep, and caribou. And they are usually after trophies rather than meat. These factors dictate the choice of rifle and cartridge.

The sheer size of the moose suggests the need for a cartridge of adequate power and relatively large diameter. The fact that it is often shot at long ranges also indicates a cartridge of fairly flat trajectory and high remaining energy. The ideal cartridges for deer—such as the .30/30 and the fine .270—might be a bit shy on power when used on an animal five or six times as large and with a comparable tenacity for life.

For most moose hunting, especially when combined with hunting other species, the minimum rifle-cartridge combination should be the .30/06 or its equivalent. For a list of good moose cartridges see the previous chapter on elk.

Shot Placement. Generally moose are shot in open areas such as meadows and along shorelines. They are huge targets and are usually standing or moving slowly. There is every opportunity for the hunter to place his bullet into the vital area. Here again, the best spot is the lungs, just behind the shoulder tip. Shots through the shoulder itself should be avoided as the heavy shoulder blade will turn bullets of even some higher-powered rifles. Brain shots are not only hard to make but will ruin the trophy and are to be avoided. Neck shots are not so good on moose, especially bulls, since the neck of a mature bull represents from 18 to 24 inches of tough meat and bone.

A lung shot with an adequate rifle and cartridge will usually kill a moose, but a finishing shot may be necessary when the hunter approaches the downed animal. The antlers of a wounded moose should be avoided.

161

The cardinal sin is to shoot a moose in the water because of the difficulty of dressing the animal after it has been killed. Often the best that can be done is to hack off chunks and drag them out. It is a bloody, laborious, muddy job. Many guides will turn over the dressing chore to a hunter who has shot a moose in the water.

Bow and Handgun. Moose have been killed with bows and handguns. More hunters who attain skill with these weapons will hunt moose with them in the future. But at this writing, the killing of either moose or elk is a job for the skilled enthusiast, not the average hunter. The killing of a moose by the ordinary hunter with either of these light weapons must be regarded as a stunt.

Moose hunting has an appeal all its own. It satisfies the human craving for hunting the "biggest." When a hunter kills this enormous beast, he will have sufficient steaks to last him until the next hunting season. Moose meat, especially of young animals, is mighty good.

Two prized delicacies of northern Indians are boiled moose tongue and boiled moose nose. The tongue is cut out whole, boiled in salt water until tender, skinned, and sliced for sandwich meat. The large gristly nose is first singed of all hair, then boiled, skinned, and eaten.

Occasionally the moose hunter will bag an old patriarch of a trophy whose headgear is most impressive but whose meat has the flavor of a gum boot—but that is one of the hazards of moose hunting.

15

Caribou

THE CARIBOU is another species of big game that has migrated northward to escape contact with man. Before the turn of the century virtually all the caribou had been exterminated or had left the northern tier of states within Continental United States. The herds are still retreating northward into the more desolate reaches of the Arctic.

The great herds no longer are seen migrating to winter feed-grounds as far southward as they used to, but stay with the summer ranges and the game refuges provided for them. Many such sanctuaries are provided now for them in Alaska, and in this new state the caribou is still the most numerous big-game animal. As late as February, 1959, this author saw caribou as far northward as Cape Lisburne, Alaska, while hunting polar bears. The caribou there were no farther than five miles inland, and were living among the high wind-swept bluffs on the sparse arctic birch and a type of tough grass found on the skimpy soil.

The enemies of the caribou include man, who continues to invade its ranges; domesticated reindeer, which compete for food; and wolves, which prey on the old and sick. Together, they have thinned the ranks of the one million caribou of 1900 to approximately half that number today. Though spot areas of heavy wolf-kill still remain, predation by wolves is now the least dangerous.

Caribou hunting in the future will be more restricted. The recent bag limits, allowing the hunter up to three animals per season in some areas, are bound to be reduced. Light aircraft used for spotting the bands will be similarly restricted. And, when necessary, the seasons will occur uniformly ahead of the late-fall migrations when hunting is too easy. Caribou hunting will remain reasonably good so long as the necessary vast ranges remain.

There are three general classifications of caribou, the segregation being made according to type of habitat: the Barren Ground caribou (*Rangifer arcticus arcticus*); the woodland caribou (*Rangifer caribou caribou*); and the mountain caribou (*Rangifer montanus*).

Antlers of the caribou have one of two palmated tines branching off each main beam. The brow tine, usually present on only one beam, is called a "shovel." Double shovels, as shown here, are a rare and prized feature of any caribou head. Scoring data is on page 394.

The Barren Ground species generally is considered the smallest, and the mountain caribou the largest. There are, however, at least a dozen subspecies, and the ranges of the species overlap. There is still diversity of opinion as to which species some of the subspecies belong. Because of such confusion, size cannot be an accurate criterion of species. For instance, the Barren Ground caribou found in the Arctic in the Point Hope area are small. A bull with 30-inch antlers is considered large. As against this, the Osborn caribou, a subspecies of the Barren Ground caribou, is one of the largest; and bulls weigh up to 600 pounds or more. Again, in the Slana River country of southeastern Alaska, this author has killed Barren Ground caribou with antlers in the 54-inch class weighing 600 pounds and over.

The caribou's migratory habits and nomadic nature add to the overlapping of ranges and species. Coloration is one means of classification: in general, the farther north the animal goes, the lighter its color; the species with the most southern habitat is darkest. There is even some confusion here, since the bulls change color with the season. In early fall the bulls are generally mouse-colored. With the coming of winter the bulls' manes turn whiter, adding greatly to the desirability of the trophy.

The overall distribution of the three species covers practically all of Alaska, 80 per cent of Canada (the exceptions being the southern parts of Alberta, Saskatchewan, and Manitoba), most all the major islands off Canada in the Arctic Ocean, and the southern coastal areas of Greenland. At present, only the states of Idaho, Montana, and Minnesota have any caribou, with the total population there being around fifty head.

In appearance the caribou is a striking animal. Both sexes are antlered. The size of the bull's antlers in proportion to its body is greater than any other deer. In general, the antlers of the bulls sweep back, then forward in a graceful curve, and are palmated in the region of the points.

The bull's antlers are not usually identical. Rather, the left brow point will leave the main antler beam, turn inward, then point straight forward over and parallel to the animal's nose. The opposing brow point is usually no more than a spike pointing in the same direction. Occasionally a bull will have two palmated brow points known as "double shovels" which add to the desirability of the trophy.

The principal food of the caribou is lichens. This "caribou moss" which the species prizes so highly is not a lush or abundant food but grows sparsely on the boggy ground. To find it and similar food in sufficient abundance, the caribou must travel great distances.

The caribou is well equipped for both traveling and changes of temperature. Its hoofs, proportionately larger than those of any other antlered game, are roundish and like pairs of cushions. These support the animal in boggy and snowy regions. Its hair is hollow, providing good insulation against extremes of temperature and giving it exceptional buoyancy in the water.

The caribou's long-striding walk, swinging trot, and awkward gallop cover a lot of ground. The trot is begun with a short upward spring. The impression one gets is that such an upward jump is necessary to get the animal in motion. When trotting, the animal holds its head high and level and its small, whitish tail erect.

The worst enemy of the caribou is the wolf, and this predator is a big factor in the movement of the herds. Caribou will leave a valley when

Rare "double-shovel" caribou taken by author in Alaska's Slana River country in 1958.

wolves move in or are on the increase and will settle down in areas of fewer wolves.

The caribou likes the high rolling plateaus above timberline in mountain country, partly for the food found in this semibarren country and partly for protection against enemies. In the generally lower bush-and-spruce country of Canada and Alaska, as the drainages dip towards the Arctic, caribou will still be found in the autumn hunting seasons well up on the bare rolling plateaus above the "bush." Their range at this season overlaps that of the grizzly, moose, and even sheep and goats. Unlike elk, caribou are not timber-loving animals.

The rut begins in most regions in early fall. Bulls are polygamous and will gather harems of a dozen or so cows. During the rut, the antics of bull caribou become so inexplicable they border on the insane. A bull standing near his harem of cows may suddenly whirl around and dash off in one direction, stop and graze for a moment, then amble back. Or he may spring high in the air and trot away, grabbing a bite of moss as he

166

Barren Ground Caribou taken by author in Alaska's Sun River area in 1965 measured 392-6/8 Boone and Crockett points— enough for older records.

goes, freeze in his tracks for a few seconds, and then bolt in another direction.

HUNTING THE CARIBOU. Distance is the biggest problem in caribou hunting. The hunter must travel far to reach the remote caribou ranges, he must often move great distances once he's there to locate the game, and after he has killed his game he has to carry out the trophy and meat.

Modern airplane travel has helped to simplify the problem. Hunters are often flown to bush landing strips where they meet their outfitter. Light planes will take them into good caribou country, land on small lakes, and even supply a spike-camp from the air. Afterwards the trophy and meat are carried out to the lake landing field on packboards with guides doing most of the lugging. This is practiced considerably in such areas as the Cassiars in British Columbia.

Recently, more and more of the big northern outfitters have begun to use horses, and this, of course, is the ideal way. Horses are trailed in to remote camps in game country, hunters are flown to the nearest lake big enough for landing, and the guides meet them there and take them to camp.

There is no better way of hunting caribou than on horseback. Good mountain-broke horses can cover up to twenty miles a day and are useful in bringing out trophies and meat. In typical caribou country the muskeg, bog, and moss on which the hunter on foot must travel will defeat an average desk-man in a few miles. Good horses, experienced in northern terrain, can take it.

The use of a bush tractor and trailer for hunting caribou is gaining rapidly in popularity. This outfit consists of a small caterpillar type of tractor with tread removed and wider tracks installed. This spreads the weight so the machine won't sink in too deeply. The exhaust is pointed high and the engine is sealed, making it possible for the machine to ford creeks and even sink in halfway up to the driver without foundering. A 6-foot bulldozer blade is attached to the tractor's front end. To this tractor is hitched a heavy trailer capable of hauling up to a ton of gear. Occasionally dual wheels which spread the weight are used instead of single wheels. The vehicle runs over light foliage and when a heavy tree blocks the way the blade uproots it. To cross glacial creeks, the bulldozer digs a ramp down to the water and, when the creek has been forded, another ramp on the opposite bank. Used in conjunction with horses, the bush tractor can penetrate inaccessible areas and is thus a boon for hunting caribou.

Spotting the Quarry.　To locate caribou, hunters must reach the high plateaus and rolling, open areas above timberline, either on horseback or on foot. The entire area is glassed from ridge tops, high knolls, and low mountain passes. The best instrument is a light spotting scope fitted with a small tripod which will fold to scope length for carrying. Often, in the absence of such a tripod, the guide will place the objective end of a high-powered scope over a packboard and steady the ocular end from a sitting position with elbows on knees. In average caribou country, vision is often unlimited and the hunter can see for miles in every direction. A spotting scope will pick up animals beyond the range of binoculars and often serves to appraise trophies.

Caribou are not hard to spot. They stand high above foliage, travel along high trails and promontory points, often etching themselves against the sky. During late fall the white manes of the bulls stand out clearly like distant white dots.

Once spotted, caribou must be approached within rifle range. Before beginning any type of stalk, however, the general course, or probable route of the animals, should be determined. This is difficult due to the animal's erratic nature. Often a band will graze, move about, and head in a certain direction but after a few minutes will abruptly shift direction and head off at another angle. This trait is aggravated during the rut.

Often by watching for a half hour, the general direction in which the herd is *apt* to move can be ascertained. If it is late in the morning by the time any animals are located, or by the time a game area is reached, a good technique is to wait until the animals bed down for the day. Once bedded down, they may remain there for an hour or so before moving on again. Favorite areas for bedding down are high slopes and just under elevated knolls where they can see most of the country below them.

Stalking.   If a band is located on the move it is best to arrange the stalk so as to intercept it rather than attempt to follow. On the move a caribou band travels fast—faster than the average hunter can follow and remain concealed. If the beasts are bedded down it is best to try to reach them before they get up to feed again.

In any approach the basic technique is to utilize the terrain to make a concealed approach. Often this requires circling a mile or more around some obstructing point, knoll, or gully bottom, to get a few hundred yards closer. This is ultimately profitable, and the guide's skill in maneuvering to the hunter's advantage is often amazing.

When hunting caribou on horseback, the mounts should only be ridden to the last place of definite concealment. Often in typical caribou country the foliage is nothing higher than scrub willows, arctic birch, and similar vegetation. If hobbles aren't brought along for the horses, a good way of tying the animals is to grasp two handfuls of birch or willow, tie them in half a square knot, then tie the steed's halter rope around this knot with three half hitches and a final slip knot. This type of vegetation, known as "shintangle," is springy and tough. A half-dozen strands will usually anchor a horse.

Once on foot, the basic procedures of stalking are followed. The hunter tries to move into, not with, the wind. He uses the unevenness of the terrain to assist his approach. He keeps low, moves slowly, and doesn't talk. Since caribou country is often open country, this technique often won't bring the hunter within range and special tricks must be employed.

Two techniques will often work with caribou. One is to watch the animals from prone and concealment until they all start to feed, or have their heads pointed in an opposing direction—then move fast for a few seconds until they raise their heads. Usually this must be on hands and knees, and over broken, boggy ground. The uneven, alternating clumps of solid, rooty ground mixed with the lower, more boggy intervals between, and the occasional clump of birch or willow, make such an approach possible. This writer and his guide once utilized the trick to get within 325 yards of seven head of Alaska caribou after going on all fours for a quarter mile. The big, well-palmated 53-inch bull was worth the effort.

Several days later the guide disclosed another productive way of getting closer to a band 400 yards away which would see us the second we left the open gully bottom where we had anchored the horses.

"There's no way of getting any closer without being seen," he concluded. "Now I'll duck down and head out slow right towards them. You come right behind, crouched as low as you can and right on my heels. If we go slow enough, they might think we're a pair of wolves. Caribou are curious cusses and might not run until they're sure."

It worked. As we left cover the beasts wheeled around to stare at us. The big, white-maned herd bull jumped, then trotted off sidewise. He stood and gaped, ready to bolt. Then he wheeled and trotted back to the others, who were engaged in similar antics. At one point the entire band broke into a trot and it appeared certain they were leaving the area. But after a 50-yard run they wheeled again, stopped, and gaped at us. We didn't break stride, raise our heads, or appear interested at all. At 196 paces, stepped off afterward, the guide shot the big bull, standing nearly broadside, from a quickly assumed prone position. I already had my own bull, but he wanted one for his own collection.

Selecting a Trophy. Most sportsmen shoot caribou for the trophy, which is magnificent in appearance. Natives of the Far North usually kill caribou for the meat. Some nonresident hunters want to save the meat as well, and this brings up a special problem.

Caribou beef is excellent meat, even from the big bulls if not taken during the heat of the rut. Caribou meat ages faster than most wild game, and the steaks of an animal may be eaten within three days of the time it was killed and cooled. For this additional reason, hunters usually want some of the trophy's steaks for camp use at least.

Most seasons on caribou, however, coincide with the mating season. During the crest of the rutting season, the bulls become thin and worn down due to excessive sexual activity. Moreover, during this season they eat little if anything and drink the urine of the cows as well as wallowing in their own. This makes them smell and taints the meat. A thin, "running" bull smells just like a decayed mouse nest, and the odor coming from a steak is overpowering.

The hunter can often pick his bull with some view toward avoiding this. A plump bull is apt to be free of the taint of the rut; a gaunt bull is apt to be a stinker. If it is possible to arrange one's hunt for caribou at the earliest part of the fall season, the chances are far better that as yet the desirable bulls haven't begun to "run" too badly.

Rifles and Cartridges. The purpose for which one hunts caribou often dictates the power of the rifle and cartridge he selects. So does the sex of the animal. Females and small bulls and yearlings don't require as much power to kill as do the aged, tough bulls weighing 600 pounds or more. Neither do migrating caribou shot at close range.

Many Eskimos shoot caribou with such cartridges as the .243 Winchester with excellent results. This does not make such a cartridge adequate as a caribou cartridge for the average hunter. Eskimos are excellent rifle shots from shooting hair seals. The caribou in the Arctic are small for their species and are often stalked to close range in snow. The Eskimo must use the same cartridge he uses for most of his hunting and which may be reloaded cheaply. All of his hunting is for meat. It is a different problem for the sportsman hunting the biggest male animals at long ranges.

Another consideration is the fact that most caribou country is also fine grizzly habitat. The silvertip is on the same high plateaus just under the snow line, digging out whistling marmots for his final feast before hibernation. In both Canada and Alaska grizzly and caribou are taken in identical areas. Numerous grizzlies have been killed at the offal remaining from caribou kills. For this reason alone, the ideal caribou rifle should be entirely adequate for grizzly bear.

For hunting caribou only, the following are fine cartridges:

.264 Winchester Magnum, with 140-grain bullets
.270 Winchester, with 130-grain bullets
.284 Winchester, with 150-grain bullets
7-mm Remington Magnum, with 150-grain bullets
7-mm Weatherby Magnum, with 154-grain bullets
7 x 61 Sharpe & Hart, with 160-grain bullets
.300 Savage, with 150-grain bullets
.308 Winchester, with 150-grain bullets
.30/06 Springfield, with 150-grain bullets

If I had to settle for a single caliber for caribou *only*, it would be the 7-mm Remington Magnum. For hunting only exceptional bulls, and where the cartridge will have to double on grizzlies, the old .300 H&H Magnum, the .300 Winchester Magnum, the .300 Weatherby Magnum, and the .338 Winchester Magnum are better choices. In these, 180- and 200-grain bullets are ideal.

Any rifle for caribou should be scope-sighted with a glass of around 4-power. It should be accurate and sighted perfectly for a minimum range of 200 yards. A good sling is a necessity.

Shot Placement. The heart-lungs area is the best target on caribou. Gut shots should be religiously avoided. Caribou have one peculiar trait

171

which causes many an inexperienced rifleman to miss his shot. As mentioned before, at the start of its trot or gallop a caribou makes a high bound. It is best to wait before shooting until after this first jump when the animal settles down to its steady gait.

Wounded caribou are usually downed in the open where both the gaudy coloration and the large antlers will show its whereabouts clearly, if the hunter watches closely and comes up hurriedly for a finishing shot. Like all antlered game, wounded caribou should be approached from above.

Bow and Handgun. For the average hunter, neither weapon is recommended for caribou because of the difficulty of stalking the animal close enough for a killing shot. But an experienced bowman or handgunner, who is also a skilled stalker, might be inspired by the challenge to try taking a caribou with his favorite weapon—and he might succeed.

16

Antelope

LIKE APPLE PIE, baseball, and the TV commercial, the pronghorn antelope (*Antilocapra americana*) is strictly an American institution. It is the only pronghorn antelope in the world, and is found nowhere except in North America.

The pronghorn is one of the smallest North American big-game species. Exceptional bucks will sometimes weigh up to 130 pounds but will average closer to 100 pounds. Does are approximately three fourths that size. Antelope are horned animals, and short nubbinlike horns often appear on adult does. These horns are grown upon a permanent core, but the outer shell is shed annually. Despite being deciduous, the buck's horns increase in length with age.

At first glance an antelope appears to be striped or semispotted. Its white belly changes abruptly into a tan-and-buff color halfway up its body line, gradually changing into a darker brown towards the back. The throat is banded with alternating brown and white bars. The underjaw is white, with the top of the face black. Under each ear is a jet-black spot, and the horns, likewise, are jet black.

The rump is white and looks like a puff of freshly exploded popcorn. The rump hairs are erectile and are used as a means of wilderness communication. When alerted by danger the animals "flash" by erecting these rump hairs and warn others of the band nearby and at great distances.

In the clear air of the West, where the pronghorn lives, it is possible to see this flashing with the naked eye for two miles or more. The antelope has eyesight comparable to that of a man using 8-power binoculars and can see the flashing of other antelope at far greater distances. This flashing is also used during the mating season as a means of keeping contact, one band with another, and one sex with the other.

The flashing of startled antelope in full flight deceives most hunters; the great white rump is enlarged out of proportion to the rest of the animal. As one old-timer put it, "A running antelope looks like he was three-fourths hinder. You always shoot behind 'im."

173

The pronghorn makes a prized trophy —but it takes careful stalking and sharp shooting to bag one. Each year the pronghorn sheds the outer hollow sheath of its horns and grows a new pair over a bony core. To score horns correctly, see page 396.

The range of the pronghorn once comprised just about the whole western half of the United States. The eastern limit of its range generally coincided with the western borders of Minnesota, Iowa, Missouri, Arkansas, and Louisiana. In a north-south direction the range extended from deep into Old Mexico to Alberta and Saskatchewan in Canada.

This range has currently been reduced at least one third in area, the shrinking generally being inward from the entire periphery. A map of the present antelope population and distribution, superimposed upon a map of the original distribution, would resemble a fried egg with the yolk broken.

As late as the 1920s the pronghorn appeared slated for extinction. Wise conservation procedures and more stringent hunting laws, together with an awakening to the danger of losing the species, all combined to save the antelope. In a broad way, today's pronghorn population is now at an optimum state, with the animals utilizing the full extent of their range: desert lands, sagebrush areas, arid flats, and dry foothills having sparse and short vegetation.

As an indication that the pronghorn has reached range capacity and must be stabilized at somewhere near its present population, most western states now manage the herds so as to harvest the entire approximate increase, except in spot regions where either a surplus or a deficiency exists. The total antelope population in 1946 was estimated to be 234,000. Today's official estimate is 237,000 animals.

Pronghorn populations in the various states are not as stable as the overall population and shift with such variables as severity of winters, hunter harvest, and periodic pressure from stockmen groups to reduce herds on lands where the antelope competes with domestic animals for food.

Currently Wyoming has nearly one third of all the antelope, with over 100,000 head. Other states having large antelope herds are Montana, New Mexico, Texas, Idaho, Oregon, South Dakota, Nevada, Colorado, and Arizona.

In recent years there has been a widespread program of trapping and transplanting the animals into regions where they are thought to "take hold" and to rehabilitate spot regions where an antelope population once existed but has been depleted.

The pronghorn, like many other species, has felt the influence of man crowding into its range. Unlike other species, the antelope had to remain in its desert range. Its retreat has been more in the form of ranging higher within the peripheries of its own range and migrating back and forth into adjacent ranges, than in moving to a completely different area.

The setting aside of lands for atomic testing has also cut into the remaining desert antelope habitat. And while there is neither shooting nor hunting of any game on these lands, the normal increase in the antelope population is kept down by the presence of protected predators such as the coyote.

One development which has reduced antelope range within the past few years has been the irrigation of desert lands for agricultural purposes. However, alfalfa, a standard crop on these new lands, provides the antelope with abundant food while they use the marginal areas for range. It is a common sight in this newly developed country to see bands of antelope feeding in the alfalfa fields at daylight. At sunup, they normally move back into the desert areas. Many ranchers don't object.

Antelope have traits common to all game species, and several peculiar to their own. Like deer, they tend to drift lower at night for water. During the heat of midday, antelope will climb to the rolling plateaus, promontory points, and jutting bars overlooking desert flats, to bed down. Like other game, they bed down in positions where they can see *downward* in all directions.

Rainfall and deep puddles cause antelope to move into higher country. As with most other species, the largest animals are found highest. This is

175

particularly true of the wise old bucks. Under pressure, they have learned to range high—as far up as the mountain-mahogany belt and fringing pines. Pursued antelope will run higher and will stay up in mountainous, bluffy country normally regarded as deer habitat.

Startled antelope will run in a generally straight line, not on an erratic course like a deer. Bands will run single file, with the best and biggest bucks usually bringing up the rear. The fleetest of all American big game, pronghorns can run effortlessly at forty miles per hour for many miles without tiring or slowing down. In shorter bursts of speed antelope can run sixty miles per hour.

The predominant characteristic of the pronghorn is its innate curiosity. The antelope is prone to stand and gape until its interest is fully satisfied, then take off if it detects danger. This trait was one of the causes of its near-extinction. The man-conditioned herds of today, however, have gradually learned that man usually means danger and have become more wary.

The pronghorn's trait of circling back to an area after it has been startled is perhaps more useful to the hunter. Often animals have been frightened out of a basin only to drift back within a matter of hours.

HUNTING THE ANTELOPE. The best single piece of equipment for the antelope hunter is a pair of good binoculars of at least 8 power. An additional tool is the light spotting scope so useful in caribou hunting. This is best used in locating game, then left in the vehicle used to reach antelope country.

Jeeps, pickups, and similar desert-going buggies are used for hunting antelope. It is illegal to shoot from motorized vehicles, but they are useful for getting deep into antelope ranges.

The procedure is to stop before each basin rim or long ridge and thoroughly glass the country ahead. Basin rims should be crept up to cautiously and the whole region glassed without disclosing the hunter's presence. Often this entails crawling up the last few yards before looking over into lower country. Once game is spotted, it is then stalked on foot.

Many times, however, antelope will be located from the vehicle. An antelope's hearing is fairly acute. Its vision is eight times as acute as man's. So it is safe to assume that any animal seen from a moving jeep has already spotted the vehicle.

Under such a circumstance, a productive way of stalking is for the hunter to slip unobserved out of the far side of the moving vehicle while the driver continues on. The hunter immediately drops low and out of sight. If conditions are such that he can remain concealed, he can circle the game, approach it from an opposite direction, and get a shot while the game still watches the "danger" of the vehicle.

176

This trick often works even if the game is mildly alerted and moves off a short distance as the vehicle comes in sight. If the driver continues on, completely out of sight, and if the concealed hunter stays put for an hour or so, the animals will often circle back within rifle range.

In most instances stalking within range of spotted game will be done wholly on foot. One basic procedure, regardless of conditions, is to maneuver within the terrain so that all changes in elevation may be utilized and the hunter comes upon the game from an unsuspected direction. Often this entails circling for considerable distance in order to come upon the animals from behind the opposite basin rim.

Occasionally antelope will be located in flat country or across a basin so large that to circle them requires too great an expenditure of time or effort. The animals probably will be watching the hunter as he comes into distant view. A hunting technique that often works is to pay no apparent attention whatever to the game, but continue walking slowly and casually at an oblique angle to the quarry. As the hunter walks leisurely forward, he also moves gradually sideways and in slow degrees cuts down some of the intervening distance between himself and the watching game. Often unpursued antelope sighted at around 500 yards can be approached to within 300 yards before they bolt. The trick here is

Near record antelope taken by author in Idaho's Medicine Lodge country in 1951.

for the hunter to give the illusion of not caring whether the game sees him or not, while moving sideways at the same time he moves forward. If he stops, looks toward the antelope, or gives any sign that he is aware of its presence, the animals will immediately bolt.

Often in rolling and broken foothills, a hunter will come upon antelope at long rifle range which see him and are immediately spooked. The rule in this situation is to drop immediately into the best concealment available, assume a solid shooting position, and wait for the animals' characteristic pause on the crest of a hill before they disappear from sight.

The best field position for shooting game is the sitting position. It allows the shooter to sight above intervening brush and small hills. It is quickly assumed and is nearly solid as the prone position. If antelope pause on a hillcrest, however, there may not be any obstructions between the shooter and his game and he can use the prone position. If a clump of sagebrush can be used as a fore-end rest, a standing antelope at 300 yards is an easy shot with a precision rifle.

Another effective hunting method is for two partners to separate at the first sight of game. One continues until he is out of sight, then doubles back to the same area and finds concealment. The other hunter circles to come behind the game, staying out of sight. If the hunter who circles makes it without detection, he is apt to get his chance. If the game is spooked into movement before, it is apt to circle back or run towards the area from which it thought the other hunter had moved.

The actual "driving" of antelope in the big open country of the West is about as productive as trying to drive the Snake River up over Teton Pass. But antelope may be *moved* by the above technique to the hunter's advantage.

In regions where the general routes of antelope are known, and especially if many hunters are expected to work the lower flat country, antelope may often be successfully hunted by the hunter posting himself at some high knoll, low saddle, or "pass" along such an anticipated route, staying hidden in some form of concealment, then waiting for game to move into range. The best time for such a technique is the morning of opening day of the hunting season. The best place is relatively high.

Another technique, for the lazy hunter, is to drive into antelope country, then leave his jeep or pickup parked in a gully, arroyo, or broken area where its top will be visible, and from where the hunter can walk away in plain sight. The hunter walks out of the sight of the game, but then doubles back at an oblique angle to a position within rifle range between the game and the vehicle. Often the antelopes' curiosity will be their undoing. Maybe it will take a couple of hours, perhaps a half day or longer. But unless antelope are molested by other hunters, they are apt to pick their way cautiously towards the vehicle to investigate.

Rifles and Cartridges. Because of their keen vision and their open habitat, antelope generally are shot at long range. Shots at antelope at 200 yards are considered close shots. More will be at 300 yards, if the animal isn't running. Opportunities at 400 yards are more common.

This requires a precision rifle with exceptionally flat-shooting bullets of reasonable weight and high performance. Pound for pound, antelope can run off with more severe bullet wounds than almost any North American big game. Also, an alerted antelope's erected rump hairs create a deceptive illusion of its size—especially when running—and the necessary lead to intercept him at extended ranges is often underestimated, causing many gut shots and shots through the hams.

The best antelope cartridges are those shooting bullets of 100 grains and over, with the flattest trajectories and the greatest accuracy. The best rifle for antelope should have a good fit and a light, crisp trigger-pull. It should be equipped with a good scope of 4 to 6 power. The new variable scopes in 2½ to 10 power do nicely and often double as binoculars.

Excellent antelope cartridges are:

.25/06 Remington, 120-grain bullets
.257 Weatherby Magnum, 100-grain bullets
6.5-mm Remington Magnum, 120-grain bullets
.264 Winchester Magnum, 140-grain bullets
.270 Winchester, 130-grain bullets
.284 Winchester, 125- and 150-grain bullets
7-mm Mauser, handloaded 130- and 139-grain bullets
.30/06 Springfield, 150-grain bullets

The 7-mm Magnum and .270 Magnum cartridges, such as the Remington, Weatherby, and 7 x 61 Sharpe & Hart, are fine for hunting trophy antelope but have an excess of power. They are fine one-rifle cartridges for doubling on antelope and larger game.

Much has been recently written of the hot 6-mm cartridges, such as the .243 Winchester and the 6-mm Remington, for use on antelope. With 100-grain bullets, such calibers are fine for antelope up to 250 yards. Beyond 300 yards a more powerful cartridge is better.

Antelope habitat is open country and windy. Often the hunter must allow for wind drift at long ranges. The drift of a bullet varies with its velocity, its own constancy, and the angle at which it is shot into the wind. The best practical way to learn wind-doping is to practice shooting at long ranges on windy days in advance of the hunt.

Here's how one old-timer put it: "Before I leave camp in the mornin', I tie an anvil onto a long log-chain, solid. If the wind comes up so the anvil stands straight out from the stake, she's too windy, for me at least, to hit antelope."

179

Wounded Antelope. A wounded antelope is harder to recover than most game. It will carry off a lot of lead, even slightly misplaced; and the animal will head for the flattest country where visibility is best and will usually continue to move until it dies.

The best procedure for finishing off a wounded antelope is not to wound one. This often can be averted by using an adequate rifle and cartridge, and by passing up chancy shots, especially running shots at long range.

If an antelope is wounded, the hunter's best technique is to get immediately onto the highest elevation nearby. From there the animal can be watched in its retreat to the lower flats. Also, from such an elevated position, prone shooting is possible with a clear view; and every effort should be made from this solid shooting position to finish off the animal before it gets completely out of range.

This, of course, means shooting at the beast's posterior. It means ham or gut shots. It means an abundance of fevered, musky fluid poured from the sebaceous glands all through the meat, tainting it, and creating an overall mess. It is the price the hunter often has to pay for an uncertain shot, and the cure is prevention.

Should the wounded animal get out of range completely before it is dispatched, the best course is to watch its retreat with binoculars until it lies down. Then it should be given an hour to stiffen before approaching.

Bow and Handgun. Hunting antelope with either bow or handgun is a challenge to the stalking skill of any hunter, and the thrill of success is intense. Those who do accomplish it in the open antelope country of the West are rare, since 99 per cent of the advantage lies with the quarry. Successful hunters with either weapon hunt in the broken dips, arroyos, slash canyons, and any terrain where it is possible to get close to the game. They wear camouflage clothing. Above all, they hunt in areas where there are few hunters so that once they've sighted an antelope and begun their stalk, the animal will not be spooked by someone else.

17

Bears

THERE ARE FOUR major species of North American bears: the black, grizzly, polar, and brown bear. Cinnamon and glacier bears are color variations of the black bear, but there are some indications that the grizzly and the Alaska brown bear interbreed. The North American bears are among the most highly prized big-game animals, and a large measure of this appeal is based on their record of being dangerous.

The real danger of the black bear lies in the way it attacks when cornered or wounded. Unlike the grizzly, which rears up to swing and swat with its forearms and claws, the attacking black bear comes at its opponent on all fours like a dog. It will close its jaws around its victim's arm, leg, or torso and will hang on like a bulldog, biting deeper, until the opponent is dead. Again, unlike the grizzly, the black bear will not leave its enemy for dead, but like the domestic hog is very apt to eat the remains.

A grizzly bear is unpredictable. A half-dozen individual grizzlies under comparable circumstances, may react in as many ways. It takes very little provocation to touch off a grizzly's rage. Suddenly surprising a grizzly on a trail may uncork its fury. Shouting or whistling at one at close range is apt to set it off. Coming between a sow and her cubs or surprising one near its cache will surely do it. And once enraged, a grizzly's ferocity is hard to overrate. No other animal within grizzly habitat can lick this huge bear. It knows no fear. Consequently its amazing physical strength and its tendency, once into a scrap, to fight to the death, have established its reputation as the "horrible bear."

The polar bear is as fearless as the grizzly and has an even greater fighting potential because of its enormous size. Hunting this great white species is a hazardous undertaking. The hunter must face the dangers of the Arctic along the ever shifting line where moving pressure-ice meets the open water and where the white bruin feeds; treacherous snow holes through which a hunter can fall into the ocean; blizzards and storms which can maroon a hunter on off-shore ice floes; sudden shifts in wind and currents which can open great gaps of water between the hunter and shore.

The danger of the Alaska brown bear lies in its great size and physical strength. It is odd that the brown bear, though so closely related to the grizzly, does not have the same ferocious, hair-trigger temperament as the silvertip.

For the big-game hunter such hazards have an intriguing appeal. In an encounter with any species of bear the element of danger lends excitement to the hunt.

BLACK BEAR. The black bear (*Eurarctos americanus*) is the most numerous of the group and the most widely distributed. Its range includes all the wooded portions of Canada and Alaska, as well as large areas in Continental United States. These are a large strip coincident with the Rocky Mountains and reaching southward into central Mexico; the Pacific Slope from the middle of California northward to Canada; large areas of the Northeastern States and about the Great Lakes; an extended belt of country along the Appalachians; and spot areas in the Florida Everglades, Mississippi, Louisiana, Alabama, the Carolinas, Virginia, and New York.

Of the states, Alaska has most black bears with an estimated population of 75,000 animals. The states of California, Maine, and Washington all have black bear populations in excess of 20,000, and Colorado, Idaho, Michigan, Minnesota, Montana, New Mexico, North Carolina, Oregon, and Wyoming all have sizable numbers.

Black bears vary in weight with adults ranging from 250 pounds to over 450. An average adult stands more than 2 feet at the shoulders and is approximately 2½ times as long as it is high.

The black bear hibernates in late fall, usually around November but depending upon altitude and severity of season. Cubs are born while the sow is in hibernation, and may include one black cub and one brown cub. Twins are common, and triplets not unusual.

Hibernating blacks are not impossible to arouse. Jarring or pounding around the den will cause them to move, and often on a sunny day in mid-winter a black will leave the den, mosey around outside for a few rods, then go back in.

Blacks leave the den in early spring. They live on a diet of dogtooth violets, grass shoots, and similar vegetation until their alimentary canals are again enlarged and conditioned for meat.

During the summer months, black bears move widely in search of food—rodents, carrion, any domestic stock they can steal, and wild fruits

Black bears sometimes seek safety in trees. This agile bruin was discovered resting in an unusual position.

and berries. Two to four weeks after emerging from hibernation the black bear's pelage is rubbed and shaggy-looking. From then until late fall, before the animal has again fattened up for hibernation, its coat is no good for a trophy. Early spring and late fall are the best times to hunt black bear for trophies.

Hunting the Black Bear. In spring, bears are hunted as they appear in the first open "slides" where small mountain avalanches have cleared the snow and the first blades of grass have appeared. Bears eat these first green shoots to condition their alimentary canals after the dormancy of hibernation, and they are often found on these slides.

Bears are great travelers. The sexes do not mingle except during mating season. The boars are not gregarious, but gruff individualists, and any adult bear seen is apt to be alone. Since black-bear habitat includes other big game, the chance of bagging one while on a hunt for other species is always good.

Fine areas to hunt black bear are high huckleberry, elderberry, wild raspberry, and similar fruit patches. So are old abandoned orchards, campsites, and the trails paralleling rivers and creek bottoms. The offal left from game-kills often produces a bear, if the hunter can get there before the coyotes. Often black bears will raid outlying ranches or forest camps for refuse, poultry, or even penned hogs. Individual bears become known as "pests" through such raids and usually won't leave the scene permanently but must be killed. In the West black bears follow the fringes of sheep herds in mountainous grazing lands to feed on carrion.

Three factors will maintain good black bear hunting in the future. First, the black bear adapts well to timbered forest lands; the annual lumbering operations do not disrupt its life cycle to any great extent. By nature a wanderer, the bear simply leaves a disturbed area and travels until it finds a more suitable habitat. Second, the black bear is now considered a game animal in almost every state and is protected by game laws. Third, the taking of cub bear, or the killing of female bears with cubs at her side, is now prohibited. This helps to increase the bear population. The state of Washington, for example, in 1937 had a black bear population of 13,000; in 1967 the number was 20,000, with indications of an increase since.

Rifles and Cartridges. The best rifles for black bear are those most suitable for mule deer and caribou, and should not include those listed as minimum for all-round deer rifles. Since the black bear is a woods-loving animal, it is often killed in timber and at relatively short range. For this reason, larger caliber, medium-powered cartridges may well be included. Suitable black-bear cartridges include:

.25/06 Remington, 120-grain bullets
.264 Winchester Magnum, 140-grain bullets
6.5 Remington Magnum, 120-grain bullets
.270 Winchester, 130- or 150-grain bullets
.284 Winchester, 150-grain bullets
7-mm Mauser, 139- or 160-grain bullets (handloads)
.300 Savage, 150- or 180-grain bullets
.308 Winchester, 150- or 180-grain bullets
.30/06 Springfield, 150- or 180-grain bullets
.358 Winchester, 200-grain bullets
.350 Remington Magnum, 200-grain bullets

Cartridges of the .250 Savage, .257 Roberts, .243 Winchester, 6-mm Remington, and .30/30 class are on the light side for black bear under hunting conditions, but will do the job at close range.

Use of Dogs. In many areas of the country, black bear are still hunted with dogs. The major reason for coursing with dogs is that the nature of the terrain or foliage is such that the hunter without the aid of dogs would not have a chance at bear. Bear are often hunted in conjunction with another species also necessitating the use of dogs, such as bear-boar hunting in the Tellico Plains region of Tennessee, or lion-bear hunting in the Southwest.

When bear are coursed with dogs, the quarry is either run past the hunters, brought to bay, or put up a tree. This is one type of hunting where a suitable handgun may be preferable to a rifle—for the anticlimactic shooting of a treed animal after the thrill of the race is over.

The .44 Magnum, the .41 Magnum, or the .357 Magnum, each shooting its heaviest bullet at maximum velocity, should be the only ordnance considered for the job.

Bow and Handgun. Both bow and handgun hunting for black bear are gaining in popularity, possibly because this species, due to its woods habitat, can be stalked closer than can open-country game. The heaviest weapon the hunter can shoot well should be his choice. An ethical standard by which the hunter using either weapon might well limit himself is that outside range at which he can regularly and surely place all his bullets or arrows into a 12-inch circle, under conditions encountered while actually hunting.

Another condition under which the handgun hunter can reasonably hunt black bear is while horseback hunting for another species. Black bears like trails, and the hunter will often surprise them at close range in horse country. The shoulder-holstered magnum handgun is then handy and effective. When the offal of game-kills is checked for bears, a pistol is easier to carry than a rifle during the stalk.

GRIZZLY BEAR. The grizzly is, on the average, larger than the black bear, weighing about 500 pounds although occasionally a bear will weigh twice as much. The identifying features of this bear are a broad head, a large hump at the withers, a dished face, and silver-tipped guard hairs along the spine. Grizzlies vary in coloration from creamy yellow to nearly jet black, but the average bear is brown.

Grizzly bears inhabit the most remote and inaccessible country remaining in North America: a belt extending from the northern part of Mexico to the Arctic circle. Most of this distribution is thinly spread, and the bulk of the population is in Alaska and British Columbia.

The grizzly bear population is declining and in many areas the animal is now considered an endangered species. The 1937 grizzly population of the United States was 1,100, but by 1967 the estimated number had dropped to 850. One reason for the decline is that the great silvertip is a prized trophy. Another is the constant whittling down of its remaining habitat. Like elk, the silvertip must have remote country to exist.

A bright spot in the hunting picture occurs within some of the great sanctuaries, such as Yellowstone Park, where the grizzlies multiply and overflow into adjacent regions. This permits the harvest of a few animals, for a few lucky permit holders. A good example of this was Wyoming's

1970 grizzly hunt. Twenty permits were issued for Park County, and ten permits were issued for those lands in Teton County which were controlled by the Grand Teton National Park.

Grizzly hunting in the future will be generally curtailed. Restrictions are apt to take the form of fewer grizzlies permitted each hunter over a lifetime, yearly limitations on how many bears an outfitter can have his clients kill in an area and possibly minimums as to the size of a trophy.

The grizzly is midway in size beween the black and brown bears, and is distinguished by silver-tipped hairs on the spine and a prominent hump on the withers.

The silvertip leads a solitary life in remote areas, usually at high elevations. It ranges wide for such food as blueberries, low-bush cranberries, wild-pea vines, rodents, carrion, grubs, and even ants from fallen logs. It covers a circuitous route up to twenty miles across. Old boars leave their claw marks on trees, indicating possession of a "private" domain. Like ursines, the grizzly goes into hibernation with the deep snow and heavy frosts of late fall and emerges in early spring. Grizzly dens are in rocky, craggy areas at the upper periphery of timber.

Two basic grizzly foods are of especial importance to the hunter since in the normal fall hunting season these staples disclose its presence. These are the blueberries found in large patches in Canada and Alaska, and the whistling marmot—a rodent comparable to the western rockchuck.

Hunting the Grizzly. In September grizzlies range far and wide, stripping ripe blueberries from their short stems. Consequently an effective way to locate a grizzly is to glass the blueberry patches. It takes a lot of fruit to fill a silvertip, and it is constantly on the move while the fruit season is on. The bear shows up well at extreme distances in the short fruit bushes.

The final fattening food for the grizzly's impending hibernation, the lowly marmots, are dug from the rocks at an elevation just under the snow line left by glaciers—the elevation at which marmots themselves hibernate. A grizzly will spend many hours during the day digging out such fat meals and is easily spotted with glasses in the relatively open country. Often the agitated noise of the rodents at being disturbed will draw the hunter's attention to a bear working their dens.

High trails, game crossings from one basin to another, creek beds, moose trails in the bush, and lake shores where the bear might find carrion are all likely places to look for grizzlies. So is the offal from recent game-kills. Perhaps the best area to look for a grizzly during the September-October period is the apexes of high basins and valley heads. Silvertips love such alpine "pockets."

Rifles and Cartridges. The "best" grizzly rifle is the most powerful rifle the hunter can shoot well. The grizzly hunter owes it to his own and his guide's safety, to say nothing of the beast itself, to use an outfit which will insure a clean, quick kill. One thing every grizzly hunter should paste in his red hat is the reminder that a grizzly must be stopped, not just killed. And the tenacity with which a grizzly clings to life is incredible. Any wounded beast may be expected to fight to the death.

Generally speaking, the right grizzly rifle is about on a par with the best trophy-elk rifles. Some adequate grizzly cartridges are:

.300 H&H Magnum, 180- or 220-grain bullets
.300 Weatherby Magnum, 180-grain bullets
.300 Winchester Magnum, 180-grain bullets
.338 Winchester Magnum, 200-grain bullets
.350 Remington Magnum, 200-grain bullets
.375 H&H Magnum, 270- or 300-grain bullets

Bow and Handgun. As such powerful cartridges are necessary to kill a grizzly, it should be apparent that the silvertip isn't bow or handgun game. An occasional grizzly has been dispatched with a heavy handgun, and a few will be killed in the future by archers—certainly it represents the greatest hunting challenge. But in such instances, a cool rifle shot with a heavy rifle habitually backs up the bowman, in case he starts something he can't finish. It is likely that one could count on the fingers of his hands the number of handgun hunters and bowmen who have the ability, basic hunting know-how, and sheer guts to take on a grizzly bear in its own bailiwick with these light weapons—and do a clean job of it.

POLAR BEAR. The great size of the polar bear, the ease of reaching by air the jumping-off areas to hunt him, and the increase of sporting dollars all make hunting this animal extremely attractive. The future depends largely on the regulations governing hunting via aircraft, and on international agreements and regulations. Alaska's Fish & Game Department at this writing is doing an admirable job of insuring the survival of this bear.

The white bruins live most of their life on the moving ice pack. Cubs are born during hibernation in rocky dens along the shoreline, but the boars seldom if ever go inland. Polar bears are great swimmers and will often swim ten to twenty miles between ice floes. They spend most of their time hunting, and their principal diet is the fat from hair seals. The lowly hair seal spends its time hunting for its main food, fish; and this determines the habitat and incidence of polar bears.

Generally speaking, polar bears are found offshore on the ice pack of the Arctic Ocean from Kotzebue, Alaska, northward around Point Barrow, and east and northward to Greenland.

One of the best jumping-off spots for hunting polar bear is the Point Hope-Kotzebue region of Alaska. Around such capes as Point Hope, Lisbourne, and Point Barrow, the ocean currents bring the fish in close to shore. The seals follow the fish, and with the anchor ice of midwinter, the favorable westerly winds, and the ice pack coming in, the big bears travel in relatively close to shore from the Siberian and Arctic sides. There the bruins hunt the seals along the open leads of water caused by currents and winds shifting the ice pack and anchor ice. Between February and March polar bears are usually within striking distance, and light aircraft or dog teams managed by Eskimo guides are used to transport the hunters.

Hunting the Polar Bear. Temperatures during hunting season are well below zero day and night. The hunting areas are usually many miles offshore, and the elements are merciless. Blizzard, fog, "white-outs" (frozen ice crystals), and frigid temperatures are the main obstacles to airplane hunting. The dog-sled hunter has these to contend with, plus the always-present possibility of being stranded on a moving ice floe by an open lead suddenly occurring between him and shore.

In dog-team hunting, the hunter and Eskimo guide generally travel ten or fifteen miles offshore into the maze of pressure-ice until they reach

Subzero cold and arctic terrain make hunting polar bear a dangerous sport.
This one was taken off Point Hope, Alaska.

open water. They hunt the edge of this moving, dangerous hunting ground during midday, then drive back to the native village at night. Arrangements for such hunting must be made through a commercial outfitter catering to polar bear hunts, who has himself made suitable arrangements with the Eskimos for dog teams, guides, and other services.

Airplane hunting is less miserable, and greater distances can be covered during the day's hunt. Two light aircraft, for safety reasons, are used, one flying above the other. One pilot scouts for game, the other surveys ice conditions and weather. When a bear is seen hunting on the ice pack, the planes are set down at a distance, and the hunter makes his stalk on foot.

The current headquarters for airplane hunting of polar bear is Kotzebue, Alaska. The sport was pioneered from there, several commercial outfitters operate out of the little Eskimo village, and bears are reached within a day's flight—usually from a hundred to two hundred miles out, west and northward. Hunters stay overnight at the modern but small hotel at Kotzebue, and the planes take off from the ice on the sound immediately out front. Outfitters for this type of polar bear hunting advertise in outdoor magazines, and the current rate for a trip, with bear guaranteed, is $2,500 to $3,000.

The most important piece of equipment for the hunter traveling either by dog team or aircraft is the down clothing he must wear to keep from freezing to death. This includes down underwear, pants, parka, cap, and mitts. Eskimo *mukluks* (double, hair-insulated boots) are also necessary.

The same rifles and cartridges suited to grizzly-bear hunting are ideal for polar bear. Rifles should be degreased before going into such subzero temperatures to prevent the actions from sticking.

ALASKA BROWN BEAR. The Alaska brown bear has for decades been considered North America's largest carnivore and a separate species from the grizzly bear. Recent exceptional specimens of polar bear, however, have challenged its position. With continued observation and study, the line of demarcation between the brown and the grizzly has diminished. Both bears have the same dished face, shoulder hump, general coloration. Their ranges overlap. In 1961 the Boone & Crockett Club flatly classified both bears as one, calling them Alaska bears, genus *Ursus.*

Brown bears are found along the coastal areas of southern Alaska, on many of the major islands, and extensively along the Alaska Peninsula. Kodiak, Admiralty, Chicagof, Afognak, Umiak, and Kruzof are some of the major islands having brown bear populations. On the Peninsula the

The Alaska brown bear, largest carnivore in North America, may attain a weight of 1,500 pounds. Like the grizzly, it has a lump on the withers.

areas around Port Heiden, Port Moller, and Cold Bay have good bear populations, and have produced some of the ranking heads.

The life cycle of these great bruins is interesting. They den high in the coastal mountains in rocky caves or dug dens, usually on northern slopes to prevent flooding from sudden chinook winds. They breed in late May, alternate years; twins are common, triplets not too unusual, and quadruplets have been observed. Coloration runs from a badgery silvertip of the true grizzly through cinnamon to a dark chocolate brown.

Brown bear males may weigh well over a half ton, with exceptional specimens reaching 1,500 pounds or more. A bear with a 10-foot-square hide (determined by laying the skin flat on the ground, totaling the measurements from nose-to-tail and from paw-to-paw, and dividing by two) is considered outstanding. The skull, the criterion by which bears are rated, is scored by adding its width and length in inches. The total is expressed in points. The Boone & Crockett Club now ranks as minimum those skulls having a score of 28 points.

Bears of 10-foot size, or even 9-foot size, are increasingly hard to obtain. Two years ago near Kizhuyak Bay on Kodiak Island I luckily took a brown bear which squared out at 9 feet 8 inches. The skull scored 28 12/16 Boone & Crockett points. The game department told me that at the time Kodiak bears were averaging only 7½ feet.

The brown bear is faced with the same forces that threaten the grizzly, and is declining in size and abundance as man cuts into its habitat, disrupts its natural cycle of living, and increases the hunting pressure. There is some evidence that more huge bears remain than is at first apparent, for while the tracks of large bear are seen often, trophy bears aren't seen as frequently during hunting season.

Outfitters are currently limited in the annual number of brown bears their hunters can harvest and in the number of camps allowed in places like the Alaskan Peninsula. Rising costs due to such restrictions discourage both outfitters and hunters, but the facts of the brown bear's decline and the need for a more controlled harvest speak for themselves.

Brown bears emerge from hibernation in April. Sows range with their cubs and the boars remain solitary. The first food is the green grass shoots growing among the alders, supplemented later by northern ground squirrels dug from the rocky hillsides. With early June the salmon begin moving up the glacial creeks, and the bruins move downward into the valleys to gorge on fish. With a late-fall fattening on salmon and berries, the bruins again are ready for the Big Sleep.

Hunting the Brown Bear. The only successful way to hunt brown bears is with a good outfitter. Relatively few outfitters cater to such hunts. Those that do, advertise in outdoor magazines. The jumping-off spot for stateside hunters is Anchorage, Alaska.

Reaching brown bear country is dependent upon transportation available, and this means that most hunting is done from temporary camps reached by light aircraft or boats. Outfitters having their own boats, or chartered craft, often cruise about the islands and into bays and inlets scouting for bears from the craft itself and sometimes using the boat as a floating camp. Once game is sighted the stalk is made on foot.

The use of aircraft has recently cut down on the time element and opened up new areas which were unavailable by boat. Hunters and

High on northern slopes, a hunter stands on a huge mound of dirt which was piled up by a brown bear making its den.

outfitter utilize the main airlines to reach the major jumping-off areas. From there private planes shuttle the outfit into the high valleys, bay heads, and creeks. There, in bear country at the base of the quick-rising mountains, the craft lands, not on an airstrip, but on a beach or creek bed. You have never really flown until you ride with a native pilot and watch him set down on an uneven, gravelly creek bed while winding his way between driftwood piles, rocks, and washouts!

Once in camp, hunters climb a hill that commands a view of the region and spend an hour or so inspecting the terrain with a spotting scope or high-powered binoculars. Trophy bears range above snow line and glaciers; they love the deep snowbanks and will slide down them like playful children. The trails they leave in the snow are easily read to determine freshness and the bear's sex. Lower country should also be carefully scrutinized. With powerful glasses moving game can be seen in thick foliage.

May is the best month for hunting brown bears. The abundance of remaining snow makes it easy to spot spoor and determine whether bears are in the area. The alders which grow in these northern climes are still bare and moving game is easy to spot. Finally, late May is the mating

Hunters take preliminary field measurements of an enormous brown bear which will rank high in the records.

season and trophy boars, traveling about in search of a mate, reveal themselves to the watchful hunter. It is a rule in any bear camp that a sow is not to be molested; a boar may find her while the hunt is still on.

Once a bear has been spotted, a campaign must be outlined for stalking within killing range. It is foolhardy to strike out after a bear until his intentions become manifest. He may be wandering in search of food and travel five miles before stopping. He may be hunting a female and travel twice that distance. But when the bear lies down and indicates that he will remain in the area, it is time to plan the stalk.

Brown bear taken on Kodiak Island by author in 1968. This trophy rates 28-12/16 score in Boone & Crockett measurements.

Brown bear should always be approached from above if the wind permits. Of all the senses, their sense of smell is the keenest and the hunter must have a favorable wind to stalk close enough for a kill.

Rifles and Cartridges. The right rifle and cartridge for brown bear is the most powerful the hunter can handle. The animal is ponderously large and possesses unbelievable vitality. The first shot may well kill the bear, but it won't *stop* him.

When a brown bear is hit he will do one of two things with blinding speed: He will make for the hunter or race away. If he heads for the hunter, the latter must have sufficient firepower to stop him. If the wounded beast tries to escape, he will head for the nearest and thickest alder thicket. This means that the finishing shots will be made at short range through heavy brush. Bullets must plow through this brush and stop an enraged and powerful animal. They should be heavy and of large caliber and high velocity. Two of the best are the .375 H&H Magnum using 270- or 300-grain bullets, and the newer .338 Winchester Magnum using 200- or 250-grain bullets. The recent .358 Norma Magnum cartridge using 250-grain bullets of suitable construction should be an effective cartridge for brown bear. The .30-caliber cartridges are less desirable, and the otherwise adequate .300 H&H and .300 Weatherby Magnum using 220-grain bullets should be considered minimum. Cartridges under .30 caliber, even in magnum power, are not adequate for brown bear. The more recent .350 Remington Magnum using 200- or 250-grain bullets, in the Model 660 Magnum Remington rifle, makes a

Huge grizzly (*left*) taken on Alaska Peninsula in 1961, and black bear taken in Wyoming near Shoshone River in 1960.

good brown-bear outfit for close range. This short-barreled rifle is lightweight and easily handled—ideal for hunting in alders.

Shot Placement.   The best possible area to hit a brown bear is through one or both shoulders. On angling shots, the hunter should either hold to break the near shoulder and have the bullet penetrate and enter the chest cavity, or go through the heart-lungs area and break the opposite shoulder. Such a hit will put the beast down at least temporarily, offering the chance for quick finishing shots. A spine shot is too difficult for the average hunter to make with dead certainty except under the most favorable conditions.

To track down a wounded brown bear in high grass and thick alders is a difficult and delicate task. In any case, all sound should be listened for intently before any follow-up—which should invariably be from the uphill side. Often the rumpus made by a bounding bear will indicate its direction, its degree of injury, and the spot where it goes down.

One man should lead the way, chamber loaded and safety off, watching every inch of terrain and the foliage ahead. The other unravels the blood or track spoor step by slow step until the beast is located. An experienced guide will insist that the hunter keep shooting until the animal quits moving.

Bow and Handgun. There is hot-stove-league talk about whether brownies can be killed with a bow or a magnum pistol—with rifle back-up, of course. A few brown bear have actually been killed with these weapons. But the average hunter, even the cool experienced game-shot, is better off just contemplating the matter. The brownie is generally a one-specimen species. Most hunters wait half a lifetime to bag their first, and one trophy is usually sufficient.

There is no more thrilling moment for the big-game hunter than to come up to his downed brown bear, contemplate that it has taken nature twenty to thirty years to produce the great animal, and regard his prize with a mixture of ecstasy and true humility. As my hunting partner said on our recent brown-bear hunt, "That 10-foot beast was the first game I've ever shot that kept getting even bigger the longer I looked at him!"

18

Mountain Sheep and Goats

THE HIGHEST HUNTING honor that can come to the North American big-game hunter is to become a "grand-slammer" on wild sheep. This means to take a legal, representative specimen of each of the four species: Dall (*Ovis dalli*), Stone (*Ovis dalli stonei*), Rocky Mountain bighorn (*Ovis canadensis*), and desert bighorn (*Ovis canadensis nelsoni, Ovis canadensis gaillardi,* etc.).

Only a few have accomplished this feat, and a few dozen hunters are trying for their second "go-round," attempting to get a ram of each species whose horns will reach 40 inches along their outside curl.

The great rams of the 40-inch class, and even those slightly smaller, are becoming more difficult to get. North America's wild sheep are limited by their peculiar type of habitat. The biggest rams generally come from remote areas which have seldom, or never, been hunted.

The availability of airplanes and bush tractors, however, for getting hunters deep into formerly inaccessible areas means that very few such high, remote areas remain. Also, the demand today for these prized species is so great that outfitters often allow too many hunters into their allotted areas. Finally, in their urgency to get a ram trophy, many hunters shoot smaller rams, preventing many from aging into real trophies.

Some relief for the future will be found in transplanting sheep to areas where they have never ranged, or to suitable ranges where previous bands have been decimated. The Rocky Mountain species especially has proven adaptable to transplanting.

North American wild sheep are classified in various ways. One classification is according to horn type, with the Dall and the Stone classed as thin-horned sheep and all others as bighorns.

197

Coloration gives another broad basis for classification. The Dall is white, the Stone blue-black, and the bighorns brown-gray. The Dall is smallest, adult rams averaging around 250 pounds; the Stone and the bighorns may reach 300 to 350 pounds. Generally the horns of the bighorn sheep are set more closely against the skull than those of the thin-horned group. Because this impairs the vision of mature bighorn rams, they often rub the tips of their horns against rocks to wear them down and broaden their field of vision.

Another broad classification of wild sheep is according to range. The Dall's range covers Alaska and as far south as the southern border of Yukon Territory; the Stone's range comprises British Columbia and Alberta, in the Peace River area; and the Rocky Mountain sheep's range is from the southern portions of British Columbia and Alberta on southward into Mexico. In a region overlapping the ranges of the Dall and the Stone is a species called Fannin (*Ovis fannini*), nicknamed "saddleback sheep," and considered by some to be the result of interbreeding between Dall and Stone sheep.

Like the antelope, the wild sheep in Continental United States were headed for extinction. They were slaughtered largely for their prized flesh, considered by most outdoorsmen to be the finest of all animals.

The bighorn sheep has massive, curling horns which are never shed throughout his lifetime. The horns are composed of a hollow sheath growing over a bony core. For scoring data see page 400.

Two of the author's prized sheep trophies, a Rocky Mountain ram (*left*) and a Dall ram, illustrate the difference in horns and pelage between the species.

Wise conservation legislation, such as protecting the ewes and permitting only a limited harvest of rams in each area (usually those with horns having three-quarters curl or more), and complete protection of the species in other regions have saved this prized animal and even made limited hunting available. Currently, several western and southwestern states permit ram hunting on a permit basis. The best areas for the hunter, however, are Alaska, Yukon, and Canada, which have the largest sheep populations.

As a species, mountain sheep are considered to be "predictable." That is, unless molested they will follow a definite pattern. They generally live at the highest areas within their habitat. In the Rockies, this means at elevations of 10,000 feet or over, usually above timberline. In Alaska and Canada, where the mountains are high compared to the "bush," but where the overall elevation is comparatively lower, sheep country begins at the 7,000-foot level and continues from there to the "top" country. In a general way, all species of sheep except the desert bighorn love the high, rolling mountaintop country above timber and foliage. Winter usually drives them off the very top country into the upper periphery of timber and brush; but in the fall hunting season they will be found on the mountaintops. Summer drought will sometimes cause sheep to move, if high water holes are dried up.

Author's best Stone Ram (*left*) and best Dall ram in his trophy room in Idaho.

Wild sheep have a life span of twelve to fifteen years. Except in mating season, the rams have nothing to do with the ewes and lambs but gang up in bunches of males from two to nearly a dozen. During the rut rams fight viciously for the ewes. Both sexes are horned.

Desert sheep generally live at the higher elevations of their lower country, in areas near available water holes.

The enemies of mountain sheep are man and wolves, and part of the species' survival strategy lies in staying at extreme elevations to escape both. Wild sheep can climb, run, and jump in treacherous cliff country along shelving ledges where neither wolf nor man can follow. The desert sheep's worst enemies are the herds of wild burros which occupy and despoil the sparse water holes in their desert habitat.

The vision of wild sheep is comparable to that of antelope. Many ram hunters swear that an old trophy ram can look through a two-foot granite boulder. And once spooked, a ram can quickly get through country no hunter can negotiate. In short, sheep hunting is most difficult, which makes bagging a trophy such a great thrill.

HUNTING MOUNTAIN SHEEP. If horses are available mountain sheep are hunted by riding the highest ridges and studying the open country with high-powered binoculars or a spotting scope. Sunup is a good hour to locate sheep as they are then in the open and show up well in the slanting rays of the sun. By mid-morning they will bed down for the day, usually in rough rimrock from where they can observe the terrain below. During mid-afternoon they come out again and graze until dusk. This is also a good time to hunt except that the trip back to camp has to be made in the dark.

In Alaskan and Canadian bush country, where horses are not available, hunters are often flown in to high-altitude lakes near known sheep habitat. Spike camps are set up and the hunters take to the hills on foot.

Desert sheep are usually hunted by using a 4WD vehicle to get into game country.

When hunting wild sheep, the best procedure is to get higher than the game and hunt down. This often means circling back a mile or so to get out of sight, doubling up and back of a cliff, mountain, or basin, then making the final stalk from an unsuspected angle. Any attempt to move directly toward game which has seen the hunters at a distance is doomed to failure.

Often sheep are located in a situation where it is impossible to stalk them without disclosing your position. The best procedure is to leave the game until it beds down or moves to another area where it can be approached safely. This may mean waiting a day, but sheep won't leave an area unless they are spooked.

Rifles and Cartridges. The rifle for sheep should be accurate, flat-shooting, and reasonably high-powered. In the broken peaks of sheep country, rams are often come upon at relatively close ranges. But it is often necessary to shoot long distances, and the rifle should be capable of handling both types of shots.

The rifle for sheep should be light for climbing where oxygen is thin and exertion excessive. It should have a relatively short barrel. Many times the sheep hunter must negotiate thin shelving ledges on semivertical cliffs and a long-barreled rifle, bumping into the spires and walls, is apt to push him into Eternity. Many ram hunters gladly sacrifice the velocity of a 26-inch rifle barrel for the handiness and safety of one 22 inches long, or even shorter.

Fine cartridges for sheep hunting include the following:

.264 Winchester Magnum, 140-grain bullets
.270 Winchester, 130-grain bullets
.284 Winchester, 150-grain bullets
7-mm Mauser, 130- and 139-grain bullets (handloads)
7-mm Remington Magnum, 150-grain bullets
.308 Winchester, 150-grain bullets
.300 Savage, 150-grain bullets
.30/06 Springfield, 150-grain bullets

The sheep rifle should be equipped with a good quality scope sight. A 4X is the best all-round scope unless the hunter wants to use it as a binocular. In this case a 6-power scope is better, and a good variable is perhaps best.

A rifle sling on the sheep rifle is a necessity. Climbing often has to be done on all fours if the hunter is to get where he wants to go. A good sling, permitting the rifle to be slung from the shoulder or across the back, allows the hunter free use of his hands.

Accessories. Other necessities for sheep hunting include a 100-foot length of light nylon rope, clothing as nearly the same coloration as the rocks in sheep country, a daily lunch of some kind of concentrated food, and slipproof boots. The rope will allow the hunter to descend and ascend places otherwise impossible to negotiate. Rams sometimes tumble or roll when shot into chimneylike crevices from where they could not be recovered without using a rope. Hunting clothes of the same general color as the rocks will help to camouflage the hunter. Often a concentrated snack of candy bars or piñole is a virtual lifesaver when getting a ram requires staying out overnight.

A spotting scope, which may be steadied on a packboard (*opposite page*), is a necessity for locating mountain sheep or goats, like the three billies above on the high cliffs of their habitat.

THE ROCKY MOUNTAIN GOAT. The Rocky Mountain Goat (*Oreamnos montanus*) is a type of antelope limited in range to an elongated strip of region coincident with the Rocky Mountain Range. Its range includes southern Alaska, Yukon Territory, British Columbia, the western edge of Alberta, and portions of Washington, Idaho, and Montana.

Like mountain sheep, mountain goats live their life cycles within a radius of from five to ten miles. As with other game species, food is the determining factor and the dizzying heights, cliffs, and ledges where they live furnish lichen, the staple of their diet.

Mountain goats are white or creamy-white in overall color, and average approximately 250 pounds in weight. Both sexes are horned, and it is difficult to tell them apart at a distance. Billies, however, generally appear larger, have a greater hump at the withers, and live a largely solitary existence.

Twinning is more rare among mountain goats than among other species. The kid stays with the nanny until its second year. With the birth of the new kid, it is butted out of the family group onto its own.

The mountain goat wears the same pair of polished black horns on its shaggy head throughout its lifetime. Present in both sexes, the horns grow to a maximum length of about 12 inches. Scoring data is on page 402.

Winter drives the goat downward from the cliffs and into the upper periphery of timber. But with early spring it heads up again. Wolves, eagles, and man are the goat's enemies, with eagles taking a heavy toll of kids. The black, spearlike horns of both sexes are dangerous fighting weapons, as people who have handled an occasional wounded goat have found out. Its main defense, however, is simply to climb away from enemies. Of all game the mountain goat and mountain sheep are the most sure-footed. Avalanches, old age, and misjudgment of footing do cause an occasional casualty.

Because of its very limited range, the mountain goat population is about at carrying capacity; harvested numbers are apt to remain at about the present level. Future harvests, despite increasing numbers of hunters, will occur on a sustained-yield basis, with given numbers of surpluses to be harvested from defined management areas.

Hunting the Mountain Goat. Goat hunting is roughly comparable to sheep hunting. The basic difference in both peaks-loving animals is that the mountain sheep likes the high rolling saddles and spines between the spires and peaks, while the mountain goat lives on the precipices and cliffs. The best hunting procedure is to get above the quarry if at all possible. Goats especially look for danger from below and know less of how to handle any hazard coming from above.

Goats are most often located by a thorough glassing from below the cliff areas of mountain country. Their white coloration makes spotting them and identifying the species relatively easy. Stalking goats usually takes an entire day. Often after the hunter makes his climb and knows for sure he is near the quarry, the craggy, rough terrain will keep the game from view.

This is aggravated by the fact that goats are phlegmatic by nature. Often they will lie or stand in one place for long periods of time without moving. After the hunter has succeeded in getting above the game, patience should be his watchword. Often if he merely waits for an hour or so the game will appear.

A simple trick to fool goats into making their presence known is to toss a small rock into a gully or crevice at ten-minute intervals. Falling rocks in goat country are common, but the repeated rattling of a stone will often arouse the curiosity of a goat, and it will come into sight to learn whether the noise is friend or enemy.

The flesh of trophy goats is usually not edible—as opposed to that of mountain sheep. Goat trophies are usually caped out and lugged back to camp.

Often the meat of wild sheep must be left overnight. Eagles and ravens will despoil such meat quickly by pecking, pulling out tufts of

hair, and even evacuating their bowels all over it unless proper preventatives are used. The best way to protect a trophy is to turn the dressed
carcass belly down over a large rock in a crevice, then pile rocks over the
exposed parts. Breezes will circulate over the carcass, allowing it to cool
without spoilage, and predatory birds cannot get at it.

Rifles and Cartridges. While mountain goats average smaller than
the large species of sheep, they are harder to kill. Pound for pound the
wild goat will take as much killing as a grizzly. Its tough, spongy flesh
absorbs bullets without the shock imparted to such thin-skinned species
as deer.

In general, the same rifles and cartridges used for sheep will be
adequate. To that list, the .30-caliber magnum cartridges might well be
added. In areas where goats can be stalked to within reasonable range,
cartridges of .35 caliber are even better—such as the .358 Winchester
and the .350 Remington Magnum—as an increase in bullet diameter,
with other factors being equal, always gives better killing power on tough
game animals.

Bow and Handgun. Mountain sheep and goats represent an extreme
challenge to the archer and handgun hunter. Both species can be taken
with either weapon, but there are few hunters with the necessary time,
patience, money, and stalking skill.

Early Indian hunters used to kill mountain sheep, especially, with the
bow-and-arrow. They did not rely on their great skill in stalking to do the
exacting chore, but they organized game drives to move the animals
through narrow passages where the hunters would lie in wait. The narrow
crevices along migration routes, the shelving ledge-trails at the base of
mountain spires and rock citadels, and the walled-in mountain passes
were the chosen spots. In these areas, within 20 to 30 yards of the trail,
blinds were built. Once the game became accustomed to the blind, the
best hunters would wait inside while others moved the game towards the
place of concealment.

An entire tribe in central Idaho, the Sheep-Eaters, once survived on
mountain sheep killed largely in this fashion. In Alaska and Wyoming
some of the ancient rock cairns built as blinds for hunting driven sheep
are still visible.

Perhaps the biggest obstacle to bow or handgun hunting of either
mountain sheep or goats is the fact that either species has to be stopped
in its tracks. A wounded animal on the high cliffs often means a lost
trophy.

19

Predators

THE PREDATORY BEASTS which prey on the various species of game have a definite place in Nature's scheme. Predators are necessary to eliminate the weak, aged, and crippled from game herds; to keep herds well scattered on their ranges and thus diminish excessive in-breeding and diseases caused by too intense a concentration; and to clean the landscape of carrion.

It is sometimes difficult for man to reconcile this function with the fact that some predators kill only the fat and the young of big game when available, or slaughter wantonly and eat only select portions of their kill.

In an overall effort to utilize big game to his own advantage, man has often sought to suppress or eradicate certain predators. But once a tampering with a wildlife balance is begun in one direction, unpredictable and often violent disturbances occur in another. Man is just beginning to understand the far-reaching effects of predation. In his manipulation of wildlife, the best he is able to suggest is the holding of all predators at a compatible level with the game on which it lives.

Within these limits, and within the scope of future knowledge of the ecological relationship of predators to game management, both predator and varmint hunting are bound to grow in importance.

WOLF. Among the largest of the American big-game predators is the wolf (*Canis lupus*). A descendant of the Pleistocene period, the wolf is the ancestor of the domestic dog and has a long and legendary record of depredations against stock.

The wolf's numbers have so steadily dwindled in the past decade that it is regarded by some as an endangered species. Wolf hunting of the future will have to be compatible with its status at any given time.

207

North American wolves may be divided into two basic groups, the red wolves and the gray wolves. Both have been exterminated from many sections of the country. The remaining red wolves—named for their russet winter coat—now inhabit the Ozark Mountains, parts of Arkansas, Oklahoma, and Texas, together with scattered spot areas in the southern Mississippi Valley states.

Like the pronghorn antelope, the red wolf is a true American species found nowhere else. Adult red wolves weigh up to 70 or 80 pounds.

The gray wolf, often called the timber wolf, has been driven northward out of the United States and is now found largely in Canada, Yukon Territory, and Alaska. The gray wolf belongs to the same family as the Scandinavian and Siberian wolves and in North America consists of twenty-four subspecies.

The coloration of wolves often changes with their habitat. Gray wolves vary in color from nearly black, with the legs washing out into a roan-blue much like moose, to black-gray, silvery-gray, and to nearly pure white. This lightening of hue generally follows the animal's progression northward. In size, the gray wolf will reach 150 pounds and over. Its lugubrious howl is a deep guttural moaning sound which will carry far on cold nights and is an awesome thing to hear.

In Canada and Alaska, gray wolves prey heavily on moose and caribou. They hunt in small family groups historically called "wolf packs." Such a group will successfully kill adult Canadian moose and regularly hunts the vast burned-over bush areas for the species.

One method wolves employ to get a moose at sufficient disadvantage is to chase it into, or locate it already in, a small shallow lake. Then by cutting off its escape route, harassing the animal until it can't feed, and keeping it in the water for days on end, the predators succeed in weakening it until they can kill it as it is finally forced to make a break. One animal grasps the moose's nose or throat, and while the quarry struggles to shake off that tormentor, others sever the tendons of its hind leg. Wolves often begin eating before a victim is dead.

Wolves also prey on caribou. Running in relays, the pack tries to tire an animal and chase it into deep snow or muskeg, or to the ice of a stream or lake. There, with the caribou at a disadvantage, the wolves can kill it.

A wolf killed with a firearm represents one of the most prized trophies. Occasionally a wolf is killed—mainly in caribou country—by a sportsman after other species. Like uranium, a gray wolf is only where one finds it. About the only preparation the hunter can make is to glass all game country thoroughly before he discloses his presence and be ready for an unexpected opportunity.

Several outfitters catering to polar-bear hunts out of Kotzebue, Alaska, will also take a sportsman wolf hunting. This is done in winter when snow and ice help to make the predators visible, and when they are working the caribou herds hardest. The technique is to fly over the caribou country just inland along the coast from Kotzebue to Cape Lisbourne, weather permitting, until a wolf is spotted. Then, if in open country—and most of it is treeless that far into the Arctic—the beast is chased at low altitude until it offers a close, straightaway target. The hunter uses a rifle, or a shotgun loaded with buckshot.

Wolves also are hunted from planes in winter in the Yukon-British Columbia region. This is an area of numerous lakes, and a choice place to catch a wolf unawares is on the ice, where an unimpeded race is possible.

COYOTE. The coyote is a western predator but has a greater north-south range than most other predators. Coyotes are now distributed from the Arctic Circle to South America.

Like the whitetail deer, the coyote has demonstrated an amazing ability to live in man's back yard and survive. The coyote has survived in spite of man's every attempt to kill it off due to its canny nature and its ability to eat almost anything. The diet of the coyote includes grasshoppers, rodents, game-bird eggs, rabbits, and the carrion of domestic or wild game. Stockmen hate coyotes and have waged a continuous war against these killers of poultry and sheep.

Coyotes are gray in color, lightening to tan along the belly and legs. The winter coat is thicker and lighter in color than the summer coat, in some instances almost white. An average-sized coyote weighs from 20 to 25 pounds, with adult males weighing well over 30 pounds. The animals are prolific, having up to a dozen or more pups in a litter.

In appearance a coyote resembles a small shepherd dog. Its three outstanding characteristics are its long thick tail, which, like a fox's, seems to float when the animal runs; its sharp-pointed ears and nose; and its eerie cry, which is a true sound of the wilderness.

Coyotes are scavengers and are often erroneously credited with killing the carrion they clean up. They serve a useful purpose, too, in keeping rodent infestation down. In many western states, the coyote keeps the prolific jack rabbit from over-populating the region. Again, such range hazards as pocket gophers in elk and domestic-stock country are currently being traced to man's virtual extermination of the coyote in those regions.

Because of its innate cunning, sagacity, and elusiveness, the coyote has won the respect of many sportsmen. Coyote hunting is a thrilling sport, and many ingenious methods of hunting the little yodel-dog have been developed.

Coyotes are hunted incidentally with such species as antelope, deer, and elk. Their ranges overlap those of the coyote, and an occasional coyote is seen by the big-game hunter. The little predator will come to the offal left from big-game kills and is often seen in primitive country, trotting along the high ridge trails at daybreak. In desert country, they are often seen moving about jack-rabbit concentrations, or staring at the hunter from a distant knoll with only their pointed ears showing.

In marginal farm areas where meadowlands meet timber or desert, coyotes will often come at daybreak to hunt for mice. In mild seasons, resident hunters in such areas often conceal themselves on top of haystacks and wait for the animals to appear with daylight. Then they shoot them with high-intensity sniping rifles. Similarly, in some desert areas of the Southwest where artificial blinds for deer hunting are available, such as stands or platforms set up high above foliage to simulate windmills or water tanks, such blinds are used for spotting and shooting desert coyotes at long ranges.

In some western states, coyotes are coursed with hounds bred especially for the purpose. Often the hounds will be hauled by vehicle in a crate through good coyote country until a yodel-dog is seen, or its tracks in fresh snow are picked up. Then the crate is opened and the dogs released. The hunter follows in the vehicle until the dogs run the animal down.

In western canyon country, rugged sportsmen hunt coyotes in winter on snowshoes. The procedure is to follow the canyon rims and scout for coyotes hunting for rabbits and mice in the semibroken areas.

In western desert areas, in deep snow, coyotes are occasionally "run" with saddle horses. The horses are hauled by trailer to the edge of the desert early in the morning, after a snowfall of several inches, and the ride begins. Once a fresh track is found, the rider trots his horse until he sights the coyote. The beast usually will run towards the roughest country available.

In good snow conditions, a tough saddle horse can often catch a running coyote within six to ten miles. The last mile is a heated race, with the coyote wringing its tail and often lying down exhausted to await the end.

In the open desert and prairie regions of the West, coyotes are often coursed in winter with light aircraft and shot at close range ahead of the low-flying plane. Pilot and hunter make up the hunting team, and the preferred weapon is a 12-gauge shotgun loaded with buckshot. In such shooting, the animal must be "led" from behind, just the reverse of wingshooting birds.

Another method gaining popularity in the West is hunting coyotes in open desert and dry farm country in winter with snowplanes. A snow-plane is a specialized little winter vehicle with a radial type of aircraft motor mounted on the rear of a fuselage large enough to seat two people in tandem. The fuselage and motor are supported well off the ground upon three laminated plywood skis.

Coyotes are also hunted from snowmobiles. These vehicles can overtake a coyote under favorable conditions. However, snowmobiles and snowplanes must be restricted to areas where they will not molest game species.

Snowplanes are often used for hunting coyotes in the open desert country of the West.

In desert areas coyotes are often hunted with some type of desert buggy. Roads are often nonexistent, but coyotes are usually found where desert travel is the hardest. A combination of light snow and heavy jack-rabbit sign in February means good coyote hunting. At this time coyotes are in their mating season and are more apt to congregate in large numbers. In the Southwest coyotes are called into rifle and handgun range by simulating the death cry of a wounded jack rabbit.

Most coyotes are killed with rifles at long range. The best weapon is an accurate, scope-equipped rifle shooting a cartridge such as the .22/250, .243 Winchester, 6-mm Remington, or the .25/06 Remington with 87-grain bullets. A coyote rifle should be capable of inch-group accuracy at 100 yards and shoot exceptionally flat to 300 yards.

BOBCAT AND LYNX. The bobcat and the Canadian lynx are two other predators which feed mainly on small game such as grouse, rabbits, and rodents but also kill fawn deer and, in deep snow, adults.

211

The bobcat is the smaller of the two, with adults averaging 20 pounds or more. It ranges from Canada to Mexico, being distributed widely throughout the country. The lynx, which is restricted to Canada, weighs twice as much as the bobcat.

In the West hunters sometimes spotlight bobcats with a jeep in rocky canyons. The cat's eyes shine in the light and it can be killed at long range. This method of hunting is only feasible in areas having no big game and where it is legal.

Another way to hunt bobcats is to find a place along the sunny side of a canyon where the animal suns itself and leaves its tracks in the snow. Hunters spread raw hamburger along the bluffs and lie in wait for the cat to emerge.

By far the most effective way to hunt bobcats is with dogs, since most hunting dogs will take up the scent of a cat immediately. In fact, one of the professional lion hunter's biggest problems is to break young lion dogs from running bobcats. An adult bobcat will give most dogs a merry chase and often prefers to stand at bay and fight instead of climbing a tree. Hunters either shoot the bobcat, let the dogs kill it, or allow the animal to escape and run another day.

COUGAR. One of the most relentless and seldom seen predators of North American wildlife is the cougar, also known as panther, mountain lion, or simply lion.

The status of the cougar has changed rapidly during the past few years due to the growing esteem with which hunters have come to regard it as sporting quarry. Currently, in six of the most heavily populated cougar states the status of the animal has been changed from predator to game. Of all the cougar states only Arizona now pays a bounty on the cat.

Males average from 140 to 200 pounds and measure up to 7 feet or over in length. A professional hunter in Arizona with over 100 cougars to his credit told me in the fall of 1960 that he once carried in a big tom on a horse just to weigh it. The beast weighed 210 pounds. Females weigh proportionately less.

Like the mule deer on which it continuously preys, the cougar is a western inhabitant. Its range lies mainly west of the Rocky Mountains and reaches from Canada on the north to Central and South America on the south. An animal is killed on rare occasions in the Florida swamps.

Cougars follow the deer concentrations and venison is their staple food. The cats prey on all three species of deer and like domestic colts and hogs when available. Horses have a deadly fear of cougars, and many a western rider in wild country has been surprised by his mount wheeling in its tracks and taking off at a sudden whiff of "cat."

An adult cougar will kill an average of a deer per week or more. The kill is made by the cat's stalking to within short running distance of a deer, then overtaking it in a short, swift rush. The cougar springs upon the animal's withers and bites into the neck at the base of the skull, sinking its teeth deeper and deeper until they sever the spinal cord.

The cat eats its fill of the deer, then rakes pine needles, oak-brush twigs, and leaves over the remainder. Unless molested or on the move, the cougar will return each day or so until the carcass is eaten. Cougars will not eat the kill of another animal or the flesh of their own kills after the meat begins to sour.

Somewhat on the order of grizzlies, cougars have a long, circuitous route which they cover within an eleven-day period. Such a circle may be from ten to fifteen miles in diameter.

The cats like rimrock country adjacent to huge canyons and gorges, in arid regions where, of course, deer are plentiful. They dislike humid climates but will nevertheless stay in drier portions of such areas if the region contains deer. Such areas as the Kaibab, Grand Canyon, and Arizona's Mogollon Rim country are noted cougar regions.

Cougars do most of their hunting by night and bed down in the high, sunny, rimrock crags by day. Because of their nocturnal hunting habits, and their habit of bedding-down during the day in such inaccessible places, man seldom sees a wild cougar until it has been coursed by dogs and treed.

The only successful hunting method is to arrange with a professional cougar hunter who has suitable dogs, then camp in cat country and let the dogs do most of the work.

The work of a cougar dog in unraveling scent is an amazing thing to witness. Good lion dogs are very rare. On an average only one out of two hundred dogs, regardless of species, will turn out to be an exceptional cougar dog. But such a dog, well trained on cougars, is priceless. It will pick up cold scent, identify the faint scent as to species, determine the direction of the cold spoor, refuse to chase deer, bobcats, bear, or small game whose fresher tracks cross the cold lion spoor, and unravel the cat's tracks for five to eight hours.

Good breeds for cougar dogs are Black-And-Tan, Walker, Plott, Redbone, and Blue-Tick hounds. But the exceptional cougar dog is as apt to come from one species as another. The animal must love to hunt. It must have the quality of tenacity, of never giving up. It must possess a wonderfully keen nose. It must also thoroughly hate cats, and hate lions and their smell enough to give up all other game smell for the scent of the "big tom."

Training a hound begins early. Often domestic cats are bought and turned loose ahead of the young dogs in simulated cat country. The dogs are encouraged to pick up the scent (a natural impulse in most hounds), give chase, tree the little feline and, if possible, kill it.

Cougar hounds are especially trained for hunting the big cats. This dog has thirty cougars to her credit.

Young dogs are trained in company with experienced cougar dogs. Once one breaks from the trail onto scent which the older dogs determine is not lion scent, it is punished severely. Deer country is cougar country, and the hardest job of the lion hunter is to break his dogs from running deer.

The most severe punishment is given dogs that run on the scent or sight of deer. After they return each time, they are beaten, hung by the neck with a lariat until nearly choked to death, and cussed with a language that would make an old salt embarrassed. Currently, "shocking collars" are being used to cure dogs that chase deer, bobcat, or bear. These are collars fitted with high-voltage batteries and time switches. When a dog picks up a deer scent and wants to run it, the owner sets the switch and lets the animal run. Several minutes later, and after the dog has the full deer scent in its nostrils, the collar gives it a shock that knocks it half off its feet. This electric current continues for several seconds and will repeat at intervals. A few such doses sends the hound looking for relief from its master.

Saddle horses or riding mules are used in cougar hunting with dogs. The dog pack, averaging anywhere from two to six dogs, follows its owner at heel and behind the horses until camp is well behind and a likely area is found. Except in snow, cougar sign is invisible. Moreover, good cougar country is fairly brushy with such predominant foliage as scrub oak, cypress, cedar, "alligator" juniper, pine, manzanita, and blackjack oak.

It would seem to the novice hunter that in such an area, one place to begin hunting would be as good as another. The professional cougar hunter, however, looks for three things: high trails, high passes between creak damages, and scratchings in the ground. These scratchings are made by a cougar pulling a small pile of dirt and pine needles into a mound. This mound resembles in size the pile of dirt that would be made by the toe of a hunter's boot if he dug one deep scoopful and moved it 6 inches. Only males scratch. Females and kittens won't, though the females may be the reason any adult tom is in that area. The freshness of the scratching can be determined by its moistness. A cougar invariably will pull the dirt and needles in the opposite direction from which it is traveling.

Cougar hunters like to pick up a track made during the previous night. If the scratchings and the interest of the dogs indicate this degree of freshness, then the chase is on. While it is true that good lion dogs will pick up scent much older—often as old as three days—the possibility of treeing the cougar is not good unless an overnight track is worked.

In any dog pack, one veteran hound which won't "open up" on anything except cougars is always used. From the sudden baying of this animal, its extent of interest in the scent, and general behavior, the course of the cougar and its whereabouts are estimated. Young dogs may "trail backwards" for a distance, but will come back and accept the experience of the veteran dog.

The cougar leaves a staggered line of tracks, with the toe pads of each paw set in a curved row in front of the large heel pad.

Where a cougar will go is anybody's guess. He may head straight up a peak, then descend in a parallel course to the bottom again. He may head up or down, sideways, or a combination of all three.

The dogs unravel the old scent, track by track, as it meanders up canyons, over rimrock, and across brushy basins. Good lion dogs bay while trailing, but oddly enough the distant sound of their baying doesn't bother the cat. Often the lion will lie undisturbed until the dogs are within a hundred yards or so—then race off with the hounds in hot pursuit.

The hunters follow the dogs as they trail the quarry. There is no more rough, bruising horseback riding on earth than following a dog pack on the scent of a cougar in rough country.

When close to the dogs, in slow trailing over rocks, the riders (often they are walkers, dragging mounts up steep, unnegotiable areas, or skidding them on their haunches off bluffs as steep as a cow's face) catch their breath for the more rapid going in places of faster trailing.

When cougars are hunted in snow the chances of success are increased. Almost any hunting hound can follow cougar tracks in snow. The real criterion of a cougar hound is what it can do in hot country, on rocky terrain, and with a cold trail.

Wind, hot sun, and rocky areas are the enemies of a cougar trail. Wind will blow the scent from a trail after an hour or so. Hot sunshine will dry out the moisture and all the scent. And a little-known characteristic of a cougar is that, in areas of hard footing, the scent glands in his footpads will close up and leave no smell whatever. In rocky areas, such as old dry washes, the trail can only be found by casting about, then cutting it where the cougar has left the hard footing and his scent glands have begun to work again. Often dogs will lick the rocks, trying to pick up faint scent.

Eventually, with luck, the cougar is started. Once it bounces out in front of dogs, a cougar is apt to run only a quarter mile or so before treeing. Usually in the dog pack, along with the veteran trailer, is a dog that is fast on treeing. The dogs bay differently when they tree a cougar than when on the trail, and the treed cat and dogs are found by this sound.

Occasionally *two* cougars are started in the same area—perhaps a female and kitten. In such instances, the dogs usually split up, tree both cats, and must subsequently be found by their owner. Many a veteran dog has left the pack to tree a second cougar, has become lost from the hunters' hearing, and has stayed with the treed cat up to two or three days. Often only thirst or starvation will cause a loyal dog to give up.

Most dog owners feed the hounds all they can eat of the fresh cougar meat at the site of any kill. This is not only a reward and a savings in costly dog food, but it encourages any hound to stay with a treed lion until the owner arrives.

A treed cougar will usually stay put until the hunters come up. Sometimes a treed cougar, depending upon the distance it has been run, its anticipated chances for escape, and the general type of country, will spring from a tree 40 to 50 feet up, then race off and have to be treed again by the dogs. A cougar nervously walking a high limb as the hunters come up is almost sure to jump.

Weapons for dispatching treed cougars vary. Some hunters use a .38 Special or .357 Magnum handgun. One Salmon River hunter used a sawed-off .22-caliber clip repeater rifle, whacked down to resemble a horse pistol. It would be illegal now, but did account for many a cougar. Another Arizona hunter prefers a standard .22 automatic pistol shooting long-rifle hollow-points. He shoots the cougar, often after some judicious climbing, from a position directly in front, exactly into the sticking spot. This allows the puny bullet to enter the chest and pierce the heart, and he simply waits for the animal to bleed and topple.

Another preferred cougar gun is a .30/30 carbine with open sights. This carries flat and handy in a saddle scabbard and is entirely adequate. Tree lions may be killed with bow-and-arrow, though most dog-pack owners advise against it. A wounded cougar can easily cripple and kill valuable dogs. There is one instance on record where a treed tom cougar took seven different broadheads before finally giving up the ghost.

JAGUAR.   Jaguar hunting is a rapidly growing sport among well-heeled hunters. The jaguar is found in Mexico and Central America, and is run by hounds much the same as the cougar. In fact, some jaguar hunters of the Southwest take their cougar dogs to Mexico during the winter.

A jaguar hunt is normally financed by a hunter who wants the big cat for a special trophy. The location of individual animals is usually learned from Mexican natives—often because of the cat's depredations against stock.

There are other smaller predators. But since they do not prey on big game, and often overlap into the varmint classification as well, they are not considered here.

20

Small Game— Pests and Varmints

A GENERATION AGO, the sport of "varminting" was in its infancy. Shooting crows, chucks, and jack rabbits was considered kids' stuff in many parts of the country and usually was done with .22 rimfire rifles. In the West, especially, a man would have been considered a sissy if he shot such small game for sport.

Two developments changed all that. First was the growing hunting pressure on big game with the ratio of hunters to animals becoming increasingly top-heavy. More dramatic was the development in the mid-thirties of high-intensity, centerfire .22 cartridges shooting jacketed bullets at the unheard-of speeds of 2,000 to 2,600 foot-seconds velocity. The .22 Hornet was a landmark and turning-point in this development.

Since that time, the sport of varminting has grown into a national institution. Today we have cartridges, rifles, scopes, and riflemen capable of laying 'em into a chuck at 400 yards; a whole army of varmint hunters; and more powder burned in the sport than in most other forms of shooting.

It is difficult to define either a "pest" or a "varmint." In some areas an animal which is a real pest to one segment of the economy would possess great virtues to another. In other areas, sheer numbers change the status of a bird or beast from that of an innocent little creature to names unfit to print. Lastly, the line of demarcation between varmints and predators is often extremely thin, even nonexistent.

For the purposes of this book, the more commonly accepted pests and varmints will be considered.

Western ground squirrels, which destroy crops and irrigation ditches, are generally hunted with rifles shooting .22 rimfire cartridges.

GROUND SQUIRRELS. One of the smallest pests is the western ground squirrel, closely allied to the prairie dog found in the Great Plains regions. These rodents breed and live in colonies, eat grain from farmlands, cause leaks in irrigation ditches and sinkholes in farmlands, and destroy high big-game ranges through their burrowing.

The small squirrels are widely spread and offer sport to many shooters. The common rifle used for shooting them is the .22 rimfire. High-speed, hollow-point bullets will *pop* them adequately, and many a youngster gets his first rifle training on this species.

In areas where experienced riflemen find little else to shoot, ground squirrels are shot at longer ranges with the recent WMR .22 cartridge, the newer 5-mm Remington Rim Fire Magnum cartridge, or even the larger cartridges suited to chucks. Archers, too, get in their practice for big game on the lowly rodent, using flu-flu arrows, or blunts made by capping arrow shafts with empty .38 pistol brass. Another form of sport rapidly growing in the West and Southwest is the shooting of ground squirrels with handguns. The "magnum" pistol shooter, like the archer, gets his practice for big game and at the same time improves his reloads and special game loads.

219

Shooting jack rabbits in the snow, the author wears white coveralls and assumes a steady position.

JACK RABBITS. The blacktailed jack rabbit is another pest of the West. It multiplies faster than an adding machine, inhabits desert and sagebrush areas, and often eats ranchers out of any profit. In many areas, jacks will girdle the bark off young orchards, graze alfalfa and grain lands into nothing, and, at night and in droves, will eat stacked hay until the stacks topple over.

Jack rabbits are wonderful quarries for the serious varminter, though they are very cyclic. Some years their numbers dwindle to virtually nothing; then within a cycle of approximately every seven years they multiply to hordes.

The .22 rimfire long-rifle hollow-point bullet, used in a repeating rifle, has long been the standard jack-rabbit outfit. During the settlement of the West, jacks were numerous enough so that a larger cartridge was hardly needed. Not over a decade ago, in some desert regions of the West, a good shot could go into the desert, on foot, and shoot up to a hundred jacks in a day, using no other outfit. Winter jack rabbits were that concentrated.

The past few years, intense pressure has diminished the jack's numbers. The pests have been mass-poisoned, shot, and slaughtered in community rabbit drives. Such virtual warfare has thinned the rabbit numbers and made the remaining animals wilder, ideal targets for the serious varminter with the precision rifles and cartridges he uses for other pests. Standing shots on jacks range anywhere from 150 yards to as far as the shooter wants to bang away. Running jacks break cover at all distances, and the shooter who can take running jacks with any consistency—say two out of five—will have no trouble hitting running big game of any species.

The best way of going about a jack-rabbit hunt in western desert country is simply to inquire locally about the pests' whereabouts—then go and shoot.

A cartridge that is rapidly replacing the humble .22 rimfire for serious jack-rabbit shooting is the .22 Magnum Rimfire, which sends a 40-grain jacketed bullet at 2,000 foot-seconds. This is the "poor man's varmint cartridge" and gives the beginning varminter an adequate load without the necessity of reloading. This cartridge is fine on jacks and similar pests to approximately 150 yards.

A similar rimfire cartridge of even more power is the new 5-mm Remington Rim Fire Magnum. This cartridge has a 38-grain bullet which moves along at 2,100 foot-seconds, making it the fastest rimfire cartridge ever developed. Like the .22 Winchester Magnum Rimfire, it is not adaptable to reloading.

The confirmed chuck hunter, of course, uses the same outfit on jacks as he uses on chucks. Good calibers include the .22 Hornet, .222

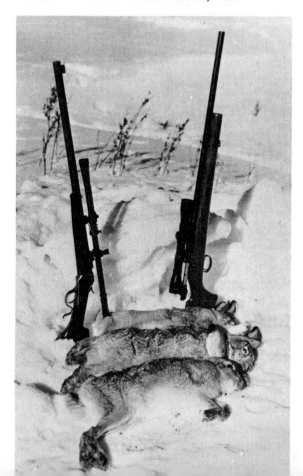

Heavy-barreled target rifles equipped with scopes will zero-in on fast-stepping jack rabbits.

Remington, .22/250, the .243, and the Remington 6 mm. Many hunters tune up these last two cartridges, frequently used on deer, for use on desert jacks.

A good scope of approximately 4 power is best for jack rabbits, and a sling is a necessity both for carrying the rifle and steadying it when shooting. The sitting position (unless shooting running animals) is by far the best. It allows the hunter to see over the ubiquitous sagebrush and hold a steady aim.

COTTONTAIL AND SNOWSHOE RABBITS. Cottontail rabbits are hunted in two ways. One is with a small-calibered rifle or handgun such as the .22 rimfire, and stalking the edible little animals along brushy dikes, in sagebrush, on rocky bluffs and in swampy areas. Unlike jack rabbits, the cottontail will usually run a short distance, then stop—often on the brink of its hole. This makes for short-range shooting at a stationary target. For this reason, and because of its fine eating qualities, head shots at cottontails are all many hunters will take.

The second way of hunting cottontails is with a small hunting dog such as the beagle. The dog flushes the rabbit from bushy terrain, and the zig-zag race is on. The hunter tries to shoot the animal as the dog drives it past him. Often two or more hunters will hunt cottontails together, to double the chances of a hunter being in the course of the running rabbit. A choice weapon is a 20-gauge shotgun with modified choke.

Snowshoe rabbits are found in the more northern timber areas, and have many of the characteristics of the smaller cottontail. They will hop a short distance, then sit up. They are hunted much as cottontails are, often in conjunction with a species of big game, as meat for the pot.

CHUCKS. The chuck, both the eastern woodchuck and its western counterpart, the rockchuck, is the favorite quarry of the varmint hunter. Chuck hunting has become a nationwide sport, and at least one national organization of chuck hunters has been formed.

Many serious and far-seeing chuck hunters will not shoot the first adult breeding animals which emerge from hibernation, but wait until well after the young animals come from their dens, and then shoot only a portion of the colony. Since the chuck is considered a pest and is given no protection, the fraternity of chuck shooters have to take such conservation measures in their own interests in many places. Otherwise they would soon be out of anything to shoot.

Chucks feed heavily on alfalfa and other hay and grain crops. They den adjacent to such feed when it is available, but the rockchuck is often found in rocky bluff country, and among the lava outcrops of desert lands

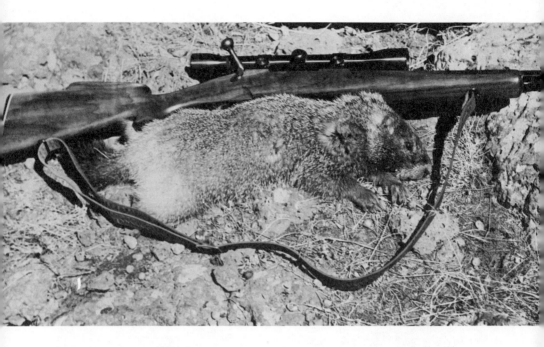

Winchester Model 70 in .243 caliber, with custom Fajen stock and Weaver
6-power scope, accounted for this big rockchuck.

far removed from agricultural. Heavy hunting pressure, drought in desert
regions, grazing sheep bands and similar factors will cause chuck populations to move. But unless such pressures are too great, the colonies will
remain in the same general areas from year to year.

Chucks are generally wilder and more wary today than formerly, and
must be shot at longer ranges. The basic procedure is to locate the
animals, either by glassing likely country or by the presence of fresh dung
and tracks around den areas; then post oneself at a considerable distance
away, assume a prone position, and wait for the animal to appear from
the den or burrow. Many times it is possible to shoot several chucks from
a single position.

Often in the desert and hill country of the West, rockchucks are
located by driving a jeep or other suitable desert buggy through rough
country, and glassing rock heaps, lava upthrusts, and areas where outlying
dry farmlands meet sagebrush. Many times two or three avid rockchuck
hunters will buy and maintain some old clunker of a vehicle to be used
for nothing else. Usually the location of the good, remote chuck country
they locate and use from year to year is kept as secret as their sins.
Adequate chuck cartridges begin with the .22 WMR and the 5-mm
Remington Rim Fire Magnum. These two cartridges, in suitable rifles
and equipped with good scopes, are reasonably good chuck outfits up to

Fine varmint Cartridges (*left to right*): .222, .223, .224 Weaherby, .22/250, .225, .243, 6 mm, and .25/06.

around 150 yards. The other cartridges mentioned for use on jack rabbits are all fine ones for chucks. The tendency today is to shoot chucks at longer ranges, and many shooters self-impose a limit of 200 yards under which they refuse to shoot at a chuck.

For such reasons, plus the fact that they double well on deer, the newer high-intensity 6-mm cartridges are gaining in favor and replacing many of the older stand-by .22 centerfires. Bullets of around 70 grains are used in the .243 and Remington 6-mm, and 100-grain bullets are loaded later for use on antelope and deer.

Three of the most popular and efficient chuck cartridges in use today are the .222 Remington, the .22/250 Remington and the .243 Winchester. The .222 is adequate up to around 225 yards; the .22/250 will take care of chucks to 300 yards, and the .243 will handle chucks regularly to 350 yards. The choice depends largely upon the intended ranges, the degree of human settlement in the chuck area, and whether the cartridge and rifle must double on large game.

FOXES. Foxes are considered fur-bearing animals in some regions, predators in others, and varmints in many sections. The two main species of foxes are the gray fox and the red fox. The ranges of the two species overlap, and in combination cover roughly 80 per cent of the entire United States, as well as the wooded portions of Canada as far north as the Arctic Circle and southward to the Mexican border. The red fox has three color phases—red, silver, and cross. Within the Arctic Circle there is another species of pure white fox, the Arctic fox. For the most part, foxes are woods-hills-forests creatures, but the Arctic fox lives in the treeless, ice-bound northland, subsisting largely upon the remains of seals killed by polar bears.

Foxes are notoriously cunning and have lived on domestic poultry at the periphery of outlying farms. Farmers have hunted them with dogs, trapped them and destroyed their dens and young.

Fox hunting as a sport began with the early history of our country, and coursing foxes with hounds became a pastime of the elite. Today the basic forms of fox hunting are hunting with dogs, trail watching, coursing with light aircraft after heavy snowfall, and driving.

The most productive way is to hunt with dogs, and the foxhound, one of America's oldest breeds, was developed for the purpose. A lone hunter may use a single hound, or several hunters may hunt as a group. Winter is the best season as fresh tracks may be easily picked up and the general location of the fox ascertained.

The general procedure is to let the dogs loose after having posted the hunters in the most strategic spots. The intention is to have the dogs chase the running fox past the hunters. In patches of woods and country where the quarry can be "contained," such a plan will work. Posted hunters use shotguns loaded with BB, Number 2, or Number 4 shot. Number 2 is "standard."

Brush and timber patches containing fox sign are similarly hunted by groups of hunters without dogs, or with possibly a single hound. The idea is to drive the animal from the protection of the woods and towards a posted hunter or hunters at the far end. This is comparable to driving whitetail deer.

Trail watching for foxes in midwinter is a cold sport, but an animal may occasionally be taken by the patient hunter who can view a large area of sign-infested country from his single position. For such hunting, and where the ranges may vary greatly, a sniping rifle similar to the one used for chucks and coyotes is the best weapon.

In less wooded country such as the Dakotas, winter-flying for foxes is becoming a popular sport. As with coyote coursing, the best time is after a fresh snowfall. The pilot pushes the animal from sparse cover with a low-flying plane, and the gunner shoots the fleeing animal as it runs ahead. A repeating or automatic shotgun is the standard weapon for this. The high cost of this type of fox hunting is somewhat offset by the payment of bounties on foxes in the regions hunted.

Recently, varmint calling has mushroomed as a sport. With the aid of a varmint call, drawing foxes up to a concealed and camouflaged hunter is a thrilling form of hunting.

SKUNKS. Another pest-predator is the common skunk, a small animal about 2 feet long with a bushy tail. The skunk is black with white stripes along the back and has white patches on its face and the tip of its tail. It can be detected by its foul odor alone, which hangs on the air almost everywhere it goes. This awesome odor is, of course, the skunk's defense against other animals and man, and few other creatures will have anything to do with it.

A skunk lives on large insects, mice and gophers, and small frogs. It also likes young birds, poultry, and game-bird eggs. It lives in wooded and swamp areas, and is often found around brushy fence lines and in or around old abandoned buildings. The animal is found in almost all of Canada and the United States. It is seen mostly at dusk and is a nocturnal hunter.

Skunks are killed by hunters with the weapon they happen to have—usually a shotgun or .22 rifle. One's main concern in any contact with a skunk is to give it plenty of room. The malodorous, acrid fluid which it expels is horrible, and may strangle and blind a person if he gets any in his face.

WOLVERINES. A larger pest resembling the skunk, but actually of the weasel family, is the wolverine, often called the "glutton" and other more colorful names.

This animal weighs approximately 30 pounds, is dark-brown in color, and except for its short legs, looks like a small bear. Pound for pound there is no more tenacious fighter on the continent, and an adult wolverine will drive many a larger animal from its kill. Its fight with any opponent is to the death. It inhabits most of the wooded country in Canada and Alaska.

Trappers, especially, hate the wolverine. In the North, trapper's caches are located at intervals of about ten miles on the trap route. These caches, often built upon three or four sawed-off trees growing close together, and consisting of a platform and boxlike hut on top, are stocked with food and equipment during summer months. Often small log cabins, dug into the ground, chinked with moss, and sod-roofed are used for the bunk and heavier camp equipment. As he travels along his winter trap line, the trapper plans on an overnight stay at each cabin and cache. A wolverine that gets into such a cache ruins it. The beast eats all the edible stuff it can gorge, then fouls the remainder with its own excreta and odor.

The wolverine hunts largely at night, is one of the hardest animals to trap, and is seldom seen by dude hunters. The animal's one virtue is that its fur won't freeze into ice under human breath in extremely cold temperatures and is therefore especially desirable for use as the ruff on parkas. In many modern down parkas meant for arctic use, a combination of wolf and wolverine fur is used, due to the relative scarcity of wolverine fur.

BADGERS. Badgers are considered pests in some western areas because they dig holes in agricultural and range lands. Badger holes are especially dangerous to horseback riders. If a horse, moving at a fast gait, steps in one, it usually breaks a leg. Many a rider has been thrown and sometimes crippled due to an unseen badger hole.

Badgers are stockily built, gray with a white stripe down the back, sharp-nosed, short-tailed, and weigh from 15 to 20 pounds. They are great fighters and will give any fighting dog a bad time. Many a youngster has tried to dig a badger from a hole, only to find that a badger in soft earth can dig faster than he can shovel.

About the only reason for a hunter to shoot a badger would be for the fine belly hairs so useful in tying trout flies.

PORCUPINES. The porcupine is a squat, quill-studded member of the rodent family weighing around 30 pounds. It lives on vegetation, preferring the bark and twigs of trees, It has earned the name of pest mainly through its habit of girdling the bark from stands of valuable coniferous timber and causing them to die. One porcupine can cause a serious economic loss.

For many years porky was given legal protection. It was considered the only edible creature which a lost hunter could kill with a club. This notion has gradually died out, and currently in any timber country a porcupine is shot on sight as a conservation measure.

Another reason for the porcupine's pest status is that it embeds its quills in the nose and face of hunting dogs. These quills are barbed like a fishhook and work deeper into the flesh until removed. Dogs love to bite porcupines and seem never to learn from the experience. The best way to remove quills is to hold the dog down and pull the barbs with hognosed pliers.

Due to its waddling movement and slow gait, a porcupine can be approached closely. Contrary to the belief of many, it cannot "throw" its quills, but sticks them into an enemy by lashing out with its tail.

A handgun is a suitable weapon for killing a porcupine. Only head shots should be taken; a porky is hard to kill with body shots.

227

MAGPIES. One of the smallest, smartest, hardest to hit, and most ubiquitous varmints is the common magpie. This black and white bird weighs only a few ounces, but will reach 18 inches in length including the long black tail. It is widely spread over big-game country, has the keenest vision and will come out of nowhere to any game-kill or offal. The bird feasts on carrion and cackles the news of any carcass to other woods scavengers.

In settled country magpies are found around domestic stock, along fencerows and in such foliage as willow patches and cottonwood groves.

This skinny little pinto predator is very gun-wise. One will sit on a fence post as a car drives slowly along a country road, but the second the car stops it will fly leisurely away. A person may wander about a field and magpies will sit within short range; but if the person carries a gun the birds will fly off. And if a half-dozen birds are working about a feed lot on a ranch, one shot will send them flying to the protection of trees where they will stay concealed high in the branches, often for an hour or more, before returning.

The magpie's biggest claim to the title of pest comes from its destruction of the eggs of pheasants and other game birds.

Two methods will often net the varminter a magpie or two. One is to conceal himself within sniping-rifle range of an old game-kill or animal carcass, and shoot an occasional bird as it comes in to peck or lights on a post nearby. Any precision chuck rifle is suitable.

The other method is to stalk through heavy growths of willows or cottonwoods where magpies are and shoot them flying overhead or sitting in the trees. A sporting gun for such hunting is either a double-barrel or repeater shotgun shooting 3-inch .410-gauge load of fine shot such as No. 7½.

CROWS. The crow is the most sought-after winged target of the varmint hunter. Like the magpie, the crow is a cunning and wise old bird with a built-in suspicion of man. There are four subspecies of crows, which together have a range covering most of the continent.

Crows are black (both sexes), weigh up to a pound and are identified by their guttural *caw-caw*-ing sound, which can be heard for up to a mile.

The pest has earned man's hatred because it destroys corn, one of the basic crops, and game-bird eggs. The fact that crows are among the best scavengers is usually overlooked because of this.

Like some other birds, the crow migrates southward during the winter and many head back northward with spring. The best chance for the varminter is to catch the flocks on these group-pilgrimages and do the bulk of his crow shooting during these seasons.

OWLS. The owl is a natural enemy of the crow, and one form of crow-hunting is based on the fact. A stuffed owl is placed on a post in a crow area; the hunter conceals himself within shotgun or rifle range nearby; then he uses an artificial call to attract the flock's attention. He does his shooting while the crows fight the stuffed owl. Live owl decoys are far more effective.

Another method is simply to locate a large crow flock, conceal oneself in camouflage clothing either in natural-appearing blinds or in sparse foliage, then call the birds into range on an artificial crow call. Crow decoys are often used in this method, and it is comparable to calling ducks into a stool of decoys.

EAGLES. The black desert, or golden, eagle was long considered a pest in the West. The great bird, which often attains a wingspread of 7 feet, killed antelope fawns and wild sheep lambs. The black eagle's numbers have diminished, however, and since the huge bird also kills innumerable rodents, it is no longer designated as a pest. Congress, in 1940, gave year-round protection to the bald eagle. In 1963 this protection was broadened to include the black eagle.

21

How to Dress and Skin Game

THE TREND IN big-game hunting today is to hunt for sport and trophies rather than for meat. This is contrary to the practice of fifty years ago when hunters shot for the skillet, chose the youngest and females of the species, and heaved the antlers of the males into the brush on the premise that "horns don't make good soup."

However, many men believe there is no better steak on earth than one from a wild ram, and the meat of elk, deer, moose, caribou, and antelope is similarly good if properly cared for. The taste of meat depends, of course, on the age of the animal, its physical condition, and general tensile strength. But in a basic way, the quality of wild meat depends on what the hunter does in the first half hour after it is downed.

MAKE SURE OF THE KILL. First, you should ascertain that fallen game is dead before beginning to carve it. A definite sight picture as the bullet was shot, how the beast reacted, and the position it assumed upon falling all help determine this. Neck-shot game falls instantly and hardly moves or quivers after hitting the earth. So does a brain-shot animal. A heart-shot animal often springs high into the air, or violently forward, usually jerking its forelegs upward under its chest. Occasionally one runs rapidly, giving little indication of a heart hit, so long as it can hold its breath, then topples over. A gut-shot animal humps up and sometimes bites at the wound. Bear especially do this, and I've seen bull caribou do it.

The position in which game falls helps to indicate whether or not it is dead. An animal that falls in a sprawled position, or rolls downhill and then lies sprawled, is usually dead upon the hunter's arrival. If its ears lie in flopped position, with mouth open and legs at loose angles, it is probably dead.

A beast that falls suddenly, or goes gradually down after a fast run, and lands in a bunched-up position with head erect and eyes alert is not dead. Neither is a beast whose head is upright and flat against the earth with the ears laid back. In the case of a carnivore, it is likely just waiting to jump the hunter once he gets in range. The rifle should be kept ready.

One of the best ways to determine whether an animal is dead is to approach it from above and pelt it in the ribs with rocks or chunks of timber. If dead, the animal will simply wobble with the rock's impact. If alive, it will generally spring up or give other indication.

Wounded game is best dispatched with a brain or neck shot unless the cape-and-antlers are to be used as a trophy. Then a heart shot is best. Never cut the throat of a trophy animal.

Pictures should be taken immediately before the beast's eyes glaze over, or before it stiffens up and begins to look like an old salt mackerel.

DRESSING THE ANIMAL. Several things will cause game meat to become tainted: body heat, blood coagulating between muscular tissues, contact with the musk glands or with the sebaceous glands, contact between flesh and intestinal fluid or body excreta. A quick, clean job of dressing the animal and cooling it rapidly will prevent tainting.

The best knife for this purpose should have a thin blade, very sharp, about 4 inches in length. Possibly the best type of knife available is a folding sheath knife. This is just like a huge two-bladed pocketknife, 5 inches long overall, and with two 4-inch blades, one thin, one heavy.

Before starting to dress the animal, decide if the headgear is to be saved as a trophy. If so, any cuts must be made so that the trophy will remain uninjured.

Once the question of a possible trophy is settled, the actual dressing is begun. This is basically the same regardless of game species, with minor differences to be considered later. Let's follow the step-by-step procedure with the most common species, deer.

First, the animal should be placed on its back, head uphill if possible. The less the carcass is moved, the better, since moving tends to spread blood into the tissues and scatter fluid from shot-punctured organs.

The carcass may be anchored on its back, either by tying the legs outward to trees or brush, or propped up by pushing lengths of wood or rocks under the lower side along the ribs.

The next step is to remove the musk glands on both sides of the metatarsal bones below the hocks. These glands appear as puffed areas of uncombed hair and are filled with a musky green fluid which will taint meat if allowed to touch it. In removing these, use only a finger and thumb to pinch and pull out the glands, while running a sharp knife under, taking all hide to the bone. Throw the glands away from the carcass and wipe or wash the hands before touching any meat. These glands occur in both does and bucks.

The testicles of bucks are removed next. Tie a length of string or a strip torn from a clean handkerchief solidly around the penis. This prevents urine from flowing. Tie a length of string around the anus, after this organ is cut around with a knife as deep as possible (without cutting the colon). This prevents excretion from the intestines from touching the meat when later moving the carcass. With does, the genitals and anus are tied similarly.

The abdominal incision is best begun by lifting the belly meat as high as possible with one hand, and a small downward cut started with the other, just ahead of the pelvis bone. This lifts the flesh away from the intestines so that they are not cut—a thing to be carefully avoided.

With the incision started, run two fingers of one hand, in forked position, under the abdominal flesh and over the intestines, pointed forward, and continue the incision through the belly meat by cutting between the two fingers with the knife point. Doing this separates the intestines and the belly meat, and prevents cutting into the intestines.

With trophy animals the abdominal incision should never be cut farther forward than the point of the sternum at the rear edge of the rib cage. With meat animals, especially the larger ones, it is often best (to promote a rapid cooling of the carcass) to cut all the way up through the ribs to the throat, opening the carcass its entire length from the anal vent.

With the beast's head uphill, the intestines have a tendency now to sag backward in the abdominal cavity, and the diaphragm may be reached. This is severed all around, largely by holding the stomach away with one hand, and cutting with the other. The diaphragm should be cut as near to the ribs as possible, each side in turn, until the back is reached.

At this point, in deer-sized game, it is now possible to reach inside the thorax past the lungs and grasp the animal's gullet and windpipe. These are pulled vigorously backward, gaining as much of their length as possible; then with the other hand cut the windpipe and gullet off as far forward as possible.

With the windpipe and gullet severed, it is possible (with one hand still holding them) to strip out the entire innards all the way back to the colon by a vigorous pull backward toward the rear of the carcass. Occasionally this will have to be helped with a judicious cutting of the tissues holding these organs against the back.

The colon is then cut all around, at the forward edge of the pelvis, and as deeply back as possible. If a small ax is available, the pelvis may be split all the way through, carefully stopping before chopping downward into the colon. If not, the colon may be pulled forward and free anyway, if it has been cut around from both sides of the pelvic bone, fore and aft. Often this cutting is helped by pulling free with the fingers the threadlike tissues holding this organ in place. In any event, sufficient cutting around the colon should be done so that it may be pulled out intact, with no danger of pulling it apart and spilling the contents.

The heart and liver, if not shot, are then removed from the offal, and the remains dragged off some distance. This is important as these remains later help to attract predatory birds away from the hung carcass.

Next, with bucks, the cape-and-antlers are removed. To do this, the skin is *never* cut by splitting the hide along the underside of the neck, or by cutting the beast's head off. This ruins the cape and is the bane of every taxidermist.

Instead, the carcass is carefully rolled over onto its side and a single cut made from a point just on top of the shoulders, or withers, up the center line of the back of the neck to 2 inches back of the antlers. Next, beginning again at the withers, a cut through the skin is made down towards the animal's chest and as far back as the center line of the shoulders on each side. These opposing cuts are brought together well back under the chest to a point well behind the brisket.

These are the only cuts necessary to save the cape; and by allowing that much hide (all of it forward of the three-way cut), the taxidermist can make a full shoulder mount without any seams showing in the finished trophy. The seam sewing up the skin at the back of the neck doesn't show in a finished mount when viewed from the lower side in normal wall position.

With these cuts made, the neck skin is carefully skinned away until the junction of the head and neck is reached. There, at the last joint behind the skull, the head is cut and twisted free, leaving the head integral with the cape.

If the animal is not to be saved for a trophy, the abdominal incision may be continued forward all the way to the throat. Too, the rib cage may be further split all the way, along the sternum. This greatly eases the chore of removing the lungs, gullet, and windpipe. If an ax isn't available, the entire rib cage may be split with the heavy blade of the knife. This is done by standing spraddle-legged over the carcass, facing the neck, using both hands on the husky knife, and lifting quickly upward after the blade has been inserted beneath each rib end in turn.

This cutting of the rib ends is not done precisely in the center of the sternum, but just to one side. At this point alongside the breastbone there is an immovable joint which permits such cutting. A similar splitting of the pelvic bone is also possible with a heavy sheath knife; the

233

HOW TO DRESS
AND SKIN A DEER

First step in dressing a deer is to cut off the musk glands, which look like tufts of hair on both sides of hind legs.

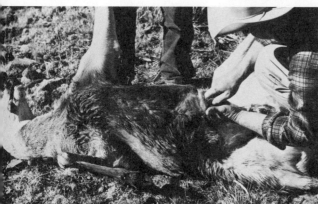

Begin the abdominal incision at the pelvis bone. Fingers of one hand reach inside belly flesh while knife hand cuts forward with sharp side of blade up.

After the animal is dressed it is laid belly-side down for a few minutes to drain blood from the abdominal cavity.

To remove only the cape-and-antlers, cut along white lines. Shoulder cuts continue beneath the animal and come together behind the brisket.

Skin hind legs at the hocks, sever the joints, and leave the legs and hoofs intact.

Hang the deer from the hocks and complete the job by rolling the hair side of the hide under and skinning downward.

After deer have been skinned, enclose the carcasses in cotton meat bags to protect them from flies and predators.

blade is simply pounded through, a half-inch longitudinally at a time, by hammering the back of the blade with a chunk of wood or rock. I've even watched men split the pelvis of a deer with a folding sheath knife, but not with *my* knife.

With the insides removed, the body cavity is wiped as free of blood as possible with the hands, available grass, pine boughs, or cheesecloth brought along for the purpose.

Dressing out a game animal immediately gets rid of a big percentage of the body heat and greatly facilitates removal of the remainder by exposing greater areas of body surfaces.

HANGING THE CARCASS. The next important step is to get the carcass immediately off the ground. With deer-size game this usually means hanging the carcass from a tree. Often in the case of trophy bucks, especially in cool weather, the cape-and-antlers are not removed from the carcass until the animal has cooled out—for convenience in getting it to camp. Care must be used in such cases to speed up the cooling-out process, since the heavy hair of trophy bucks, plus only a small abdominal opening, tend to insulate the body heat inside.

Partly for this reason, bucks are best hung by the antlers. This keeps the unopened part higher off the ground, allowing the body cavity to drain better and shed rain or snow.

Deer meat meant for immediate skinning should be hung by a gambrel run through the thin skin at the hock joints. Slit the hide in the hind legs along its forward edge from hoofs past hocks (and similarly along the knees in the front legs); skin out the hide around each of the hock and knee joints; break and sever the legs at these points, leaving the leg bones right *in the hide*; then complete the skinning. The finished job will leave the carcass free of hide and legs.

IMPROVISED HOISTS. There are several ways for the lone hunter to get his deer off the ground. One method, in hill country, is to skid the dressed carcass downhill, head first, to an available tree. Then, with the heels uphill, the head is tied as high up the tree as possible. With that done, the heels are moved around the tree to its downhill side. Where the steepness of the hill is not acute enough to permit complete hanging, the hams are propped away from the tree trunk and off the ground.

A better way is to carry a tiny block-and-tackle in the rucksack or on the packboard. This can be homemade from two 2-wheel awning pulleys and 30 feet of nylon rope. This gives a ratio of 3 to 1 and can hoist any deer off the ground. One pulley is tied on a tree, the other to the game.

Another method is especially useful in jackpine country and requires only a length of rope and a pole, say, 12 feet long. Three feet from the butt end of this pole, tie a length of rope, or better, doubled rope. Tie another length of the rope to the pole's butt and the longest length to the small end. The rope tied 3 feet from the butt is tied as high up a tree—to a limb or around the bole—as possible; the butt rope is tied to the deer's antlers, pulling the butt end as far down as possible, and allowing the small end of the pole to rise upward. The rope tied to the smaller end of the pole is pulled all the way down and tied to the trunk, raising the deer off the ground.

A big buck also may be lifted with some rope and three 7-foot poles sharpened on the butt ends, and tied together with several half hitches at their tops to form a tripod. The tops are laid over the deer's head, with the poles pointing outward like the spokes of a wheel. The deer's head or antlers is tied short to the tops. Next, the deer is lifted as high as possible, so that the pointed butt ends of the poles will dig into the ground. Each pole in succession is raised a foot or so, and its butt end again dug sharply into the earth. But alternating on the poles, and keeping the whole arrangement even, the deer is finally hoisted up under a nearly upright tripod.

The "Spanish windlass" is another device for lifting a heavy animal. First a gambrel (length of sapling or pole) is shoved through cuts made between tendon and bone at the hock joints of the deer so it protrudes on either side. A 2-foot length is about right. Next take a length of rope just long enough so that, when both ends are tied to a heavy tree limb, the loop formed in the bottom will just reach the gambrel when it is lifted as high as possible. An 18-inch green stick approximately 2 inches in diameter is run into the lower loop of the rope, just *under* the gambrel. This forms a lever, with the gambrel as the fulcrum. By twisting the stick around and around the gambrel, as it itself revolves, the "winch" cranks up the beast to sufficient height. The lever must be lashed to the rope or the limb once the deer is hoisted.

The last way of getting a carcass off the ground if nothing better is available, is to drape it over an available blowdown, brush heap, or rock pile, and insert a stick to hold the abdominal cavity open.

Hanging the carcass overnight, or for several nights, completes the cooling process. The meat is then placed in clean cotton bags taken along for the purpose and hauled home to cold storage. In hot weather, when cooled game can't immediately be transported home, it should be unwrapped and hung in the open air at night and wrapped in canvas and hung off the ground in the shade during the day.

With larger species, the carcass must always be opened up completely from pelvis to throat (necessitating chopping it with an ax at the pelvic

237

Utilizing the lever principle, a hunter can hoist his deer with only a 12-foot pole and a length of rope tied to a tree limb. The rope is secured to the tree trunk when the deer is off the ground.

A lone hunter can hoist a deer on a pole tripod. Antlers are lashed to top of spread poles (*above*), then each pole is raised a little at a time until deer is off the ground.

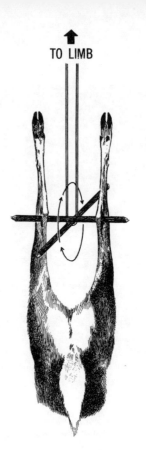

TO LIMB

Two short strong poles and a length of rope can be converted into a Spanish windlass to hock-hang a deer.

bone and the sternum) after the cape has been removed. This speeds up cooling. With elk, the gullet must be removed soon after the beast is killed, as it sours first. Moose and caribou are handled similarly.

Such large species are usually quartered and hung in trees to cool. Wherever possible it is always best to skin out the meat and transport it in clean bags. Where there are no such bags and horse packing is necessary, the skin is usually left on the quarters to protect them.

SKINNING. The skinning of any animal, whether for meat or for pelage, is done in one of two ways: either the animal is skinned "open" or it is "cased."

To open-skin an animal, two basic cuts are made. One reaches from the anal vent to the point of the chin. The other cut is in two parts. One cut goes across the animal's chest from one forefoot to the opposing foot. The other part of this cut goes across from one hind foot to the root of the tail, and on across to the opposite hind foot. This cut is made just inside the thin hair of the pelage—that is, on such animals as bear, just forward of where the thick hair of the pelt along the hind legs meets the thinner "belly" hair. These leg cuts end below the knee and hock joints (unless the feet and legs are to be saved for any special reason such as making a gun rack) where each leg is girdled and the skin peeled away.

240

With furred game such as bears, the leg cuts go all the way to the feet. Each foot is then carefully skinned (after girdling the soft pad) to the final toe joint. The claws are left integral with the hide for mounting into rugs. Mountain goats are skinned on each leg down to the hoof, which is severed at the last joint, and the hoofs left attached to the hide.

Smaller furred animals such as foxes and coyotes are skinned "cased." This means that the skinned hide resembles an envelope or case, and is achieved without any cuts being made up the belly line or down the front legs.

To do this, the feet are first girdled at "ankle" height, unless they are to be saved for any reason. Next, a single cut is made from the girdling on one hind foot to the root of the tail, and across the opposite hind leg to the foot. All skinning from there is done by peeling and skinning the hide down over the animal's head, with the hide rolling hair side in.

The tail bone is *not* cut off at its root. Neither is the hide cut across the tail at its back, or top. Instead, the tail must be left attached to the hide and the tail bone removed. This is accomplished by skinning around the root of the tail, up the animal's back, and up the tail bone itself, until a space large enough to insert your toe is made. Next, a pair of pliers with the jaws semi-opened is placed around the tail root. With the toe holding down the carcass and hide at the back of the tail, and a good solid pull made against the folded hide of the tail with the pliers, the entire tail bone will "strip" out in one slick movement.

Where pliers aren't available, a length of willow or sapling, split through the center and the flat halves placed over the tail bone like the bread of a sandwich, then pulled against the hair and hide of the tail, will do the job.

With that done, the hide is simply skinned away over the entire animal. The front legs are skinned without any further cutting—the legs being pulled from the doubled hide. Especial care must be used at the ears, eyes, and nostrils. The ears are cut off flush with the cranium. The eye skin comes off after carefully cutting the conjunctiva (thin skin holding the lids), and the entire snout cut off where the septum between the nostrils joins the skull and left integral with the hide.

With antelope, the hair must never be allowed to touch the flesh or it will taint it. This can be accomplished by skinning the antelope while it is hung by the neck, and rolling the hair side of the pelt under in a roll as one skins. Or, if in the usually flat terrain where nothing is available for hanging the carcass, the animal can be propped flat on its back over a piece of canvas or clean cloth brought along for the purpose. Then it is skinned completely on one side, all the way to the spine, tipped a bit and the other side skinned out, and then the entire carcass carefully lifted off the skin, and placed in a clean cotton "deer sack." Here, too, care must be used to make sure no hair touches the meat.

241

BONING OUT THE MEAT. With the largest species and in remote areas with limited transportation, it is possible to bone out the meat and leave all the bony skeleton. This is occasionally useful, too, for an animal which has been badly shot up.

First, the beast is skinned out. Next the ham is disconnected, cut off at the hock, and boned. The shoulder is similarly cut off on either side. Then, with sort of a filleting procedure the entire strip of the back meat is cut away from the spine, neck to tail, on each side of the animal. It is then peeled down the ribs as far as the ends of the loin and chop cuts reach; then it is cut away and carried in as a strip of boned meat the full length of the animal on each side.

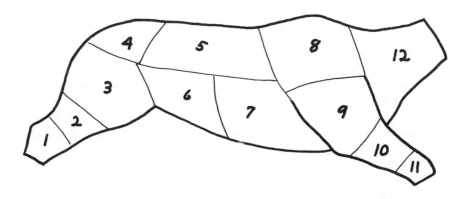

Various cuts in a meat animal: **(1)** hock bone, throw away; **(2)** shank, for stew; **(3)** round, for steaks; **(4)** rump, for roasts; **(5)** loin, for chops and steaks; **(6)** flank for stew or steaks; **(7)** ribs, for stew or roast; **(8)** shoulder, for roast or steaks; **(9)** knuckle, for roast; **(10)** shank, for stew or ground meat; **(11)** knee, for dog food; **(12)** neck, for ground meat.

The best way of doing this is to skin out one side, leave the carcass lying on its other side, and pare away all meat; then roll the carcass over and remove the meat from the opposite side in the same manner. For badly gutshot beasts, this may be done without even disemboweling the animal. Before resorting to this method, the hunter should exhaust every other, and even then make certain that it is legal in his state or area.

CARE OF SKINS AND HEADS. Special care must be used after removal of either pelts or skins to prevent subsequent "slipping" of the hairs during taxidermy. First, all meat should be pared away from the hide or pelt. Fat should be pared away from bearskins. With trophy capes, the head should be completely skinned out at camp, all flesh removed from all portions, the ear cartilages taken out, and the cape aired and heavily salted. The only delicate part is the removal of the ear cartilages. This is accomplished by folding the ear forward as one works, and separating the *rear* skin of the ear all the way to the ear's edges and tip. The remaining white gristly cartilage, which gives the ear its shape, may be left with the skin, and the front portion of skin, on the ear's forward side, need not be skinned out. No skin cuts are made.

Taxidermists use a pointed stick, anchored solidly, to help in doing this work. The ear is shoved downward over the stick as they work, exposing the junction of skin and cartilage. Most hunters simply use their fingers.

The basic way of keeping any hide or pelt in good shape before it can reach the taxidermist is to salt it *too much*. Use pailfuls, working the salt (common table salt is best) all over the flesh side of the pelt, clear to the edges, and thoroughly into every pocket, nostril, fold, and orifice.

With the pelt salted with a thick layer, it may be rolled into a compact bundle, with the legs folded inward onto the meat side so the brine won't run out. The bundle should never be laid on the ground or exposed to bright sunlight, but kept in cool shade on a box or canvas.

After it has been kept this way for a couple of days, it is wise to unroll the hide, check for folds and unsalted spots, then re-salt the entire pelt (the same salt which rolls off may be used again), and roll it up once more. In the normally cool weather of hunting season, this will insure its getting back to the home taxidermist in good shape.

This all sounds like work, which it is. But the care of meat, trophies, and pelts is the small price the big-game hunter pays for the thrills of the chase. After all, it can't be *all* fun.

II

HUNTING GAME BIRDS

22

Planning the Bird Hunt

G AME BIRDS are divided into two basic groups, the
upland birds and waterfowl. Upland birds are
affected by the same problems that disturb many game animals—
dwindling habitat, increasing hunter pressure, and such natural rigors as
severe winters, predation, and inadequate food supply. Several species of
native upland birds have proven amenable to transplants into decimated
areas, and into spot areas which previously had no bird populations.
Along with this, the singular success of foreign transplants, such as the
pheasant and chukar, should keep upland-bird hunting relatively good for
the foreseeable future.

Despite this, tomorrow's bird hunters will have to accept gradually
smaller bags and more restrictive seasons on public lands. These limitations will be offset, though, by the pleasures enjoyed away from the
growing problems of urban living. The bird hunter of the future will
probably derive more real benefit from a day's hunting, getting into the
fields and bagging a brace of birds, than did the market hunter of the
past who could kill birds by the bushel but who had no emotional need
for hunting.

When planning a hunt, it is advisable to consider species of secondary
importance to the main one desired. A disappointing pheasant hunt will
often be saved by a fine duck, goose, or grouse hunt in the same area. For
this reason, wise bird hunters check the legal open-season dates on all
game birds in the area they wish to hunt.

HUNTING AREAS. Broadly speaking, today's bird hunter will hunt
upon one or more of three classifications of land—public lands, private
lands, and hunting preserves.

247

In many regions, the public lands where much big-game hunting is done also contain upland game and waterfowl. Multiple use of these lands is permitted and encouraged by the Forest Service and allied agencies. No permission is necessary to hunt on these public lands so long as fire regulations, hunting laws, and local restrictions—such as no hunting around campgrounds—are observed. In checking areas and general regulations, the state hunting maps issued by license vendors are the best source of information. Local game wardens are another authoritative source.

Hunting on private lands is another matter. In a majority of states the upland birds are the sovereign property of the state but live on private property. The landowner controls the right to enter and hunt on that property, and the trespass laws are basically very strict though not always enforced. Waterfowl, of course, are federally owned (that is, by all the people), but the rights of the private landowner as regards hunting and trespass are the same as with upland birds.

The hunting fraternity may as well face the fact that the unfortunate situation of increasing posted lands, and the growing antagonism between hunters and property owners, was caused by hunters. The few have spoiled the privileges of the many by such thoughtless acts as leaving gates open, shooting too close to houses and stock, driving jeeps over planted lands, trampling over crops, breaking fences, and often such sheer acts of vandalism as shooting livestock, dogs, and poultry. Such trouble often comes from the city-dweller who seeks to get a year's shootin'-urge out of his system in one day, goes hog-wild, and forgets to treat others' property as his own.

The various state fish and game departments are constantly trying to better relations between hunters and landowners. This is often done by such cooperative movements as planting wind-breaking tree rows and hedges, as well as wildlife food and cover, on farmlands, in cooperation with the soil conservation movement. In return, benefitting farmers grant a reasonable amount of hunting privileges. As one example of how this helps, Idaho has since 1953 opened up more than 157,000 acres of new hunting lands in this way.

In planning for any hunt on private lands, the hunter should contact the landowner well in advance of the hunting season. This is best done by visiting him and politely asking for the privilege of hunting on his property. Often helping a busy farmer for a few minutes, or expressing genuine interest in him and his work, will open the doors to hunting privileges.

If personal contact can't be made, then a letter, and if possible the recommendation of a mutual friend, is next best. Any contact and arrangement should be made early. Often landowners want only a limited number of hunters on their lands and will deny all late comers.

Once the privilege to hunt is granted to any hunter, it is his responsibility to keep his hunting manners on a high level. The main consideration is, of course, to treat the landowner's property with the respect it deserves, and to keep all promises made to him in return for the privilege of hunting his lands. Such additional friendly gestures as habitually giving the landowner a bird from the hunt or a present for his wife help to make the hunter welcome and the privilege of hunting continuous.

Planning for a hunt on a shooting preserve should be done early, and reservations made well in advance. Currently, many of the best bird regions are those farthest removed from cities and suburbs, and the hunting is done out of small villages, resort areas, hunting lodges, and guest ranches. Overnight reservations during the hunting season may have to be made well in advance, and this should be included in the planning.

Another aspect of bird hunting which differs from big-game hunting is the use of dogs. One of the pleasures of any bird hunt is the use of a trained hunting dog. Not only is a dog often needed to get any game, but is vital to conservation in that the animal can recover cripples.

The number of trained hunting dogs is small compared to the number of hunters taking to the field. Buying, owning, feeding, and training a dog are all costly in time and money. Moreover, the mortality rate of dogs is high. For these reasons, not every hunter has a dog, much as he would like to own one. Often in planning a bird hunt it is possible to have the use of a dog through hunter partnerships in which a dog owner invites another hunter or two along.

CHECKING EQUIPMENT. Hunting gear receives hard use. Small mishaps and minor damage seem habitually to occur while equipment is in use, and since hunting equipment is in the field when any damage occurs, repairs ordinarily cannot be made right then. Usually, the average hunter brings the gear home with the firm resolve to fix it the next weekend. If he is fortunate enough to go hunting the next weekend, the item is often left somewhere around home and forgotten until needed again.

Wintertime is a good season to check all hunting equipment. The fall's hunts may be relived and future hunts anticipated through such pleasant chores as mending hunting coats, putting laces in hunting boots, patching rubber waders, or replacing that duck call someone borrowed and didn't return.

Winter is also a good season for gun repairs, alterations, and even replacement. Good gunsmiths are most rushed just prior to the opening day of game seasons and are often swamped with work. The best ones often won't promise delivery for months, and getting damaged guns into their hands early is smart planning. The same applies for changes in stocks, installation of choke devices, or custom stocking.

Guns are like any other commodity in that the prices, especially of used equipment, follow the seasonal demand and supply. The hunter who buys his shotgun well ahead of the hunting season, or during the winter months following the close of the hunting season, can usually get a better buy than the hunter who rushes in the last day or so, planks his money down and says, "I want a good shotgun."

Testing the Shotgun. Shotgun tubes, like people, are individualistic. No two barrels, given the same length, choke, and shell, will produce identical patterns at any given range. Due to minute manufacturing differences, variations in metal stress, variables in gun assembly, and similar factors, each shotgun is different.

The only way to learn about any gun is to test it with various loads and combinations of components. The usual way of patterning shotguns is to set up a target at 40 yards, fire the loads onto a paper target, then scribe a 30-inch circle around the thickest part of the entire pattern. The pellets within the circle are counted and their total number considered as a percentage of the total number of shot in the load.

This method works fine in theory but has shortcomings. First, the shooting is deliberate and with aimed shots much like rifle shooting. It may show what the gun will do if aimed perfectly at the target, but does not indicate whether the shooter, in fast wing shooting, shoots where he

Proper form with the shotgun should be acquired during practice shooting. Spread the legs comfortably and stand with the feet pointing at a 45-degree angle from the line of sight.

thinks he is pointing. Neither is the densest part of the pattern always in the center of the spread, nor does this way of patterning give any indication of shotgun fit.

A far more practical way of testing is to shoot at life-size targets in a way that simulates field shooting. First, a suitable backstop is needed—either a target-butt or a square frame set on legs in a field. One of the most inexpensive papers for targets is newsprint, which may be obtained cheaply in end rolls left over from newspaper printing. A damaged end roll usually contains enough paper for several targets, and can be obtained at any large newspaper plant. It comes in 30-inch width.

Targets may be either cut-out silhouettes made from building paper and pasted onto the target paper, or may be drawn in outline right on the newsprint. They need not be artistic, but should be the correct size and general contour of the species to be hunted.

Chinese pheasants average 3 feet in overall length. Bobwhite quail are from 8 to 10 inches in length. Ruffed grouse are 15 inches. A Canadian honker reaches 3 feet in body length and attains a wingspread of 6 feet. And a male redhead duck will average around 20 inches in length. In sketching these targets, it is best to have them in the flying position.

When firing at the targets, it is practical to duplicate field conditions as far as possible. The shooter should mark off 40 yards, or other distance

Testing the shotgun on paper targets will reveal flaws in stock fit. Gun here patterns to the left, indicating stock is too long. Charge is No. 6 shot at 40 yards, modified choke, 20 gauge.

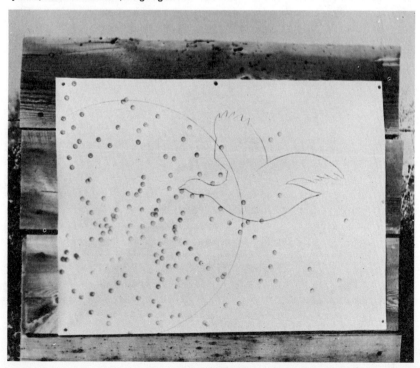

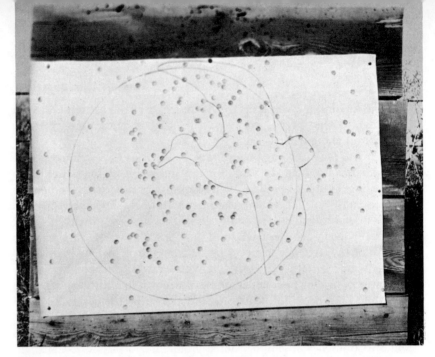

Better stock fit is indicated by greater density of shot charge on the bird. Charge is No. 6 shot at 50 yards, full choke, 12 gauge.

Low shot pattern suggests that comb of stock may be too low. Charge is No. 2 shot at 60 yards, 3-inch Magnum 12 gauge.

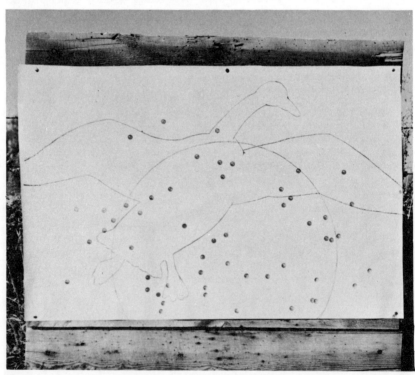

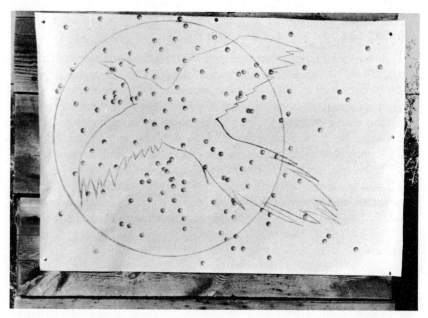

Dead center pattern means good stock fit. Charge is No. 4 shot at 40 yards, full choke, 12 gauge.

at which he wants to pattern, with a plainly visible mark. Then, after backing off some distance at a reasonable angle, he should begin walking towards the target and pretending not to see it until he approaches the distance mark. Once this mark is reached, the shooter should "discover" the paper bird; swing quickly up at it, and fire without deliberate aim.

To get an indication of what the gun does, numerous targets should be used, at varying distances, with the shooter approaching the target from different angles. The same kind of upper garments habitually worn in the field should be worn. One mistake of the beginning shotgunner is that he usually buys a shotgun while wearing city clothes, but uses the weapon while wearing bulky shooting coats or cold-weather garments. The fit is not the same.

While practice testing, fire a few rounds with the eyes shut. The approach to the target is made the same, and a good shooting stance quickly taken—an easy position with the feet at approximately 45-degree angle to the target. However, just before the gun is raised, the eyes are closed and the actual shooting is done quickly and from the remaining impression of where the target is. This particular type of practice is splendid for determining shotgun fit.

The targets may be read easier if the pellet holes are marked plainly with an ink pad and an eraser-tipped pencil. The eraser is inked on the pad, then pushed against each pellet hole, making a plainly visible mark.

A dozen or so targets shot in this manner will reveal much. It is true that the factor of lead, or forward allowance, must be disregarded in such static shooting. But the immediate purpose is to determine the gun's pattern and fit.

In this type of testing, the general evenness and uniformity of patterns may be learned. Again, one brand of shell or size of shot can be tested against another. Most beginners are surprised to find that often one brand of shells works best in one particular gun.

Next, the density of patterns at the outside shotgun ranges can be learned from a study of the punctured targets. Often a shooter will discover that he has been shooting too far for his gun's pattern at a given species. Or again, that he is using the wrong gauge of gun for his particular quarry.

If such testing is alternated between quiet and windy days, the gunner can see that wind affects shot charges by blowing them laterally. But more important, such testing brings to light whether the shooter's gun fits properly, and where the shot charge is actually going in relation to where the shooter *thinks* he is pointing.

Shotgun Fit. Often a shooter will learn in a half-dozen targets that he habitually shoots to the left. Or maybe he shoots right and higher than he thought, or under. If such a difference is constant, his problem is likely that the gun doesn't fit.

It is an unhappy fact that only a fraction of the total number of shooters can be well fitted by a shotgun of standard factory dimensions. It is a price we pay for mass production. The standard dimensions in factory shotguns are a length of pull of 14 inches; a drop at the comb of 1½ inches; a drop at the heel of 2½ inches; and a "pitch" of 2 to 3 inches depending upon barrel length.

These dimensions are meant to fit the "average" shooter and represent a fair compromise. Unfortunately, there is no average shooter. Shooters range from stocky, short-armed people to gangling, skinny types. Obviously the gun that fits one won't fit the other.

With the deliberate aim used in most rifle shooting, this isn't quite so serious a matter. Often in the time-lag between when game is sighted and when the shot is taken, the shooter can virtually make the rifle's dimensions fit *him*, and get the sights lined up. In wing shooting there usually isn't that much time, and unless the fit of the gun makes it point naturally at the target, the shooter will miss.

Stock dimensions on a shotgun can easily be altered to fit the individual shooter. And testing will bring the faults of fit to light.

The length of the stock should be such that when the butt is held in the crook of the arm, and the gun pointed vertically, the finger fits comfortably on the trigger. This should be checked with the same coat used when shooting. If the stock is too long, the shooter will shoot to the left. Or to put it another way, if the charges on the paper targets have consistently gone to the left, the stock is too long. Oppositely, if the shot charges have gone right, the stock is too short. If the charges consistently have printed high, the stock is too high on the comb. Oppositely, if the shot charges regularly have gone low, the comb is too low.

A good gunsmith can alter a stock to fit the individual shooter at nominal cost. Stocks can be sawed off and refinished if too long. Recoil pads can be attached to stocks that are too short. Combs are easily worked and refinished if too high, and can be built up and refinished if too low. Some firms will soften and bend the stock to overcome these last faults. Or a custom stock can be installed.

Improvement always comes when using a gun that fits, and there is also a magic "feel" about a well-fitting gun which adds materially to the shooter's confidence.

Wing Shooting Practice. For the beginner, any pre-season practice should be based on an understanding of the principle of lead. In wing shooting, one never shoots at a target, except in those rare instances when a bird is flying directly at or directly away from the shooter. Instead, the shotgunner must shoot where the moving game will be when his charge arrives. This involves a complex combination of angles and speeds.

A good way to understand the principle of leading is to go onto a baseball field and study the players. The fielder doesn't stand in his tracks and catch a fast ball headed somewhere else. He runs to where it will be and intercepts it. Or if the fielder is running, the thrower doesn't heave the baseball to where he is, but throws it to where he will be.

This applies not only to a ball moving in a horizontal plane, but moving in a vertical plane at the same time. Often an object's speed in one plane is vastly different from its speed in the other, which determines the necessary lead for each of the two directions. For example, a second-baseman to catch a hot line-drive headed several yards away from him might have to run 10 feet laterally, but only drop his glove from the original line-of-flight a matter of 18 inches.

A good stunt on a ball field for understanding shotgun lead is to have one person throw a ball much as a bird might fly, then have the "gunner" try to hit this flying ball with another ball. Practice must be done at short range, of course, since the "shot" ball won't be as fast as a shotgun charge. Throwing practice forward-passes with a football involves the same principle, and is helpful to a beginner. Or have a partner throw tin cans into the air and try to hit them with rocks. Later, if in an out-of-the-way area, practice on cans with the shotgun.

255

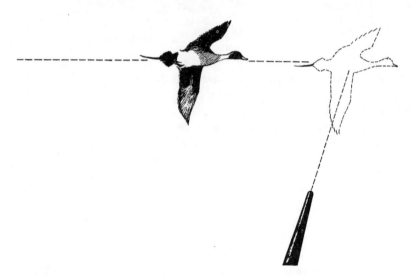

Two methods of leading a flying bird with the shotgun. With the sustained lead (*above*), the gunner swings ahead of, and at the same speed as, the bird and shoots when he feels his lead is right. With the fast swing (*below*), the gunner begins his swing behind the bird, swings faster than the bird, shoots when his lead is right, and follows through.

When a bird flushes from below and ahead of the hunter, he must lead above the target.

A low-flying overhead bird might seem like a dead-on hold. Actually, the hunter must shoot slightly under.

Hunter must shoot ahead of an overhead, incoming bird, even though his gun barrel will momentarily obscure the target.

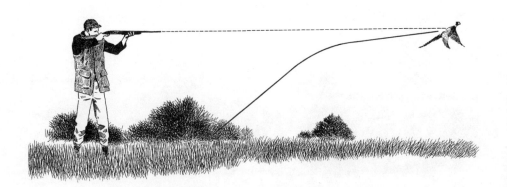

When a bird flushes in front of the hunter and flies straightaway, no lead is required. This is a true dead-on hold.

It is often advisable to have an experienced shotgun hunter stand directly behind the shooter and study his actions. Many times the veteran can tell the novice whether he shoots high or low, over or under, or whether he stops his follow-through on pulling the trigger. Again, shooting over water, either at ducks or thrown objects, will disclose errors of lead—the splashing of the water showing where the charge went.

For the strictly urban resident, pre-season practice is often difficult but not impossible. Even if he can't shoot clay targets, he can stand the gun in a corner, pick it up a few times a day, and swing at imaginary targets, or moving targets outside his window. This will help make all motions with the gun come naturally and improve his field shooting.

If the hunter can walk about a field devoid of game, but practice pointing and swinging at imaginary birds, mentally pulling the trigger and endeavoring to continue his follow-through, he will find that this dry practice pays off.

23

Clothing and
Equipment

THERE ARE A few basic differences between the
clothing best suited to big-game hunting and the
best clothing for upland bird and waterfowl hunting. Generally speaking,
the bird hunter will be hunting at lower altitudes and in warmer weather
than the big-game hunter. Bird hunting is generally done early in the fall
before snow, usually in brushy terrain. Thus the bird hunter's clothing
may be lighter than the big-game hunter's. It doesn't have to be brightly
colored for safety purposes but it should be more snag-resistant.

The clothing for waterfowl hunting, too, serves a different purpose
than the big-game hunter's duds. Waterfowl hunting involves water. And
around lakes, rivers, and ponds there are always winds, and often howling
gales. The air moved by these currents is always high in humidity, more
so than inland. The waterfowl hunter spends a greater proportion of his
hunting time just sitting, or in some cramped and immobile position,
than the upland-bird or big-game hunter, and often he must remain
concealed.

Such conditions dictate the type of clothes for the duck and goose
hunter. They must be drab in coloration to match the foliage in which
he conceals himself. They must protect him from moisture and water,
yet keep him from becoming cold and clammy inside his outer shell.

CLOTHING FOR THE UPLANDER. Cotton underwear is generally
best, either the shirt-and-shorts worn at home or the two-piece thermal-
knit cotton garment for slightly cooler weather. Seldom in upland-bird
hunting is it necessary to wear woolen underwear. The hunter's movement usually keeps him warm, and during midday or any other time he

becomes too warm it is always easier to shed an outer garment than to stop and change underwear. For this reason, as well as for the fact that wool itches next to the skin, the upland-bird hunter is generally more comfortable if he starts the day in underwear a bit too light or skimpy than in a garment too warm or heavy. An extra shirt, on cool mornings, will make up any difference and is easily removed later.

Shirts, similarly, should be chosen according to the weather and climate. A hard-finished cotton shirt of gingham or denim is fine. A lightweight woolen shirt is adequate for cooler days.

Pants for upland-bird hunting are very important. Since briars, brush, snags, thistles, burrs, and similar pants-grabbers are common, hunting pants should be tough but lightweight. Pants should also be relatively loose-fitting for ease in walking and climbing over fences and other obstructions. Because weeds and burrs always find their way into boot tops and socks, pants should be tapered, or snug-fitting at the ankles, to go inside the boot tops. Bird-hunting pants are best without cuffs. Heavy-cotton duck, denim, and similar fabrics of hard finish and tough weave make fine bird-hunting pants. For the worst briars, cotton pants faced on the leg fronts with Naugahyde are better and are entirely snagproof. Marsh brown or tan is one of the best colors.

Footwear. The bird hunter's boots are most important. They must be light, must keep weeds and burrs from his feet and ankles, must be comfortable and keep his feet free from galling during long hours of walking and hot hunting, and relatively waterproof.

A long-time favorite in a hunting boot which fills all these needs is a leather boot, 8 or 10 inches high, with light, water-resistant uppers, moccasin-type bottoms, light cord or crepe soles. Such boots come in two types, insulated and regular. For most bird hunting, the insulated boots are not necessary.

Any boot meant for hunting should be ample in size to accommodate the natural swelling of the feet during prolonged walking. New boots should be broken in before the hunt. One way of quickly breaking in a hunting boot is to put it on, wade quickly in water so that the leather just begins to become wet, then wear the boot continuously until it dries.

Lightweight socks of cotton or wool are adequate for upland-bird hunting. Their reasonable bulk, plus the "breathing" of unwaterproofed boots, will prevent excessive perspiration from wetting the feet. Care should be taken that socks used for hunting should fit perfectly. Few things are more annoying than a sock that gradually works down inside a hunting boot.

Headgear and Gloves. Most bird hunters use the standard peaked hunting cap made of canvas or heavy duck. Some prefer a light leather cap such as is used in big-game hunting. Any waterproof cap should have ventilation eyelets, and an adequate peak for a sunshade.

Many westerners like felt hats, either fedora or ten-gallon type, for upland-bird hunting. Hats provide better sunshades for the eyes than caps, and better run-off for water in case of sudden rain. The single fault of hats is that they are harder to push through heavy brush.

Hunting gloves are generally unnecessary for upland-bird hunting. Where they are needed, a light, tight-fitting glove is best, or one of the special shooting gloves having provision for the quick removal of the trigger finger.

Suitable clothing for the upland-bird hunter: woolen shirt, light jacket, strap-on bird bag, and Naugahyde-faced pants.

Coats. The coat for upland-bird hunting should be water repellent but not waterproof. Perspiration caused from waterproof clothing produces a miserable clamminess. The coat should be amply large to go over adequate underclothing and to allow freedom of movement when shooting. The shoulders should be wide and not bind.

A hunting coat must provide space for bagged birds, a supply of heavy shells, and such incidentals as a small camera, dog whistles, and lunch. Most hunting coats have a variety of large pockets in the front and a bigger game pocket in the back.

Over the many years, and the combined experience of numerous hunters, a more or less standard hunting coat for upland-game hunting has evolved. This garment, though a compromise, does the overall job fairly well. It is a coat made of cotton duck having the necessary hard finish and tight weave. Collar and wristbands are of softer corduroy, for comfort at these points and for appearance. The garment is cut full across the shoulders for its chest dimension and has provision for weight distribution. This consists of a half-dozen or more large pockets on the front and a waterproof game pocket in the back. The load may be shifted between front and rear pockets as game is collected. Often a recoil pad is built into the shoulder.

A lighter version is a sleeveless vest made on the same order. In some vests, individual loopholes are sewn in series around the front to hold shotgun shells. The vest is a fine hunting coat for milder days when a full coat would cause too much perspiration.

Instead of the game pocket, many hunters use a neck-loop for lugging dead birds from the belt, but this is usually unwieldy.

CLOTHING FOR THE WATERFOWLER. The seasons for waterfowl hunting vary more than for upland-bird hunting, often running from October well into winter. This is especially true for split seasons. Because of the wide range of temperatures and weather, clothes for waterfowl hunting are more varied.

As in some forms of big-game hunting, the waterfowler's clothes must perform three functions. They must keep him warm. They must keep him waterproof. And in order to do both, clothing must provide some means of soaking up perspiration or allow it to evaporate. An additional function of the waterfowler's clothes is that they must camouflage him.

Underwear. Temperature control, for the duck and goose hunter, is best regulated at his hide; and the most important garment for keeping him warm is his underwear. By a correct choice of underwear, the waterfowl hunter can be comfortable regardless of weather or season.

For the cool days of October, in most areas, a two-piece suit of woolen underwear is perhaps the best. If the weather is exceptionally balmy—making it poor waterfowl weather—the thermal-knit cotton underwear, either in two-piece or union-suit type will often suffice.

As the cold weather increases, heavy woolen underwear is needed with the necessary bulk and insulation both to absorb any perspiration and to keep the coldness of outer garments away from the skin. Two-piece garments may be used one piece without the other, regulating the warmth to the type of outer coat and pants.

For hunting in late season, often in snow and blizzard conditions, the newer insulated underwear is a boon to the waterfowler. The two popular materials in this garment are Dacron and down. Dacron is easier to launder, with down having a bit better insulation. Insulated underwear allows the hunter to keep down excessive bulk in outer clothing, which is an aid to better shooting.

With suitable underwear, geared to the expected weather and seasonal conditions, outer clothing can be chosen. Usually a light wool shirt and woolen pants will take care of most weather and temperature conditions. In balmy weather even cotton shirts and pants may do, especially during midday.

Socks. Special care should be taken in selecting socks. In bad weather the heaviest woolen socks or several pairs of lighter woolen socks will keep the feet warm inside rubber boots or waders. In freezing weather insulated socks, or small boots made of the same down or Dacron construction as insulated underwear, are better. They may be worn as is or over light socks. For older hunters with poor circulation, electric socks will keep the tootsies warm when other socks fail. These are battery-operated from cells carried at the belt and can be turned on or off like an electric blanket.

Gloves and Headgear. Gloves and mitts for keeping the hands warm range in material from cotton jersey gloves, to fur-lined driving gloves and down-filled mitts. A useful mitt for most temperatures is a new plastic-outside, insulated-inside mitt with knitted wristbands and an opening in the palm of the hand for getting the trigger finger out in a hurry. This opening is closed by a flap when not in use.

For extremely cold weather, pocket hand-warmers are excellent. These little metal gadgets cost only two or three dollars, slip handily into a side pocket, and will operate all day on a filling of cigarette-lighter fluid or even white lantern gasoline. One in each side pocket will keep a goose hunter happy when others have to give up.

Caps for the waterfowler should be at least fairly waterproof. They are made of cotton duck, corduroy, and leather. A good cap for mild wet weather is a rubber Northwester hat such as sailors use. For the coldest weather, a down-insulated cap is warmest of all. Any cap for cold weather should be equipped with ear flaps.

Footwear. For pits, permanent blinds, and other places where deep wading is unnecessary, foam-rubber insulated rubber pacs 10 or 12 inches high are often sufficient and keep the feet warm over well-chosen socks.

The most common footwear for the waterfowler are hip-length rubber boots. These boots are useful in setting out decoys, launching and beaching boats, wading out to retrieve birds, or going to and from shallow-water blinds. Nothing though is colder than a gum-boot in frigid weather, unless amply insulated inside with adequate socks. Especially if they get wet inside.

For this reason, rubber boots should be amply large to accommodate heavy socks. Ankle-fitting rubber boots are more comfortable *if* they allow enough socks to be worn. For standard wide-ankle boots it is often necessary to take a pair of small webbed straps along. These, buckled snugly around the ankles, will keep the boots from pulling off when walking in deep water and mucky bottoms.

Waist waders such as fishermen use are often used in waterfowl hunting, either in going back and forth to shore blinds or for standing midstream in sparse concealment. They, too, should be amply large to prevent binding and splitting at the crotch when used over heavy clothing. Web straps around the ankles are often useful.

Coats. The coat for hunting waterfowl must serve several important functions. It must keep rain and snow out. It should have ample pockets for the inevitable small items. It must allow freedom of movement for good shooting. And the coat must keep out wind, not only from the upper part of the body, but from that vital area around the neck and face.

Some hunters use a hip-length sheepskin-lined coat with mouton-fur collar. The high collar is turned up against wind and cold, and a light raincoat is worn over the coat during rain or snow.

A better hunting coat is a hooded parka of a material suited to the cold. It should be waterproof and hip length so that no appreciable gap is left between coat and rubber boots.

Camouflage Suits. All hunting clothes should be chosen to conform in color as closely as possible to the expected surroundings. Marsh brown is the best all-round color for coats and caps. Brown-green boots are preferable to black rubber boots.

265

The new rubberized two-piece camouflage suits made especially for hunting are excellent. The mottled, green-brown design makes contour-identification impossible at any distance and blends the waterfowl hunter with his surroundings. Only the coat may be worn with waist waders.

In some of the northern country, late flights or a split hunting season may make it necessary for the waterfowl hunter to hunt in snow. Then a white costume is the best camouflage available.

Some hunters simply take a bed sheet, cut a hole in the middle for their head, and drape it over them. A 25-pound-size flour sack pulled or tied over the cap completes the outfit. Another style is a white cotton cape like a judge's robe sewed loosely at the sides with hood.

There are hazards in both types of white costumes, as a personal experience may indicate. A partner and I were hunting geese along a river in deep snow, concealed in snowbanks along shore, and whanging at the honkers as they passed up and down the stream. My partner's costume, conceived and executed within ten minutes after I had asked him to go along, was made of a bed sheet. My own was patterned after the cape design.

We had waited perhaps an hour when six honkers came down the river, and luckily we rolled a couple. One of them fell, only winged, into the middle of the river and immediately began swimming downstream. My partner let out a yell and started to lope out to midstream in pursuit. The river there was 2 feet deep, with mush-ice running and smoking fog and below zero temperature.

At this inauspicious moment, my partner discovered that his costume was too long. He repeatedly stepped on the sheet, tearing it into strips and ripping it half off him. But in a sprinting splash, with sheet strips flaying like banners behind him, he overtook that flapping gander.

I was of much less help. At the first stride I took riverward, I made a momentous discovery. While standing in the shore water, the white shroud had frozen all around, just water edge, in a 2-inch circle of ice. In truly masculine manner, I neglected to lift my skirts before take-off, and stepped on the frozen skirt-hem. I landed in the river with a greater splash by far than the gander.

Accessories. Other items for the waterfowl hunter include decoys, duck or goose call, and usually lunch for the day. Generally speaking, the more decoys the better. Hunting partners often combine their decoys, cutting down on the equipment of each. With regard to calls, it is always wise to know the right tune to play when decoying waterfowl. Unless the hunter knows from the "talk" of the wild birds which calls will attract them, he should learn the calls in advance, either from an experienced caller or from a phonograph record of authentic bird calls. A good idea is to tie any call to the hunting coat with a thong to prevent losing it overboard.

Lunches vary in elaborateness. For an all-day hunt, one of the very best containers is the two-bottle sandwich-box. The vacuum bottles may be filled with a quart each of something hot, and the entire kit fits together nicely in a case with carrying handle. Such a kit, used with a beverage cooler, makes an ideal lunch-carrying combination for the upland-bird hunter. Block-ice for cooling beverages can ordinarily be purchased en route, or the box may be filled with cube-ice from the home refrigerator. The kit and a small cooler will hold lunches for two or three hunters and is usually left at the vehicle till lunch time.

24

Guns and Loads

THERE ARE SIX types of shotguns; the basic differences are distinguished by the kind of action and number of barrels:

1. Double barrel
2. Slide, or pump, action
3. Autoloading
4. Over-under
5. Single-shot
6. Bolt action

In addition there are the multi-barreled guns consisting of a rifle and a shotgun barrel in combination, called "drillings" in England, and Paradox guns with a single tube capable of shooting either shot charges or a ball. These are rifled near the muzzle.

THE DOUBLE. In Britain and in the early days of American shooting, the double was considered the standard smoothbore. Its virtue was that in a single gun, having one fit, stock length, trigger-pull, and feel, the shooter had a choice of two degrees of choke and two quick shots.

The double is still preferred by many shooters. It comes in all standard gauges, in a variety of chokes, and in all grades from plain to fancy. Doubles begin at around $100 and run to several thousand dollars for custom-grade guns with gold and silver engraving.

SLIDE ACTION. The repeating slide-action shotgun took the fancy of American shooters around the turn of the century and has grown in popularity ever since. The Winchester Model 97 hammer shotgun was

Noble Model 420 double-barreled shotgun.

largely responsible and, until it was discontinued in 1957, was one of the most popular models ever built. Nearly one million were manufactured.

Advantages of a repeater were obvious. Up to a half-dozen shots were quickly available, in an era when birds were numerous and game bags liberal. More, the repeater utilized only a single trigger as opposed to the long-standard twin triggers of the double, and it had the advantage of a single sighting plane. Its lone disadvantage, compared with the double, was that only one degree of choke was available.

The popularity of the slide-action repeater has continued ever since. The basic change in the slide-action shotgun has been that it was made hammerless, for safety and appearance. It is hard to surpass a good slide-action shotgun for any kind of wing shooting.

Slide-action shotguns (*from top*): Winchester Model 12 Field, Remington Model 870AP, Ithaca Model 37.

AUTOLOADER.   The genius of the inventor John M. Browning was responsible for the self-loading, or automatic, shotgun. He modified the slide action by harnessing the kick, allowing the recoil of the gun to eject the empty shell and reload. Besides the autoloader sold under the Browning name, Browning patents were also sold and used by other manufacturers in the production of similar guns. By 1970, over two million Browning autoloaders had been sold to American sportsmen.

The biggest change since Browning's original auto has been the shift from a mechanically operated mechanism to a gas-operated action, accomplished in the fairly recent Winchester Model 50 self-loading shotgun.

A feature stressed in the sale of autoloading shotguns was its speed of fire. Actually, a good shotgun man could operate a slide-action repeater and get on target as fast as one could with the auto. The real advantage of the autoloader was that all thought of reloading could be disregarded in fast shooting, and that the use of recoil in operating the mechanism appreciably reduced that same recoil.

Autoloading shotguns: (*from top*) Browning Automatic-5, Remington Model 58ADL, Savage Model 775-SC.

Over-under shotguns: Browning Superposed (*top*), Italian-made Beretta Silver Snipe.

Self-loading shotguns in their original styles were not as streamlined along the sighting plane as repeaters. That is, the receiver, due to the straight back-thrust of the barrel-bolt, had to be high, the barrel somewhat lower, and a ramp front sight elevated to conform to the receiver's height. This fault was alleviated by using an elevated rib. However, many shooters claimed that the high-rising front sight, after a dip along the barrel, was a real advantage in pointing. Often larger sighting blocks were installed to augment the advantage. Later models of the self-loader have been made more streamlined in appearance, and resemble the slide-action, hammerless repeaters.

The original self-loaders, like the repeaters, were made to hold many shells; the autoloaders five. With dwindling waterfowl supplies, restrictions were made and both models were plugged to an overall capacity of no more than three shells in chamber-and-magazine. Today's self-loaders are built to that smaller capacity.

Current prices for slide-action shotguns begin around $125; prices for autoloaders start at $175. With either, one may go as high as he wishes, depending upon styles, engraving, and accessories.

OVER-UNDER. Interest in the over-under shotguns increased with the manufacture of a reasonably priced American over-under, and the federal restriction on waterfowl shooting requiring the shotgun to be limited to three shells. The over-under had the repeating shotgun's advantage of a single sighting plane; it had the double's advantage of two degrees of choke; and it now approached the auto and slide action's amount of firepower. Presently, there is a growing use of the over-under, both for upland-bird and waterfowl shooting. Most over-unders have single triggers. Prices for over-under shotguns begin at around $200 for the plainer models.

BOLT ACTION. Bolt-action shotguns are relatively inexpensive to manufacture, and were based on the popularity of military bolt-action rifles. They come in either clip or tube magazine, are ordinarily "rougher" in functioning than the slide-action and autoloading repeaters, but are worth their modest cost for the beginner, or the person who cannot afford a more expensive gun. Bolt-action repeating shotguns cost approximately $50.

Stevens Model 85 bolt-action shotgun.

SINGLE-SHOT. The single-shot, hammer type of shotgun is one of the least expensive, but is an ideal beginner's gun. His limitation to but one shot without reloading is often a blessing, both for safety reasons and to make him shoot better. Many of today's veteran scattergun artists started out as boys with such a single-shot, likely in "long Tom" barrel length.

Barrels in modern shotguns vary in length from 25 to 32 inches. The longest barrels are used mostly in waterfowl shooting. The biggest gauges ordinarily have the longest barrels, and the popular length is 28 or 30 inches for most field shooting. The longest tubes retain the shot-velocity a trifle better, but often this advantage is more than compensated for in the shorter barrels by virtue of their increased handiness.

CHOKES. A vital part of the shotgun is its choke—the constriction in bore size at the muzzle. A shotgun having no choke would be fit only for use as a riot gun. One with too much choke would funnel-and-spray its charge over a wide area and be similarly useless.

Chokes are of three types: standard boring, swage choke, and recess choke. In a standard boring, the constriction is begun 2 to 3 inches behind the muzzle. The bore proper is tapered slowly into a mild cone, or "lede," reducing the tube's inside diameter by a few thousandths of an inch. From the forward, smaller end of the lede to muzzle, the barrel is left untapered and of this smaller diameter. This final section may run in length anywhere from ½ inch to an inch or more, and is called the "parallel."

This system of boring was accidentally hit upon by the late Fred Kimble, one of the greatest shotgun artists of all time, while he was really trying to ream *all* the choke out of a barrel, and has never been improved upon.

Winchester Model 37 single-shot shotgun (*top*) and the Stevens Model 94 single-shot shotgun.

A swage choke is a simple constriction in barrel size put onto the muzzle end by cold-swaging the barrel to a smaller diameter. It is a make-shift, usually placed on inexpensive guns or sawed-off weapons.

The recessed choke is a mild, barrel-like shape bored into a barrel an inch or so behind the muzzle, with both the bore proper and the parallel left identical in diameter. Both a recessed choke and a swage choke are sometimes useful in salvaging a barrel which has been cut off at the muzzle end behind the choke. A far better way of helping the gun, however, is to install a choke device, as we'll come to.

The extent of choke in the barrel determines the spread or density of the pattern at a given range. Chokes range from full, improved-modified, modified, quarter choke, and improved cylinder, to straight cylinder. That is in theory. Actually these borings overlap; charges and patterns will vary from one brand of shell to another; and a straight-cylinder choke usually has *some* degree of constriction.

The criterion for a full-choke, 12-gauge shotgun is that it should put 70 per cent of the total number of pellets in a shot charge into a 30-inch circle at 40 yards. Many full-choke guns will do better than that, and some gun makers will guarantee a greater percentage.

Improved-modified choke is supposed to pattern 65 per cent; modified, 60 per cent; quarter choke, 50 per cent; improved cylinder, 45 per cent; and cylinder, 35 per cent.

273

In order to give the shooter having a single-barreled shotgun a variety of chokes, several variable-choke devices have been perfected. Some of the most popular are the Cutts Compensator, the Poly-Choke, and the Weaver. Savage and Mossberg currently build some models of their shotguns with integral choke devices.

Variable-choke devices are of two basic designs. One type has a series of ventilated slots or holes, plus individual tubes containing built-in degrees of choke, which may be interchanged. The other type, with or without the series of ventilated slots or holes, is based on the principle of a collet which can be screwed down by degrees onto separated or split ends of a tube, giving the desired constriction.

These devices are installed by threading the unit onto the threaded end of a barrel which has been cut off behind the original choke. In either type, almost any degree of choke may quickly be had, the range often including full-choke or extra full-choke. Their use converts the single gun into one of many uses. An added advantage of a ventilated choke device is that it reduces recoil.

Recently, Winchester developed an even simpler type of choke device for use at the muzzle of its single-barrel shotguns. This is a small knurled tube, having a certain degree of choke, which is screwed into the inside-threaded muzzle of the barrel. When in place, it is scarcely noticeable.

GAUGES. "Gauge" in shotguns is comparable to caliber in rifles, and in today's guns is limited to six—10, 12, 16, 20, 28, and 410. The gauge number is based on the number of round balls of pure lead it takes to make a pound. For example, it would take 12 balls the diameter of a 12-gauge shotgun barrel to make a pound. The 410 gauge is an exception and indicates that the bore is .410 caliber, or .410 of an inch in diameter. Following are the gauges and equivalent diameters:

10 gauge	.775 inch
12 gauge	.730 inch
16 gauge	.670 inch
20 gauge	.615 inch
28 gauge	.550 inch
410 bore	.410 inch

The controversy over which is the right shotgun gauge has raged for years and will continue to do so. Today, of all the gauges, the 12 gauge is most popular and will cover the widest range of field uses. The 20 gauge is second in popularity. The 16 gauge, which could be made to duplicate both these other gauges, has for some reason largely lost out. Likely it is

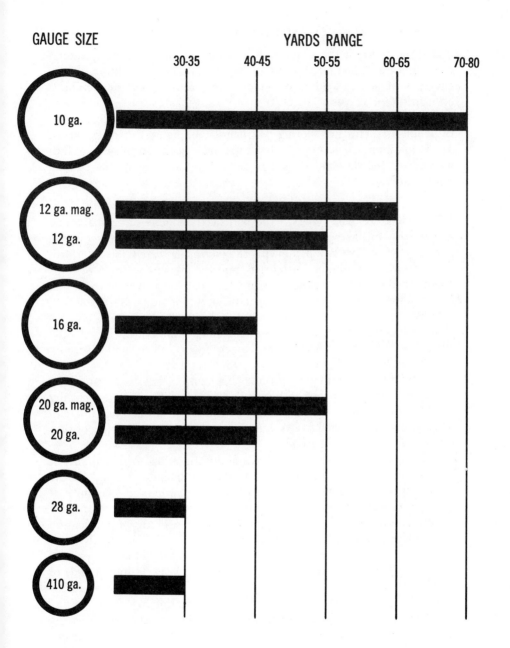

GAUGE SIZE

YARDS RANGE

30-35   40-45   50-55   60-65   70-80

10 ga.

12 ga. mag.

12 ga.

16 ga.

20 ga. mag.

20 ga.

28 ga.

410 ga.

Actual sizes of the six standard shotgun gauges, with the range at which
each is most effective.

due to the fact that the 20 gauge is handier, and in "magnum" loadings can duplicate almost anything the 12 gauge can do. In addition, the 20 gauge, with lighter loads, can serve more pleasantly on smaller birds ordinarily shot at closer ranges.

The new 3-inch magnum 20 gauge is another shotgun rapidly gaining in popularity. This new boring will handle the lightest 20-gauge loads, and in addition will accommodate all the loads of the 16 gauge as well as all loads of the standard 12 gauge. Some consider it to be the coming all-round shotgun.

SELECTING A SHOTGUN. Inexperienced shooters often make one of two basic mistakes in purchasing a new gun, or in changing from one gun to another. One group, knowing the increasing scarcity of waterfowl, the mushrooming number of hunters, and the growing wariness of birds conditioned to heavy hunting pressure, feel that the answer lies in a gun having longer range, tighter choke, and shooting more powerful loads.

Such a gun, however, used with the heaviest "big-bump" loads— those maximum for the gauge—does not automatically teach the difficult art of leading birds at their longer ranges; and the added severity of recoil usually starts, or aggravates, a flinching habit.

Consider the recoil impact of these "big-bump" loads: A 20-gauge gun weighing 7 pounds, if shot with its mildest load of 2¼ drams of powder and ⅞ ounce of shot, has only 15.7 foot-pounds of recoil. The same gun fired with a load boosted to 2¾ drams of powder and a full ounce of shot has 26.4 foot-pounds of recoil.

A 16-gauge gun weighing 7 pounds and using a load of 2½ drams of powder and 1 ounce of shot has but 19.6 foot-pounds of recoil. If the load is its near-maximum charge of 3 drams of powder and 1⅛ ounce of shot, recoil jumps to 31.4 foot-pounds.

Again, recoil in a 12 gauge using a charge of 3¼ drams of powder and 1¼ ounce of shot—a good average load—is only 26 foot-pounds in an 8-pound gun. But boost that charge to 3¾ drams powder and 1¼ ounce shot, and that same gun will kick to the tune of over 38 foot-pounds of recoil!

On the other side of the fence, often a man wanting to start his wife or son field shooting will buy the smallest gauge. He wants them to have a light, handy weapon which won't kick too hard. Also, such a puny gauge is thought to be more "sporting." But the owner finds that a gun with a tiny gauge instead of being sporting is often a bird-crippler, if it doesn't miss altogether. It takes far more skill to hit with the smaller pattern, and initial disappointment over constant missing results in discouragement.

Actually, both the tightly bored gun shooting the heaviest loads, and the smallest gauges, are weapons for the specialist. The beginner, and in fact a majority of upland-bird shooters, is far better off with a gun of reasonable choke, shooting loads of average power. The best all-round choke is modified.

For any bird shooting, there is little need for the average shooter to go below 20 gauge, or above 12 gauge. In bird hunting, the 28 gauge and the puny .410 bore are for the experienced shotgun artist who wants to impose self-limitations. The larger 10 gauge is needed only for pass shooting at waterfowl, and is likewise a gauge for the experienced shotgun hunter.

Shotgun weight can be a burdensome thing for the upland-bird hunter, and should be less than the one-twentieth of the hunter's weight suggested as maximum for the rifle. Twenty-gauge shotguns should run between 6¼ and 7 pounds for a maximum, and 12-gauges average from 7½ to 8 pounds at the outside, except for magnum versions.

As to shot sizes, type of load, and best choke for each bird species, the following recommendations are based on the experience of numerous observing hunters:

Game	Type of Load	Shot Size	Choke
Turkey	Heavy	BB, 2, 4	Full
Geese	Heavy	BB, 2, 4	Full
Ducks	Heavy	4, 5, 6	Full or Modified
Pheasants	Heavy	5, 6	Modified
Grouse	Medium	5, 6, 7½, 8	Modified or Improved Cylinder
Quail	Medium	7½, 8, 9	Modified or Improved Cylinder
Doves	Medium	6, 7½, 8	Modified
Woodcock	Medium	7½, 8, 9	Improved Cylinder
Rail	Medium	7½, 8, 9	Improved Cylinder

Before getting into the usable ranges of each gauge, it would be well to consider some of the physical properties of shot pellets, and some of the exterior ballistics of the more common shot charges.

Here is a table of the various shot sizes:

Size of Shot	Diameter in Inches	Pellets per Ounce
9	.08	585
8	.09	410
7½	.09½	350
6	.11	225
5	.12	170
4	.13	135
2	.15	90
BB	.18	50

The following exterior ballistics for three of the most popular shot sizes and for the four most useful gauges in bird hunting, were taken from information supplied by the Winchester Arms Company and relate to their most powerful Super Speed shells. Data for the most powerful Remington and Peters loads, and those of other brands, may be considered comparable:

Gauge	Shell Length	Drams Powder	Ounces Shot	Shot Size	Muzzle Vel (FPS)
10	2⅞	4¾	1⅝	BB, 2, 4	1330
12	2¾	3¾	1¼	2, 4, 6	1330
12	2¾ Mag	4	1½	2, 4, 6	1315
12	3 Mag	4	1⅜	2, 4, 6	1315
12	3 Mag	4¼	1⅝	2, 4, 6	1315
16	2⁹⁄₁₆	3	1⅛	2, 4, 6	1240
16	2¾	3¼	1⅛	2, 4, 6	1295
16	2¾ Mag	3½	1¼	2, 4, 6	1295
20	2¾	2¾	1	2, 4, 6	1220
20	2¾ Mag	3	1⅛	2, 4, 6	1220

At each of these five velocities, here is how each of the three shot sizes will perform in flight:

Shot Size	Muzzle Velocity	Velocity (FPS) 40 yds.	Pellet Energy 40 yds.	Drop in Inches 40 yds.
BB	1330	915	16.27	2.4
2	1330	860	7.98	2.6
4	1330	815	4.77	2.7
2	1315	855	7.86	2.6
4	1315	810	4.71	2.8
6	1315	760	2.47	3
2	1295	845	7.71	2.6
4	1295	800	4.62	2.8
6	1295	750	2.43	3.1
2	1240	820	7.28	2.8
4	1240	780	4.38	3
6	1240	730	2.30	3.3
2	1220	815	7.13	2.9
4	1220	775	4.29	3.1
6	1220	725	2.26	3.6

Less powerful loadings, in all gauges and in the type of medium-powered shells ordinarily used in upland-bird hunting, will show a corresponding decrease in velocities and energies.

These tables do not include all the shot sizes or gauges. They are, however, representative of the performance of high-speed shot pellets in flight.

A study of these tables will disclose several important facts to the beginning shotgunner. First, the larger pellets retain their velocity and energy proportionately far better at useful killing ranges than do the smaller shot. Secondly, in standard gauges the velocity of the charges increases proportionately to the increase in gauge. Lastly, the smaller gauges generally throw smaller shot charges. All three factors have a definite bearing on the useful killing range of a shotgun.

Pattern is likely the most limiting factor as to range. If, for example, it takes a certain large-sized shot to kill a species at long range, then the small gauge cannot contain in its load a sufficient number of pellets to make a dense enough pattern at that range. Or to put the matter another way, if it takes the velocity and energy of a large-sized shot to do the job at an extended range, then it also takes sufficient number of that shot to make a pattern dense enough to insure a kill.

Because each individual barrel determines to some extent what the pattern will be, even at identical ranges and with the same degree of choke, it is impossible to lay down hard rules as to shotgun range. However, some generalities will be useful to the beginner.

Broadly speaking, a 10-gauge shotgun is useful out to a limit of 70–80 yards. The 12-gauge 3-inch magnum has an overall range of 60–65 yards. The standard 12 gauge is considered to be a 50–55 yard gun. The 16 gauge has a useful range up to 45–50 yards, and the standard 20 gauge is basically a 40–45 yard gun. The new 20-gauge 3-inch magnum, handling everything from the light ⅞-ounce charge of the standard 20 to the heaviest 1¼-ounce load of the standard 12 gauge, becomes adequate to a range of 50–55 yards. The 28 gauge, and .410 bore using 3-inch shells, are usable on the smallest birds such as doves up to 30–35 yards.

It is true that kills are often made at ranges beyond these. However, the actual *measured* range of each is a considerable distance and farther than many a shooter suspects. Shooting at ranges beyond the capabilities of any gauge is but an invitation to the missing, and worse, crippling of game birds. Depending upon the toughness of the species, it takes from three to six pellet-hits to insure a clean kill—this number assuring that one or more will penetrate the vital organs.

Copper-plated shot is now available to the handloader, and recent tests indicate that this more expensive shot will give better results at longer ranges. Shot deformity is less than with black shot, hence there is improvement in both pattern and consistency.

Regardless of the gauge, the load, or the combination, the shooter is the most important element in good shotgun shooting. Only one thing will make a good shotgun hunter and that is intelligent practice, both "dry" and on game.

25

Dogs for
Upland Game
and Waterfowl

PART OF THE joy of bird hunting is the use and companionship of a good dog. A hunting dog will find birds where no hunter could, follow their scent into brush and foliage where no hunter would enjoy going, set or flush the birds at decent gun range before the hunter, then run down cripples and bring the dead game back to its master's hand. In the case of waterfowl, the good hunting dog will plunge into water icy cold enough to chill the hunter's ancestors, and retrieve downed birds which would otherwise be lost.

More thrilling even is the fact that a good hunting dog enjoys all this effort and gladly does it, often for little more than a word of appreciation from its master. And aside from the work a hunting dog does, the pleasure of its companionship is worth the price of ownership.

Hunting dogs are specialists and as such have been bred through many generations both to preserve and to accent certain desirable qualities. Individual strains have been developed for certain uses, and in many breeds a combination of useful traits has been bred in.

Dogs for use on birds may be divided into two broad groups—those for use on upland game and those adapted to waterfowl hunting. Some species may be used on both.

In the upland game division, dogs are further separated into those that "set" or "point" game, and those that only find, then flush birds. Those in the first group are, of course, the setters and pointers.

Beautiful and strong-willed, the Irish setter is a long-haired breed popular with many bird hunters. *Courtesy of David Michael Duffey.*

SETTERS AND POINTERS.   The English setter is the oldest bird dog used in America. These dogs are long-haired with wavy but not kinky hair, with thin feathering on the legs. Adults average around 60 pounds in weight, and stand approximately 2 feet tall. In color an English setter may vary from black, white, or tan, to a combination of liver and white, lemon and white, or black and white. This breed is considered a one-man dog and worships the owner who treats it kindly.

The Llewellin setter, named after its originator, is similar to the English setter. It often has English setter blood mixed in, and is usually blue-ticked in coloration.

The Irish setter is another beautiful breed and is characterized by its rich mahogany-red color, silky feathering, and strong will.

Gordon setters are comparatively rare today, and not too often used as field dogs. This breed, named after the Duke of Gordon, is black with tan markings, slightly smaller and more racy in appearance than the English setter, and is used more for show purposes than in the field.

The basic difference between the setter and the pointer is that the pointer is short-haired. This breed is English in development and rivals the setter for field use. Because of the pointer's short hair, it can take hot weather and does not pick up burrs like the setters do. Oppositely, it can't stand severe cold weather as well as long-haired dogs, or the beating a dog takes in heavy brush. Pointers love to hunt, are stronger willed than the setters and less easily offended. In color, pointers range from white and black, to white and liver, white and orange, and white and brown.

The stylish English pointer is an avid hunter. Here one retrieves a pheasant for his master.

A more recent pointer coming to the American scene is the German short-haired pointer. This is a hard-working breed, not as fast as the English pointer, but adaptable to pointing and retrieving both upland species and waterfowl. The German pointer is short-haired, as its name indicates, and relatively stocky. A large dog, it sometimes weighs as much as 70 pounds. It has a mild disposition but is a good scrapper. In color, German pointers range from solid liver to combinations of liver and white.

The German wirehaired pointer, a recent arrival, works well on both upland game and waterfowl. *Courtesy of David Michael Duffey.*

These are the main species of setters and pointers. Both classes are bred for intelligence, keen scent, stamina in the field, and tractability. Their common denominator is that upon smelling the hot scent of sitting birds, both will freeze into immobility. The sight of a statuesque animal, holding birds until he comes up, is one of the hunter's great thrills.

FLUSHERS. There are other dogs that neither point nor set birds, but which are most useful in hunting birds that won't hold for a dog but run ahead. Those breeds of dogs that find game, scare it up, and can be taught to retrieve dead birds, might well be called the "flushers."

One of the most popular of these is the cocker spaniel. This affectionate little species weighs from 20 to 30 pounds, is solid black, golden, or multicolored, and has a cheerful disposition, which makes it unexcelled as a pet. Cockers hunt both by body scent and trailing. Dogs that develop the habit of depending on the bird scent left in air currents are preferable. One of the desired traits of the cocker is that, because of its small size, it of necessity hunts slowly. This allows the hunter to keep up without too great an effort and within range of the game as it flushes.

The affectionate cocker spaniel is a fine flusher and retriever for upland game.

The springer spaniel, one of the best dogs for Chinese pheasants, is tops in heavy brush, swamplands. *Courtesy of David Michael Duffey.*

The springer spaniel is another fine hunting dog for upland game. It is larger than the cocker, often weighing up to 50 pounds and standing 20 inches high at the shoulder. The springer varies in color from black and white to liver and white. This breed is one of the best Chinese pheasant dogs imaginable. Where a setter or pointer will often break point in order to keep up with a skulking ringneck, the springer keeps right on after it until the bird flushes. Like the cocker, the springer hunts both by body scent and by trailing. The pheasant leaves both kinds of scent, and the springer's popularity in America followed closely the rise of the pheasant as a growing game-bird species. Due to the springer's larger size, it is a better worker in heavy brush and swamplands than the cocker.

The Brittany spaniel is another fine flushing dog, which might also have been included with the pointers and setters, since it has an instinct to point game. This spaniel is a short-tailed species reaching a shoulder height of 18 inches on an average, and runs in color to combinations of liver, white, and orange. This species ranges wider in field use than the springer or cocker, and is very adaptable to work on pheasants. The dog has a good disposition and makes a friendly hunting companion.

The Brittany spaniel, imported from France about thirty years ago, is both a flusher and a pointer. *Courtesy of Paradise Brittany Kennels.*

The Labrador retriever is another fine flusher of game birds, especially pheasants. As its name suggests, the Labrador was originally known for its use on waterfowl, but it adapts easily to upland hunting. This is a big, relatively short-haired dog, rather stockily built and usually pure black overall. Occasionally a Labrador will be pure tan or other solid color. This dog has a mild temperament, making it an ideal family dog.

The Chesapeake retriever, similarly, is noted for its work in retrieving waterfowl, but makes a good dog for flushing upland game. This dog, too, is large, reaching 70 pounds and over. The predominant colors are solid tan, brown, or straw color. Both the Labrador and the Chesapeake make good children's dogs as they have a patience and tolerance not found in many other species.

The Weimaraner is a late-comer to the American hunting scene but is an exceedingly popular breed. This is a large, short-haired dog, with males reaching as much as 80 pounds in weight. This German-originated breed is silver-gray to dark blue-gray, is highly intelligent, and most striking in appearance. It learns easily and has an instinct for pointing. Weimaraner owners are very careful not to allow the strain to become contaminated, and currently Weimaraners bring high prices.

These are the principal breeds of hunting dogs used for hunting upland game. As with any animals, both deliberate and accidental crossbreeding has been extensive. Sometimes hunters try to breed out unwanted traits and breed in others by crossing two definite breeds or bloodlines. More often, and especially in the more rural areas, crossbreeding comes about through the freedom given dogs.

As with lion dogs, the exceptional bird dog is apt to appear in any bloodline or within any breed. Dogs are individualistic, with varying degrees of hunting instinct and receptiveness to training. Because of this, mongrel dogs sometimes make fine hunting dogs, especially dogs born on ranches or farms which are used in hunting early. There is many an instance of some lowly mongrel pup whose sire was likely the best half-dozen dogs in the community becoming a real hunter on pheasants. Many a farm boy has been given a puppy of such democratic ancestry, has grown up with it, loved the animal, romped with it over the fields, and had a "scarer-upper" on pheasants worth its weight in biscuits and gravy. The chances, however, are smaller than when starting with a young dog of good hunting bloodlines. The percentages lie with the pure-blood breeds in which good hunting qualities have long been in-bred.

DOGS FOR WATERFOWL. For use on waterfowl, the various pure-blood retrievers are best. Two of the very best, as indicated above, are the Labrador and the Chesapeake. The Irish water spaniel is one of the oldest breeds used in this country on waterfowl and is also a fine retriever

Adaptable to waterfowl and upland game, the Labrador retriever is also a fine family dog.

on upland-game birds. This breed is fairly large, with males weighing up to 60 pounds. The curly coat of hair all over the body and ears is the most striking feature. This coat is liver-colored all over, including the ratlike tail. The abundance of the coat makes work in cold water relatively comfortable, and is one of the useful, as well as ornamental, assets of the breed.

Another retriever useful on both upland birds and waterfowl is the golden retriever. This is a large, intelligent dog, distinguished by its pure golden color. The breed has abundant wavy hair. Adult males weigh up to 65 pounds and like Labradors and Chesapeakes make fine companions.

BUYING A HUNTING DOG.   There are two ways of obtaining a good hunting dog. One is to go to a reputable dog trainer and buy the dog of one's choice. For this the new owner pays not only for the dog, but for the hours which have gone into the dog's training, the general understanding of dogs, and the necessary patience in educating a young animal for the hunting field.

For many bird hunters, all this is an advantage. Often they haven't the space or the time necessary for dog training. Moreover, they are naturally less proficient than an expert, and the training of a professional usually brings the dog to a high level of field ability.

287

There are, however, drawbacks to buying a trained dog. First, the trusting loyalty common to a puppy has gone not to the new owner who will use the animal, but to someone else. The adult dog is less apt to treat the new owner with the affection that is a most pleasant part of the man-dog association. Also, the trained dog, under the less skilled handling technique of the new owner, is apt to perform less efficiently than for his original trainer.

These are factors which must be considered. However, in any case the prospective owner should give the new dog a trial workout in his own hunting area before final purchase. In addition, the word of a reputable trainer as to the dog's capabilities and probabilities should be accepted as the kennel's reputation is at stake.

For some, a better way is to buy the animal as a puppy, to be trained by the owner. This applies especially when the dog is to be a companion, a family pet as well, or double as a child's dog. All pups worship human beings who treat them well, and by starting with a pup, this bond of affection begins growing from the very first; and the grown dog not only will perform better for his owner but will be a better companion.

In choosing a pup for hunting, several important decisions should be made. First, the breed should be chosen for the game to be hunted and the owner's housing accommodations. No use buying a Great Dane for hunting teal if one lives in an apartment. Again, the probability of the dog's being a companion for children or wife should be considered. The new owner's skill in training a dog should not be forgotten. If the owner has little experience and expects to devote a minimum of time to the chore, he is better off with a flusher breed than one of the pointing breeds. It takes less time to bring a flusher to the point of field use than it does to perfect the pointing-and-holding ability of a pointer or setter.

In choosing a puppy from a litter, things to look for are general liveliness, eager, intent eyes, a relatively wide head and nostrils, its general actions within the litter, the condition of its coat, and whether or not it seems to like people. These all indicate intelligence, healthiness, tractability, and desire to please. Any pup chosen should be given its shots for distemper and similar ailments before purchase.

DOG TRAINING. Pups, like children, are individualistic. No two are exactly the same and each must be treated a bit differently. The new owner's first job is to understand his pup. Some breeds are strong-willed and this shows in puppyhood. A strong-willed breed like the English pointer will take harsher commands and corrective punishment better than the setters, for example. But any dog should be taught to obey. An adult hunting dog which won't mind is worthless. In teaching a dog anything, the owner should be kind but firm; and the type of discipline should fit the individual dog.

A puppy is a playful bundle and should be allowed to play without serious training until it is from six to ten months old. For later hunting purposes, the more a pup can be taken into the field while young, the quicker it will learn to hunt. Many a young pup will pick up bird scent or fresh tracks, show interest, and "root" along, mesmerized by the strange appealing scent. This should be encouraged.

When actual training begins, the person who wants to give his dog an adequate and correct training, especially if he has a setter or pointer, should purchase an authoritative book on dog training, study it, and follow the directions. Such a text will show step-by-step the technique for teaching the new dog the fundamentals, as well as methods to correct basic faults.

Actually, the basic training consists in the dog's mastering a few fundamentals. These are to mind a command; to heel when not hunting; to point or set birds and hold them (if a pointer); to hunt and flush them within shotgun range of the hunter (if a flusher); and to retrieve dead birds.

Dogs, like people, learn by association and repetition. They learn more slowly because of a lesser intelligence. Consequently, teaching a dog anything boils down to patience in getting it to understand what is wanted; praise for its accomplishments; the necessary discipline for disobedience; repetition of lessons; and more praise for each success.

A dog's first lesson, that of obeying, comes gradually and through the word-association of a command coupled to an appropriate action. If the command is "Come!" or "Come here!" and the trainer lightly pulls the pup towards him on the training cord, the dog soon gets the idea. After a few times, and suitable praise, the young dog learns to come without any pulling on a cord, or without any cord.

Similarly, in teaching a dog to lie down, the instructor says clearly, "Down! Down!"—all the while pushing the dog gently to the ground by the collar. Eventually the association of ideas takes over and the dog will lie down at the simple command, "Down!" Or, to break an eager dog of jumping on one with its forepaws, one commands, "Down!" while stepping on the animal's hind toes with increasing pressure until it gets the association.

Teaching a dog to heel likewise requires the repetition of the command-action association. While leading the dog by the neck cord, each time it starts to run ahead the command "Heel!" is given. At the same time, the running end of the cord or a length of heavier rope is whirled in front like a propeller. It takes only a few times of running its sensitive nose into the whirling rope for the dog to understand that "Heel!" means to stay behind.

Making a dog learn to stay reasonably close in front of the hunter, to stop, or to come back, is one of the most difficult lessons. The situation is aggravated by the very nature of a bird-hunting dog's most priceless feature—its nose. Once the dog scents game, it naturally wants to come upon that game at once and set or flush it, regardless of its master's ability to keep up.

Often, too, pointers and setters are allowed to run wide, find game, and set it; but they are *also* taught both to hold such birds on point until the shooter comes up and to come back when called.

This lesson, too, is taught by association and with a training cord of 40 feet or so attached to the dog's collar. A simple leather collar is usually sufficient for most young dogs. Some require collars with in-pointing studs, so that when pulled by the cord, the studs dig into the animal's neck.

The dog is allowed to wander or hunt until the command "Ho!" is given. The command is not given often enough to be confusing, but each time it is given the rope is tightened until it stops the dog. Eventually the dog will stop each time at the word-command only, without the use of the cord.

Pointing breeds have the built-in instinct to set or point birds when they come close upon them. But most young dogs, until trained differently, have the built-in yen to break point and chase the birds into the adjoining township. The training cord is used, together with a word-command, to break this habit. The command "Hold!" is given, the birds flushed (usually by a helper), and if the dog breaks to run them, it is jerked back with the cord.

Often severe jerking is necessary. One method is to fasten the cord's end to a solid object once the dog is on point. Then if it breaks and runs to the full length of the cord, it is stopped short. A dog whistle is used to call dogs back from too far afield, and response to it also is taught with a training cord.

At each successful performance, some form of reward should be given the learning dog. Usually a kind word or two of real praise and a pat on the head is all the dog wants. Most dogs want to please.

The final important lesson of retrieving is taught in comparable fashion, through the association of ideas. Any young dog is playful and likes to pick up objects in its mouth, drag them playfully, or wrestle with them. Many a boy teaches his dog to bring the newspaper simply by putting it into the animal's mouth a few times, then saying, "Come on." The general procedure with a bird dog is the same. The young dog is given something it likes to hold in its mouth, such as a rubber bone or soft stick. Often, after one plays with a dog with such an object a few minutes, then tosses it away a few feet, the pup will naturally race for it.

Once the dog will run for or grab an object, its lesson in retrieving is well under way. Next, the neck cord is attached to the collar and the object again tossed a few feet away. After the dog has gone for it and picked it up, the cord is gently pulled while giving the command, pleasantly, "Fetch!" Gradually the animal sees the connection between holding the object in its mouth, and coming to the owner for his word of praise.

Later, as it practices, the dog will come to do the trick without the use of the cord. At this stage, the object may be tossed farther away, and eventually hidden from its sight until the command "Fetch!" is given. As the dog improves further, a feathered dummy "bird" is given it and the words "Dead bird!" and "Fetch!" are used in combination. When the animal will find a hidden "bird" and bring it in at these commands, it is ready for practice on live birds. Retrievers for use on waterfowl are taught in the same way.

Other field manners, such as sitting down when presenting the bird to the shooter, are taught in a similar word-action manner. In all training, the dog must be given the notion that its work is pleasant. Lessons should be kept fairly short, say a half hour a day, and any lesson should be stopped after a success rather than a failure.

When hunting birds, the same kindness, care, and firmness should continue in the field as in the yard. It is important to control the dog's tendency to run wide in the presence of game.

While hunting, the dog is waved into likely-looking cover and allowed to work, and when moving from one field to another it is made to heel. The whistle is used to call it back when it gets too far away. Some handlers use a couple of toots on the whistle, like a starting train, to signal the dog to hunt.

To keep a dog from becoming gun-shy, the first shots during its field training should not be fired directly over it but at a distance of several yards. The first shooting should be done with a BB rifle or cap gun while someone else stands near the dog. If the animal tends to run or tremble, it is rubbed and assured that it is all right. The next step is to shoot from a closer distance, possibly with a .22, until gradually the animal becomes accustomed to gunfire.

Hauling dogs to and from hunting areas presents quite a problem for the one-car owner. Pickup trucks and station wagons with the rear seats removed are perhaps the best vehicles for hauling dogs. If the family car must be used, large sheets of plastic neoprene placed over all seats and upholstery will protect them from hair and toe scratches while the dogs are inside.

Truck cages are not so good, as dust from the tires rises into the dog's nostrils, and fumes from the exhaust are apt to make it sick. Periodic

291

stops should be made so that dogs can be taken out on leash and allowed to move about to search for trees.

Regardless of the training of any bird dog, or the shooting and handling skill of the hunter, there will be those inevitable "off" days afield when neither seems able to do anything right. The hunter cannot hit the broad side of the proverbial barn, and the chief ability of his prized setter or pointer seems to be sitting on its hind end and pointing at the lunch box. Instead of cussing the birds or walloping the dog, it is always wisest simply to say, "Old boy, we're a couple of bums today, aren't we?" Then go home and try it again another day.

26

Field Guide to Hunting Upland Birds

IN HUNTING any species of bird, two techniques will put the hunter within range. One is to locate and approach the birds, the other is to let the birds find the hunter.

With upland birds, only the first is successful. Hunting upland birds in the hope that they might come to the hunter is comparable to sitting on a stool in the lower pasture and waiting for a cow to back up to be milked.

The best way to stalk upland birds is with dogs, but if dogs aren't available the hunter must do the job himself on foot. With most species of birds this is far less efficient.

First, the general location of the birds is determined. This may be done from a knowledge of the hunting area, local information, the recognition of suitable bird cover, sometimes from the call of the birds themselves, from recent tracks in the soft earth, or from fresh dusting bowls. Some species, like the bobwhite, remain in definite localized areas.

Once the hunter is within the general habitat, he should look for the cover in which the birds hide, feed, and skulk. Such areas include fencerows, weedy ditch-banks, brush patches which cannot be tilled at fence intersections, brush-choked gullies, weedy dikes in otherwise open fields, row-crops such as ripened potato fields which contain dried weeds or vegetation, perennial field crops of thick cover such as alfalfa and bull clover, and stubble fields. These are all likely cover for game birds.

Depending on the time of day, the birds may either be shaded up or feeding within such cover. Or, like big game, they may be feeding at the edges of such concealment. Most game birds will, at the sight of the hunter, head for the nearest available cover if it can be reached in safety. If not, they may sit tight, hoping to avoid detection. Once within cover, upland birds will either lie low, move farther away within the concealment, or move completely through the cover patch and flush away on the opposite side.

For example, the chukar partridge, if the cover is sparse, will race away for several hundred yards from an approaching hunter, then either flush or hide. The Chinese pheasant is more apt to duck immediately into cover, then pop out again on the opposite side and race or fly away unseen. Oppositely, a sage grouse is more likely to walk a few steps, sit tight in the first available sagebrush, then flush well ahead of the oncoming hunter.

HUNTING WITH A PARTNER.   All such characteristics dictate that the best way of stalking upland birds without a hunting dog is with a partner. Almost any situation can be handled far more efficiently with a partner than when hunting alone. For example, fencerows can be worked with a hunter on each side, each preventing birds escaping. (The pheasant is master of this strategy.) Also, long-stretching willow rows, canal banks, and similar areas of cover can be handled in a comparable manner.

In many areas of row-crops, long ditches, etc., with birds that run instead of sitting tight, another technique is to have one hunter circle and move to the far end before any hunting is begun, then head back along the cover as his partner begins working the opposite end. As they come closer together, hidden birds will usually flush, and one or the other is apt to get a shot.

Often with running or skulking birds, the very presence of a hunter at either end of a ditch or dike, working closer together, will cause birds to change strategy and sit tight. Then, of course, they have to be kicked out, often at close ranges.

Many times the nature and density of cover will indicate another technique of getting birds up. One hunter posts himself at some vantage point, usually at the far end of small, patchy foliage, while his partner walks through and kicks about in every yard of foliage. Birds sit tight in direct ratio to the density of brush. Often the "working" hunter has to kick the birds out literally from beneath his feet before they will fly. The first bird, cackling or chirping into the air in an explosion of wings, will cause the other birds to bounce up, and the "standing" hunter gets his chance.

Many times a party of three or four hunters, working without dogs, can cover individual brush patches and get the birds up. Usually they are divided into those who post themselves at vantage points, ordinarily called "blockers," and those who move through the cover, called "drivers."

HUNTING ALONE. The lone hunter, working without a dog, is at a great disadvantage. His best procedure, with most upland species, is to work through the edge areas of any type of cover. He should move slowly so that birds are not spooked too far ahead of him by any undue commotion, and always be ready to shoot. The fresh tracks, dung, and dustings in or at the margin of cover all indicate the amount and proximity of game.

Stalk upland birds along fencerows and the edges of heavy foliage where they tend to seek shade and food.

Narrow fencerows, ditch-banks, brushy dikes, and field margins are the types of cover that the lone hunter can work to best advantage. The best technique is for him to move slowly and work slender-shaped areas of cover so that he will eventually come to where they terminate in an open area. Many times the birds, detecting his presence but not unduly alarmed by his slow movement, will move ahead but not flush until he reaches the last few rods of cover.

Once upland birds are flushed, any missed birds should be carefully marked down, to be hunted later. Often with short-flying birds, the nature or size of the new concealment is sufficient marking. But in more open country the far-flying birds become difficult to mark down and find later.

A good technique is first to establish a beeline to the new location by mentally marking down any available object directly beyond the spot where the birds have lit—such as a distant mountain, knoll, or tree. Next, before striking off, a careful estimate of the distance should be made. For example, if you conclude that a bird headed straight towards a distant ridge end and lit, and estimate the ridge end to be about 400 yards away, by pacing off the distance as you head for the spot you are very apt to arrive close to the new location of the bird.

When hunting with a partner, your estimation will be more accurate. Each hunter marks the bird down in a direct line towards a distant object. When the hunters converge along the two lines, the spot where their paths intersect will be *it*.

Upland birds which have been flushed, especially if they fly considerable distance, will tend, in many instances, to sit tighter when again located. Often, when hunting them in the new location, the hunter will swear they have evaporated. Actually they often have to be almost stepped on to make them flush again. The best procedure, once at the new location, is to begin at the estimated spot and continue working the entire area of cover in increasing, concentric circles, until the bird is found. The usual behavior of many species is to "explode" virtually from underfoot.

These are all broad generalities applicable to most upland birds in average hunting circumstances. The exceptions only provide additional spice to the hunting effort.

Our upland birds fall into the general categories of the doves, quail, partridges, grouse, ptarmigan, pheasants, and wild turkey. In addition to the above generalities, each species has its own characteristics and eccentricities. These, of course, determine the techniques for hunting that particular species.

MOURNING DOVE. Our smallest upland game bird is only slightly larger than a robin; its body is dusty-gray with darker wings and face

Mourning Dove

D.A.

markings. It is hunted in all forty-eight of our original states. Like many other birds, the mourning dove lives in a moderate climate and migrates back and forth. In the summer this dove will be found throughout the northern tier of states. In fall it moves southward; and with the warmth of spring it again travels northward.

This movement not only causes the mourning dove to be hunted in a wide variety of foliage and terrain; it also provides "migration" shooting for all the Nimrods of the northern states. That is, the legalized hunting season must coincide with the bird's southern migration or else there is no hunting. The recent annual kill of mourning doves is estimated at over 20 million, placing it high on the list of game birds. As the supply of larger upland birds diminishes in proportion to hunting pressures, more hunters are turning their attention to doves.

When the birds are present, they will be found in loosely defined flocks anywhere from a pair of birds up to a dozen or so. Regardless of the region, the birds will generally be found close to their food supply during the day, and characteristically they will make an evening flight towards water.

The food of mourning doves includes weed seeds, some insects, and the seed of grain crops. Doves like to feed in fairly open areas, and they need grit to grind their seed-food. When alerted or resting, they like to alight on fence wires, telephone wires, and the topmost bare branches of trees.

One good way of hunting mourning doves is to drive in a car or jeep and use a pair of high-powered binoculars. Good country includes outlying grain fields, stubble, dirt roads, willow rows, cedar patches, and desert creeks and creek beds.

If doves are in the country they will often be flushed from dirt roads where they pick grit; they will be seen resting on fence wires and phone lines; they will be spotted on bare willows and tree tops; and during the last hour or so before sundown, they will be found in a somewhat definite flight pattern towards water. The binoculars are most useful in studying distant tree tops, willow rows, and the evening flight pattern.

Birds that are found via the vehicle may be hunted after they are flushed and have alighted in an adjacent field. Or, having located a suitable area, hunters can return to it and thoroughly hunt out the region on foot. The location of the evening flight pattern gives an important clue to where any hunting should be done the following evening. In semidesert country, the best area for doves is any available creek bed. The hunter simply "works" the foliage along the watercourse, scouting for birds along the willow or brushtops, or shooting them as they flush before him. In grain country a fine procedure is to hunt along the fencerows hemming in any large areas of wheat stubble.

It doesn't take a large shotgun to kill mourning doves. However, the bird's swift erratic flight makes it tricky to hit, even at close ranges, with a puny shot pattern. A 20 gauge is ideal for doves, and No. 7½ and 8 shot sizes are the most used. Many hunters of larger birds use their 12-gauge shotguns on doves, and the tiny .410 and larger .28-gauge guns are fine for the hot-shot gunner. The dove is one species for which the .410 shotgun may be said to be adequate.

WHITE-WING DOVE. Another member of the dove family, larger and browner than the mourning dove, with many of the same characteristics, the white-wing's most notable habit is its daily flight to water. In the desert and semidesert, where the white-wing lives and is hunted, the hunter can take full advantage of this characteristic. By acquainting himself with the terrain, any available water, and the evening flight pattern of the birds, he can post himself in a strategic position—often in some form of natural blind—and shoot at passing birds.

In Mexico and many areas of the Southwest, the only water in much of the desert country is to be found at water holes. These may be natural or man-made, and consist largely of hollowed-out depressions meant for catching rain water. White-wings use them and will fly in regularly to such "tanks."

Shooting at white-wings makes many a shotgunner tear his hair. These birds are fast and erratic in flight. The 12-gauge and 20-gauge guns are most commonly used, in conjunction with No. 6, 7½, and 8 shot sizes.

THE QUAIL FAMILY. The many species of quail make up one of our most important upland birds. Quail range in species from the much-loved bobwhite of the South, to the Gambel quail of the arid lands of the Southwest, to the mountain and valley quail of the Northwest and Pacific Coastal country. Quail range from the hottest country to moderate and cool regions. They inhabit country whose foliage ranges from cactus to burrs, to palmetto to sagebrush, and from wheatland to weeds.

The most popular quail is the bobwhite quail, so called because its call simulates the sound *bob-white*. This is a small bird, averaging around 9 inches overall length, mottled in belly coloration with brown back, and light throat, face, and neck markings. The bobwhite's range is over most of eastern North America.

The mountain quail, much larger than the bobwhite, is plumed, with bright scarlet throat patches fringed in white reaching downward upon a

D.A.

Bobwhite

gray-colored chest, darker, mottled belly and brownish wings. As the name suggests, this species is found in mountainous country and is largely confined to the West.

The valley quail is another species very popular with West Coast hunters. This quail is of contrasting coloration and sports a top-knot. The male has a dark, white-ringed throat patch, light-gray chest, mottled belly, and gray-brown back. Its original range along the West Coast has been extended with transplantings to cover most western states.

Gambel quail is another top-knotted species, often called desert quail, and is widely spread in the arid regions of the Southwest from Utah to Mexico.

Massena, or Mearns', quail, and scaled quail are two other southwestern species.

Like other upland species, quail will be found adjacent to their food supply, which consists of berries, fruits, weed seeds, domestic grain, and insects. The species is gregarious, and the birds live together and are found during hunting season in coveys. Certain of the subspecies, such as the bobwhite in the South, will complete their life cycle often in an area no larger than a half-section. Others, such as some of the western species, will range much farther afield.

If ever there was a species that required a hunting dog, it is the quail. A good hunting dog relieves the hunter of the effort of finding the birds; it will "set" the quarry until the hunter comes up ready to shoot and will then retrieve the dead game for him.

Some species like the bobwhite and Massena quail will hold for a dog. Others like the mountain quail and scaled quail are not so accommodating and will run ahead of pointing dogs, hide, skulk and refuse to fly—until they drive a good dog crazy.

However, in a broad way, all quail are hunted in much the same fashion with dogs. The dogs are hauled to a likely area and turned loose at the edge of game cover. Once released, the dogs cast about, working the areas shortly ahead of the hunters, trying to pick up the ground-scent, or scent of the birds themselves. For species that will hold, pointers and setters are the most used quail dogs, and the classic conception of bird hunting is a brace of such good dogs, one honoring the point of the other, holding a covey of bobwhites for the anxious hunter. With the dog on point, the hunter flushes the covey by walking in, and then the shooting begins.

Once the covey flushes and scatters, it is important to mark down as many singles as possible, which are then hunted down, set again and flushed.

On species that will not hold for a dog, and that will not flush easily but continue racing ahead, other breeds of dogs are more useful than pointers or setters. Flushers like the Springer spaniel will keep moving with the scattering birds of the alerted covey and oust them into the air.

Which direction a flushed quail will fly is anybody's guess, but usually it will be towards the nearest available cover. Like any upland bird, the quail utilizes heavy foliage as a protection from enemies; and the hunter should remember this after marking down flushed birds.

Because of the quail's coloration, its affinity for relatively thick foliage, its ability to run ahead and lie low, the hunter without dogs has an almost impossible job. The best he can do is to work the likely thickets, fencerows, and edge country, hoping to kick out a bird or so.

In the West and Southwest, the modern 4-wheel-drive jeep has helped the hunter without dogs. Hunters working country which these little desert buggies will negotiate simply drive through cactus, sagebrush, and similar arid terrain until they come upon birds. At the sight of one crossing the "road" or buzzing off in flight, they pile out and lope after it, trying to make that bird, or others, take to the air.

Jeeps and saddle horses, too, are often used in quail hunting, in conjunction with dogs. The hunters cover the mileage on horses or in the vehicle, with the dogs either trailing the horses or riding in the jeep until birds are located. This is a good way to cover distances in desert country where, as one hunter put it, "Everything that grows either sticks or bites you"—referring to the cacti and poisonous insects and snakes.

Quail are normally shot at close ranges. This, together with their fast, startling flight, dictates a gun of moderately open bore and fast-handling qualities. The 12-gauge shotgun, in modified and improved-cylinder choke, tops any other gauge, and a good double is one of the very best types on quail. The over-under, however, is gaining popularity, as are the lightweight 20-gauge autoloaders. One of the best of these is Remington's new lightweight Model 1100. Number 7½ and number 8 shot are good all-round choices.

HUNGARIAN PARTRIDGE. This is an important upland game bird which has adapted itself well to the northern tier of states, the West, spot areas in the Midwest and East, and vast areas of the wheat-belt section of southern Canada. It is a small bird, mottled gray-and-red on the belly, with brown, mottled wings.

In some ways the Hun is hunted like quail—that is, a good hunting dog is almost a must. The biggest difference, so far as hunting is concerned, is that the Hun likes the more open prairie areas, where it uses its strategy to outwit the hunter. Flushed coveys will light in open fields again and, like mountain quail, will strike off and run from dogs. As with open-country hunting of big game, the hunter usually has to

Hungarian Partridge

D.A.

maneuver in the terrain so that he can come upon a Hun covey again from an opposite and unsuspected direction—or find himself another covey.

A good gun for Huns is also a good quail gun. Both the 12 and the 20 gauge are popular, and should be of modified choke. Number 7½ shot is ideal for Huns.

CHUKAR PARTRIDGE. This is one of the newest upland game birds in this country. Originally from Asia, this newcomer gives every indication of catching on as a coming species in the arid regions of the West. The chukar is dove-colored, with dark barred markings along the flanks. Its legs and feet are vermillion-red, giving it the nickname "redlegs." The adult chukar is about two-thirds the size of a Chinese pheasant, and very delicious.

Hell's Canyon, the deep river-boundary between Idaho and Oregon, is one area where the chukar is firmly established. Because of the steep country and difficulty of access, it is improbable that hunters will ever be able to decimate its growing chukar population.

Unlike the Hun, which likes flat and rolling country, the chukar likes bluffs, arroyos, and high spiny ridges having sparse cedar, mahogany, and sagebrush foliage. Dry dirt bluffs in such semiopen areas seem preferred spots.

The first thing to do in hunting chukars is to learn in what regions the chukar has been planted and has caught on. Once into an area which chukars use, it is best to hunt this wily bird with a good dog. Any dog that will work on Huns will be a good one on chukars. So will the flushers used on quail. However, the chukar may be successfully hunted without a dog. Identified by its peculiar *chuk-a-chuk, chuk-a-chuk* calling, the chukar is easily heard on a still autumn morning at distances well over a half mile. The call is most deceptive. It sounds over here, but is just as likely over there.

Chukar Partridge

D.A.

In trying to approach the distant birds, it is well to move slowly in their general direction, but also to zig-zag laterally while listening. From several different positions the area from which the calling comes can usually be pinpointed.

In bluffy country, this bird likes the very edge where foliage leaves off and dirt slides begin. Often the birds may be seen running around in the upper bluffs, much as mountain sheep work the upper crags in rocky terrain. It may be that this is a part of their escape strategy—when threatened, the birds simply sail out, like overgrown bumblebees, across the open void of the canyon.

When hunting such areas, it is wise to move along the very brink of the canyon, moving up each tiny slash-gully coming in from the side. By staying close to the brink, the hunter can cause flushed birds to fly along the top, rather than across the canyon, affording a better shot and enabling him to retrieve downed birds.

The chukar likes to stay in sparse foliage and on the high spines of bluffy ridges rather than in thick cover. Often in sparse cover the birds will detect a hunter or dog at some distance and will run ahead, almost as fast as a pheasant, for several hundred yards before taking to the air or stopping to hide.

When approaching a flock of chukars to within shotgun range, old-timers use the trick of not shooting at the first bird that rises. Invariably such a bird, like the cow guard of an elk band, will be situated at a vantage point some distance from the main flock. When this one flushes first, it often brings the first shot from the startled gunner, exploding the rest of the flock while he is unloaded. For this reason, many veteran hunters pass the first bird of a flock and shoot at subsequent birds.

Despite the fact that chukars will often run ahead and out of range, they also will sit tight in cover which the hunter swears could not hold a bird. Such tactics make a dog invaluable.

Perhaps the chukar's most exasperating trick is that when flushed it does not fly in a straight line but follows both the lateral and the vertical contour of the ridge over which it buzzes. This makes it one of the hardest birds in America to hit.

A good shotgun for chukars is the 12-gauge repeater, with modified choke, and shooting either No. 6 or 7½ shot . . . with lots of ammunition in the coat pockets.

RUFFED GROUSE. This is the most popular of the numerous grouse species due to its widespread range, which includes the entire eastern part of Canada and northern United States, and the canny way it can outwit the hunter.

Ruffed Grouse

Inhabiting thickets and moderate underbrush, the ruffed grouse, like other wildlife, lives close to its food supply, which includes wild raspberries, grapes, strawberries, acorns, and snowberries, as well as insects and buds of bushes. The ruffed grouse spreads its tail in fanlike fashion when it struts and can erect the neck feathers into an enormous puff. During courtship, the male will drum its wings while sitting on a log to attract the females. This drumming sound carries far and sounds like a distant motorcycle taking off.

One key to the whereabouts of ruffed grouse is the fact that they are never found far from water. Experienced grouse hunters follow the small creeks rather than the ridges, especially in pine-belt country. If these tiny creeks are bounded on either side with patches of wild raspberry bushes or similar thickets, or are adjacent to edge country where forests meet semiopenings, then the combination indicates good grouse country. It takes experience to recognize good grouse areas, and another key to success is to hunt those areas that have produced birds in previous years.

Grouse, like black bears, like man-made trails. They use them in thicket country for strutting about, and the dust in them for dusting bowls. Often the hunter slowly walking such a trail will find the telltale signs of "small chicken tracks" or a stray feather. The thickets nearby are good grouse cover.

The grouse is one species that may be hunted without a dog. Ruffed grouse will not run too far ahead of the hunter as will other species of birds, nor will it sit unduly tight. Rather, at known danger or the close proximity of the hunter, it explodes away. Like certain species of big game, the ruffed grouse will fully utilize any available trees in its escape route. Invariably, the flushed bird will dart in between trees, leaving timber between it and the hunter. If flushed at the margin between timber and open areas, this bird displays an uncanny ability to use the terrain to its advantage. If the hunter happens to be on the *open* side, the bird will fly momentarily into the timber; but if the hunter happens to be within the timber fringe, the bird will escape just along the *outside* of the timber belt.

This calls for snap-shooting. It takes a gun that is light and handy, has reasonably open choke, and will throw a good pattern. A light double—there are few repeat shots at flying ruffed grouse—in 12 gauge, with modified or improved-cylinder boring, and used with medium-power loads containing No. 6 or 7½ shot, is one of the best choices.

Unhit birds will seldom fly beyond 300–400 yards and will normally sit tight until again flushed. If the hunter marks them down, hunts toward them in a straight line, and carefully hunts the expected area in increasing, concentric circles, he is very apt to flush them again.

Unlike crippled pheasants, wounded grouse will not run very far. Downed birds usually can be located by the sound of their fluttering wings.

BLUE GROUSE. With the exception of the desert sage grouse, the blue grouse is the biggest member of the grouse family—large cocks will weigh as much as a mallard duck. This species is gray-blue with mottled brown. It lives in the conifer country of western United States, and is often called the pine hen or fool hen. Big-game country and blue grouse go together, and in recent years some western states have opened the blue grouse season to coincide with the elk and deer season and have permitted hunters to kill these big birds with rifle or pistol. Often this was the only way blue grouse in remote areas could be harvested.

FRANKLIN GROUSE. Found in the wooded section of western America, the Franklin grouse has an overall range from the Northwest to Alaska. This grouse is smaller than the blue grouse and is characterized in the males by the nearly black barred breast. Often called the "fool hen," this bird offers little sport to the hunter. Big-game hunters often get a mess of this species with no other weapon than a six-foot stick with which the bird may be hit on the head after a careful approach. Other hunters heave rocks at these birds until they hit one for the skillet.

SHARP-TAILED GROUSE. This species is identified by its speckled appearance and sharp-pointed tail. Until recently this grouse has been confined largely to Alaska and Canada. Recent plantings have caught on in the West, however. For example, by 1960 Idaho's plantings of the species had caught on enough for a limited, weekend open season with a bag limit of two birds. There have been open seasons in the area ever since, and in 1970 the general open season lasted nine days, with a bag limit of three birds.

A major enemy of this species is the range fire, which often destroys chokecherry bushes, sagebrush, and other low foliage which sharp-tailed grouse use for cover.

PRAIRIE CHICKEN. The prairie chicken, or pinnated grouse, is unlike most other species in that it likes open prairies and fields. This fact was its undoing in many of the early prairies of the United States. The plowing of prairies and wheatlands destroyed the nests and otherwise moved the birds from normal ranges. The species now inhabits only certain prairie areas of Canada and scattered spots within the United States.

SAGE GROUSE. The sage grouse is the largest of the grouse family, and in the West is called the sage hen. The future of this species depends on the amount of sagebrush lands which will be available to it. Range fires in summer have a disastrous effect on populations. Also, the airplane spraying of sagebrush lands, which kills the sage and allows the growth of natural grasses for domestic stock, has an adverse effect on the sage-hen population.

Currently the sage grouse is about holding its own, with an occasional annual increase under optimum hatching conditions, weather, etc. For example, although the average bag limit during the 1960s for many western states was about two birds, in 1970 some permitted three birds per hunter.

This species is mottled gray in appearance, which blends perfectly with the sagebrush of their habitat.

Old cock birds weigh as much as 7 or 8 pounds and are tough as a rubber boot to chew. In the past, when their numbers were greater, hunters would only shoot the smaller, younger birds because the adult birds were so tough and tasted strongly of sage from the bird's diet. Currently, sage grouse are not as strong-flavored due to their living at the

307

Sage Grouse

fringes of outlying and marginal farmlands, where they eat green alfalfa leaves. Incidentally, drawing the birds immediately after shooting removes most of the strong sage taste, and hanging a dressed bird with an onion inside the cavity overnight helps also. The modern pressure-cooker helps greatly in unbending the noble old cocks into something fairly palatable.

One of the most amazing of wildlife spectacles is the sage grouse's courtship. Annually, about April, the big dusky birds will congregate in open desert areas adjacent to high sage, called "booming grounds." There, in the eerie period between daybreak and sunup, the cocks put on a magnificent show to attract the hens.

The male bird will puff out the air sacs on his chest until he looks grotesquely like an overdone pouter pigeon. The white-feather covering of these extended air sacs covers his entire front and makes the bird, at a distance, look like some big white ball. While thus puffed up, and with tail spread like a semicircular picket fence, the cock will make a gurgling sound which carries far and resembles the distant booming of cannon—for which booming grounds were named.

During the booming, cocks remain in a small area, though a dozen males may be booming within a few square rods. Once a hen is attracted to the male of her choice, she goes to him, sits at his feet, and waits there until her hero has attracted as many hens as he can, often three to a half dozen. Occasionally a hen will change partners during this show, which causes a terrific fight between the rival males.

With full sunrise, the birds all retreat into the nearby sagebrush. Only rarely is the actual mating consummated on the booming grounds.

The hunter after sage grouse should first determine what states have legal hunting on this species. Next he should consult a fish and game map of that state and locate the areas open to hunting. The last step is to find out where the largest stands of virgin sagebrush are within these regions. These are apt to contain the most plentiful populations of this scarce species.

Recent sprinkle-irrigation, and the reclamation of sagebrush lands under the Desert Act, have had an influence on sage-grouse hunting. On the one hand, this agrarian encroachment has cut the bird's range, but, in outlying country, the margins between sage and irrigated lands are among the finest places to hunt for sage grouse. The big dusky birds love alfalfa.

Like the ruffed grouse, the sage grouse can be hunted without a dog, though a good dog is an advantage if it can be controlled. Many an otherwise good pooch, seeing all that open country for the first time, wants to lope over all of it in the first hour.

Within sagebrush lands, the best areas to look are the low bluffs, the flats containing sparse sagebrush, the mild promontory endings, any fence lines dividing sagebrush lands and cultivated fields, areas where alfalfa fields join creeks or irrigation ditches, and even the alfalfa fields themselves, *if* a cutting of hay has been recently harvested and *if* the owner grants permission. No hunter should ever trespass through an uncut alfalfa field.

The signs denoting the presence of birds are fresh tracks in the dust—the size of domestic chicken tracks—black or pinto splotches of dung, and large dusting bowls such as other grouse use. Then the principal chore is walking, for sagebrush lands are vast in area, and bird populations are relatively scarce.

The first indication of game usually is a huge mottled fowl bolting up from the sage, shedding a few feathers, probably some dung, and emitting a startling *cuk-cuk-cuk*. To the uninitiated, the bird looks as big as a turkey and as easy to hit as a barn.

About the time it levels off and the hunter is ready, the bird makes its characteristic dip sidewise and, when the hunter fires, is usually just under the shot charge. Such a flight-dip usually occurs at just about reasonable shotgun range. It is better to wait out that first pause in the bird's getaway flight.

Sage grouse do not get up together when a flock is flushed, but rise in singles, doubles, or any unreasonable combination. For this reason, all the area where the first bird has been flushed should be rehunted carefully, using the increasing concentric-circle technique. And, as with other species, flying birds should be well marked down. Sage grouse will fly from several hundred yards to nearly a mile before realighting.

309

The best shotgun for sage grouse is the 12-gage, full-choke, and either in standard chambering or in the 3-inch Magnum type. Number 4 and 6 shot is best for this species. The newer 20-gauge Magnums are increasing in popularity, but probably will not overtake the 12 gauge while we have available sage-grouse hunting.

PTARMIGAN. Ptarmigan are native residents of the Far North, mainly Alaska and Canada, with a few making it across the border into the United States. The ptarmigan is the size of a medium grouse, and changes color with the seasons. In late fall, it is a mottled gray color, often with patches of pure white showing as it goes into winter plumage. A ptarmigan in its pure-white winter coat can be detected only at a distance of a few feet, and only by its dark eyes. The species is usually found in willows, arctic birch, and similar sparse vegetation. It utters a *tuk-tuk . . . tuk* sound when alerted, and is more wary than many of the woodland grouse species.

This bird is usually hunted during the fall season in conjunction with big game. Ptarmigan love the high mountainous pass-type country and the bunches of alpine willows common to such beginnings of water. Good places to hunt them are along glacial creek beds having willow and alder foliage. Other likely spots are the open promontory points in the plateau country above the creek bottoms.

Ptarmigan

310

When flushed, ptarmigan emit a stuttering *tuk-tuk-tuk-tuk* and will usually realight within view of the hunter, sometimes on the ground and many times on the bare willow tops. An unusual feature of the ptarmigan's flight is that, like a small "bullet hawk," it can fly laterally over a ridge, then suddenly stop its wings, change its "feathering," and fly straight downward and alight immediately below.

On a big-game hunt for such species as sheep, grizzly, and caribou, ptarmigan are often shot with a .22 rimfire rifle. The puny rifle doesn't spook big game, yet it will take care of the ptarmigan pot-meat. For serious hunting of this species, any light shotgun, 12 gauge or 20 gauge, preferably in modified choke, and using No. 6 or 7½ shot would be adequate.

RINGNECK PHEASANT. Like the chukar partridge, the ringneck came from Asia, and was the first bird to be successfully transplanted into America to replace dwindling native species of upland birds. The first birds were brought into America in 1881. Since that time, the ringneck pheasant has become America's number one upland game bird. Thanks to this gaudy Asiatic transplant, thousands of people now own guns, hunt, and enjoy the outdoors.

The future of its habitat is bright. The pheasant takes to cultivated cornfields and other farmlands like a duck to a puddle. But in 1970 another kind of threat to the species was detected—mercury. The mercury used in fertilizers and sprays has been absorbed by the crops on which pheasants feed. Beyond very minute levels, mercury can be toxic to humans who eat the birds. Several western states delayed scheduling the current fall season until it could be determined if the mercury level in the pheasants was dangerous.

Even infinitesimal amounts of mercury in flesh will register on an atomic Materials Testing Reactor. The Atomic Energy Commission offered the use of a reactor to the National Reactor Testing Station near Arco, Idaho, as a laboratory for measuring mercury in game birds. At this writing, part of the testing has been done on Idaho pheasants, and the national spotlight is on the experiment. It is very likely that reactors will be useful nationwide in ascertaining relationships between farm chemicals and game birds.

The ringneck has a wide range, occupying the northern half of the United States. It is found in greatest abundance in the agricultural areas, chiefly in the Corn Belt, and its range extends westward well beyond the Rockies. South Dakota is the leading ringneck state, and ringneck hunting there, especially for nonresident hunters who make annual treks, has been fabulous.

311

Ringneck Pheasant

Perhaps the biggest asset of the ringneck—in addition to its sporty hunting qualities and palatability—is that it has proven to be so adaptable that it can live in numbers virtually in man's back yard, survive, and in many respects even outwit him.

Ringneck females are mottled gray-white-brown and have a speckled appearance. They will weigh 2 pounds or more. Tails on the hens will run from one-third to one-half the bird's overall length. The cock bird is larger, approximating the weight of a mallard duck or a blue grouse. The extremely long tail of the cock makes him appear larger than he is, and makes him somewhat difficult to hit when flying—many hunters shoot where the tail is but where the bird has been.

The coloration of the cock is gaudy and brilliant. He has a green-black head, tufted "ears" and a bright red patch around the eye. The breast is a burnished orange-red with dark feather-tip markings. The back varies from orange-brown to blue-green feathers resembling peacock herl over the tail base. The streaming tail is black-barred its full length and may be 22 inches or more in length.

The basic techniques of upland-bird hunting mentioned at the beginning of this chapter can all be applied to pheasant hunting. That is, it may be hunted with dogs, by the hunting-partner method, by the lone hunter working without a dog, or by a party of several hunters working down a field in rank.

The fundamental traits of this bird, upon which any successful hunting procedure depends, are that it loves to skulk, to run, and to fly considerable distances; and also that it will double back like a whitetail deer, and will also upon occasion sit tight. What a ringneck will do under any given condition is quite like sticking a spoon into your morning grapefruit and predicting which way the juice will squirt.

Because of its unpredictable behavior, the pheasant will drive a good pointing dog, experienced on birds that hold, to distraction. The dog locates game and slams into a point; the pheasant sits a second, runs off a few rods; the dog breaks point, sneaks up, and points again; the bird again breaks and skulks away farther, then runs; and Rover again breaks point, then either gawps up at his master or breaks and chases the fleeing ringneck into another township.

For this reason many hunters prefer a flushing type of dog like the springer spaniel for work on pheasants. Some slow-working mongrels, farm-trained on pheasants, make wonderful pheasant hunters—they snoop 'em out, oust 'em up, and run 'em down when winged.

The ringneck has adapted itself to civilization and farmland. The best method of hunting this bird depends on the type of terrain, the availability of dogs, and the number of hunters. For long narrow cover, such as single ditch-banks, dikes, and fencerows, one hunter without a dog can usually flush any pheasant within the foliage. It is always better to have another hunter "block" the bird's escape at the far end, as touched upon earlier.

There is a special method of hunting pheasants adapted to such row-crops as corn and potatoes, and is aimed both at preventing the birds' cutting back, like deer, within the field, and at having them fly out beyond range at the end of the field. This is the party method. Several hunters, spaced a few rods apart, will slowly "comb" down the full length of a row-crop field. Before beginning, other hunters sufficient to cover the open end of the field will be stationed in the open just beyond the crop.

Several hunters will make considerable noise while working the field. This will either cause the birds to flush or run ahead. If they flush, the hunter ahead of whom they fly is entitled to the shot. If he misses, the next hunter in line, if within range, has a chance at the bird.

313

In most instances, the majority of birds will move towards the far end of the field. There, finding their skulk route cut off, they will sit tight and be flushed the last minute by the drivers coming through. This method is widely used in the Corn Belt, and modifications of it are adapted to most other row-crop hunting areas.

One form of pheasant hunting is a contradiction to all accepted forms. Its success depends entirely upon a fall of fresh snow during hunting season. The morning following such a storm, pheasant hunting can become an exciting solo affair.

The birds will huddle during the storm, then with sunup and clearing weather will begin to move about to feed. Any movement will show plain, fresh tracks; on the other end of those tracks will be a bird. The technique is simply to walk slowly along the tracks, making sure they do not double back. Usually the trail will end in some sort of bush, clump of foliage, or the bottom of a ditch—often a few yards from the bird. The hunter either stands until the bird can no longer sweat it out and flushes, or moves in and kicks it out.

A winged pheasant can outrun the hunter unless he's a good sprinter. If he does not have a dog, that winged bird is surely going to escape unless the hunter can race up within range and shoot again as it runs.

The ability of the hunter to sprint fast is also an aid, under certain conditions, in getting the bird into the air. Often a bird will skulk and run along the bottom of an irrigation ditch. If the hunter sees the bird and sprints ahead, he can often come within range before the bird flushes. Otherwise it would run out of range before taking to the air.

The 12 gauge is the most used shotgun on pheasants and for all-round shooting should be full-choke. Many hunters like the old standby double, but either the pump or automatic is hard to beat. A single-shot on pheasants is only an inducement to profanity. As cocks are normally the only sex hunted, and are often tough as boiled owl, No. 4 and 6 shot are the two preferred sizes. Some hunters have gone to the 3-inch Magnum 12 as an adequate tool for long-range pheasant shooting.

Two tendencies often cause the hunter to miss, especially if he is inexperienced on this species. One is the tendency to undershoot the fast-rising bird; the other, because of the bird's streaming tail-feathers, is to shoot behind.

WILD TURKEY. This bird is similar in appearance to the domestic bronze turkey, except it is more racy in form and a richer bronze in coloration. Wild toms will average around 15 pounds in weight, with the hens correspondingly smaller.

The overall range of the wild turkey extends from Pennsylvania to the Gulf of Mexico, westward beyond the Black Hills of South Dakota and

Wild Turkey

Arizona, and over a considerable area of Old Mexico. Of recent years spot plantings of wild turkeys have been made in additional western states including Wyoming and Idaho (first plant in 1960–61). These plantings were made in the hope that the wild turkey population would be of more than scenic value, someday reaching a level which would allow limited hunter-harvest. This objective has been realized; the wild turkey has caught on. In some of the most remote areas the laws have expanded from permit hunting to open seasons.

Similar plantings are becoming popular in the Midwest and other areas. The success has been due in great measure to a recently discovered fact—that *really* wild turkeys, trapped in a turkey area and moved to a comparable habitat, will increase. Farm-raised wild turkeys will not.

Unexcelled vision and keenness of hearing, coupled with its uncanny instinct for knowing when it is being hunted, make the wild turkey perhaps the most difficult to bag of all our upland birds. If the hunter should possess one qualification, it is unlimited patience.

Turkeys are hunted with both rifle and shotgun. Cartridges such as the .22 Hornet and .222 Remington, if used with relatively heavy-jacketed bullets, make good turkey rifles. The old .32–20 was considered good for turkeys, since its bullet would not destroy much meat. The recent military M1 carbine using factory loads has proven to be a fine turkey rifle. Almost any .30-caliber sporting rifle is effective and won't cause too much destruction if a heavy-jacketed bullet, handloaded to decrease the velocity to approximately 2,000 feet per second, is used. In shotguns, the

315

12-gauge standard and its magnum version are among the best. Some hunters prefer the 10 gauge. The best shot sizes are BB, 2, or 4.

A popular technique is to stillhunt the birds in areas where they are known to be. This is determined from hearing their gobbling, or locating their spoor as they work certain ridges for food. Another method is to hunt them from a blind built of natural materials to look as unobtrusive as possible, situated within range of a known watering hole.

Another much-used technique is to scatter a flock of birds, either wittingly or unwittingly, then patiently call individual birds into range on an artificial call using judiciously spaced yelps to simulate the natural call of the separated birds. One old Arizona turkey hunter used nothing more elaborate than the simple stem of his old tobacco pipe. After years of listening and practice, he had perfected his calling into an art.

The future of upland-bird shooting lies largely with the public and the price that shooters and an interested citizenry are willing to pay for a perpetuation of the sport. Our large areas of public land are dwindling. More and more, upland birds are being hunted upon private lands. In most instances, the birds are the sovereign property of the state; but adequate and increasingly enforced trespass laws protect the landowner and serve as a basis for keeping hunters from harvesting their own game.

One solution that has gained ground and provoked criticism is the establishment of private shooting preserves. These are lands either leased or purchased by private interests upon which pen-raised birds are released for shooting. Private preserves range in size, elaborateness, and guest fees from simple fields where the hunter may find ample birds in suitable cover for a modest day-charge, to luxurious establishments with family accommodations on the order of high-class resorts.

The virtues of private hunting preserves are that they provide bird shooting at reasonable cost close to the heavily urbanized areas where hunting would otherwise be impossible. Their drawbacks are that the game is pen-raised and not wild; the cost is necessarily high per day; and the hunting of game birds at so much per bird is not compatible with the American tradition of free public hunting of native game.

It is, however, interesting to note the growth of private shooting preserves within the past few decades. Currently, there are almost 3,000 shooting preserves for upland birds and waterfowl in North America. Four of the Canadian Provinces have shooting preserves, and only five of the contiguous forty-eight states do not permit the establishment of private hunting preserves and the trend has been towards gradually whittling down the remaining number. Perhaps the private shooting preserve is, to date, the most workable answer to a mushrooming growth in population coupled with a corresponding decrease in game-bird habitat and population.

27

Field Guide to Hunting Waterfowl

WATERFOWL HUNTING HAS always been a favorite sport of most American hunters. A major milestone in waterfowl hunting was reached in 1900 when, by the passage of the Federal Lacey Act, which controlled interstate shipment of game, market hunting about reached the end of its rope.

Later, in 1918, a treaty known as the Migratory Bird Treaty Act was signed by Britain and the United States, providing basic bag limits and limitations on the length of shooting seasons. These two acts, more than any other legislation, changed the complexion of waterfowl hunting.

Other important legislation was the Duck Stamp Law in 1934 and the Pittman-Robertson program in 1937. The Duck Stamp Law made it mandatory that every duck hunter over sixteen years of age purchase a migratory waterfowl hunting stamp. The P-R program, as it is popularly called, provided for an excise tax of 11 per cent on sporting arms and ammunition. The funds from both are used to acquire and restore waterfowl habitat.

Bold legislation was necessary, and continues to be needed, not only to make waterfowl hunting a sport instead of a commercial proposition but to insure game bags to future generations of hunters.

Currently, the duck population is holding its own. In 1936 the U.S. duck population was estimated at 33 million. By 1965 their numbers had fallen to just over 29 million, but by 1967 the population had recovered and grown to slightly over 38.5 million. A large share of the credit for this increase must go to the National Wildlife Refuge System. In 1937 we had approximately 11.5 million acres of refuges. Through its efforts, the amount nearly tripled to over 30.5 million acres by 1969, with much of the land being used for propagation as well as for sanctuary.

North American waterfowl nest and reproduce in the northern portions of the continent and winter in the southern part. There is some overlapping of the nesting and wintering areas, resulting in "resident" waterfowl.

The migrations of these birds assume four broad patterns, referred to and regulated as the Atlantic, Mississippi, Central, and Pacific Flyways. The recovery of banded birds indicates that waterfowl heading northward to the nesting grounds in spring may be harvested that fall in another flyway. Again, they may take a different route back. But the management of waterfowl is based upon the habitual use of these four routes.

Waterfowl may be divided into four categories: ducks, brant, geese, and shore birds.

DUCKS. Compared with other waterfowl species, ducks are found in a wide variety of habitat. Individual species will change this broad pattern according to migration habits, season, food preference, and whether they are of the diving-duck group or surface feeders.

Methods of hunting ducks include stalking and jump-shooting, hunting with decoys, boats, and dogs, using blinds, or any possible combination of these methods. All these techniques will be covered in subsequent chapters.

For all forms of duck shooting, the 12-gauge, full-choke, repeating shotgun, either pump or autoloading, has long been the most popular duck gun. For close-in shooting over decoys, the 20 gauge is handy and effective in the hands of a good shotgun man. With the development of the 20 gauge, there has been a great spurt of interest in the trim twenty, and the magnum version is bound to increase in popularity for duck hunting.

Similarly, many duck hunters facing increasingly wary and scarce birds have gone to the 12-gauge, 3-inch Magnum, or duck gun, in full choke, especially for pass-shooting. For those who like the two-choke virtues of the double, but also like a single sighting plane, the over-under has provided the answer and is now popular as a duck gun. The best shot sizes for all-round duck shooting are No. 4, 5, and 6.

Greenwinged Teal. Also called greenwing and mud teal, are distributed from the Arctic to central Mexico. Their habitat includes ponds, lakes, marshes, and streams, and, in cold weather, salt water. Sometimes they are found a distance from the water.

Coloring of the male and the female differs: the male's breast is tan with brown spots, with a white vertical crescent behind, gray sides, and buffy undertail coverts. The female is brownish gray on top and pale speckled gray below.

The voice of the male is a piping whistle; that of the female a high-pitched quack.

Greenwing are swift in flight and dart in a zig-zag fashion, wheeling like pigeons in compact flocks. They sometimes walk around on the ground, feeding in mud. Their food consists of crustaceans, aquatic plants, shellfish, seeds, etc.

Bluewinged Teal. Also called summer teal, are slightly larger than greenwinged teal. Distribution in nesting season is southern Canada and northern United States, and wintering grounds include Mexico, Central America, and northern South America. Their habitat is fresh water, marshes, ponds; very seldom are they found in salt water.

The male is grayish on top, tan with darker tan below, a white patch on the end of the flank, with black tail and undertail coverts. The female is brownish-gray on top and pale gray mixed with darker gray below.

Bluewinged Teal

The voice of the male is a peep-like whistle; the female has the same shrill quack as the green-winged teal. Their flight is erratic.

Food of the bluewing consists of crustaceans, aquatic plants, snails, and seeds.

Bufflehead. Also called butter-ball, dipper duck, spirit duck, dipper, dapper, marionette, shot bag, Scotchman. Their nesting range is north-western Canada and southern Alaska, wintering range the southern half of the United States. Their habitat includes lakes, bays, oceans, and rivers.

The male has black and white glossy feathers, with a large head with black, purplish-toned feathers, and a triangular white patch from below the eye around back of the head. There is a white patch on its wing, which can be seen in flight. The female is dusky brown in color, with a large head and a white patch in back of the eye. Its bill is bluish gray and comparatively short. Bufflehead range in size from 12 to 15 inches. They nest in hollow trees; their eggs are cream-colored.

The voice of bufflehead is seldom heard; the female quacks and the male whistles. On shore this duck usually gathers in flocks. On the water they float lightly when not disturbed and can take off into the air from under the surface of the water.

Food consists of fish, aquatic insects, and shellfish.

Goldeneye. Also called whistler; brass eye; great-head; carrot; quandy (female); and whistlewing (because of the whistling sound its wings make in flight). Nesting area is central Canada, wintering grounds, central United States. Their habitat include bays, oceans, rivers, and lakes.

The goldeneye is 18 inches long and has a stocky body and a short neck, with a long thin bill. The male's upper parts are black, the rest of the body is white, and the head has a greenish gloss on top. The bill is black. The female has a brown head, yellow eyes, gray back and sides. The belly, collar, breast, and split wing are patched with white; the outer part of the bill is yellow.

Goldeneye make a running take-off, rise together in flocks, and stay together in flight. They dive frequently when feeding. The voice of the male is penetrating and shrill; the female's is a deep quack. Food consists of aquatic insects, plants, crustaceans, etc.

Ruddy Duck. Known by nearly a hundred other names, nests in southern-central Canada and central-northern United States, winters in Mexico and along the full length of both the Pacific and the Atlantic Coasts. Their habitat is lakes, streams, rivers, ponds, and sheltered bays.

Measuring 15 inches in length, with a broad, upturned, blue bill and a thick neck, the male has a chestnut-brown body, black-crowned head with white cheeks, and a tail shaped like a fan. The female is similar to the male in the winter but has a dark stripe along the cheek.

The ruddy duck's eggs are dull white to buffy color, and from five to fifteen are laid. Their voice is silent except for a low cluck when courting. They swim with their tail often cocked, and can sink slowly underwater or dive quickly; on land they require a long run for take off into the air. Food consists of insects, aquatic animals, and vegetation.

Scaup. (Greater and Lesser). The lesser scaup's other names are little blackhead, little bluebill, raft duck, creek broadbill, river bluebill, cove bluebill, bluebill coot.

The lesser scaup has a far greater distribution than the greater scaup, with nesting grounds in northwestern Canada, and wintering grounds in southern United States, Mexico, and along each coast. Their habitat is in fresh water, and very seldom salt water.

The male has a purplish-black head, neck, chest and rear ends. The back and scapulars are white mixed with black, giving a grayish effect. The eggs range from a greenish gray to olive coloring.

Both male and female are usually silent during the day, but the male utters a loud *scaup* when startled. They fly swiftly and erratically, often twisting and turning, and stay in large compact flocks. They are good divers and swimmers.

Food consists of aquatic vegetation, snails, and insects, and small aquatic animals.

The greater scaup's other names are bluebill widgeon, broadbill, raft duck, big blackhead, troop fowl, greenhead. Their habitat is oceans, bays, lakes, rivers and ponds.

Their size is 18 inches. An identifying characteristic is a large wing with a white strip that extends almost down to the end. The male's head and neck are similar to that of the lesser scaup except that the head has a greenish iridescence. Body is same as that of the lesser but sides are white. The bill is blue. The female is dark brown with a clearly defined white area across face at base of bill. The eggs and voice are the same as the lesser.

They collect in large rafts and generally stay on large bodies of fresh water and salt water rather than small bodies of water as the lesser does. Food consists of mollusks, crustaceans, and seeds.

Ringnecked Duck. Also called ringnecked scaup, bastard broadbill, ringnecked blackhead, blackie, ringbilled blackhead, ringbill. They have a limited nesting ground in central Canada and Maine. Their habitat is wooded lakes, streams, and ponds in the North; saltwater bays in the South.

The drake's chest, back, and rump are black, its breast is white, merging into brownish black on the belly. The sides are gray. The head and neck are black with purple iridescence, and the neck has a narrow chestnut collar, which gives this duck its name. The bill is grayish blue with a black tip separated by a white band. The female is brown with a white eye-ring, cheeks and belly. The eggs are dark olive-buff. Their voice, which is seldom heard, is similar to the lesser scaup, and they travel in small flocks and land without circling.

Food consists of seeds and aquatic vegetation.

European Widgeon. Also called redheaded widgeon and widgeon, are often found along the Atlantic, but do not have any true distribution pattern. Their habitat is lakes, streams, rivers, marshes, and bays. They prefer fresh water but are sometimes seen on salt water.

This duck measures 19 inches, the male has gray on top and flanks, a pinkish breast, whitish rump, rear flanks, belly and wing coverts. The head is cinnamon-red with cream-colored forehead and crown. Primaries

Widgeon

and tail coverts are black, and the speculum is green, shading to black toward the rear. The female's body is dusky brown edged with gray on the back, scapulars, and rump; buffy brown on the chest and sides; white on breast and belly; and the head is cinnamon-buff, darker around the eye and back of head.

The male's voice is a shrill whistling sound; the female quacks.

Widgeons fly in close, irregular flocks and circle in when landing. They sit high on the water. Their food consists of aquatic plants, seeds, and widgeon grass.

Wood Duck. Also called summer duck, wood widgeon, acorn duck, and tree duck, nests in eastern United States from Canada to Florida, and in the Northwest. Their habitat is freshwater marshes, swamps, and creeks. They nest in hollows in trees.

The size of this bird is 18 inches. The drake's head is maroon, purple, green and white, with feathers at the back of the head draping like a hood. The body is bronze-green on the back and rump, purplish-chestnut on chest with a black and white vertical bar in front of folded wing, pale buffy sides and large patch of purplish chestnut on each flank. The

Wood Duck

female is white on the throat and underparts, and ashy gray on neck. The head is brownish with greenish gloss on top and the eye is circled by a white ring. The back, rump, and scapulars are brown, glossed with bronze and greenish-purple. Chest and sides are olive-brown and the breast and belly are white. The eggs are dull white.

The male normally emits a long series of whistles and a sharp *hoo-eek* when startled. The female emits a *crr-ek cr-r-ek*.

D.A.

Shoveler

They sit high on the water and hold the head high above the level of the body in flight, which is swift and direct. They eat aquatic plants, seeds, and nuts.

Gadwall. Also called gadwell, gray duck, specklebelly, creek duck. Nesting grounds includes northwestern United States and southwestern Canada; they winter in southern United States and the northern half of Mexico. Habitat is lakes, ponds, streams, and fresh and brackish marshes.

Their size is 20 inches; the male's head and neck are light brown, its shoulders are red-brown, and its undertail and rump coverts are black. Distinguishing features are a chestnut patch on middle wing coverts and white on the lining and axillars. The female is brown on top with whitish breast and belly. Chestnut and white on wings are similar to the male. The eggs are creamy color.

The voice of the male is a whistle and trill, and the female has a loud quack. Their flight is direct and swift, in small compact flocks. Their wingbeat is rapid and in flight the wings appear long and pointed. When alarmed they spring immediately into the air. They eat grass, grain, and aquatic plants.

Shoveler. Also called spoonbill, broadbill. They nest in Central Alaska, a strip of Canada including Yukon, British Columbia, and Saskatchewan, and northwestern United States. They winter in Mexico and southern United States. Their habitat is shallow water and fresh or brackish marshes.

This bird is identified by its pronounced shovel-like bill. Its size is 19 inches. The drake has a green head, brown belly and white breast and wings with a dark strip extending the entire length. Tail coverts and primaries are black. This bird shows more white on water than any other surface-feeding duck. In flight an alternating dark and light pattern from head to tail can be seen. Hens are brown above and paler brown below. The eggs are pale olive-green to gray-green in color.

The voice of the male is a low *woe-woe* and the female a quiet quack. Their flight is rather slow, somewhat hesitating except when frightened. They fly and also swim with their bill pointed down. They sit low on the water, and use their shovel-type bill for surface feeding. Their food consists of snails, aquatic insects, seeds, crustaceans, aquatic plants.

Pintail. Also called springtail, pheasant duck, gray duck, pickettail, sea widgeon. Their nesting range includes all of Alaska, western Canada, and northwestern United States. Wintering grounds include Mexico and Central America, and a fringe area around all the coastal areas of the United States. Their habitat is lakes, ponds, rivers, marshes, and saltwater bays in winter.

The size of this bird is 22 to 27 inches. It can be identified by its pointed "stem" tail and its long slender neck with a distinctive line on the side. The drake has a white breast and belly, brown head, gray back and sides, and black, white-edged feathers. The female is light brown, darker brown on top, and white on the belly.

Pintail

The male's voice is a loud *qwa, qwa* in flight. The female utters a subdued quack. They fly fast and gracefully and sit high on the water. When startled they spring neatly from the water. Their food consists of shellfish, grain, and seeds.

Black Duck. Also called black mallard, English duck, inhabits the eastern part of the continent, with nesting grounds in eastern Canada and the United States and wintering grounds in southeastern United States. Any water is suitable habitat for this duck.

Both males and females have brown heads and black bodies, white underwings, dusky legs, and a yellow or greenish bill. Their voice is a low, reedy *kwek, kwek, kwek*; they fly high in the air with their neck slightly lowered. Like mallards, they take off from the water vertically.

Black ducks feed on aquatic plants, grass, grain, seeds, and mollusks.

Black Duck

Mallard. Also called greenhead, the most popular of all ducks and is found the world over. They are the most widely distributed on our continent of all the ducks; nesting grounds include the western portions of Alaska and Canada and the northern half of the United States. Wintering grounds include southern United States and northern Mexico.

One of the largest wild ducks, drakes weigh over 3 pounds and are 23 inches in size. The male has a green head, white collar, brown breast, gray body, and black rump, with a tight curl of feathers on top of the tail.

327

Mallard

The female is brown and only has a little white in its tail.

Their voice is similar to the black duck. They feed on seeds, grain, grass, and aquatic vegetation.

Redhead. Known as fiddler duck, grayback, and American pochard, also has an extended distribution. Nesting grounds include all of Alaska, western Canada, and northwestern United States. Like several other species, the redhead winters in Mexico and around the coastal fringes of the United States. Hens are brown with gray wings. The drakes have gray bodies with black breast and rump. The bill is blue in color.

Canvasback. Two identifying features of the canvasback, sheldrake, or "can" are the drake's white body with both ends black; and the sloping, long bill which meets the head with little "jump" in contour. Female canvasbacks are gray in color. The drakes have red heads, in addition to the black and white bodies which resemble "belted" hogs. Canvasbacks winter in the southern half of the United States, and have nesting grounds in western Canada and Alaska.

Canvasback

In addition to these species are the scoters, including the surf scoter; the white-winged scoter; and the American scoter, commonly called a "coot."

Mergansers. (American merganser, hooded merganser, redbreasted merganser). All three species are commonly called sheldrakes, and the redbreasted merganser is also commonly known as a fish duck.

BRANT. Of two species, the American brant and the black brant, these birds are midway in size between ducks and geese, with the American brant resembling a goose, and the black brant considerably darker. Both species nest in the Arctic and migrate to the United States' coastal areas in winter. The American brant lives on the eastern side of the continent, the black brant stays on the western half. These big birds like the protection afforded by off-shore islands. One of their preferred foods is eel-grass, and the incidence of this gives a clue to where the greatest concentrations of birds are apt to be.

329

Both species of brant are hunted by the use of duck boats, decoys, and blinds. The best guns are those suitable for large ducks and geese, and if one were to be picked above all others it would be a standard 12-gauge, pump-action, full-choke repeater.

Brant

D.A.

GEESE. The largest and most important wild goose is the Canada goose, known as the Canadian honker. This goose will run to a yard in body-length, with a wingspan of twice that. Size varies as between the males and females, but will average around 8 to 10 pounds. From records of banded, sanctuary birds, a Canadian honker may live to an age comparable to that of man.

The Canada goose has a striking appearance. Both sexes are light gray on the breast, tapering to a white along the underbelly and to the tail. The back and wing coverings are a darker gray. The bird has an unusually long neck, which changes coloration at the body line to become a pure black. This extends all over the head with the exception of a large vertical white patch extending from near the crown, all the way down the face. This head-and-neck shows up plainly for long distances, either in stubble or on water—and especially so if the bird is alerted, and stands with head upright.

Honkers fly habitually in V wedges, and can attain a speed up to 50 or 60 miles an hour. The "cry of the wild goose" sounds something like *Eaur-awk, eaur-awk* . . . and once heard, simply isn't forgotten. It can be heard for nearly a mile on a still day.

Canada Goose

The Canada goose is widely distributed, with an annual range from Alaska to Mexico. Nesting grounds are the marshes of almost all Canada, and the honker winters as far south as Mexico. Like elk, honkers can predict weather. Consistent temperatures of 28 degrees and lower will start them on their southward migrations; their spring migrations northward indicate general warming trends. Of all waterfowl, the Canada goose is one of the smartest and hardest to approach within shotgun range.

Besides stalking and jump-shooting, the methods used for hunting geese of all species include the use of blinds of all sorts, boats either from which to hunt or to tend off-shore blinds, and the use of many types of goose decoys.

Geese are especially hard to stalk and catch in smaller waters such as ponds and potholes. When they alight they habitually choose some position where they can see in all directions—long sandbars in lakes, open fields of stubble, the middle of large rivers or near tiny islands. These strategic positions are abandoned only when the built-in suspicions of the species are entirely allayed.

One place geese may occasionally be stalked is from the curving bank of a sizable river, and after the birds haven't been molested for some time. The method is to spot them as they alight, allow an hour to pass, then stalk through the foliage off each bank bend until the birds are located. This calls for careful stalking and concealment. Many an ardent waterfowler crawls on his belly the last quarter-mile.

The 12-gauge, 3-inch Magnum duck gun is a fine tool for shooting geese, and should be in full-choke boring. The standard 12 gauge has also long been a fine weapon, and is still adequate if geese can be decoyed in reasonably close.

On either side of the 12-gauge lovers are the 20-gauge specialists who claim that the 20-gauge Magnum will do anything the 12 gauge will on decoyed geese; and this group usually are exponents of No. 6 and 7½ shot, trying for neck shots only. Many a gunner will claim that the smaller shot sizes at close to medium ranges will cut through goose feathers where the bigger shot will ball up and slow down.

Oppositely, there are many veteran hunters who swear by the bigger 10 bores for all goose shooting. They like the better pattern this gauge will impart to larger shot, at the long ranges geese often have to be taken. For pass-shooting, the 10 gauge will do more than the 12 gauge.

From the standpoint of actual use, BB shot, No. 2 and 4 are the most popular for shooting geese. On any gun large enough for geese, a soft-rubber recoil pad is a sensible investment.

SHORE BIRDS. The shore birds may be grouped broadly into the snipes, gallinules, rails, and coots. These birds, as the name suggests, live at the junction of shallow water and shorelines. They belong to the Rallidae family, whose numerous species are distributed in most parts of the world. Most species are smaller than the duck family and have sharp, pointed bills.

The snipes have long curving bills, necessary to feeding on beaches and in matted vegetation. Two of the more common varieties are the curlew snipe and the Wilson snipe.

The gallinules are the largest shore birds. These birds are relatively short-billed and look more like coots than do snipes and rails. The Florida gallinule and the purple gallinule are two of the most prominent.

One of the most important shore birds, so far as the hunter is concerned, is the Carolina rail, or sora. Another, more widely distributed, is the Virginia rail. Both birds nest in southern Canada and migrate to southern parts of the United States for wintering.

The American coot is one of the most widely distributed of the shore birds, being found in Alaska, Canada, the United States, and Mexico. They are far less migratory than other waterfowl. The coot, or mud hen as it is popularly known, is a squat, slate-colored bird with a white bill. Coots swim and dive well and are often seen with ducks. They are among the most vicious of birds, and while being trapped and banded, will peck the hands of the handler. When leaving the water to fly, coots take off in a long paddling run along the surface, and are easily hit with a shotgun charge. There is a wide divergence of opinion about their edibility, which depends largely upon their diet.

The woodcock, commonly called the timberdoodle, is sometimes considered an upland bird but is more of the snipe family. This odd-appearing bird is bug-eyed, has only an excuse of a tail, but has a somewhat paunchy belly and extremely long bill. The bird is mottled black, brown, and rust, and is generally found along the Atlantic Coast. Due to its fine eating qualities, the woodcock was heavily hunted in early days by market hunters.

Woodcock

Generally shore birds are hunted by stalking them along shorelines. Sometimes groups of hunters, walking a shoreline into the wind, will push the birds towards a concealed hunter posted in a strategic position. A species like rail can be hunted by two men in a shallow-draft boat among the marsh grasses, one poling, the other shooting.

The 20-gauge shotgun of any preferred action, having improved-cylinder choke, and using No. 7½, 8 or 9 shot is a popular combination for most shore-bird shooting.

The future of waterfowl hunting seems destined to incur ever-increasing restrictions, even smaller bag limits (periodically, at least), and the occasional removal of a dwindling species from the legal bag. Waterfowl, like other game, is not a product which can be manufactured, stored, and spread evenly so as to harvest over the years. It is, rather, an annual crop. As such, it requires brood stock, suitable conditions for reproduction, food, and resting areas along the major flyways.

The biggest cause for the dwindling supply of waterfowl has been the draining of wetlands in the interests of agriculture. The main reason waterfowl do not stop in the fall on their southward migration is that there are no suitable places. In the absence of resting places and feeding grounds en route from Canada and Alaska to Mexico many species can make the long annual journey nonstop. To the degree they do this we will have less shooting.

Such organizations as Ducks Unlimited, and such money-providing programs as the Duck Stamp Law and excise tax on sporting arms and ammunition, have started to show the way towards a restoration of "duck factories" and resting areas. The rest is up to the citizenry.

28

Stalking and
Jump-Shooting

STALKING WATERFOWL ON foot entails a different problem than stalking upland birds. While upland birds will often run directly into cover or sit tight at the approach of a hunter, waterfowl, once they spot him, will fly before he comes into range. Nature tells upland birds that their camouflage coloration will prevent detection while they are immobile in the foliage of their natural habitat, but waterfowl instinctively know that their camouflaging is inadequate when they are on water. Consequently, the successful stalking of waterfowl depends on getting within shotgun range entirely unseen and unsuspected.

There are only limited types of habitat conducive to such an approach. The most common of these are inland potholes, creeks, water holes such as irrigation ponds on cultivated fields, the intermittent ponds and small lakes of marsh country and flooded lowlands, and inland rivers.

The use of potholes, creeks, and small water of any type by waterfowl is dependent on such factors as resident bird population, fall flights of migrating birds, and the relationship between areas and species-distribution. Weather, and any adjacent feeding grounds such as stubble fields, also have a direct bearing on the degree of bird concentration. Often the general incidence of birds may be determined for distances up to a mile or so by observing them hovering over and alighting on such inland waters. During foul, cold weather, normally coincident with the northern flights, birds will tend to group and rest more than in balmy weather. In short, waterfowl's use of inland waters is variable and may be heavy, spotty, or seldom.

The hunter's problem, once he sees birds alight on inland waters, is to sneak up within range, utilizing available cover, then jump-shoot the birds as they fly off. During any stalk, flying birds overhead will give the hunter's presence away; and while stalking it is best, when detecting such a flock, to lie low and immobile until it has either alighted or taken off.

Changes in elevation, available foliage, and the changing contours of streams, creeks, and ponds can help the hunter approach birds unseen, if he knows how to use them. From their low position on the water, waterfowl cannot see very far inland, and this is an advantage to the hunter. Consequently, the stalker's approach is generally easy except for the last 50 to 100 yards. As the final distance is the most difficult, the biggest lament of the stalker is that he can't make it undetected, and the birds get up just out of range.

In sneaking up on inland waterfowl, the best technique is to crawl for the final yards up to a stream bank, lake shore, or creek bed, from where the game can be viewed. As the hunter gets close to his objective, he should limit his movement as much as possible. At the last cover, where the hunter "takes a look," he should be very careful not to disclose himself.

If the birds have swum out of range or sight, or if there are no birds where he expected them, then the hunter must alter the direction of any subsequent stalking so as to intercept them at other positions along the stream, creek, or pond. Usually this means cautiously moving back along the route he has come, circling about, then coming up again to some other vantage point.

The hunter should exercise extreme care in carrying his shotgun when approaching waterfowl. There is always the possibility of inadvertently poking the gun's muzzle into snow or mud. When the plugged gun is fired, it will blow up the barrel and may injure the shooter.

One of the sporting aspects of stalking and jump-shooting waterfowl is the fact that, even after a perfect and successful stalk is made and the hunter comes within range, one or two quick shots is all he gets. Thereafter, birds of the same flock won't return to that spot again, and he often has to wait in the same area for others to fly in.

Stalking and jump-shooting take another form in marshes which are interlaced with tule beds and similar vegetation. A light boat with a pointed bow and narrow beam is often poled quietly from pothole to pothole, and the birds are shot as they jump from sudden view of the craft and hunters. This type of jump-shooting depends upon a quiet approach, and is most profitable where large areas of water and marsh can be covered.

Retrieving dead birds which fall into rivers, creeks, and small inland potholes is always a problem. Many may be recovered simply by wading out after them, wearing hip boots or waders. Many birds that are out of reach will be blown or drift with the current to where they can be picked up closer to shore. Even a light breeze will eventually move a dead bird a considerable distance, if the hunter is patient. Throwing sizable rocks just *over* a dead bird in calm water will move it towards the hunter a few yards.

A simple gadget to carry along for those birds that are hard to reach is a small coil of chalkline equipped at the end with a huge treble hook and a few ounces of lead sinkers. Such a rig, heaved out and over a dead bird, will hook the feathers and enable the hunter to pull it in.

29

Shooting from Blinds

IN BLIND-SHOOTING, as against stalking and jump-shooting of waterfowl, the birds invariably must come to the hunter. This means that any blind, if it is to be successful, must be situated so that birds will pass closely by it.

For pass-shooting, this means that the blind must be in line with the normal flight course of birds as they travel back and forth. For shooting shallow-water ducks, the blind must be in shallow waters where ducks are known to feed. For sound or bay shooting, the blind must often be floating, so that it may be towed to within the normal courses of the flights. For hunting migrating geese in stubble fields as they head southward in the fall, pit blinds must be situated as close as possible to the most used areas, with decoys and a goose call serving to bring the birds in the final distances.

Before locating any blind, then, the pattern of the moving birds should be carefully plotted; and the blind placed in the closest, most natural position possible for their expected flight. This takes observation, a knowledge of bird habits, and often several seasons of trial-and-error before the best blind locations can be established. Good permanent blind locations include reefs, points of land jutting into open water, necks of land between two water areas, the inside bends of acutely curving rivers, and similar spots that waterfowl habitually cross.

PERMANENT BLINDS. Permanent blinds are more often used for such shallow-water species as mallard, widgeon, teal, and pintail because the areas these birds "work" can be more easily pinpointed than those of diving ducks. And such blinds should be built only after observation has shown that the birds will use the areas annually.

Permanent blinds may be as elaborate as the hunter wishes but are built to accommodate only one or two hunters. More hunters are a nuisance in a blind, and the size necessary for over two makes the blind too conspicuous. Blinds may be in the form of sunken boxes or elevated platform-huts. They can be built of a variety of materials, such as posts-and-planking, plywood, or wooden frames lined with tar paper and covered with chicken wire for inserting brush camouflage.

Often in mountain or pothole lake country, a good permanent blind can be constructed largely of rocks piled in seemingly haphazard fashion into a small cairn, then covered with brush or limbs to look like part of the natural landscape.

In conifer country bordering lakes and rivers, a permanent blind may be nothing more than a brushy pine tree situated at some strategic bend or point. Limbs on the "shooting" side are cut out and laced with others from nearby trees of the same kind into a hutlike enclosure at the tree's base, with a small aperture left in front.

In the same type of country, small blinds can be made to resemble natural pines or spruces. These are built by erecting a tripod of strong light poles a man's height, then strengthening them with other saplings. This frame is covered with green pine boughs, leaving an aperture for the gunner.

On brushy lake shores, islands, or points of land jutting into open water, permanent blinds are often built of stakes driven into the earth to form the blind's outside; then this skeleton is laced with brush.

In the building of any blind, whether permanent or temporary, the main idea is to cover it with an outside layer which is in harmony with the surroundings. In short, the successful blind must not only be situated so that flying waterfowl will naturally pass it; it must seem to be an integral part of the landscape.

For example, in tule country, the tule covering should be laced vertically, not horizontally, into the blind skeleton. Similarly, rock or driftwood blinds constructed along coastal waters or lake shores should be made to look as casual and unobtrusive as other clumps of driftwood or piles of rock—not finished up in fine houselike shape. Also, the blind should be the same general size as the natural piles of wood or stone. For a similar reason, a blind built high (such as the pine-tree blind mentioned before) would be entirely conspicuous and out of place if built in an area of normally low vegetation. A better type might be a small shore pit laced with brush on top.

Many permanent blinds in shallow water may be reached by wading. Others must be reached by boat, and in this case provision must also be

The permanent blind above is built of stakes driven into the river bottom and covered with cypress bark to blend with the terrain. The blind below, also of cypress bark, is built around the trunk of a large cypress tree.

made for concealing the boat. Many times the craft is pulled alongside the blind, then covered with brush common to the blind and area.

For waterfowl shooting in coastal waters, floating permanent blinds are used. These often have to withstand rough water, and are solidly built upon raftlike foundations with elevated platforms to resemble small floating islands. Sides are made of plywood, or mesh laced with brush common to the shore, and lined with tar paper. Some are large enough to accommodate a small rowboat and in big water are often used in conjunction with a sea-worthy mother boat anchored within the area.

Generally a blind is made larger at the bottom than at the top for the convenience of the hunters. A small opening is left at the top through

Built of two logs cleated together, with room for a duck boat between, the raft blind is camouflaged with rushes and grass woven through a chicken-wire fence.

which the hunter shoots. Many permanent blinds are heated by a gasoline lantern or small portable heater.

Like good violins, permanent blinds get better from year to year due to weathering, normal breaking down, and winds which mold them to the contour and harmony of the surroundings.

A permanent blind should be built well ahead of the waterfowl season. This allows the birds native to an area, as well as migrating birds, to get used to it.

TEMPORARY BLINDS. Suppose a hunter discovers that birds habitually cross a wooded strip of land between two separated areas of a river.

341

Often the reason cannot be determined until the hunter flies over the area in an airplane, but the fact can be established by merely watching the birds' flight.

In such a situation many times the best possible "blind" is simply a large tree directly under the birds' route. The hunter posts himself tightly against the tree, in suitably colored outer clothes, and waits. His opportunity comes in pass-shooting any birds that eventually cross.

Pit blinds dug in stubble fields and covered with straw provide excellent concealment for goose hunters.

Again, consider the rancher who irrigated his fields each fall for plowing and discovered that after a few days waterfowl migrating through the area paid no attention whatever to an occasional canvas dam lying spread out to dry along a ditch bank. Such a dam, incidentally, is a rectangle of heavy canvas, 6 by 9 feet or larger, with a light pole shoved through a loop sewn along one side. It is used to dam off ditch water.

Having discovered that the birds paid the dams no heed, this fellow simply left a canvas dam or two spread out innocently along a ditch near ponded water. Each evening, especially during foul weather, he would stick his shovel upright into the ground near a dam, as though he had left the field. Then he would crawl under the canvas, lie on his back with only his face showing and Old Betsy by his side, and wait. When a mallard or gander came sailing in, he would kick off the dam, sit up, and give the bird a bad time.

Similarly, when migrating autumn birds congregate in wet stubble, a hollowed-out shock of unthreshed wheat, oats, or barley makes one of the best one-man blinds imaginable. The hunter simply arranges the bundles so that he can hunch down, partly inside the shock, and hope the cramps do not get to him before the birds do.

Recently, most farmers have taken to combining their grain in the fields instead of stack-threshing it, and baling the straw. Straw bales piled together, in a field of baled straw, do not look suspicious and make fine one-man blinds. Only enough bales are piled together to conceal the hunter.

The natural straw of grain fields can deceive birds which use these fields. The hunter must first learn, as nearly as possible, the exact spots which the migrating birds are beginning to use most. This can be done by watching from a distance and not molesting the birds for the first day or two. Having established a likely spot for a blind, the hunter, after dark, digs a narrow, shallow pit.

Such a pit need only be deep enough to sit or lie in. All dirt removed is carefully covered with straw from the stubble field. A blanket for covering the hunter is then made by stuffing straw into the mesh of a rectangle of chicken wire. Lastly, the decoys are set out close to the pit in strategic positions and left overnight.

Just before daylight, the hunter gets into the pit, covers himself with the straw blanket, and waits for a flight of waterfowl. A honk or two on the goose call, once a flight comes into view, will help lure the birds within shotgun range. An advantage of this type of blind is that the blanket is portable and can be used in another location.

Islands in rivers pick up driftwood from the early spring run-off which can be used for a blind. A blind on an island has the advantage over a shore blind in being closer to passing waterfowl and in permitting the shooter to see long distances up and down river without being seen.

Driftwood in such locations should be disturbed as little as possible. Any blind made of driftwood should be located on the upstream end of an island, not the downstream end where current ordinarily would never deposit it.

Often such a heap of driftwood can be improved and made more comfortable with a tarp of suitable color draped over the top and held down by other sticks. Camouflage sheets can be purchased. Or canvas can be dyed a suitable color—tan in tule country, white during snowstorms, or dirty gray to match the driftwood itself. Often an old canvas which is stained with mildew or mold will blend perfectly. In using any cloth as a covering for a blind, it is best to drape it loosely so that surface planes will not show up clearly from above nor reflect light unduly.

343

A blind may be merely a pile of sticks and brush (*left*) to break the outline of the crouching hunter before he rises for incoming birds, or a clump of cattails in which a hunter can conceal himself (*right*).

In marsh and lake country, either muskrat or beaver houses make good temporary blinds. The shooter simply climbs on top, drapes a suitably colored sheet of camouflage cloth around him, and lies in wait. Birds are used to the permanent stick-house, and unless the hunter shows up too plainly, will not pay too much heed.

Similarly, haystacks along river banks and lake shores in meadow country make fine shooting blinds, *if* they happen to be located in the path of any consistent flight pattern. The shooter simply climbs on the stack via a ladder, covers himself with hay, and waits. Stacks of bundled wheat or oats in stubble land are often found to be ideal blinds for foul-weather flights of waterfowl coming in to the fields, and are used, often in conjunction with decoys, like the haystacks.

In open prairie country, the lowly tumbleweed, piled in quantity along fencerows and dikes, makes a fine blind and is ubiquitous enough to be highly useful.

Temporary blinds are applicable to almost any hunting situation. The problem is to utilize materials available on the spot, and the best tool is imagination. The recent use of camouflage cloth helps greatly to accomplish this, and this item is easily portable.

344

A blind should be arranged so that the hunter has his back to the wind. This allows him to face birds coming in naturally upwind, and it is more comfortable. Often the ability to wait out a spell of gusty, bitter weather spells the difference between getting a bag of ducks or geese and getting a cold. Few places are colder than an unheated blind with the wind blowing in one's face.

Provision must always be made for a shooting aperture in the blind's top, large enough for a swing with the gun. Few men can hit a flying duck through something resembling a knothole.

Often when using temporary blinds for long hours or even several days in succession, many hunters get careless and inadvertently spoil the blind's effectiveness by tramping down the natural grasses and vegetation around it and leaving articles of equipment unconcealed. It is said that a Canadian honker can spot the shiny brass of an empty shell a quarter-mile away if it is flying high.

345

30

Decoys and
Duck Boats

THERE ARE THREE fundamental reasons why
waterfowl will come to artificial decoys. They are
gregarious and like to be in groups with their kind. They assume that
flocks of similar birds indicate the presence of food. And the sight of
unmolested birds gives them a sense of safety from predators.

Imitation duck and goose decoys have been made from many diverse
materials ranging from stuffed canvas, old shoe boxes, tin cans, and
crumpled paper, on up to lifelike statues carved in wood and painted
with the skill and fidelity to detail of a Renaissance artist.

SIMPLE DECOYS. Some of the simplest decoys have shown results.
Canadian honkers have been successfully decoyed into a field in which
old mail-order catalog pages or balls of crumpled newspapers were
scattered. Similarly, a dozen brown paper bags, blown up and tied shut,
and placed on the stubble of grain fields with their crushed tops bent
upward like a crude head, have brought in birds.

Another simple decoy is a bunch of grain straw tied with "straw
strings" taken from grain bundles; the straw is fashioned into the rough
shape of a duck, then rolled in earth or mud for darker coloration. A few
of these, scattered among other decoys, adds to the overall effectiveness
of the set.

For use in stubble fields during the fall flights, another simple decoy is
the head decoy. This is either the head of a live bird killed a day or so
previously, an imitation head carved of wood or cut of dark pasteboard,
or even knots of dark-colored wood. In any case the head is staked with a

wooden or wire pin into the earth at such a height to resemble a duck's or goose's head sticking above the stubble. Seen at a low and oblique angle, the decoy looks authentic.

On sandbars or muddy beaches, a simple decoy often is made by bunching up mud into the approximate shape of a bird and equipping it with wing tips cut from previously killed birds and saved for the occasion. The shadows and coloration afforded by the mounded "birds" and real feathers are often sufficient to draw in passing birds.

In all instances where such simple decoys are used, the set is always added to with real birds as they are killed. A proven way of placing the real bird is to lay it breast down and prop the head up with a forked stick shoved into the earth, or to fold the head under the wing as though the bird is resting. By the position of the stick, the dead bird could either be made to look ahead, or better, have its head dropped over as if feeding. The addition of a number of propped birds adds to the stool's effectiveness.

An interesting thing about makeshift decoys is that their use follows the hunting pressure northward along the "line of necessity" created by the increasing awareness of waterfowl to the incidence and ways of man. In the Arctic and Alaska, the use of decoys has been negligible. Farther down into the nesting grounds of northern Canada the need for decoys has not been acute, due largely to the top-heavy ratio of birds to population and hunters. But in southern Canada (due partly to increasing nonresident waterfowl hunters) and in the adjacent states, decoys are necessary to any consistent success. That is the situation today. With birds scarcer and hunting pressure increased, the greater the need for more and better decoys.

SILHOUETTE DECOYS. As its name suggests, the silhouette decoy is cut from light metal or cardboard and will cast a shadow. The cardboard kind is usually painted to resemble the live bird. Silhouettes are staked with a wooden slat nailed to the back into the earth or shallow water. Their advantage is that they are cheap, easily made, and portable. Their portability is an advantage when used in stubble fields, where considerable walking is required.

A popular decoy today, either for geese or ducks, is the folding cardboard decoy. This decoy is made of two sheets of cardboard, suitably painted on the outside, spread apart to form a thin A-shape, with the bottom portions either held open on a forked metal stake or formed into a flat base to float on the water. Usually the goose versions are used with metal wire stakes in shallow water or on sandbars. Duck decoys of this type are usually floated by means of a flat, light board which spreads the decoy at the bottom, to which the cord is attached. Seen from the front,

Folding silhouette decoys are becoming popular with waterfowl hunters because of their portability.

these "folders" look like open isosceles triangles, but viewed at any angle they appear entirely lifelike. A real virtue of the goose decoy is that, for purposes of folding, it is constructed with a movable head-and-neck. This allows the staked decoy to be used upright, simulating a goose in natural feeding position.

RUBBER AND PLASTIC DECOYS.   Other portable decoys are made of rubber and are blown up, like toy balloons, into life-sized shapes. Rubber decoys ride high on the water and are virtually unsinkable. Their drawback is the normal tendency of rubber to puncture and deteriorate, though there are few instances of a hunter using them having a blow-out.

Plastic decoys are commonly used and are popular because of their portability. Like rubber decoys, they are usually short-lived, especially when used in freezing weather.

WOODED DECOYS.   It is hard to better the old-fashioned wooden "block" decoys, and many old hand-carved blocks are still serving well into the second or third generation. Block decoys are often made of a light, straight-grained wood such as Port Orford cedar, or of hollowed-out pine. Sometimes they are shaped out of one piece; often the body is made first than the carved head is installed on a wooden dowel.

Wooden blocks have the advantages of standing abuse very well, and wood takes paint beautifully. The action of blocks on water is realistic, too, since their weight is comparable to that of a live bird. Lack of portability is their only drawback, but when used in conjunction with permanent blinds and boats they are ideal.

PLACEMENT OF DECOYS. The placement of decoys to simulate live birds is an art taking many seasons to master. The best possible way to learn, of course, is to study the live birds themselves; then utilize the artificial decoys in a way comparable to their habits.

Broadly speaking, waterfowl will decoy to large numbers of their own kind. This means that the more decoys the hunter has, the better his chances to pull flying birds in. For this reason, the pooling of the decoys of two hunters will result in more birds than if each shot alone from separate blinds.

An exception to this is shallow-water ducks feeding in potholes. Often a half-dozen to a dozen decoys in a single pothole is sufficient—simply because that is the way the live birds would work the spot.

Another fundamental is that each species will decoy best to birds of its own species. There are exceptions to this, also. Mallards, as one example, will often decoy well to a setup containing Canadian honker decoys. Or

Decoys along a bank should be arranged in natural feeding positions. The three at right are too uniform to be effective.

again, one species of shallow-water duck may decoy if decoys of another shallow-water species are included in the stool. However, it is basic that the decoys of the shallow-water ducks and those of the diving ducks should not be mixed. The reason is simply that the two groups do not mingle while feeding or resting.

A few goose decoys mixed in with a set of duck decoys will help to bring in the mallards.

The decoys for diving ducks may be set closer together than decoys used for shallow-water ducks. Mallards, as an example, spread out into small groups when feeding and only bunch up tightly just prior to taking off. To bunch up mallard decoys, while trying to simulate feeding birds, would look unnatural. An exception to this is that mallards resting along shorelines and river banks during foul, bitter weather tend to bunch far more than during feeding.

Again, when placing decoys to simulate feeding birds, it is apparent that some of the decoys should be placed with heads down as though feeding. All decoys with heads up would resemble a flock just set down or ready to take off and would not suggest the security of a feeding flock to birds overhead.

On large expanses of water, the V-spread decoy layout is very effective. The legs of the V can extend for about 75 feet, with female decoys placed up toward the point.

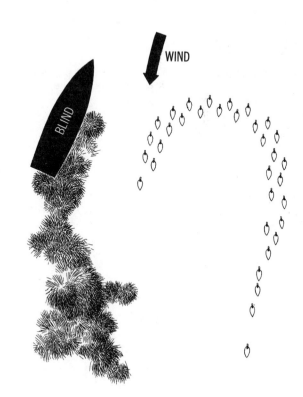

The J spread should be used when there is not much water in front of the hunter and therefore only a limited feeding area. It is good for divers in deep water and for dippers in shallow water.

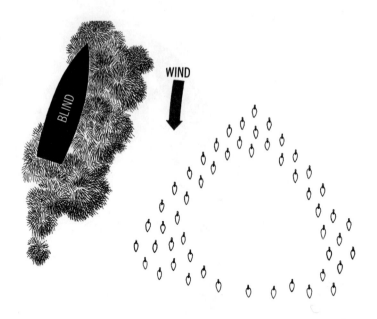

Effective on small bodies of water, the triangle spread leaves an opening for incoming birds. It should be placed opposite blind.

For deep-water ducks in Chesapeake Bay, many hunters have been successful with a spread that simulates a few stragglers swimming up to join the large feeding group.

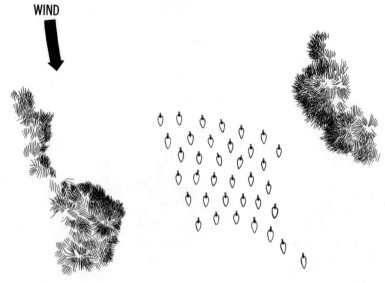

Ducks and geese flock to realistic-looking decoys better than to those that look artificial. While it is true that waterfowl in virgin country will come to most anything that looks like their kind, heavily hunted birds will not; and in most areas today, the better the decoys the more chance of attracting birds. This applies in proportion with the season's progress. The younger birds coming at the beginning of the season will decoy better than those at season's end.

The placement of decoys in relation to the blind is most important and should be compatible with the habits of live waterfowl. Birds like

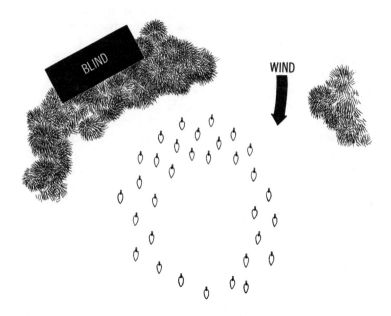

When a large set of decoys is placed offshore on a lake or river, use the oval spread 2 or 3 yards offshore slightly downwind of the blind and covering an area about 20 yards wide and 25 yards long.

mallards and honkers, as well as many other species, will make their final swing into decoys upwind. The position of the stool should take advantage of this fact.

Experienced hunters have found that such details as the color of the decoy anchoring cords has a bearing on the ultimate success. Cuttyhunk and similar light-colored line has often been used. But from a bird's-eye view, such cord in dark water often shows up as an unnatural white line and tends to keep wary birds suspicious. Better color for the cords are green, dark brown, or even black. The best cord is monofilament nylon fishing line of ample strength, which won't show at all.

Often a stool can be made less suspicious-looking to flying birds simply by placing a stuffed owl or crow or magpie decoy in tree or on a post along a river bank where such a bird would normally sit. Flying waterfowl soon learn to interpret the behavior of these wary birds, and suspicions are allayed if such a bird is unalarmed—an example of the brotherhood of the wilds.

CALLING. The final step in decoying waterfowl is to call them in once they have spotted the decoys. This applies only to "talking" species. Calling, like the arrangement of decoys, is an art in itself. The skill to do it successfully and consistently comes with observation and practice.

Calling can be learned from a veteran waterfowler, from phonograph records of experienced callers, from the sounds of the birds themselves, and from practice.

Generally speaking, the low, happy gabbling of feeding ducks is imitated—not the *quack, quack* made by alerted or frightened birds. With Canadian honkers the pitch, intensity, and duration of the habitual *eaur-onk, eaur-onk* is different when coming from a startled bird, such as one jumped from water, and that of a bird flying contentedly to others of its kind. These differences have to be learned, and it is best to learn the delicate shades of meaning in waterfowl calls from the birds themselves.

As with bugling for elk, calling should not be overdone. Decoys simulate feeding birds. Too much of an invitation means less available food for the resting birds and sounds suspicious. A basic rule of calling is: Once the birds turn to come in to decoys, *never* call again as long as they continue to come in.

Beginning hunters often figure that once the birds are within range it is time to shoot. Veteran shooters prefer to let any incoming birds, especially geese, come as close as they will. Birds settling to decoys are slower-moving and easier to hit than birds farther out.

DUCK BOATS. Boats for duck and geese hunting are specialized craft and vary in design and size according to the conditions of different areas. Some boats are used to approach sitting rafts of ducks. Some are used largely to tend floating blinds. Others must be highly portable for cartop use in prairie pothole country. And some must be highly stable for stand-up shooting in marsh bullrush country. All must be seaworthy and generally are low in height, pointed at at least one end, and decked over. Their purpose is to conceal the hunter and remain inconspicuous.

One popular form is the sneak-box. This is a low, shallow-draft, pointed-end boat decked over fore and aft, with an open cockpit in the middle for the hunter, and is propelled by oars. It is usually made of wood.

Another highly useful craft is the scull-boat. This, too, is a shallow-draft boat with either a mild round or V bottom, square stern, decked over bow, and an open cockpit towards the rear in which the hunter lies supine. In this position, he can just see over the coaming around the cockpit and can propel the craft with a short paddle through a hole in the square transom. It is used to slip up noiselessly on sitting birds.

The punt is another craft used considerably on inland lakes. This is a double-end boat, decked over fore and aft, low at midship, with high coaming around the open cockpit in which the hunter stands and propels the craft with a long slender pole.

All these types and their variations may be grassed over along their decks for camouflaging. In use they look like drifting logs or patches of marsh. These craft are normally painted a drab green, brown, or varying shades, to resemble the natural foliage, and of a dullness which won't reflect sunlight. Some hunters paint their craft a mottled brown-green and use them with camouflage hunting clothing. During late season snow and ice, scull-boats are sometimes painted white, draped over with white canvas, or iced over. When used by a hunter wearing a white costume, the result looks like a floating iceberg. The pointed ends of all these craft are necessary for the penetration of marsh grasses, tules, etc.

The Eskimo version of these basic waterfowl crafts is the kayak, which he uses in much the same fashion except that propulsion is by means of a long double-ended paddle. The kayak's cockpit is exceptionally small and a capelike parka is often spread over the coaming to make the craft watertight.

Farther north in the Arctic Circle, Eskimo hunters use a tiny, pointed, one-man skin boat. This puny craft is made by stretching the single skin of an *oogruk*, or bearded seal, over a wooden skeleton. The entire craft is approximately 7 feet long, and is moved by short oars.

Southward in Canada the standard canoe is usually used as a duck boat. This slender craft is easily moved, goes handily into shallow-water foliage, and is most useful on the sheltered lakes so common to the Dominion. Square-sterned canoes, adaptable to outboard motors, are often used, minus the motor, for fall duck shooting, then double in summer as fishing craft.

For use in marshy country, the flat-bottomed skiff makes a good duck boat. This boat rides low on the water, is decked fore and aft, has the shooter's cockpit towards the stern, and has a square transom. Most skiffs are around 14 feet long.

The rail boat is patterned after the ancient dugout canoe. It is long for the beam width and has a slender stern. Usually it is pushed along with a long pole by a hunter standing on a pusher's platform near the stern. The shooter often sits on a stool near the center of the undecked craft.

Weighted boats, held down nearly flush to the water's surface by water ballast or metal weights, and called "sink-boxes," are not used much any more, due to their hazards in choppy water.

Since World War II, and the availability of rubber life rafts, this sea-worthy form of craft has been tried for hunting waterfowl. It has the virtues of being inexpensive, safe, highly portable, and rides low to the water. When draped over with camouflage cloth and used by camouflaged hunters, it often will suffice for such purposes as float-hunts on rivers, tending blinds, or crossing lakes and streams to good shooting locations.

But the rubber life raft's drawbacks are many. It is blunt and will not penetrate grasses and bullrushes. Having no keel, but with extremely highriding qualities, it handles and moves like some big wooden chip. And the surest way to get a wetting is to stand up in one of the popular two-man sizes—it kicks out sidewise from under a person as if on ball bearings. Its chief utility is its portability. Weighing only 50 to 60 pounds, it can be backpacked into inland lakes.

31

Plucking and
Preparing Birds

PLUCKING, DRAWING, and dressing game birds
in preparation for cooking them is one of the less
romantic chores connected with hunting. Some hunters shy away from
the task in the hope of giving the birds away, or persuading someone else,
perhaps the lady of the house, to take care of it. Others make a full
production out of it, winding up with feathers scattered all over the
house.

Actually, dressing upland birds or waterfowl can be a short, neat job.
Many hunters field-dress their birds immediately after killing them.
Before doing this, however, one precaution should be observed. Some
states require that evidence of sex in an upland bird be maintained until
it is checked by an official. This regulation was passed to prevent the
killing of female pheasants.

To comply with the ruling, it is necessary to leave the feathers on the
bird during transit. If the hunter elects to skin his birds later, rather than
pluck them, yet still wishes to draw the birds immediately after shooting
them, then they are simply drawn in the field but dressing is finished at
home.

Another precaution is in order. Occasionally, the lucky hunter will bag
an unusual specimen—an extraordinarily large bird, one of exceptional
coloration, or even an albino or a melanistic mutation. Such birds are
prizes and the hunter may wish to have the bird mounted.

PREPARING BIRDS FOR TAXIDERMY. The field preparation necessary to the later work of the taxidermist is quite simple and allows the
hunter to eat his cake and have it, too.

357

For hunts of one day's duration, when the bird may be taken to the taxidermist that evening, all that is necessary is to draw the bird. This is not accomplished by cutting a hole or making a cross-slit at the rear of the abdominal wall as in field-dressing, but by making a longitudinal incision from the anal vent along the belly line at the sternum. The insides are carefully removed through this single incision. Later, when this is sewn by the taxidermist and the feathers smoothed back into place, no seam is visible.

When a prized bird cannot be taken to the shop for several days, it must be skinned. To skin a bird for taxidermy, two incisions are made. One is from the anal vent to the forward end of the breast bone along the center line of the belly. Through this one incision all necessary body-skinning is done. The tail is cut off at its "narrows," leaving all feathers intact in the small diamond-shaped piece of gristle. The body is carefully skinned all around and brought out through this one incision. Legs are severed at the upper end of the drum sticks. Wings are cut off where they join the body. The back section is skinned by working upward from each side through the abdominal incision.

The second incision is made at the base of the skull—a longitudinal cut in the skin over the back of the skull and neck, about 2 inches long for birds the size of ducks and pheasants. Through this second incision, the neck is cut at the junction with the medulla and the brains scratched away with a knife point. The body may now be removed from the whole skin. All flesh is next pared off the leg bones down to their final junction with the skin, and the meat is removed from the wings down to the second joint. The leg and wing bones are left integral with the skin and are later reinforced with heavy wire to shape up the final bird. The incision at the back of the skull, like the belly incision, is sewed up later and will not show.

With the skin, head, wings, and legs all left in one piece, and all meat pared away, salt is copiously rubbed over all the inside of the skin. Particular attention is given to all folds, pockets, and junctions of skin bones. Feathers are stroked down into normal position, and the skin is then placed in a cooler, if possible, or other cool places, awaiting transit.

Prepared this way, a bird skin will last for several days until it can be shipped or taken to a taxidermist. The body of the bird may be dressed and eaten, if desired.

PREPARING BIRDS FOR COOKING. When birds are to be prepared for the table, without regard for plumage, first decide whether the game is to be skinned or plucked. Many consider it a sacrilege to *skin* any game bird. They religiously pluck the feathers off both upland birds and waterfowl, then cook them with the skin intact. The fat covering most game birds, especially waterfowl, does add to the final flavor and succulence of the cooked fowl. Another group, possibly the lazier ones, pluck their waterfowl but simply skin upland birds, removing all feathers and hide in one simple operation. Thin-skinned upland birds, such as pheasants, sage grouse, and forest grouse, are the ones most often skinned rather than plucked.

Regardless of the hunter's preference, the procedure for both upland birds and waterfowl is similar.

First, any bird should be cleaned as soon as possible after killing—at least the same evening. Birds dress easier if they are still a bit warm. Immediately after death, and especially in warmer weather, the gases begin forming in the abdominal cavity. These, with the intestinal fluids released by shot-puncturing, will tend to taint the flesh if not removed. The action is greatly hastened by moving the bird after it is dead. Incidentally, with sage grouse, this intestinal fluid smells and will give the bird a strong flavor if left inside for any appreciable time. Most hunters will disembowel the bird immediately after it is killed.

Before starting to dress a bird at home, a large newspaper should be spread over the work surface. This will catch feathers, blood, viscera, etc., and can be disposed of by burning. Another handy item is a large paper bag rolled halfway down to form an open-mouthed container for feathers.

Plucking. If the bird is to be plucked, not skinned, the first step is to pull out the breast feathers. This is accomplished by taking "pinches" of feathers out, using the thumb and first two fingers. The feathers are pulled with the grain of the position in which they lie, not against it—except for tough birds. Otherwise, the skin may tear. The pinches of feathers are put into the open sack and usually saved. Nothing, incidentally, makes a better pillow for the sleeping bag than the breast feathers of several ducks or a noble old gander or two. Even the breast feathers of grouse and pheasants, mixed with duck feathers and down, make a good pillow filler. And the breast down of waterfowl is, of course, best of all.

Scalding. With the breast feathers and other handiest feathers removed, it expedites the plucking chore to scald the bird. Scalding makes the feathers come out easier and dampens them, preventing their scattering all over the kitchen. Any feathers meant for saving should not be scalded.

The easiest way to scald a fowl is to dunk it into a bucket of scalding water; or place it into the bucket and pour the scalding water over it. The right temperature for average birds is 145 degrees Fahrenheit, and the average time is 20 seconds. Household detergent added to the water will aid the scalding water to penetrate the feathers on waterfowl, which are oily. Birds should not be over-scalded, as the skin will break.

359

With the fowl scalded, the remaining feathers are plucked off until the carcass is free of all feathers and down.

Most birds, even after feathers and down are removed, will still have a remaining fuzz of thin hair sticking out from the flesh. The fuzz is easily removed by the same method women once used to singe the short pin feathers from a domestic chicken. They would roll up a newspaper and twist it into a stick about 16 inches long by an inch or so in diameter. This newspaper torch was lighted with a match over the kitchen stove (to catch the ashes). While holding the bird aloft by the feet, they would pass the flame closely under it, but not long enough to burn the skin. This singed the hen clean of all pin feathers, and will work as well on game birds.

Back in the days when waterfowl were plentiful, many hunters speeded up the de-feathering process by using paraffin wax. The whole bird was dipped into a mixture of hot water and melted paraffin and allowed to cool. The wax-plus-feathers was then peeled off, much as you would peel an orange. The wax was saved, melted again, skimmed of feathers, kept in a galvanized bucket, and used over and over again.

Drawing. With the bird de-feathered, it is then drawn. This is done by making an incision in the skin around the anal vent, including enough of the rear abdominal wall to make an opening large enough to reach into. Through this, the inner organs are pulled.

At the rear of the bird's abdominal wall will be found a pair of riblike small bones—the equivalent of the pelvic bones in man. It helps in the cleaning process to cut off these bones on each side and close to the back, when making the rear-end incision, and allowing them to come away with the belly flesh. These two matching bones will be found around the intestines, in the belly flesh, and supporting the intestines like two curving ribs; and their removal makes an adequate opening.

With the bird dressed, and such portions as the liver and heart saved, the viscera is rolled up in the newspaper, and the carcass washed clean of all blood in cold water. The bird is then ready for a final cooling out. The head, and feet up to the drum-stick joint, are, of course, chopped off before the fowl is cooked.

This is the procedure most often used in preparing ducks, geese, and other waterfowl, for cooking. The fat and skin covering waterfowl not only are a vital part of the overall flavor, but add greatly in basting the bird as it cooks.

Upland birds may be cared for in the same way, but a great many of them aren't. Numerous hunters prefer to remove the viscera from the bird shortly after killing it, while in the hunting field, and finish at home; or they choose to wait and do both chores that evening at home.

When plumage isn't wanted, it is a simple job to draw a game bird afield. Beginning at the back, the tail is cut off at its "narrows" with a sharp pocket knife. As this cut goes downward, it is continued all the way around the anal vent on either side; and on each side the small riblike bone is severed close up against the back. The incision is extended forward, including most of the belly flesh in this cut-away portion, until both sides of the incision meet at the point of the rib cage. Care is used, in all cases, to make sure no intestines are cut.

With the cut completed, all the insides can be pulled out in a single stroke, simply by reaching forward and stripping them out with the fingers.

Many hunters have even simplified that. With the incision completed, they grasp the pair of wings folded across the bird's back; then with a mighty swing, quite like cracking a bull-whip at arm's length, they whip out the entire mass of innards in one stroke. This can be done afield but is not recommended in the kitchen.

In either instance, the inside of the body cavity is then wiped free of all blood, juices from punctured intestines, and other moisture, with a handful of the bird's dry feathers.

Skinning. When both the skinning and the drawing are done at home, the bird first is skinned completely, then drawn. With the point of a sharp knife, the skin is first cut longitudinally along a leg. With the fingers, the skin is then pulled off, up towards the body of the fowl, and on over the entire carcass. The skin on most upland birds, unless they are tough old fowls, will pull off in fairly large hunks of skin-and-feathers combined. Such areas as the drum-stick ends have to be girdled with the knife; and at such points as the wings the stripping motion of the fingers has to be helped by some bits of skin cutting.

The skin on waterfowl, if they are skinned instead of plucked, has to be cut away with a knife. Skinning is easy with upland birds, somewhat difficult with waterfowl, but with either, a little patience and a sharp knife are all that are necessary.

With the bird skinned, it is then drawn as with plucked birds, washed free of all blood and feathers in cold water, and cooled for cooking.

Palatability. The palatability of game birds depends on many factors. What the bird eats, for one thing, will determine its general flavor. As examples, mallards which have fed for some time before harvest in grain fields will be far better eating than if the same birds had lived in a muddy swamp. Sage grouse which have fed predominantly on sagebrush will be stronger in flavor than birds which hatch and grow up near alfalfa fields.

Toughness, too, has a bearing on edibility; and in at least a few instances the hunter can regulate this factor to some extent. For example, the oldest birds, other factors being equal, will be toughest to eat. Under today's hunting competition, the hunter often has to be content with what shots he can get. On good days when he may choose a bit, he can to some extent pick his birds for the skillet. Here are some tips worth remembering:

With wild geese, the oldest, most wary gander will lead the V of birds through the sky. Often such a bird on the table will taste like a gum boot. If the hunter shoots one of the birds near the tail end of the V, it will be young and tender.

The age of sage grouse may be estimated in a general way by size and breast coloration. If the bird gets heavily off the ground, has nearly a pure black breast, and lumbers off looking like a small turkey, it will be an old cock. A younger bird will appear to be much smaller and more uniformly speckled (dark and light) all over.

Pheasants may be differentiated by the length of tail feathers. In most areas only cocks are legally hunted. If a male pheasant explodes and cackles away and his tail feathers stream out approximately 2 feet, and his overall coloration is brilliant, he is apt to be an old bird. Oppositely, cock birds with short tail feathers and a dusky hue, are the younger birds. They will be far better eating.

COOKING.   The best way to learn how to cook game birds is by using a good cook book containing proven recipes, or by consulting the outdoor journals, which repeatedly publish fine recipes for cooking both upland birds and waterfowl.

Here, utilizing basic, proven recipes, are three additional touches which will lift the finished product out of the ordinary:

Sage grouse are best fried, or sautéed in butter. The evening before cooking this species, place a half onion in the body cavity and hang the cleaned and washed bird in the open air overnight. The onion must be cut to expose a moist, absorbent surface. This takes up the strong, sagey taste of the bird, and is later discarded. It also leaves a mild onion flavor to the meat which is most appropriate and delectable. Forest grouse are often killed in a big-game hunting camp for pot-meat. A fine way to prepare such birds is to clean and cool them, then split each bird's breast bone with a clean ax until the bird may be laid out flat, using the back as a hinge. Next, heat a Dutch oven until ⅛ pound of butter will "sing" as it runs over the hot bottom. Place the flattened bird in, searing it until it turns golden brown, then turn it and sear the opposite side to the same extent. Lastly, place the cover on the oven and slow-cook until the entire bird is sautéed to a golden yellow. One bird per hunter is the correct serving.

A final recipe, meant to change wild ducks into something special, was given me by my friend Joe Foss. Only the breasts of the birds are used, with the bird uncoupled at the small of the back, and the legs and backs used in some other fashion.

Each breast is rubbed with a mixture of salt and pepper, placed in a roaster containing sufficient water to begin the cooking, as with any normal roasting, and placed in a hot oven. The secret is to baste the bird repeatedly as it cooks with chokecherry jelly. The jelly is placed, at the beginning, on each upturned breast and during the cooking will turn thin and mix with the natural fat and juices of the bird, as well as the water. Each bird is basted sufficiently so that it never becomes dry and is cooked until medium well-done.

APPENDIX

1

How to Take Care
of Firearms

THE SENSIBLE CARE of firearms begins with a
consideration of the safety involved in their use.
There are many safety rules and codes which, if followed, will prevent
gun accidents; probably every conscientious shooter has developed his
own precautions and methods which have become habitual in practice.

However, if but a single gun-safety rule were strictly and continuously
followed by everyone, gun accidents would be eliminated. That rule is:
Never allow a gun to be pointed at a human being.

Such a rule is simplicity itself but takes some understanding and
attention to detail in field application. It means never to point a loaded
or unloaded gun at a person. It means never allow a gun to be placed or
to fall accidentally so that its muzzle is pointed at any person. This
means not to lay guns in car seats. It means not to stand guns muzzle up
against tree boles, bushes, and similar skimpy supports where they *may*
topple over. And it means not to point gun muzzles at oneself even while
cleaning them.

If such a simple rule were put religiously into practice, with all its
implications and possibilities understood, all such tragic gun accidents as,
"he didn't know it was loaded," "he shot himself while cleaning his
gun," and "kids were allowed to play with a loaded gun," would be
eliminated. Except for ricochets, guns won't kill people if they don't
point at them.

The single exception to this basic rule is, of course, looking through
the bores of guns whose actions have just been opened, to make sure
there are no barrel obstructions—a basic safety rule in itself.

The time to instill safety in gun handling is not when a youngster gets his first .22, shotgun, or big-game rifle. It is not in the hunting field with adults. The time to begin the conditioning for a lifetime of safe gun handling is when the toddler gets his first toy gun for Christmas or his birthday and points it at anybody. The child who is stopped in his tracks *then*, told why and instructed firmly and continuously thereafter that he must never do such a thing, is not the person who later becomes involved in a gun accident.

The actual care of all firearms may be roughly divided into three categories—home storage, transportation, and field use. Different conditions exist in each situation which must be understood to prevent gun deterioration and injury.

Broadly speaking, the enemies of guns are rust, corrosion, and mechanical damage. Dampness induces rust. The incidence of salt in the air speeds the rusting process. Corrosion is caused by chemical action. And gun damage comes from inadequate protection. Rusting, corrosion, and damage must be prevented.

HOME STORAGE. In home storage, perhaps ninety per cent of all rifles and shotguns are stored in upright position in cabinet, cupboard, closet, or room corner. When stored in this position, gravity is always at work, and any oil on a gun tends to work downward.

For this reason, thin gun oils are not ideal to use on stored guns. They drain downward into the action, eventually gumming it up, and also leave the muzzle of the gun unprotected from the oxidizing effect of the air and the changing humidity within the room. From the action, thin oils work down into the stock, often changing the coloration of a prized finish.

Because of this, the best rust preventatives for stored guns are high-quality gun greases which will spread thin and filmlike and will retain their viscosity. "Rig" is one of the best.

In preparing guns for storage, it should be basic procedure that the longer the gun is to be stored, the thicker the coating of this gun grease. As an example, for a gun shot today and expected to be used again during the same game season, the thinnest film possible is all that is required (especially in dry climates away from the ocean) for both bore and outside metal. The same gun, if it is to be stored until the next season, should receive a liberal coating of the same gun grease.

Here is the basic procedure for home storage of a gun after use: First, before entering the home with it, remove all shells or cartridges and leave the action open. Next, make sure the gun is dry, or immediately dry it out. Thoroughly wet guns should first be wiped all over with some kind of dry cloth to remove most of the moisture. Then the gun should be placed near some kind of mild heat—never intense heat such as an open flame.

With the gun completely dry, one or more patches should be run through the inside of the bore to remove the powder particles. This applies to ninety-nine cases out of a hundred. In the exceptional instance where corrosive ammunition has been fired, or thought to have been fired (such as ancient military rifle ammunition), then the bore must be cleaned of the mercury remaining from the corrosive primer. This is best done by inverting the muzzle into a bucket or pan of hot soapy water and running a cleaning rod with a brass brush up and down from the receiver end. This action suctions the hot water up the entire length of the bore and, combined with the scrubbing of the brush, effectively removes the corrosive material. The bore then is thoroughly dried by running dry cloth patches through it.

In the occasional instances where the bore is heavily fouled or mildly rusted, it is best to begin the cleaning by running a patch saturated with a good rust solvent through the bore, then allowing a few minutes time

Always clean a bolt-action rifle from the receiver end, otherwise the continued friction of the rod may damage the muzzle. Lever, pump and semi-automatic rifles must be cleaned from the muzzle end.

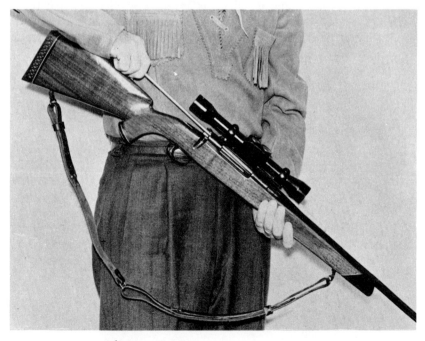

for the solvent to work before proceeding with the cleaning and oiling. Rust pits can never be removed from a rifle barrel, but the rust itself can.

Quantities of suitable patches may be homemade, if desired, from flannel yardage bought at the corner dry-goods store. Patches for .30-caliber rifles, as one example, may be made by cutting the cloth into squares measuring exactly 2½ inches each dimension. For larger or smaller calibers, the size may be varied accordingly.

Such material will also provide the larger patches needed for shotgun cleaning, as well as the necessary wiping cloths.

With the bore cleaned of all fouling and dry, a patch should be lightly oiled with suitable gun grease and pushed through the bore several times, so that all the inside surface and especially the rifling is completely filmed over.

If at all possible with rifles, cleaning and oiling should be done from the receiver end of the barrel. The friction of cleaning rods banging away on the crown, while cleaning it from the muzzle end, has taken the gilt-edge accuracy out of many a fine rifle long before it could be shot out.

Cleaning rods for rifles should be of polished metal so their surfaces won't pick up grit and dirt particles. Hardwood rods are fine for shotguns and pistols, if the wood is similarly smooth.

A patch of cloth coated with the same type of grease is then used to wipe all outside metal surfaces of the gun. The inside of opened actions, clip magazines, bolts, and metal sights are likewise wiped to coat them with a thin film of grease. Care should be used to see that the optics of scope sights are *never* touched with these oiled cloths, though the scope tube is similarly wiped. The soft lens tissue used for camera lenses is best to wipe the scope lenses. Ordinary facial tissue will do. Each lens is blown free of dust with a puff of the breath; the glass is next breathed upon at close range and the surface carefully wiped clean. Too heavy a wiping motion will scratch or remove the fluorescent coating with which all good scope lenses are coated today.

To protect the wood of the gunstock during storage, all that is necessary is to wipe it all over, after drying completely, with the same lightly coated patch which has finished the bore. In addition, every six months or so it is a good notion to put about four drops of boiled linseed oil in the palm of the hand, spread it out, and then rub the entire stock's surface with hard strokes. Linseed oil penetrates the wood during storage, and tends to bring out the original finish of the wood.

In going over the stock with linseed oil, care should be used that no metal is touched, as linseed oil on metal tends to gum.

With the gun completely cleaned and filmed all over with the oil, the action should be re-assembled (in the case of bolt actions) and closed.

The firing pin should be released. No gun should be stored with the action cocked—as a safety precaution, and to prevent strain on the cocking spring.

The gun is then stored by placing it in position without letting any ungreased fingers touch the gun's metal. Handle it with greased fingers and by the stock.

A gun cared for in this way will remain rust and corrosion free (assuming a good quality of gun grease was used) until needed again. In cases where the gun is taken down to display or show to friends, it is not too much to ask that they handle it only by the stock. The salt in the perspiration of some people is pronounced, and coming from their hands onto the gun's metal, it will cause rusting. Many gun owners have an oiled or silicone-treated cloth of ample proportions always handy in the gun cabinet for just this purpose. Once the gun has been handled, they immediately wipe it before replacing it in storage.

Recently there has been considerable experimentation with silicones as rust-preventatives for guns. Several name brands of silicone products are now on the market, and guns cleaned and stored according to the directions on the package will similarly be safe in storage. There also has been a lot of development in rifle-scope covers. These are useful, too, during gun storage for keeping the lenses free of accumulating dust.

The final precaution is, of course, to make sure that any stored guns are beyond the accessibility of small children, and curious adults as well. It's a good notion, too, to leave one notch in the gun cabinet for a handy club—to use over the head of anyone who simply cannot resist opening the gun cabinet, running his sweaty hands over your scope lenses, and turning the "cute little knobs" on your sight adjustments.

TRANSPORTATION. Perhaps more guns are injured during trans portation than during any other phase of their ownership. You won't believe this, but the worst gun injury this author ever had occurred within sixty miles of his home after a fine rifle had been shipped three thousand miles. At a nearby railway station, some attendant with the manual dexterity of a Brahma bull allowed the boxed gun to fall off an express wagon onto the tracks. A locomotive ran over it! The stock was gnawed into two and the rifle barrel was bent till it would have shot around a square corner. Of course, the company was very nice about it and wrote that "if any damage has occurred to the rifle—" to fill out the following forms . . .

Briefly, guns shipped to and from gunsmiths, and back to the company for possible repairs and alteration, are generally safe if shipped in the nested double-carton boxes which the factory used in the original shipment. They should always be shipped by express and insured for full value. If such cartons aren't available, it is less expensive in the long run to make light wooden boxes of plywood with inch-thick ends. Before shipping, the gun should be cleaned, lightly oiled, and packed all around inside with some springy material such as excelsior, foam rubber, or even wadded newspaper.

For car transportation of guns, cases of solid plastic, wood, or heavy leather are best. There is a tendency in loading cars or station wagons to heave in articles hastily—and something always seems to ride on top of someone's gun. A heavy case not only protects the gun from dust during a long trip, but prevents mechanical damage.

Often when combined modes of transportation are used, a dual-purpose case fills the bill. As an example, I once had a rifle scabbard made after not being able to find one manufactured which would serve the purpose. This scabbard was made of heavy steer leather. It covers the entire rifle and scope, buckles over the butt, and his straps for hanging it on a stock saddle. This case-scabbard has traveled thousands of miles on planes, boats, saddle horses, buses, trains, and over seven hundred miles by dog sled. No rifle inside it has ever been damaged during transit.

Because of the rugged nature of rifle transportation during big-game hunting, the light leather, cloth, plastic, and sheepskin gun cases are inadequate. The collective damages to guns inside them will run to many times the purchase price of the cases themselves. The once popular sheepskin gun cases—those having the soft-hide outside and the fleece inside—are particularly ruinous to guns, if subjected to any kind of wet weather. The fleece inside soaks up the moisture coming through the soft hide like a sponge, and holds it against the gun itself.

Many big-game hunters today travel to hunting grounds by airplane as a matter of course. For both private and commercial airplanes the gun case should be as light as possible, but rugged. The best cases for plane travel are made of tough fiber, aluminum, or high-impact plastic, and are lined inside with foam rubber.

Due to the numerous plane hijackings, commercial airlines will no longer allow hunters to carry their guns on board. Rifles and shotguns now must go with the baggage, where they are often subjected to rough treatment. Some airlines, however, do take special care of sporting equipment. I have found an added precaution helpful in protecting guns on planes. Tape several paper labels marked "GLASS, Handle with Care" in conspicuous places on the outside of the guncase. These labels are available at any five-and-ten.

A light vinyl or neoprene gun case placed over the gun and then placed inside a regular gun case is a useful addition and becomes handy at camp for protection against rain or snow, or condensation at night.

In all transportation of rifles, shotguns, and handguns, the basic thing to remember is that *some* form of protection must be given them to insure against injury from drops, moisture, crushing, and all forms of intense pressure.

FIELD CARE. The care of firearms at camp and while hunting is a continuation of this, and the same factors must be considered. Perhaps the biggest hazards are rain, snow, fog, and moisture from condensation accruing from rapid and extreme changes in temperature.

The author's scabbard, made of heavy steer leather, completely encloses the rifle and has straps for attaching it to a stock saddle.

Much of the best big-game hunting involves stormy weather and wet climate when the hunter must expose his weapon. While horseback hunting, the best possible protection for a rifle is the heavy-leather scabbard mentioned before. If treated beforehand with several applications of Neatsfoot oil, the scabbard will shed water for the duration of each day's hunt. In extremely wet weather, such as some places in Alaska and the Canadian bush, inserting a plastic liner around the rifle and inside the scabbard is better. The one fault of this arrangement is that the rifle is slower to get into operation. However, this drawback is offset by the fact that game spooks less easily and generally moves slower in extremely wet weather.

For hunting on foot in rain or snow, the rifle's best protection is the light, overall coating of a good gun grease, applied as for gun storage by wiping it with a greased cloth. This will generally keep all moisture off the metal, even in rain, for as long as the hunter wishes to stay out in such weather. When rain or snow is immediately in the offing, a patch liberally greased and quickly run over the rifle just before leaving camp will help.

The bore, however, should not be coated. Instead, either the evening before, or before beginning the day's hunt, the bore should be wiped clean of practically all oil or grease, as a surplus of grease or oil in the bore will cause pressures to jump dangerously when the rifle is shot. An ideal way is to run a single dry patch through the bore, lightly, before any day's hunt and after the bore has been lightly filmed with grease for storage. This removes all excess, but allows enough to remain to prevent rusting.

Upon reaching camp after any wet day's hunt, the gun should be wiped free of moisture, dried thoroughly, then lightly filmed all over with grease. Care must be taken to get this light coating into all crevices, such as the junction of stock and metal, and around small working parts. Rain will go into places where fingers won't.

Rifle scopes represent a special problem in wet-weather hunting. Scope covers help prevent the lenses from fogging or getting wet, but are a handicap in fast shooting. Also, scope covers are no good in a scabbard. A substitute is to carry the scoped rifle muzzle downward with the scope's ocular lens carried high in the armpit. This prevents rain from striking it, and the objective lens below is protected by the scope tube and gravity.

In violent storms, or for general wet-weather hunting, the muzzle can be kept free of rain or snow simply by placing a tiny piece of cellulose tape over it. An inch-long piece of Scotch tape will cover the bore, with enough extending so that it can be quickly jerked off for a shot. Even if the tape remains over the muzzle during a quick shot, there is no danger of increased pressure, as tests have shown. Hunters have often tied a piece of waxed paper from sandwiches over the gun's muzzle during a storm when there is small likelihood of a shot to prevent moisture from getting into the barrel.

IN CAMP. Camp storage of firearms is always a problem. In many hunting camps there never seems to be a handy and adequate place to put the guns. As a consequence, guns are ordinarily stacked in a tent corner, tossed upon a bed, or laid over some article of duffel. Extremes of temperature cause trouble. When metal is brought suddenly into a warm temperature from a cold temperature, condensation forms on the metal, and the rusting process begins. The salt in perspiration also causes rapid rusting.

There are several ways to prevent firearms from rusting in camp. First, in large hunting camps where there is at least one unheated tent (such as a storage tepee), a good way of preventing condensation on guns is to place all firearms inside the unheated tent each night, and take them out each morning for the day's hunt. Such a tent tends to maintain the temperature of the outside regardless of the heat or cold, and firearms placed inside will not be subjected to any abrupt change.

Where trees are adjacent to a tent, a fine storage rack for guns can be quickly made. A simple crossbar is nailed between two trees at a height of approximately 30 inches and a row of 8D nails hammered partly in along its length. Each gun is stood between two of the nails so it won't fall over; a canvas manta or tarp is thrown over the muzzles to protect them. The firearms gradually change temperature with the outside air and condensation does not form.

In hunting camps with a wall tent which is heated during the night, firearms can be safely stored in the tent overnight without danger of condensation. The rifle is brought immediately inside the tent when the hunter gets in and is ready to start a fire in the stove. The gun warms up gradually with the tent and is similarly cooled off before leaving the tent the next morning. In extremely cold weather, where the tent will still be quite warm when the hunters leave each morning, the rifles should be removed before the morning fire is kindled.

In instances where it is next to impossible not to bring cold firearms into hot rooms or tents, it may be done without condensation forming if the firearm is first wrapped inside a heavy coat, parka, or even a manta. The covering causes the temperature change on the rifle to be gradual instead of abrupt.

When firearms stay overnight inside the tent where hunters sleep, hang them well off the ground by the slings from heavy nails half-driven into the rear tent pole. Any contact with the earth will draw moisture.

Letting a firearm lie on top of a bed or sleeping bag is a mistake, as the metal will similarly draw moisture on the rifle's underside from the heat below. Standing a rifle butt down with its muzzle propped against the canvas of a tent's corner is not wise. The rifle may topple over and be injured. Also, any storm during the night will soak through the tent where the gun muzzle draws it taut, and moisture will run down the bore.

In horseback hunting, rifles should be removed from the saddle scabbards every night. The normal sweating of the animal softens the leather, allowing the salt of the perspiration to come through against the rifle's metal.

While mentioning salt, any unheated tent where rifles and other gear are placed overnight should be completely closed and made animal-tight.

Porcupines, rats, and other rodents like salt and will gravitate with darkness to where they may acquire it by chewing on anything which has been perspiration-soaked. Porcupines like to gnaw gun slings, pack-saddle rigging, and ax handles.

CHECK THE BORE.   One of the best safety rules is to look through the bore of any gun before starting to hunt—with the *action open*. Obstructions in barrels will cause guns to rupture and often cause injury to the shooter. In normal hunting, the possibility of getting snow, mud, or twigs into a gun muzzle is always present.

Many of the wisest and most experienced hunters have a ritual for making certain the bore of their gun is clear. At the moment of leaving camp, they open the chamber, look through the bore towards the light, then load the cartridges or shells into the magazine. The practiced movements, in that order, become as habitual as tying their boots.

In extremely cold horseback hunting, it is a good policy also to check the bore any time conditions seem to warrant it. Snow will fall into some types of scabbards, melt, and run down to the muzzle of a rifle where it can freeze into ice. The animal's body heat causes the melting along the body of the rifle, but the muzzle end is far colder. This author once saved blowing his head off on an Alberta ram hunt by catching such a condition in time. Melted snow in the scabbard had run down and frozen solidly in the bore for over an inch!

Similarly in extreme cold, such as the Arctic or the Far North in winter, the grease remaining inside rifle bolts will cause them to freeze up and refuse to function. It is a simple matter to clean a rifle bolt prior to such a hunt. The bolt is removed from the rifle and swished about in a pan filled with white gasoline, removing all grease. It should be remembered that a clean bolt will rust easily and should be re-oiled after the hunt is over. Powdered graphite sprinkled into the bolt or action of a rifle, after the grease has been removed, will add to its slickness of operation.

CLEANING KIT.   A suitable gun-cleaning kit is a necessity on a hunting trip. Cleaning kits may be as involved as one likes. Experience has indicated, however, that the larger and more bulky the kit, the bigger its chances are of being left at home or not used in the field.

For an average hunt, the only necessary kit is either a pull-through or a strong leather thong slotted at one end, and a half-dozen patches of a suitable size. With the pull-through (metal dropper attached to a strong cord), a dry or a lightly oiled patch can be run through the rifle bore.

The same lightly greased patch can be used afterward for wiping a thin film onto the rifle's outside. Greased patches may be saturated at home and carried in a small plastic box, or typewriter-ribbon box. Two small tools, an Allen wrench and a small screwdriver, are important additions to the kit. These are seldom used afield, but when the need does arise, they are worth their weight in dollars.

Remember, any rifle that has been fired or wet during the day, should *always* be cleaned, dried, and oiled before you go to bed that night. A little care and time will pay big dividends at home and in the field in preventing gun accidents and assuring the sure functioning of shooting equipment.

SHOTGUNS AND HANDGUNS. While most of the above information relates to the care of rifles, the field and home care of shotguns and handguns is similar and the same procedures may be followed.

Cleaning rods for shotguns will be generally longer than those for rifles and much larger patches are necessary. Home-cut flannel patches measuring 6 by 6 inches are the right size for 12-gauge shotguns and proportionately smaller ones should be used for the smaller gauges. A good one-piece cleaning rod may be made from a suitable length of hardwood dowel. One end is glued into a shaped wooden handle and a small eye-screw (for holding the patch) is screwed into the opposite end. In cleaning a shotgun, use one dry patch to wipe the burned powder particles from the bore before using an oiled patch to protect the metal.

Cleaning rods and patches for handguns are proportionately sized, but the same oils, grease, and solvent used for the protection of rifles will be suitable for handguns and smoothbores.

After a season's use, it is a good procedure to disassemble a shotgun that breaks down; clean it, and lightly oil every part before putting it in storage.

2

Hunting in Mexico

M exico has varied, unusual, and somewhat limited hunting. There are several species of upland game birds, waterfowl, varmints, and medium-sized game animals. For the stateside hunter, the main interest lies in the desert ram, the larger cats, especially the jaguar, the whitewing dove, and waterfowl.

Game management and hunting regulations in Mexico lag far behind similar programs in the United States and Canada, primarily because game there is tied up with the economy, the government and the military. Game laws have been few and historically hard to enforce through the meager game department.

There is not in Mexico the economic variation among the citizenry that is found in the United States. Mexico has always had a poor class and a small, extremely wealthy class. Only during the last decade or so has a substantial middle class begun to develop. This has greatly affected the hunting there in the past, and still does to a lesser extent.

For the average low-income Mexican with only a few hundred dollars annual earnings, a game bird or animal traditionally meant meat. He balanced any game against 30c for the price of a .30/30 shell and harvested as a matter of course. Poaching was common and widespread. The national sport of Mexico was never hunting, but bull-fighting, car racing, etc. Actual hunting done by the wealthy often became "shoots" verging on slaughter. The American concept of hunting for sport and conservation for the future, did not exist in the same way south of the border.

The bad manners of some wealthy Americans, however, about fifty years ago, practically sealed off Mexico as a hunting area for the nonresident. Aware of the general laxity and absence of hunting laws, these few went to Mexico and killed some species with no regard for sportsmanship. This finally led to the effective closure of hunting to the nonresident.

Mistrust of American hunters by many Mexicans grew as well from another factor. The Mexican economy was mixed in with government, which in turn was connected with the military, and this combination gave rise to unfortunate activities. Illegal hunting was allowed in key areas, for prized species such as desert rams, when American dollars were passed under the table to officials with a higher regard for the favorable dollar-peso exchange rate than for the game.

This situation remained until approximately 1950. About that time, Colonel Marshall (Tex) Purvis, an American big-game outfitter, decided to try to convince Mexico to reopen its lands to American sportsmen, on an up-to-date, responsible basis. In Mexico, Purvis assembled a half-dozen top political and economic leaders into a corporation whose objectives were to readmit American hunters and receive the resulting flow of American dollars. There would be new conditions, however, in the form of restrictive game laws with proper enforcement and a new concept of game management, aimed towards shaping Mexico's game as a national asset. The guide lines would derive from what existed in the United States.

The change was accomplished in 1954. I was invited to Mexico City during the final planning meetings, to meet with the members of the corporation and to cover the story. Finally, Mexico was reopened to American hunters under a new set of restrictions, and for the first time in approximately fifteen years Americans could legally hunt in Mexico.

Colonel Purvis, more than any other person, was instrumental in effecting this change, and he became the first outfitter on whom the government issued a brochure. This experienced man believed that Mexico had sufficient game to attract the better class of American hunters and itself profit handsomely. Purvis actually wanted to establish himself as an outfitter in Mexico and cater to this clientele. After 1954, Purvis outfitted for such prized species as jaguar. Currently, and with the continuing support of Mexicana Airlines, he is opening up an area of unexploited fishing-grounds in the Yucatan-Cozumel area of the Gulf.

The ground rules for nonresident hunting established in 1954 have generally set the pattern since. There has been, however, an unfortunate trend in the hunting restrictions. Although Mexico is still far behind the United States in its game programs, hunting laws and enforcement procedures, the focus of these controls, and their enforcement in particular, has been directed at the nonresident American. The country regards American hunters as rich and better able to bear heavy fines for violations than native residents. Any nonresident who wishes to hunt in Mexico should expect rigid regulations and high costs for the privilege of hunting there.

The procedures for hunting in Mexico are not unduly complex. They relate principally to positive identification and proof of citizenship, to permits to take firearms into the country for use in specified areas, and of course the license to hunt. The nonresident hunter at this time can take his own firearms into Mexico on a temporary basis. He may also take with him up to 150 rounds of ammunition, but he cannot take any .45, 7 mm, or .22 caliber arms or ammunition. The first two are Mexican military calibers. The government does not want the populace armed, especially with guns capable of shooting military ammunition.

Accessory equipment, including game calls, hunting dogs, fishing gear, etc. may be taken along, though all game calls require an easily obtainable special permit. All gun permits and licenses to hunt in specified areas must be in the owner's possession before he can cross the border.

There are three acceptable ways to obtain and clear the necessary papers. The easiest is to contact an American outfitter who operates in Mexico, make arrangements to hunt with him as a paying client, and then let him advise as to the necessary documents and requirements. Several outfitters have begun to work in Mexico, especially for the big cats, and advertise in the larger outdoor journals.

The second way is through the Mexican Consul. Most sizable cities in the United States, especially in the West, have a Consul. The travel department of any major airline can advise the hunter as to where to find the Mexican Consul with jurisdiction over his area. On request, the Consul will forward the necessary forms to applicants. It is recommended that when making the request, the hunter ask what will be needed, what probable costs will be, etc. Dates, areas, and intentions of a projected hunt should be stated. Before issuing any permits, the Consul will require two things: a birth certificate or photostat copy; a letter from the local police department or home sheriff's office, stating that the bearer is a law-abiding citizen in good standing. Upon payment of the fees, the Consul will issue the papers. Unnecessary waiting at the border is far shorter if this procedure is followed.

The third and perhaps least desirable method is to obtain the necessary licenses and permits at the point of entry at the Mexican border. This often involves aggravating delays, especially if the visitor doesn't speak Spanish.

A sheep license for the nonresident currently costs $450. A license to hunt jaguar, though the animal is a predator there, is $150. A good guide and outfitter for sheep for ten days will cost around $3,000, and to pay less or accept inferior service is usually a waste of money.

An American hunter with clearance can normally hunt additional species, such as quail, ducks, deer, etc., within his specified area, much the same as the nonresident of the West can do. The warm climate of Mexico and absence of the winter-range problem means that some species of birds, game, and varmints may be hunted legally all year.

3

Boone and Crockett Club Scoring Charts

This Appendix contains reproductions of the official scoring charts of the Boone and Crockett Club. The Club's scoring system is accepted as the standard for evaluating North American big-game trophies. The charts are reprinted with the approval of the Boone and Crockett Club and may be purchased by writing to the Club, c/o Carnegie Museum, 4400 Forbes Avenue, Pittsburg, Pa. 15213.

OFFICIAL SCORING SYSTEM FOR NORTH AMERICAN BIG GAME TROPHIES

RECORDS OF NORTH AMERICAN BIG GAME COMMITTEE

Minimum Score: Deer
Whitetail: Typical 170
Coues: Typical 110

BOONE AND CROCKETT CLUB

Boone and Crockett Club
Records of North American Big Game Committee
c/o Carnegie Museum
4400 Forbes Ave.   Pittsburgh, Pa.   15213

WHITETAIL and COUES DEER

KIND OF DEER

DETAIL OF POINT MEASUREMENT

SEE OTHER SIDE FOR INSTRUCTIONS	Supplementary Data		Column 1	Column 2	Column 3	Column 4
	R.	L.	Spread Credit	Right Antler	Left Antler	Difference
A. Number of Points on Each Antler						
B. Tip to Tip Spread						
C. Greatest Spread						
D. Inside Spread of MAIN BEAMS — Spread credit may equal but not exceed length of longer antler						
IF Inside Spread of Main Beams exceeds longer antler length; enter difference						
E. Total of Lengths of all Abnormal Points						
F. Length of Main Beam						
G-1. Length of First Point, if present						
G-2. Length of Second Point						
G-3. Length of Third Point						
G-4. Length of Fourth Point, if present						
G-5. Length of Fifth Point, if present						
G-6. Length of Sixth Point, if present						
G-7. Length of Seventh Point, if present						
H-1. Circumference at Smallest Place Between Burr and First Point						
H-2. Circumference at Smallest Place Between First and Second Points						
H-3. Circumference at Smallest Place Between Second and Third Points						
H-4. Circumference at Smallest Place between Third and Fourth Points or half way between Third Point and Beam Tip if Fourth Point is missing						
TOTALS						

ADD	Column 1		Exact locality where killed
	Column 2		Date killed By whom killed
	Column 3		Present owner
	Total		Address
SUBTRACT Column 4			Guide's Name and Address
FINAL SCORE			Remarks: (Mention any abnormalities)

I certify that I have measured the above trophy on _____ 19 _____
at (address) _____ City _____ State _____
and that these measurements and data are, to the best of my knowledge and belief, made in accordance with the instructions given.

Witness: _____ Signature: _____
Boone and Crockett Official Measurer

INSTRUCTIONS

All measurements must be made with a flexible steel tape to the nearest one-eighth of an inch. Wherever it is necessary to change direction of measurement, mark a control point and swing tape at this point. To simplify addition, please enter fractional figures in eighths. Official measurements cannot be taken for at least sixty days after the animal was killed. Please submit photographs.

Supplementary Data measurements indicate conformation of the trophy, and none of the figures in Lines A, B and C are to be included in the score. Evaluation of conformation is a matter of personal preference. Excellent, but nontypical Whitetail Deer heads with many points shall be placed and judged in a separate class.

A. Number of Points on each Antler. To be counted a point, a projection must be at least one inch long AND its length must exceed the length of its base. All points are measured from tip of point to nearest edge of beam as illustrated. Beam tip is counted as a point but not measured as a point.

B. Tip to Tip Spread measured between tips of Main Beams.

C. Greatest Spread measured between perpendiculars at right angles to the center line of the skull at widest part whether across main beams or points.

D. Inside Spread of Main Beams measured at right angles to the center line of the skull at widest point between main beams. Enter this measurement again in "Spread Credit" column if it is less than or equal to the length of longer antler.

E. Total of lengths of all Abnormal Points. Abnormal points are generally considered to be those nontypical in shape or location.

F. Length of Main Beam measured from lowest outside edge of burr over outer curve to the most distant point of what is, or appears to be, the main beam. The point of beginning is that point on the burr where the center line along the outer curve of the beam intersects the burr.

G-1-2-3-4-5-6-7. Length of Normal Points. Normal points project from main beam. They are measured from nearest edge of main beam over outer curve to tip. To determine nearest edge (top edge) of beam, lay the tape along the outer curve of the beam so that the top edge of the tape coincides with the top edge of the beam on both sides of the point. Draw line along top edge of tape. This line will be base line from which point is measured.

H-1-2-3-4. Circumferences - If first point is missing, Take H-1 and H-2 at smallest place between burr and second point.

* * * * * * * * * *

TROPHIES OBTAINED ONLY BY FAIR CHASE MAY BE ENTERED
IN ANY BOONE AND CROCKETT CLUB BIG GAME COMPETITION

To make use of the following methods shall be deemed UNFAIR CHASE and unsportsmanlike, and any trophy obtained by use of such means is disqualified from entry in any Boone and Crockett Club big game competition:
  I. Spotting or herding game from the air, followed by landing in its vicinity for pursuit;
  II. Herding or pursuing game with motor-powered vehicles;
  III. Use of electronic communications for attracting, locating or observing game, or guiding the hunter to such game.
* * * * * * * * * *

I certify that the trophy scored on this chart was not taken in UNFAIR CHASE as defined above by the Boone and Crockett Club.

I certify that it was not spotted or herded by guide or hunter from the air followed by landing in its vicinity for pursuit, nor herded or pursued on the ground by motor-powered vehicles.

I further certify that no electronic communications were used to attract, locate, observe, or guide the hunter to such game; and that it was taken in full compliance with the local game laws or regulations of the state, province or territory.

Date _____ Hunter _____
Copyright 1965 by Boone and Crockett Club

A-5M-12/68

Reproduced by permission of Boone and Crockett Club.

OFFICIAL SCORING SYSTEM FOR NORTH AMERICAN BIG GAME TROPHIES

RECORDS OF NORTH AMERICAN BIG GAME COMMITTEE

BOONE AND CROCKETT CLUB

Boone and Crockett Club
Records of North American Big Game Committee
c/o Carnegie Museum
4400 Forbes Ave. Pittsburgh, Pa. 15213

☐ NON-TYPICAL WHITETAIL DEER Min. Score 195
☐ NON-TYPICAL COUES DEER   Min. Score 105:15 = 120

DETAIL OF POINT MEASUREMENT

ABNORMAL Points Line E	
R	L
Totals To E	

SEE OTHER SIDE FOR INSTRUCTIONS	Supplementary Data		Column 1	Column 2	Column 3	Column 4
	R.	L.	Spread Credit	Right Antler	Left Antler	Difference
A. Number of Points on Each Antler						
B. Tip to Tip Spread						
C. Greatest Spread						
D. Inside Spread of MAIN BEAMS	Spread credit may equal but not exceed length of longer antler					
IF Inside Spread of Main Beams exceeds longer antler length, enter difference						
E. Total of Lengths of all Abnormal Points						
F. Length of Main Beam						
G-1. Length of First Point, if present						
G-2. Length of Second Point						
G-3. Length of Third Point						
G-4. Length of Fourth Point, if present						
G-5. Length of Fifth Point, if present						
G-6. Length of Sixth Point, if present						
G-7. Length of Seventh Point, if present						
H-1. Circumference at Smallest Place Between Burr and First Point						
H-2. Circumference at Smallest Place Between First and Second Points						
H-3. Circumference at Smallest Place Between Second and Third Points						
H-4. Circumference at Smallest Place Between Third and Fourth Points						
TOTALS						

ADD	Column 1		Exact locality where killed	
	Column 2		Date killed	By whom killed
	Column 3		Present owner	
	Total		Address	
SUBTRACT Column 4			Guide's Name and Address	
	Result		Remarks: (Mention any abnormalities)	
Add Line E Total				
FINAL SCORE				

I certify that I have measured the above trophy on _____ 19_____
at (address)_____ City _____ State_____
and that these measurements and data are, to the best of my knowledge and belief, made in accordance with the instructions given.

Witness: _____ Signature: _____
Boone and Crockett Official Measurer

INSTRUCTIONS

All measurements must be made with a flexible steel tape to the nearest one-eight of an inch. Wherever it is necessary to change direction of measurement, mark a control point and swing tape at this point. To simplify addition, please enter fractional figures in eighths. Official measurements cannot be taken for at least sixty days after the animal was killed. Please submit photographs.

Supplementary Data measurements indicate conformation of the trophy, and none of the figures in Lines A, B and C are to be included in the score. Evaluation of conformation is a matter of personal preference.

A. Number of Points on each Antler. To be counted a point, a projection must be at least one inch long AND its length must exceed the length of its base. All points are measured from tip of point to nearest edge of beam as illustrated. Beam tip is counted as a point but not measured as a point.

B. Tip to Tip Spread measured between tips of main beams.

C. Greatest Spread measured between perpendiculars at right angles to the center line of the skull at widest part whether across main beams or points.

D. Inside Spread of Main Beams measured at right angles to the center line of the skull at widest point between main beams. Enter this measurement again in "Spread Credit" column if it is less than or equal to the length of the longer antler.

E. Total of Lengths of all Abnormal Points. Abnormal points are considered to be those nontypical in shape or location. It is very important, in scoring nontypical heads, to determine which points are to be classed as normal and which are not. To do this, study carefully the character of the normal points on the diagram, which are marked G-1, G-2, G-3, etc. On the trophy to be scored, the points which correspond to these are measured as normal. All others over one inch in length (See A, above) are considered abnormal. Various types of abnormal points are shown (marked with an E) on the diagram. Measure the exact length of each abnormal point, over the outer curve, from the tip to the nearest edge of the beam or point from which it projects. Then add these lengths and enter the total in the space provided.

F. Length of Main Beam measured from lowest outside edge of burr over outer curve to the most distant point of what is, or appears to be, the main beam. The point of beginning is that point on the burr where the center line along the outer curve of the beam intersects the burr.

G-1-2-3-4-5-6-7. Length of Normal Points. Normal points project from main beam. They are measured from nearest edge of main beam over outer curve to tip. To determine nearest edge (top edge) of beam, lay the tape along the outer curve of the beam so that the top edge of the tape coincides with the top edge of the beam on both sides of the point. Draw line along top edge of tape. This line will be base line from which point is measured.

H-1-2-3-4. Circumferences - If first point is missing, take H-1 and H-2 at smallest place between burr and second point. If fourth point is missing, take H-4 half way between third point and beam tip.

* * * * * * * * * * * * * * * *

TROPHIES OBTAINED ONLY BY FAIR CHASE MAY BE ENTERED
IN ANY BOONE AND CROCKETT CLUB BIG GAME COMPETITION

To make use of the following methods shall be deemed UNFAIR CHASE and unsportsmanlike, and any trophy obtained by use of such means is disqualified from entry in any Boone and Crockett Club big game competition:

    I. Spotting or herding game from the air, followed by landing in its vicinity for pursuit;
    II. Herding or pursuing game with motor-powered vehicles;
    III. Use of electronic communications for attracting, locating or observing game, or guiding the hunter to such game.   * * * * * * * * * *

I certify that the trophy scored on this chart was not taken in UNFAIR CHASE as defined above by the Boone and Crockett Club.

I certify that it was not spotted or herded by guide or hunter from the air followed by landing in its vicinity for pursuit, nor herded or pursued on the ground by motor-powered vehicles.

I further certify that no electronic communications were used to attract, locate, observe, or guide the hunter to such game; and that it was taken in full compliance with the local game laws or regulations of the state, province or territory.

Date_____ Signature of Hunter _____

Reproduced by permission of Boone and Crockett Club.

385

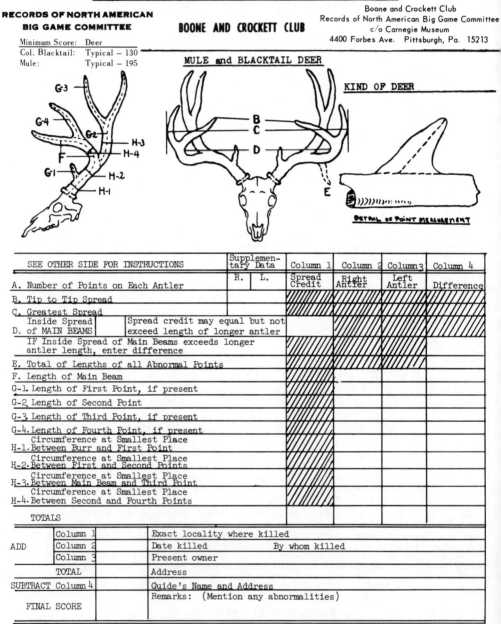

OFFICIAL SCORING SYSTEM FOR NORTH AMERICAN BIG GAME TROPHIES

RECORDS OF NORTH AMERICAN BIG GAME COMMITTEE

BOONE AND CROCKETT CLUB

Boone and Crockett Club
Records of North American Big Game Committee
c/o Carnegie Museum
4400 Forbes Ave.   Pittsburgh, Pa.   15213

Minimum Score: Deer
Col. Blacktail: Typical — 130
Mule: Typical — 195

MULE and BLACKTAIL DEER

KIND OF DEER

SEE OTHER SIDE FOR INSTRUCTIONS	Supplementary Data R.	L.	Column 1 Spread Credit	Column 2 Right Antler	Column 3 Left Antler	Column 4 Difference
A. Number of Points on Each Antler						
B. Tip to Tip Spread						
C. Greatest Spread						
D. Inside Spread of MAIN BEAMS	Spread credit may equal but not exceed length of longer antler					
If Inside Spread of Main Beams exceeds longer antler length, enter difference						
E. Total of Lengths of all Abnormal Points						
F. Length of Main Beam						
G-1. Length of First Point, if present						
G-2. Length of Second Point						
G-3. Length of Third Point, if present						
G-4. Length of Fourth Point, if present						
H-1. Circumference at Smallest Place Between Burr and First Point						
H-2. Circumference at Smallest Place Between First and Second Points						
H-3. Circumference at Smallest Place Between Main Beam and Third Point						
H-4. Circumference at Smallest Place Between Second and Fourth Points						
TOTALS						

ADD	Column 1		Exact locality where killed
	Column 2		Date killed By whom killed
	Column 3		Present owner
	TOTAL		Address
SUBTRACT Column 4			Guide's Name and Address
FINAL SCORE			Remarks: (Mention any abnormalities)

I certify that I have measured the above trophy on _____ 19 _____
at (address)_____ City _____ State _____
that these measurements and data are, to the best of my knowledge and belief, made in accordance with the
instructions given.

Witness: _____ Signature: _____
Boone & Crockett Official Measurer

INSTRUCTIONS

All measurements must be made with a flexible steel tape to the nearest one-eighth of an inch. Wherever it is
necessary to change direction of measurement, mark a control point and swing tape at this point. To simplify
addition, please enter fractional figures in eighths. Official measurements cannot be taken for at least sixty
days after the animal was killed. Please submit photographs.

Supplementary Data measurements indicate conformation of the trophy, and none of the figures in Lines A, B and
C are to be included in the score. Evaluation of conformation is a matter of personal preference. Excellent, but
nontypical Mule Deer heads with many points shall be placed and judged in a separate class.

A. Number of Points on Each Antler. To be counted a point, a projection must be at least one inch long AND
its length must exceed the length of its base. All points are measured from tip of point to nearest edge of beam
as illustrated. Beam tip is counted as a point but not measured as a point.

B. Tip to Tip Spread measured between tips of main beams.

C. Greatest Spread measured between perpendiculars at right angles to the center line of the skull at widest part
whether across main beams or points.

D. Inside Spread of Main Beams measured at right angles to the center line of the skull at widest point between
main beams. Enter this measurement again in "Spread Credit" column if it is less than or equal to the length of
longer antler.

E. Total of Lengths of all Abnormal Points. Abnormal points are generally considered to be those nontypical in
shape or location.

F. Length of Main Beam measured from lowest outside edge of burr over outer curve to the tip of the main beam.
The point of beginning is that point on the burr where the center line along the outer curve of the beam intersects
the burr.

G-1-2-3-4. Length of Normal Points. Normal points are the brow (or first) and the upper and lower forks as shown
in illustration. They are measured from nearest edge of beam over outer curve to tip. To determine nearest edge
(top edge) of beam, lay the tape along the outer curve of the beam so that the top edge of the tape coincides with
the top edge of the beam on both sides of the point. Draw line along top edge of tape. This line will be base
line from which point is measured.

H-1-2-3-4. Circumferences — If first point is missing, take H-1 and H-2 at smallest place between burr and second
point. If third point is missing, take H-3 half way between the base and tip of second point. If the fourth is missing, take H-4 half way between the second point and tip of main beam.

TROPHIES OBTAINED ONLY BY FAIR CHASE MAY BE ENTERED
IN ANY BOONE AND CROCKETT CLUB BIG GAME COMPETITION

To make use of the following methods shall be deemed UNFAIR CHASE and unsportsmanlike, and any trophy
obtained by use of such means is disqualified from entry in any Boone and Crockett Club big game competition:

  I. Spotting or herding game from the air, followed by landing in its vicinity for pursuit;
 II. Herding or pursuing game with motor-powered vehicles;
III. Use of electronic communications for attracting, locating or observing game, or guiding the hunter to
     such game.

I certify that the trophy scored on this chart was not taken in UNFAIR CHASE as defined above by the Boone and
Crockett Club.

I certify that it was not spotted or herded by guide or hunter from the air followed by landing in its vicinity for
pursuit, nor herded or pursued on the ground by motor-powered vehicles.

I further certify that no electronic communications were used to attract, locate, observe, or guide the hunter to
such game; and that it was taken in full compliance with the local game laws or regulations of the state,
province or territory.

Date _____ Signature of Hunter _____

A-2M-3-69

Reproduced by permission of Boone and Crockett Club.

OFFICIAL SCORING SYSTEM FOR NORTH AMERICAN BIG GAME TROPHIES

RECORDS OF NORTH AMERICAN
BIG GAME COMMITTEE

BOONE AND CROCKETT CLUB

Boone and Crockett Club
Records of North American Big Game Committee
c/o Carnegie Museum
4400 Forbes Ave.   Pittsburgh, Pa.   15213

Minimum Score: 195:45 = 210

NON—TYPICAL MULE DEER

DETAIL OF POINT MEASUREMENT

ABNORMAL		
Points Line E		
R		L
TOTALS		
To E		

SEE OTHER SIDE FOR INSTRUCTIONS	Supplementary Data		Column 1	Column 2	Column 3	Column 4
	R.	L.	Spread Credit	Right Antler	Left Antler	Difference
A. Number of Points on Each Antler						
B. Tip to Tip Spread						
C. Greatest Spread						
D. Inside Spread of MAIN BEAMS Spread credit may equal but not exceed length of longer antler						
IF Inside Spread of Main Beams exceeds longer antler length, enter difference						
E. Total of Lengths of all Abnormal Points						
F. Length of Main Beam						
G-1. Length of First Point, if present						
G-2. Length of Second Point						
G-3. Length of Third Point, if present						
G-4. Length of Fourth Point, if present						
H-1. Circumference at Smallest Place Between Burr and First Point						
H-2. Circumference at Smallest Place Between First and Second Points						
H-3. Circumference at Smallest Place Between Main Beam and Third Point						
H-4. Circumference at Smallest Place Between Second and Fourth Points						
TOTALS						

Column 1		Exact locality where killed
Column 2		Date killed By whom killed
Column 3		Present owner
Total		Address
SUBTRACT Column 4		Guide's Name and Address
Result		Remarks: (Mention any abnormalities)
Add Line E Total		
FINAL SCORE		

I certify that I have measured the above trophy on _____ 19_____
at (address)_____ City_____ State_____
and that these measurements and data are, to the best of my knowledge and belief, made in accordance with the instructions given.

Witness: _____ Signature: _____

Boone and Crockett Official Measurer

INSTRUCTIONS

All measurements must be made with a flexible steel tape to the nearest one-eighth of an inch. Wherever it is necessary to change direction of measurement, mark a control point and swing tape at this point. To simplify addition, please enter fractional figures in eighths.

Official measurements cannot be taken for at least sixty days after the animal was killed. Please submit photographs.

Supplementary Data measurements indicate conformation of the trophy, and none of the figures in Lines A, B and C are to be included in the score. Evaluation of conformation is a matter of personal preference.

A. Number of Points on Each Antler. To be counted a point, a projection must be least one inch long AND its length must exceed the length of its base. All points are measured from tip of point to nearest edge of beam as illustrated. Beam tip is counted as a point but not measured as a point.

B. Tip to Tip Spread measured between tips of Main Beams.

C. Greatest Spread measured between perpendiculars at right angles to the center line of the skull at widest part whether across main beams or points.

D. Inside Spread of Main Beams measured at right angles to the center line of the skull at widest point between main beams. Enter this measurement again in "Spread Credit" column if it is less than or equal to the length of longer antler.

E. Total of Lengths of all Abnormal Points. Abnormal points are considered to be those nontypical in shape or location. It is very important, in scoring nontypical heads, to determine which points are to be classed as normal and which are not. To do this, study carefully the markings G-1, G-2, G-3 and G-4 on the diagram, which indicate the normal points. On the trophy to be scored, select the points which most closely correspond to these. All others over one inch in length (See A, above) are considered abnormal.

Measure the exact length of each abnormal point, over the outer curve, from the tip to the nearest edge of the beam or point from which it projects. Then add these lengths and enter the total in the space provided.

F. Length of Main Beam measured from lowest outside edge of burr over outer curve to the tip of the main beam. The point of beginning is that point on the burr where the center line along the outer curve of the beam intersects the burr.

G-1-2-3-4. Length of Normal Points. Normal points are the brow (or first) and the upper and lower forks as shown in illustration. They are measured from nearest edge of beam over outer curve to tip. To determine nearest edge (top edge) of beam, lay the tape along the outer curve of the beam so that the top edge of the tape coincides with the top edge of the beam on both sides of the point. Draw line along top edge of tape. This line will be base line from which point is measured.

H-1-2-3-4. Circumferences — If first point is missing, take H-1 and H-2 at smallest place between burr and second point. If third point is missing, take H-3 half way between the base and tip of second point. If the fourth point is missing take H-4 half way between the second point and tip of main beam.

* * * * * * * *

TROPHIES OBTAINED ONLY BY FAIR CHASE MAY BE ENTERED
IN ANY BOONE AND CROCKETT CLUB BIG GAME COMPETITION

To make use of the following methods shall be deemed UNFAIR CHASE and unsportsmanlike, and any trophy obtained by use of such means is disqualified from entry in any Boone and Crockett Club big game competition:

I. Spotting or herding game from the air, followed by landing in its vicinity for pursuit;

II. Herding or pursuing game with motor-powered vehicles;

III. Use of electronic communications for attracting, locating or observing game, or guiding the hunter to such game.

I certify that the trophy scored on this chart was not taken in UNFAIR CHASE as defined above by the Boone and Crockett Club.

I certify that it was not spotted or herded by guide or hunter from the air followed by landing in its vicinity for pursuit, nor herded or pursued on the ground by motor-powered vehicles.

I further certify that no electronic communications were used to attract, locate, observe, or guide the hunter to such game; and that it was taken in full compliance with the local game laws or regulations of the state, province or territory.

Date_____ Signature of Hunter_____

Reproduced by permission of Boone and Crockett Club.

389

OFFICIAL SCORING SYSTEM FOR NORTH AMERICAN BIG GAME TROPHIES

RECORDS OF NORTH AMERICAN BIG GAME COMMITTEE

BOONE AND CROCKETT CLUB

Wapiti Minimum Score: 375

Boone and Crockett Club
Records of North American Big Game Committee
c/o Carnegie Museum
4400 Forbes Ave. Pittsburgh, Pa. 15213

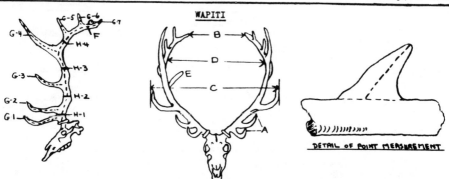

WAPITI

SEE OTHER SIDE FOR INSTRUCTIONS	Supplementary Data R.	L.	Column 1 Spread Credit	Column 2 Right Antler	Column 3 Left Antler	Column 4 Difference
A. Number of Points on Each Antler						
B. Tip to Tip Spread						
C. Greatest Spread						
D. Inside Spread of MAIN BEAMS — Spread credit may equal but not exceed length of longer antler						
IF Inside Spread of Main Beams exceeds longer antler length, enter difference						
E. Total of Lengths of all Abnormal Points						
F. Length of Main Beam						
G-1. Length of First Point						
G-2. Length of Second Point						
G-3. Length of Third Point						
G-4. Length of Fourth (Royal) Point						
G-5. Length of Fifth Point						
G-6. Length of Sixth Point, if present						
G-7. Length of Seventh Point, if present						
H-1. Circumference at Smallest Place Between First and Second Points						
H-2. Circumference at Smallest Place Between Second and Third Points						
H-3. Circumference at Smallest Place Between Third and Fourth Points						
H-4. Circumference at Smallest Place Between Fourth and Fifth Points						
TOTALS						

ADD	Column 1		Exact locality where killed
	Column 2		Date killed By whom killed
	Column 3		Present owner
	TOTAL		Address
SUBTRACT Column 4			Guide's Name and Address
FINAL SCORE			Remarks: (Mention any abnormalities)

I certify that I have measured the above trophy on _____ 19 _____ ____
at (address) _____ City _____ State _____
and that these measurements and data are, to the best of my knowledge and belief, made in accordance with the
instructions given.

Witness: _____ Signature: _____
Boone and Crockett Official Measurer

INSTRUCTIONS

All measurements must be made with a flexible steel tape to the nearest one-eighth of an inch. Wherever it is
necessary to change direction of measurement, mark a control point and swing tape at this point. To simplify
addition, please enter fractional figures in eighths.

Official measurements cannot be taken for at least sixty days after the animal was killed.

Please submit photographs.

Supplementary Data, measurements indicate conformation of the trophy, and none of the figures in Lines A, B
and C are to be included in the score. Evaluation of conformation is a matter of personal preference.

A. Number of Points on Each Antler. To be counted a point, a projection must be at least one inch long AND
its length must exceed the length of its base. All points are measured from tip of point to nearest edge of
beam as illustrated. Beam tip is counted as a point but not measured as a point.

B. Tip to Tip Spread measured between tips of Main Beams.

C. Greatest Spread measured between perpendiculars at right angles to the center line of the skull at widest
part whether across main beams or points.

D. Inside Spread of Main Beams measured at right angles to the center line of the skull at widest point between
main beams. Enter this measurement again in "Spread Credit" column if it is less than or equal to the length of
longer antler.

E. Total of Lengths of all Abnormal Points. Abnormal points are generally considered to be those nontypical
in shape or location.

F. Length of Main Beam measured from lowest outside edge of burr over outer curve to the most distant point of
what is, or appears to be, the main beam. The point of beginning is that point on the burr where the center line
along the outer curve of the beam intersects the burr.

G-1-2-3-4-5-6-7. Length of Normal Points. Normal points project from main beam. They are measured from
nearest edge of main beam over outer curve to tip. To determine nearest edge (top edge) of beam, lay the tape
along the outer curve of the beam so that the top edge of the tape coincides with the top edge of the beam on
both sides of the point. Draw line along top edge of tape. This line will be base line from which point is
measured.

H-1-2-3-4. Circumferences - self explanatory.

* * * * * * * * * *

TROPHIES OBTAINED ONLY BY FAIR CHASE MAY BE ENTERED
IN ANY BOONE AND CROCKETT CLUB BIG GAME COMPETITION

To make use of the following methods shall be deemed UNFAIR CHASE and unsportsmanlike, and any trophy
obtained by use of such means is disqualified from entry in any Boone and Crockett Club big game competition:

I. Spotting or herding game from the air, followed by landing in its vicinity for pursuit;

II. Herding or pursuing game with motor-powered vehicles;

III. Use of electronic communications for attracting, locating or observing game, or guiding the
hunter to such game.

* * * * * * * * * *

I certify that the trophy scored on this chart was not taken in UNFAIR CHASE as defined above by the Boone
and Crockett Club.

I certify that it was not spotted or herded by guide or hunter from the air followed by landing in its vicinity for
pursuit, nor herded or pursued on the ground by motor-powered vehicles.

I further certify that no electronic communications were used to attract, locate, observe, or guide the hunter to
such game; and that it was taken in full compliance with the local game laws or regulations of the state,
province or territory.

Date _____ Hunter _____

A-5M-12-68

Reproduced by permission of Boone and Crockett Club.

391

COMPLETE BOOK OF HUNTING

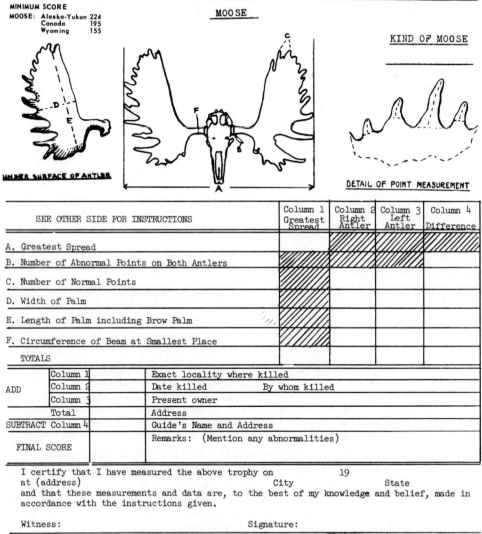

OFFICIAL SCORING SYSTEM FOR NORTH AMERICAN BIG GAME TROPHIES

RECORDS OF NORTH AMERICAN
BIG GAME COMMITTEE

BOONE AND CROCKETT CLUB

Boone and Crockett Club
Records of North American Big Game Committee
c/o Carnegie Museum
4400 Forbes Ave. Pittsburgh, Pa. 15213

MINIMUM SCORE
MOOSE: Alaska-Yukon 224
Canada 195
Wyoming 155

MOOSE

KIND OF MOOSE

UNDER SURFACE OF ANTLER

DETAIL OF POINT MEASUREMENT

SEE OTHER SIDE FOR INSTRUCTIONS	Column 1 Greatest Spread	Column 2 Right Antler	Column 3 Left Antler	Column 4 Difference
A. Greatest Spread				
B. Number of Abnormal Points on Both Antlers				
C. Number of Normal Points				
D. Width of Palm				
E. Length of Palm including Brow Palm				
F. Circumference of Beam at Smallest Place				
TOTALS				

ADD	Column 1		Exact locality where killed
	Column 2		Date killed By whom killed
	Column 3		Present owner
	Total		Address
SUBTRACT Column 4			Guide's Name and Address
FINAL SCORE			Remarks: (Mention any abnormalities)

I certify that I have measured the above trophy on   19
at (address)   City   State
and that these measurements and data are, to the best of my knowledge and belief, made in
accordance with the instructions given.

Witness: Signature:

Boone & Crockett Official Measurer

392

INSTRUCTIONS

All measurements must be made with a flexible steel tape to the nearest one-eighth of an inch. Wherever it is necessary to change direction of measurement, mark a control point and swing tape at this point. To simplify addition, please enter fractional figures in eighths.

Official measurements cannot be taken for at least sixty days after the animal was killed. Please submit photographs.

A. Greatest Spread – measured in a straight line at right angles to the center line of the skull.

B. Number of Abnormal Points on Both Antlers – Abnormal points are generally considered to be those non-typical in shape or location.

C. Number of Normal Points. Normal points are those which project from the outer edge of the antler. To be counted a point, a projection must be at least one inch long and the length must exceed the breadth of the point's base. The breadth need not be computed from the deepest adjacent dips in the palmation. The length may be measured to any location -- at least one inch from the tip -- at which the length of the point exceeds its breadth.

D. Width of Palm – taken in contact with the surface across the under side of the palm, at right angles to the inside edge of palm, to a dip between points at the greatest width of palm. Measure width of palm from mid-points of edges of palm.

E. Length of Palm including Brow Palm – taken in contact with the surface along the under side of the palm, parallel to the inner edge from dips between points at the greatest length of palm. If a deep bay is present in the palm, measure palm length across the open bay if the proper line of measurement crosses the bay.

F. Circumference of Beam at Smallest Place – needs no explanation.

* * * * * * * * * * * * *

TROPHIES OBTAINED ONLY BY FAIR CHASE MAY BE ENTERED IN ANY BOONE AND CROCKETT CLUB BIG GAME COMPETITION

To make use of the following methods shall be deemed UNFAIR CHASE and unsportsmanlike, and any trophy obtained by use of such means is disqualified from entry in any Boone and Crockett Club big game competition:

I. Spotting or herding game from the air, followed by landing in its vicinity for pursuit;

II. Herding or pursuing game with motor-powered vehicles;

III. Use of electronic communications for attracting, locating or observing game, or guiding the hunter to such game.

* * * * * * * * * * * *

I certify that the trophy scored on this chart was not taken in UNFAIR CHASE as defined above by the Boone and Crockett Club.

I certify that it was not spotted or herded by guide or hunter from the air followed by landing in its vicinity for pursuit, nor herded or pursued on the ground by motor-powered vehicles.

I further certify that no electronic communications were used to attract, locate, observe, or guide the hunter to such game; and that it was taken in full compliance with the local game laws or regulations of the state, province or territory.

Date_____ Signature of Hunter _____

Reproduced by permission of Boone and Crockett Club.

OFFICIAL SCORING SYSTEM FOR NORTH AMERICAN BIG GAME TROPHIES

RECORDS OF NORTH AMERICAN BIG GAME COMMITTEE

BOONE AND CROCKETT CLUB

Boone and Crockett Club
Records of North American Big Game Committee
c/o Carnegie Museum
4400 Forbes Ave. Pittsburgh, Pa. 15213

MINIMUM SCORE: Barren Ground - 400
Mountain - 390
Quebec-Labrador - 375
Woodland - 295

CARIBOU

KIND OF CARIBOU

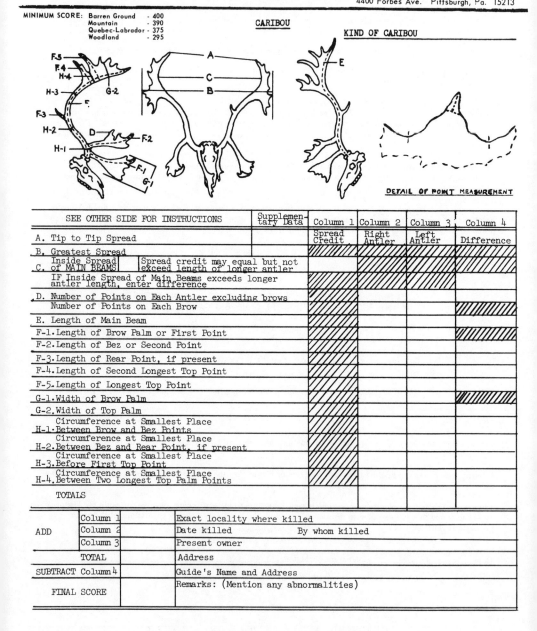

DETAIL OF POINT MEASUREMENT

SEE OTHER SIDE FOR INSTRUCTIONS	Supplementary Data	Column 1 Spread Credit	Column 2 Right Antler	Column 3 Left Antler	Column 4 Difference
A. Tip to Tip Spread		/////	/////	/////	/////
B. Greatest Spread					/////
C. Inside Spread of MAIN BEAMS — Spread credit may equal but not exceed length of longer antler					/////
IF Inside Spread of Main Beams exceeds longer antler length, enter difference		/////	/////	/////	
D. Number of Points on Each Antler excluding brows		/////			
Number of Points on Each Brow		/////			/////
E. Length of Main Beam		/////			
F-1. Length of Brow Palm or First Point					/////
F-2. Length of Bez or Second Point					
F-3. Length of Rear Point, if present					
F-4. Length of Second Longest Top Point					
F-5. Length of Longest Top Point					
G-1. Width of Brow Palm					/////
G-2. Width of Top Palm					
H-1. Circumference at Smallest Place Between Brow and Bez Points		/////			
H-2. Circumference at Smallest Place Between Bez and Rear Point, if present		/////			
H-3. Circumference at Smallest Place Before First Top Point		/////			
H-4. Circumference at Smallest Place Between Two Longest Top Palm Points		/////			
TOTALS					

ADD	Column 1		Exact locality where killed	
	Column 2		Date killed	By whom killed
	Column 3		Present owner	
TOTAL			Address	
SUBTRACT Column 4			Guide's Name and Address	
FINAL SCORE			Remarks: (Mention any abnormalities)	

394

I certify that I have measured the above trophy on _____ 19 _____
at (address)_____ City _____ State _____
and that these measurements and data are, to the best of my knowledge and belief, made in accordance with the instructions given.

Witness: _____ Signature: _____

Boone and Crockett Official Measurer

INSTRUCTIONS

All measurements must be made with a flexible steel tape to the nearest one-eighth of an inch. Wherever it is necessary to change direction of measurement, mark a control point and swing tape at this point. To simplify addition, please enter fractional figures in eighths.

Official measurements cannot be taken for at least sixty days after the animal was killed. Please submit photographs.

Supplementary Data measurements indicate conformation of the trophy.

None of the figures in Lines A and B are to be included in the score.

Evaluation of conformation is a matter of personal preference.

A. Tip to Tip Spread measured between tips of Main Beams.

B. Greatest Spread measured between perpendiculars at right angles to the center line of the skull at widest part whether across main beams or points.

C. Inside Spread of Main Beams measured at right angles to the center line of the skull at widest point between main beams. Enter this measurement again in "Spread Credit" column if it is less than or equal to the length of longer antler.

D. Number of points on each antler. To be counted a point, a projection must be at least one-half inch long and this length must exceed the breadth of the point's base. The breadth need not be computed from the deepest adjacent dips in the palmation. The length may be measured to any location -- at least one-half inch from the tip -- at which the length of the point exceeds its breadth. Beam tip is counted as a point but not measured as a point.

E. Length of Main Beam measured from lowest outside edge of burr over outer curve to the most distant point of what is, or appears to be, the main beam. The point of beginning is that point on the burr where the center line along the outer curve of the beam intersects the burr.

F-1-2-3. Length of Points. They are measured from nearest edge of beam on the shortest line over outer curve to tip. To determine nearest edge (top edge) of beam, lay the tape along the outer curve of the beam so that the top edge of the tape coincides with the top edge of the beam on both sides of the point. Draw line along top edge of tape. This line will be base line from which point is measured.

F-4-5. Measure from the tip of the point to the top of the beam, then at right angles to the lower edge of beam.

G-1 Width of Brow measured in a straight line from top edge to lower edge.

G-2 Width of Top Palm measured from rear edge of main beam to the dip between points at widest part of palm.

H-1-2-3-4. Circumferences — If rear point is missing, take H-2 and H-3 measurements at smallest place between bez and first top point.

* * * * * * * * * * * *

TROPHIES OBTAINED ONLY BY FAIR CHASE MAY BE ENTERED IN ANY BOONE AND CROCKETT CLUB BIG GAME COMPETITION

To make use of the following methods shall be deemed UNFAIR CHASE and unsportsmanlike, and any trophy obtained by use of such means is disqualified from entry in any Boone and Crockett Club big game competition:

     I. Spotting or herding game from the air, followed by landing in its vicinity for pursuit;

    II. Herding or pursuing game with motor-powered vehicles;

    III. Use of electronic communications for attracting, locating or observing game, or guiding the hunter to such game.

* * * * * * * * * * * *

I certify that the trophy scored on this chart was not taken in UNFAIR CHASE as defined above by the Boone and Crockett Club.

I certify that it was not spotted or herded by guide or hunter from the air followed by landing in its vicinity for pursuit, nor herded or pursued on the ground by motor-powered vehicles.

I further certify that no electronic communications were used to attract, locate, observe, or guide the hunter to such game; and that it was taken in full compliance with the local game laws or regulations of the state, province or territory.

Date _____ Signature of Hunter _____

Reproduced by permission of Boone and Crockett Club.

OFFICIAL SCORING SYSTEM FOR NORTH AMERICAN BIG GAME TROPHIES

RECORDS OF NORTH AMERICAN
BIG GAME COMMITTEE

BOONE AND CROCKETT CLUB

Boone and Crockett Club
Records of North American Big Game Committee
% Carnegie Museum
4400 Forbes Ave.   Pittsburgh, Pa. 15213

Minimum Score
Pronghorn: 82

PRONGHORN

SEE OTHER SIDE FOR INSTRUCTIONS	Supplementary Data	Column 1	Column 2	Column 3
		Right Horn	Left Horn	Difference
A. Tip to Tip Spread				
B. Inside Spread of Main Beams		////////	////////	////////
IF Inside Spread of Main Beams exceeds longer horn length, enter difference.		////////	////////	
C. Length of Horn				
D-1. Circumference of Base				
D-2. Circumference at First Quarter				
D-3. Circumference at Second Quarter				
D-4. Circumference at Third Quarter				
E. Length of Prong				
TOTALS				

ADD	Column 1		Exact locality where killed	
	Column 2		Date killed By whom killed	
	Total		Present owner	
SUBTRACT Column 3			Address	
			Guide's Name and Address	
			Remarks: (Mention any abnormalities)	
FINAL SCORE				

I certify that I have measured the above trophy on   19
at (address)   City   State
and that these measurements and data are, to the best of my knowledge and belief, made in
accordance with the instructions given.

Witness:_____   Signature:_____

A-1M-7-65

Boone and Crockett Official Measurer

INSTRUCTIONS

All measurements must be made with a flexible steel tape to the nearest one-eighth of an inch. Wherever it is necessary to change direction of measurement, mark a control point and swing tape at this point. To simplify addition, please enter fractional figures in eighths.

Official measurements cannot be taken for at least sixty days after the animal was killed. Please submit photographs.

Supplementary Data measurements indicate conformation of the trophy.
None of the figures in Lines A and B are to be included in the score.
Evaluation of conformation is a matter of personal preference.

A. Tip to Tip Spread measured between tips of horns.

B. Inside Spread of Main Beams measured at right angles to the center line of the skull at widest point between main beams.

C. Length of horn is measured on the outside curve, so the line taken will vary with different heads, depending on the direction of their curvature. Measure along the center of the outer curve from tip of horn to a point in line with the lowest edge of the base.

D-1. Measure around base of horn at right angles to long axis. Tape must be in contact with the lowest circumference of the horn in which there are no sierrations.

D-2-3-4. Divide measurement of LONGER horn by four, mark BOTH horns at these quarters even though one horn is shorter, and measure circumferences at these marks. If the prong occurs at approximately D-3, take this measurement immediately above the swelling of the prong.

E. Length of Prong — Measure from the tip of the prong along the upper edge of the outer curve to the horn; thence, around the horn to a point at the rear of the horn where a straight edge across the back of both horns touches the horn. This measurement around the horn from the base of the prong should be taken at right angles to the long axis of the horn.

* * * * * * * * * * * *

TROPHIES OBTAINED ONLY BY FAIR CHASE MAY BE ENTERED IN ANY BOONE AND CROCKETT CLUB BIG GAME COMPETITION

To make use of the following methods shall be deemed UNFAIR CHASE and unsportsmanlike, and any trophy obtained by use of such means is disqualified from entry in any Boone and Crockett Club big game competition:

    I. Spotting or herding game from the air, followed by landing in its vicinity for pursuit;

    II. Herding or pursuing game with motor-powered vehicles;

    III. Use of electronic communications for attracting, locating or observing game, or guiding the hunter to such game.

****

I certify that the trophy scored on this chart was not taken in UNFAIR CHASE as defined above by the Boone and Crockett Club.

I certify that it was not spotted or herded by guide or hunter from the air followed by landing in its vicinity for pursuit, nor herded or pursued on the ground by motor-powered vehicles.

I further certify that no electronic communications were used to attract, locate, observe, or guide the hunter to such game; and that it was taken in full compliance with the local game laws or regulations of the state, province or territory.

Date_____ Signature of Hunter_____

Reproduced by permission of Boone and Crockett Club.

OFFICIAL SCORING SYSTEM FOR NORTH AMERICAN BIG GAME TROPHIES

RECORDS OF NORTH AMERICAN
BIG GAME COMMITTEE

BOONE AND CROCKETT CLUB

Boone and Crockett Club
Records of North American Big Game Committee
% Carnegie Museum
4400 Forbes Ave.   Pittsburgh, Pa. 15213

Minimum Score:	Bear
Alaskan Brown	– 28
Black	– 21
Grizzly	– 24
Polar	– 27

BEAR

KIND OF BEAR
_____

SEX _____

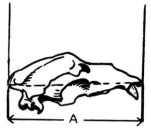

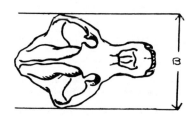

SEE OTHER SIDE FOR INSTRUCTIONS	Measurements
A. Greatest Length Without Lower Jaw	
B. Greatest Width	
TOTAL and FINAL SCORE	

Exact locality where killed
Date killed _____ By whom killed _____
Present owner
Address
Guide's Name and Address
Remarks: (Mention any abnormalities)

I certify that I have measured the above trophy on _____ 19____
at (address) _____ City _____ State _____
and that these measurements and data are, to the best of my knowledge and belief, made in
accordance with the instructions given.

Witness: _____   Signature: _____
Boone and Crockett Official Measurer

INSTRUCTIONS

These measurements are best taken with calipers to the nearest one-sixteenth of an inch.

Official measurements cannot be taken for at least sixty days after the animal was killed.

Please submit photographs.

A. Greatest Length measured between perpendiculars to the long axis of the skull WITHOUT the lower jaw and EXCLUDING malformations.

B. Greatest Width measured between perpendiculars at right angles to the long axis.

All adhering flesh, membrane and cartilage must be completely removed before official measurements are taken.

*   *   *   *   *   *   *   *   *   *   *   *   *   *

TROPHIES OBTAINED ONLY BY FAIR CHASE MAY BE ENTERED IN ANY BOONE AND CROCKETT CLUB BIG GAME COMPETITION

To make use of the following methods shall be deemed UNFAIR CHASE and unsportsmanlike, and any trophy obtained by use of such means is disqualified from entry in any Boone and Crockett Club big game competition:

     I. Spotting or herding game from the air, followed by landing in its vicinity for pursuit;

    II. Herding or pursuing game with motor-powered vehicles;

    III. Use of electronic communications for attracting, locating or observing game, or guiding the hunter to such game.

* * * * * * * * * *

I certify that the trophy scored on this chart was not taken in UNFAIR CHASE as defined above by the Boone and Crockett Club.

I certify that it was not spotted or herded by guide or hunter from the air followed by landing in its vicinity for pursuit, nor herded or pursued on the ground by motor-powered vehicles.

I further certify that no electronic communications were used to attract, locate, observe, or guide the hunter to such game; and that it was taken in full compliance with the local game laws or regulations of the state, province or territory.

Date _____ Hunter _____

A-2M-2-69

Reproduced by permission of Boone and Crockett Club.

OFFICIAL SCORING SYSTEM FOR NORTH AMERICAN BIG GAME TROPHIES

RECORDS OF NORTH AMERICAN BIG GAME COMMITTEE

BOONE AND CROCKETT CLUB

Boone and Crockett Club
Records of North American Big Game Committee
c/o Carnegie Museum
4400 Forbes Ave. Pittsburgh, Pa. 15213

Minimum Score: Sheep
Bighorn — 180
Desert — 168
Stone — 170
White or Dall — 170

SHEEP

KIND OF SHEEP

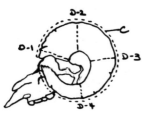
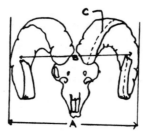

SEE OTHER SIDE FOR INSTRUCTIONS	Supplementary Data	Column 1	Column 2	Column 3
A. Greatest Spread (Is often Tip to Tip Spread)		Right Horn	Left Horn	
B. Tip to Tip Spread (If Greatest Spread, Enter again here)				Difference
C. Length of Horn				////////
D-1. Circumference of Base				
D-2. Circumference at First Quarter				
D-3. Circumference at Second Quarter				
D-4. Circumference at Third Quarter				
TOTALS				

ADD	Column 1		Exact locality where killed	
	Column 2		Date killed By whom killed	
	TOTAL		Present owner	
SUBTRACT Column 3			Address	
FINAL SCORE			Guide's Name and Address	
			Remarks: (Mention any abnormalities)	

I certify that I have measured the above trophy on _____ 19___
at (address) _____ City _____ State _____
and that these measurements and data are, to the best of my knowledge and belief, made in accordance with the instructions given.

Witness: _____   Signature: _____

Boone and Crockett Official Measurer

400

INSTRUCTIONS

All measurements must be made with a flexible steel tape to the nearest one-eighth of an inch. Wherever it is necessary to change direction of measurement, mark a control point and swing tape at this point. To simplify addition, please enter fractional figures in eighths.

Official measurements cannot be taken for at least sixty days after the animal was killed. Please submit photographs.

Supplementary Data measurements indicate conformation of the trophy. None of the figures in Lines A and B are to be included in the score. Evaluation of conformation is a matter of personal preference.

A. Greatest Spread measured between perpendiculars at right angles to the center line of the skull.

B. Tip to Tip Spread measured from outer edge of tips of horns.

C. Length of Horn measured from lowest point in front on outer curve to a point in line with tip. DO NOT press tape into depressions. The low point of the outer curve of the horn is considered to be the low point of the frontal portion of the horn, situated above and slightly medial to the eye socket, (not on the outside edge of the horn.)

D-1 Circumference of Base measured at right angles to axis of horn. DO NOT follow irregular edge of horn.

D-2-3-4. Divide measurement C of LONGER horn by four, mark BOTH horns at these quarters even though other horn is shorter, and measure circumferences at these marks.

*   *   *   *   *   *   *   *   *   *   *   *   *   *

TROPHIES OBTAINED ONLY BY FAIR CHASE MAY BE ENTERED IN ANY BOONE AND CROCKETT CLUB BIG GAME COMPETITION

To make use of the following methods shall be deemed UNFAIR CHASE and unsportsmanlike, and any trophy obtained by use of such means is disqualified from entry in any Boone and Crockett Club big game competition:

I. Spotting or herding game from the air, followed by landing in its vicinity for pursuit;

II. Herding or pursuing game with motor-powered vehicles;

III. Use of electronic communications for attracting, locating or observing game, or guiding the hunter to such game.

* * * * * * * * * *

I certify that the trophy scored on this chart was not taken in UNFAIR CHASE as defined above by the Boone and Crockett Club.

I certify that it was not spotted or herded by guide or hunter from the air followed by landing in its vicinity for pursuit, nor herded or pursued on the ground by motor-powered vehicles.

I further certify that no electronic communications were used to attract, locate, observe, or guide the hunter to such game; and that it was taken in full compliance with the local game laws or regulations of the state, province or territory.

Date _____ Hunter _____

Copyright 1965 by Boone and Crockett Club

A-2M-2-69

Reproduced by permission of Boone and Crockett Club.

OFFICIAL SCORING SYSTEM FOR NORTH AMERICAN BIG GAME TROPHIES

RECORDS OF NORTH AMERICAN BIG GAME COMMITTEE

Goat Minimum Score: 50

BOONE AND CROCKETT CLUB

Boone and Crockett Club
Records of North American Big Game Committee
% Carnegie Museum
4400 Forbes Ave.   Pittsburgh, Pa. 15213

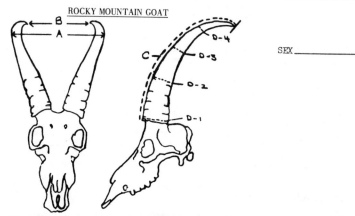

ROCKY MOUNTAIN GOAT

SEX _____

SEE OTHER SIDE FOR INSTRUCTIONS	Supplementary Data	Column 1	Column 2	Column 3
A. Greatest Spread		Right Horn	Left Horn	Difference
B. Tip to Tip Spread				
C. Length of Horn				
D-1. Circumference of Base				
D-2. Circumference at First Quarter				
D-3. Circumference at Second Quarter				
D-4. Circumference at Third Quarter				
TOTALS				

ADD	Column 1		Exact locality where killed		
	Column 2		Date killed By whom killed		
	TOTAL		Present owner		
SUBTRACT	Column 3		Address		
FINAL SCORE			Guide's Name and Address		
			Remarks: (Mention any abnormalities)		

I certify that I have measured the above trophy on
at (address)   City   State   19
and that these measurements and data are, to the best of my knowledge and belief, made in
accordance with the instructions given.

Witness:_____ Signature:_____

A-1M-7-65

Boone & Crockett Official Measurer

INSTRUCTIONS

All measurements must be made with a flexible steel tape to the nearest one-eighth of an inch. Wherever it is necessary to change direction of measurement, mark a control point and swing tape at this point. To simplify addition, please enter fractional figures in eighths.

Official measurements cannot be taken for at least sixty days after the animal was killed.

Please submit photographs.

Supplementary Data measurements indicate conformation of the trophy. None of the figures in Lines A and B are to be included in the score. Evaluation of conformation is a matter of personal preference.

A. Greatest Spread measured between perpendiculars at right angles to the center line of the skull.

B. Tip to Tip Spread measured between tips of horns.

C. Length of Horn measured from lowest point in front over outer curve to a point in line with tip.

D-1 Circumference of Base measured at right angles to axis of horn. DO NOT follow irregular edge of horn.

D-2-3-4. Divide measurement C of LONGER horn by four, mark BOTH horns at these quarters even though other horn is shorter, and measure circumferences at these marks.

* * * * * * * * * * * *

TROPHIES OBTAINED ONLY BY FAIR CHASE MAY BE ENTERED IN ANY BOONE AND CROCKETT CLUB BIG GAME COMPETITION

To make use of the following methods shall be deemed UNFAIR CHASE and unsportsmanlike, and any trophy obtained by use of such means is disqualified from entry in any Boone and Crockett Club big game competition:

    I. Spotting or herding game from the air, followed by landing in its vicinity for pursuit;

    II. Herding or pursuing game with motor-powered vehicles;

    III. Use of electronic communications for attracting, locating or observing game, or guiding the hunter to such game.

* * * * * * * * * *

I certify that the trophy scored on this chart was not taken in UNFAIR CHASE as defined above by the Boone and Crockett Club.

I certify that it was not spotted or herded by guide or hunter from the air followed by landing in its vicinity for pursuit, nor herded or pursued on the ground by motor-powered vehicles.

I further certify that no electronic communications were used to attract, locate, observe, or guide the hunter to such game; and that it was taken in full compliance with the local game laws or regulations of the state, province or territory.

Date_____ Signature of Hunter _____

A-5M-12-68

Reproduced by permission of Boone and Crockett Club.

OFFICIAL SCORING SYSTEM FOR NORTH AMERICAN BIG GAME TROPHIES

**RECORDS OF NORTH AMERICAN
BIG GAME COMMITTEE**

BOONE AND CROCKETT CLUB

Boone and Crockett Club
Records of North American Big Game Committ
% Carnegie Museum
4400 Forbes Ave.   Pittsburgh, Pa. 1521

Minimum Score:
Cougar 15
Jaguar 14½

COUGAR and JAGUAR

KIND OF ANIMAL _____

SEX _____

SEE OTHER SIDE FOR INSTRUCTIONS	Measurements
A. Greatest Length Without Lower Jaw	
B. Greatest Width	
TOTAL AND FINAL SCORE	

Exact locality where killed
Date killed   By whom killed
Present owner
Address
Guide's Name and Address
Remarks: (Mention any abnormalities)

I certify that I have measured the above trophy on   19
at (address)   City   State
and that these measurements and data are, to the best of my knowledge and belief, made in
accordance with the instructions given.

Witness: _____   Signature: _____

Boone and Crockett Official Measure

INSTRUCTIONS

These measurements are best taken with calipers to the nearest one-sixteenth of an inch.

Official measurements cannot be taken for at least sixty days after the animal was killed.

Please submit photographs.

A. Greatest Length measured between perpendiculars to the long axis of the skull WITHOUT the lower jaw and EXCLUDING malformations.

B. Greatest Width measured between perpendiculars at right angles to the long axis.

All adhering flesh, membrane and cartilage must be completely removed before official measurements are taken.

* * * * * * * * * * * * *

TROPHIES OBTAINED ONLY BY FAIR CHASE MAY BE ENTERED IN ANY BOONE AND CROCKETT CLUB BIG GAME COMPETITION

To make use of the following methods shall be deemed UNFAIR CHASE and unsportsmanlike, and any trophy obtained by use of such means is disqualified from entry in any Boone and Crockett Club big game competition:

I. Spotting or herding game from the air, followed by landing in its vicinity for pursuit:

II. Herding or pursuing game with motor-powered vehicles;

III. Use of electronic communications for attracting, locating or observing game, or guiding the hunter to such game.

****

I certify that the trophy scored on this chart was not taken in UNFAIR CHASE as defined above by the Boone and Crockett Club.

I certify that it was not spotted or herded by guide or hunter from the air followed by landing in its vicinity for pursuit, nor herded or pursued on the ground by motor-powered vehicles.

I further certify that no electronic communications were used to attract, locate, observe, or guide the hunter for such game; and that it was taken in full compliance with the local game laws or regulations of the state, province or territory.

Date _____Signature of Hunter _____

Reproduced by permission of Boone and Crockett Club.

OFFICIAL SCORING SYSTEM FOR NORTH AMERICAN BIG GAME TROPHIES

RECORDS OF NORTH AMERICAN
BIG GAME COMMITTEE

BOONE AND CROCKETT CLUB

Boone and Crockett Club
Records of North American Big Game Committee
% Carnegie Museum
4400 Forbes Ave.   Pittsburgh, Pa. 15213

Minimum Score: 115   BISON   SEX _____

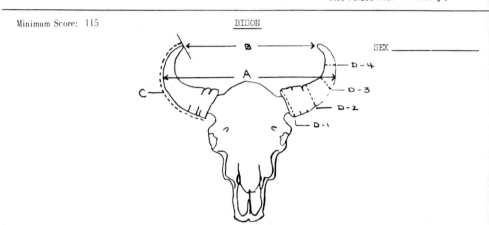

SEE OTHER SIDE FOR INSTRUCTIONS	Supplementary Data	Column 1	Column 2	Column 3
A. Greatest Spread		Right Horn	Left Horn	Difference
B. Tip to Tip Spread				
C. Length of Horn				
D-1. Circumference of Base				
D-2. Circumference at First Quarter				
D-3. Circumference at Second Quarter				
D-4. Circumference at Third Quarter				
TOTALS				

ADD	Column 1		Exact locality where killed
	Column 2		Date killed By whom killed
	TOTAL		Present owner
SUBTRACT Column 3			Address.
			Guide's Name and Address
FINAL SCORE			Remarks: (Mention any abnormalities)

I certify that I have measured the above trophy on _____   19_____
at (address) _____   City _____   State _____
and that these measurements and data are, to the best of my knowledge and belief, made in
accordance with the instructions given.

Witness:_____   Signature:_____

Boone and Crockett Official Measurer

A-1M 7-65

INSTRUCTIONS

All measurements must be made with a flexible steel tape to the nearest one-eighth of an inch. Wherever it is necessary to change direction of measurement, mark a control point and swing tape at this point. To simplify addition, please enter fractional figures in eighths.

Official measurements cannot be taken for at least sixty days after the animal was killed.

Please submit photographs.

Supplementary Data measurements indicate conformation of the trophy.
None of the figures in Lines A and B are to be included in the score.
Evaluation of conformation is a matter of personal preference.

A. Greatest Spread measured between perpendiculars at right angles to the center line of the skull.

B. Tip to Tip Spread measured between tips of horns.

C. Length of Horn measured from lowest point on under side over outer curve to a point in line with tip.

D-1. Circumference of Base measured at right angles to axis of horn. DO NOT follow irregular edge of horn.

D-2-3-4. Divide measurement C of LONGER horn by four; mark BOTH horns at these quarters even though the other horn is shorter, and measure circumferences at these marks.

* * * * * * * * * * * * *

TROPHIES OBTAINED ONLY BY FAIR CHASE MAY BE ENTERED
IN ANY BOONE AND CROCKETT CLUB BIG GAME COMPETITION

To make use of the following methods shall be deemed UNFAIR CHASE and unsportsmanlike, and any trophy obtained by use of such means is disqualified from entry in any Boone and Crockett Club big game competition:

    I. Spotting or herding game from the air, followed by landing in its vicinity for pursuit;

    II. Herding or pursuing game with motor-powered vehicles;

    III. Use of electronic communications for attracting, locating or observing game, or guiding the hunter to such game.

****

I certify that the trophy scored on this chart was not taken in UNFAIR CHASE as defined above by the Boone and Crockett Club.

I certify that it was not spotted or herded by guide or hunter from the air followed by landing in its vicinity for pursuit, nor herded or pursued on the ground by motor-powered vehicles.

I further certify that no electronic communications were used to attract, locate, observe, or guide the hunter to such game; and that it was taken in full compliance with the local game laws or regulations of the state, province or territory.

Date _____ Signature of Hunter _____

Reproduced by permission of Boone and Crockett Club.

OFFICIAL SCORING SYSTEM FOR NORTH AMERICAN BIG GAME TROPHIES

RECORDS OF NORTH AMERICAN BIG GAME COMMITTEE

BOONE AND CROCKETT CLUB

Boone and Crockett Club
Records of North American Big Game Committee
℅ Carnegie Museum
4400 Forbes Ave.   Pittsburgh, Pa. 15213

Minimum Score: Muskox
  Barren Ground 90
  Greenland   90

MUSKOX

KIND OF MUSKOX _____

SEX _____

SEE OTHER SIDE FOR INSTRUCTIONS	Supplementary Data	Column 1	Column 2	Column 3
		Right Horn	Left Horn	Difference
A. Greatest Spread				
B. Tip to Tip Spread				
C. Length of Horn				
D-1. Width of Boss				
D-2. Width at First Quarter				
D-3. Circumference at Second Quarter				
D-4. Circumference at Third Quarter				
TOTALS				

ADD	Column 1		Exact locality where killed
	Column 2		Date killed By whom killed
	TOTAL		Present owner
SUBTRACT Column 3			Address
			Guide's Name and Address
FINAL SCORE			Remarks: (Mention any abnormalities)

I certify that I have measured the above trophy on   19
at (address)   City   State
and that these measurements and data are, to the best of my knowledge and belief, made in
accordance with the instructions given.

Witness:_____ Signature:_____

Boone and Crockett Official Measurer

A-1M-7-65

408

INSTRUCTIONS

All measurements must be made with a flexible steel tape to the nearest one-eighth of an inch. Wherever it is necessary to change direction of measurement, mark a control point and swing tape at this point. To simplify addition, please enter fractional figures in eighths.

Official measurements cannot be taken for at least sixty days after the animal was killed.

Please submit photographs.

Supplementary Data measurements indicate conformation of the trophy. None of the figures in Lines A and B are to be included in the score. Evaluation of conformation is a matter of personal preference.

A. Greatest Spread measured between perpendiculars at right angles to the center line of the skull.

B. Tip to Tip Spread measured between tips of horns.

C. Length of Horn measured from inner edge at center of boss on outer curve to a point in line with tip.

D-1. Width of Boss — best measured with calipers at greatest width of base. If calipers are unavailable, use steel tape between perpendiculars.

D-2-3-4. Divide measurement C of LONGER horn by four, mark BOTH horns at these quarters even though other horn is shorter, measure width at D-2 and circumferences at D-3 and D-4.

* * * * * * * * * * * * *

TROPHIES OBTAINED ONLY BY FAIR CHASE MAY BE ENTERED
IN ANY BOONE AND CROCKETT CLUB BIG GAME COMPETITION

To make use of the following methods shall be deemed UNFAIR CHASE and unsportsmanlike, and any trophy obtained by use of such means is disqualified from entry in any Boone and Crockett Club big game competition:

    I. Spotting or herding game from the air, followed by landing in its vicinity for pursuit;

    II. Herding or pursuing game with motor-powered vehicles;

    III. Use of electronic communications for attracting, locating or observing game, or guiding the hunter to such game.

****

I certify that the trophy scored on this chart was not taken in UNFAIR CHASE as defined above by the Boone and Crockett Club.

I certify that it was not spotted or herded by guide or hunter from the air followed by landing in its vicinity for pursuit, nor herded or pursued on the ground by motor-powered vehicles.

I further certify that no electronic communications were used to attract, locate, observe, or guide the hunter to such game; and that it was taken in full compliance with the local game laws or regulations of the state, province or territory.

Date _____ Signature of Hunter _____

Reproduced by permission of Boone and Crockett Club.

OFFICIAL SCORING SYSTEM FOR NORTH AMERICAN BIG GAME TROPHIES

**RECORDS OF NORTH AMERICAN
BIG GAME COMMITTEE**

BOONE AND CROCKETT CLUB

Boone and Crockett Club
Records of North American Big Game Comm
% Carnegie Museum
4400 Forbes Ave.   Pittsburgh, Pa. 152

Minimum Score:
    Walrus: Atlantic 95
            Pacific 100

WALRUS

KIND OF WALRUS_____

SEX _____

SEE OTHER SIDE FOR INSTRUCTIONS	Supplemen-tary Data	Column 1	Column 2	Column 3
A. Greatest Spread		Right Tusk	Left Tusk	Difference
B. Tip to Tip Spread				
C. Entire Length of Loose Tusk				
D-1. Circumference of Base				
D-2. Circumference at First Quarter				
D-3. Circumference at Second Quarter				
D-4. Circumference at Third Quarter				
TOTALS				

ADD	Column 1		Exact locality where killed
	Column 2		Date killed By whom killed
	Total		Present owner
SUBTRACT	Column 3		Address
			Guide's Name and Address
FINAL SCORE			Remarks: (Mention any abnormalities)

I certify that I have measured the above trophy on   19
at (address)   City   State
and that these measurements and data are, to the best of my knowledge and belief, made in
accordance with the instructions given.

Witness:_____   Signature:_____

Boone and Crockett Official Measurer

A-1M-7-65

INSTRUCTIONS

All measurements must be made with a flexible steel tape to the nearest one-eighth of an inch. Wherever it is necessary to change direction of measurement, mark a control point and swing tape at this point. To simplify addition, please enter fractional figures in eighths.

Official measurements cannot be taken for at least sixty days after the animal was killed.

Please submit photographs.

Supplementary Data measurements indicate conformation of the trophy.
None of the figures in Lines A and B are to be included in the score.
Evaluation of conformation is a matter of personal preference.

A. Greatest Spread measured between perpendiculars at right angles to the center line of the skull.

B. Tip to Tip Spread measured between tips of tusks.

C. Entire Length of Loose Tusk measured over outer curve from base to a point in line with tip.

D-1. Circumference of Base measured at right angles to axis of tusk. DO NOT follow edge of contact between tusk and skull.

D-2-3-4. Divide measurement C of LONGER tusk by four, mark BOTH tusks at these quarters even though other tusk is shorter, and measure circumferences at these marks.

* *

TROPHIES OBTAINED ONLY BY FAIR CHASE MAY BE ENTERED IN ANY BOONE AND CROCKETT CLUB BIG GAME COMPETITION

To make use of the following methods shall be deemed UNFAIR CHASE and unsportsmanlike, and any trophy obtained by use of such means is disqualified from entry to any Boone and Crockett Club big game competition:

  I. Spotting or herding game from the air, followed by landing in its vicinity for pursuit;

  II. Herding or pursuing game with motor-powered vehicles;

  III. Use of electronic communications for attracting, locating or observing game, or guiding the hunter to such game. * * * * * * * * * * *

I certify that the trophy scored on this chart was not taken in UNFAIR CHASE as defined above by the Boone and Crockett Club.

I certify that it was not spotted or herded by guide or hunter from the air followed by landing in its vicinity for pursuit, nor herded or pursued on the ground by motor-powered vehicles.

I further certify that no electronic communications were used to attract, locate, observe, or guide the hunter to such game; and that it was taken in full compliance with the local game laws or regulations of the state, province or territory.

Date_____ Signature of Hunter _____

Reproduced by permission of Boone and Crockett Club.

Bibliography

Dalrymple, Byron, *Complete Guide to Hunting Across North America,* 1970, Outdoor Life, Harper & Row

Elliott, Charles, *Outdoor Observer,* 1970, Outdoor Life, E. P. Dutton

Fennell, James, *Guide to Hunting Rocky Mountain Mule Deer,* 1970, Okie Enterprises

Hibben, Frank, *Hunting American Bears,* 1950, University of New Mexico Press

Holland, Dan, *Upland Game Hunter's Bible,* Doubleday

Koller, Larry, *Fireside Book of Guns,* 1959, Simon & Schuster

Koller, Larry, *Shots at Whitetails,* 1970, Alfred A. Knopf

Laycock, George, *Shotgunner's Bible,* 1969, Doubleday

Laycock, George and Bauer, Erwin, *Hunting with Bow and Arrow,* 1965, Arco

Mattis, George, *Whitetail: Fundamentals & Fine Points for the Hunter,* 1969, Outdoor Life, World

Merrill, William K., *Hunter's Bible,* 1968, Doubleday

O'Connor, Jack, *Art of Big Game Hunting in North America,* 1967, Outdoor Life, Alfred A. Knopf

O'Connor, Jack, *Big Game Hunts,* 1963, Outdoor Life, E. P. Dutton

O'Connor, Jack with Goodwin, George, *The Big Game Animals of North America,* 1960, Outdoor Life

O'Connor, Jack, *Complete Book of Rifles and Shotguns,* 1966, Outdoor Life, Harper & Row

O'Connor, Jack, et al., *Complete Book of Shooting,* 1965, Outdoor Life, Harper & Row

Ormond, Clyde, *Hunting Our Biggest Game*, 1956, Stackpole

Ormond, Clyde, *Hunting Our Medium Size Game*, 1957, Stackpole

Ormond Clyde, *Small Game Hunting*, 1967, Outdoor Life, E. P. Dutton

Outdoor Life Editors, *The Story of American Hunting and Firearms*, 1959, Outdoor Life

Popowski, Bert, *Varmint & Crow Hunter's Bible*, Doubleday

Rice, Philip and Dahl, John, *Hunting Dogs*, Outdoor Life, Harper & Row

Vale, Robert B., *How to Hunt American Game*, 1936, Stackpole

Wulff, Lee, ed., *Sportsman's Companion*, 1968, Harper & Row

INDEX

Index